EMILY RIDDELL/LONELY PLANET IMAGES ©

Sculpte… moss-gr… lined with vivid turquoise lagoons, sultry French Polynesia is a place to take it slow and experience warm, laid-back island chic.

(left) Intercontinental Bora Bora Le Moana Resort (p135)
(below) Girls set to perform a traditional dance (p231) on Tahiti

JEAN-BERNARD CARILLET/LONELY PLANET IMAGES ©

of aqua imaginable. Coral atolls have this same calibre of lagoon minus the big clunky island in the middle. Fish, dolphins, rays, sharks, turtles and more inhabit these clear-water coral gardens that are as excellent for snorkelling as they are for diving and swimming. Surfers ride glassy wave faces at reef passes while kitesurfers and windsurfers fly across the water terrain with the trade winds.

To Luxe or Not to Luxe

Over-the-top indulgence has become French Polynesia's – or more specifically Bora Bora's – signature, and often overshadows what the rest of the country has to offer. Resorts on the 'Pearl of the Pacific' are a honeymooner's dream, with private overwater bungalows, every luxury trapping and spectacular views of the island's iconic, square-topped peak. But if this isn't your cup of coconut water, or simply not in your budget, don't let that dissuade you from visiting French Polynesia. Small, family-run hotels and bed and breakfasts offer a closer-to-the-culture experience at prices that require a financial output similar to what you'd need for a midrange trip to Europe.

❯Tahiti & French Polynesia

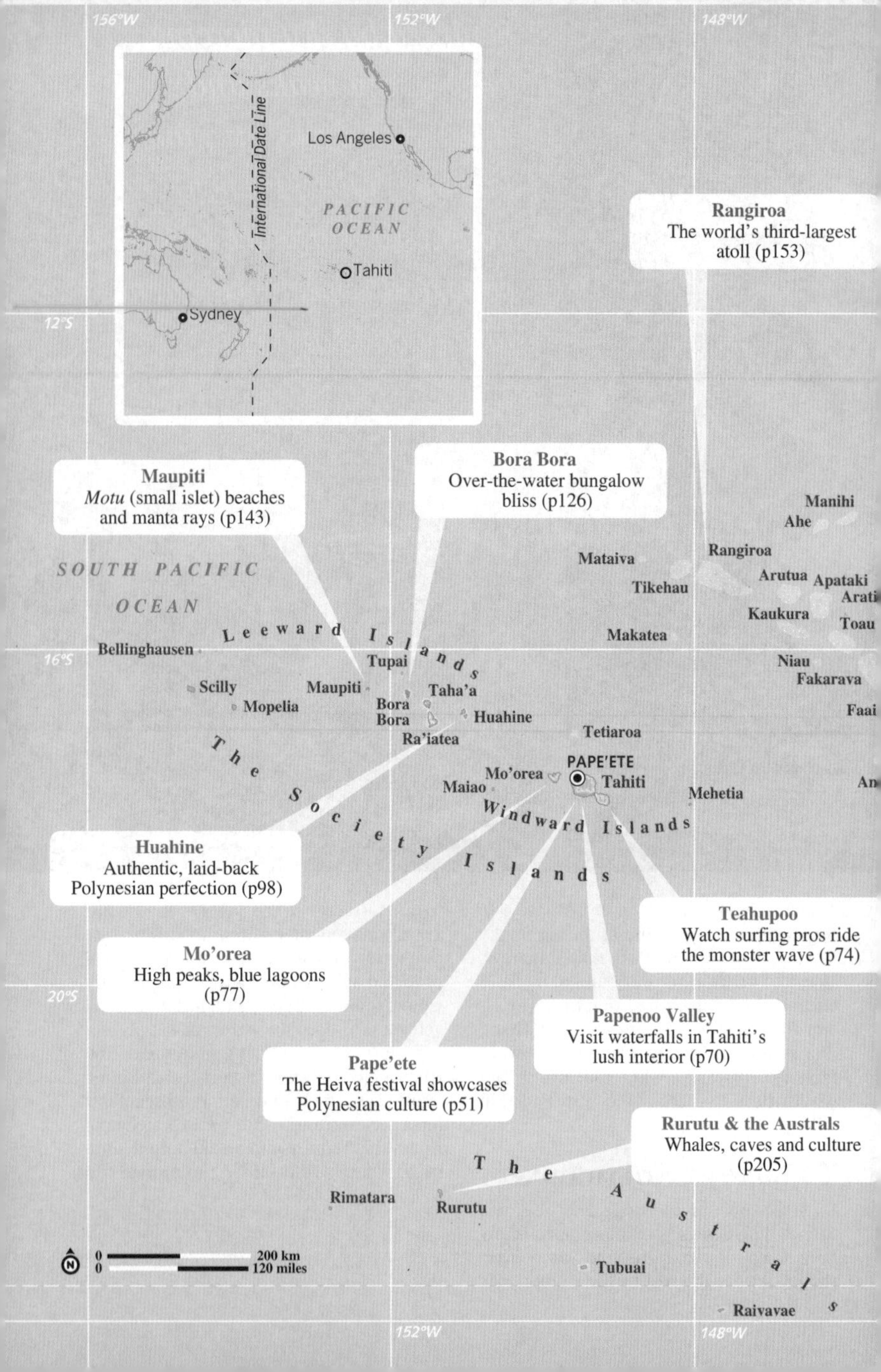

156°W
152°W
148°W
International Date Line
Los Angeles
PACIFIC OCEAN
Tahiti
Sydney
12°S
16°S
20°S
Rangiroa
The world's third-largest atoll (p153)
Bora Bora
Over-the-water bungalow bliss (p126)
Maupiti
Motu (small islet) beaches and manta rays (p143)
SOUTH PACIFIC OCEAN
Manihi
Ahe
Rangiroa
Mataiva
Arutua
Apataki
Arati
Tikehau
Kaukura
Toau
Makatea
Leeward Islands
Bellinghausen
Tupai
Niau
Fakarava
Scilly
Maupiti
Taha'a
Mopelia
Bora Bora
Huahine
Faai
Ra'iatea
Tetiaroa
The Society Islands
PAPE'ETE
Mo'orea
Tahiti
Maiao
Mehetia
Windward Islands
Huahine
Authentic, laid-back Polynesian perfection (p98)
Teahupoo
Watch surfing pros ride the monster wave (p74)
Mo'orea
High peaks, blue lagoons (p77)
Papenoo Valley
Visit waterfalls in Tahiti's lush interior (p70)
Pape'ete
The Heiva festival showcases Polynesian culture (p51)
Rurutu & the Australs
Whales, caves and culture (p205)
The Australs
Rimatara
Rurutu
0 200 km
0 120 miles
Tubuai
Raivavae

PAGE 46

ON THE ROAD

YOUR COMPLETE DESTINATION GUIDE
In-depth reviews, detailed listings and insider tips

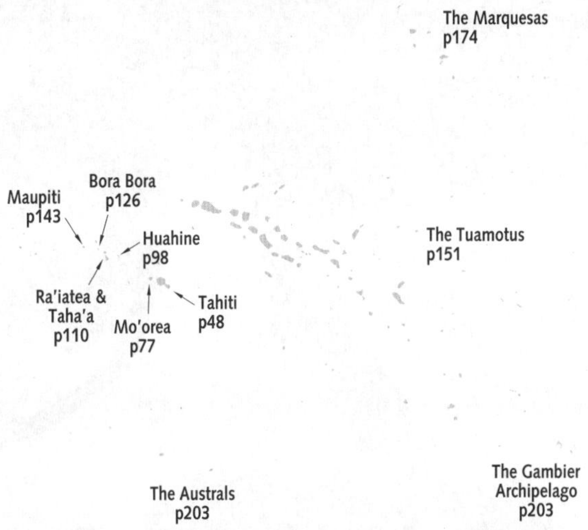

PAGE 235

SURVIVAL GUIDE

VITAL PRACTICAL INFORMATION TO HELP YOU HAVE A SMOOTH TRIP

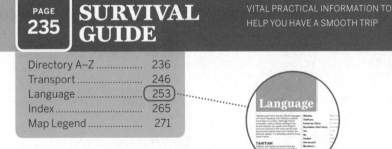

THIS EDITION WRITTEN AND RESEARCHED BY

Celeste Brash

Jean-Bernard Carillet

welcome to Tahiti & French Polynesia

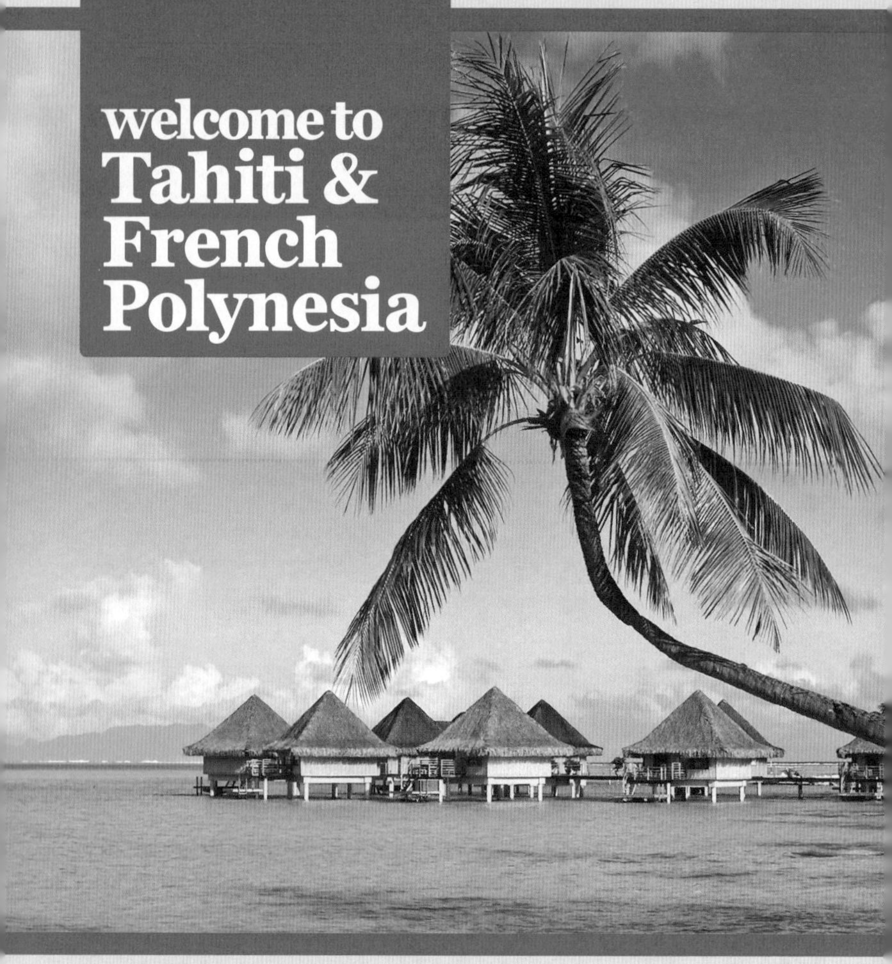

The Dream

Tahiti: just the word conjures up centuries' worth of images: hibiscus flowers; svelte, bronzed dancers in grass skirts; a humid breeze over turquoise sea. The islands of French Polynesia became legends the minute the first European explorers reached their home shores with tales of a heaven on earth where the soil was fertile, life was simple, and sex was plentiful and guilt-free. While the lingering hype is outdated, French Polynesia is still about as dreamy as reality gets. The trees are still heavy with fruit, the mountains rise as majestically as ever and the lagoons are just as blue. Today, however, there are freeways, Christianity has instilled more conservative values and people work nine-to-five jobs. French Polynesia has not escaped the modern world but embraced it. True, it's not the perfect, untainted paradise of explorer lore, but at least there's a pretty fast internet connection.

Lagoon Spectacular

While there are plenty of slim stretches of white-, pink- and black-sand beaches in French Polynesia, they are just pretty springboards into the real draw: the lagoons. Most high islands are surrounded by fringing reef that creates a protected swimming pool of the most intense hue

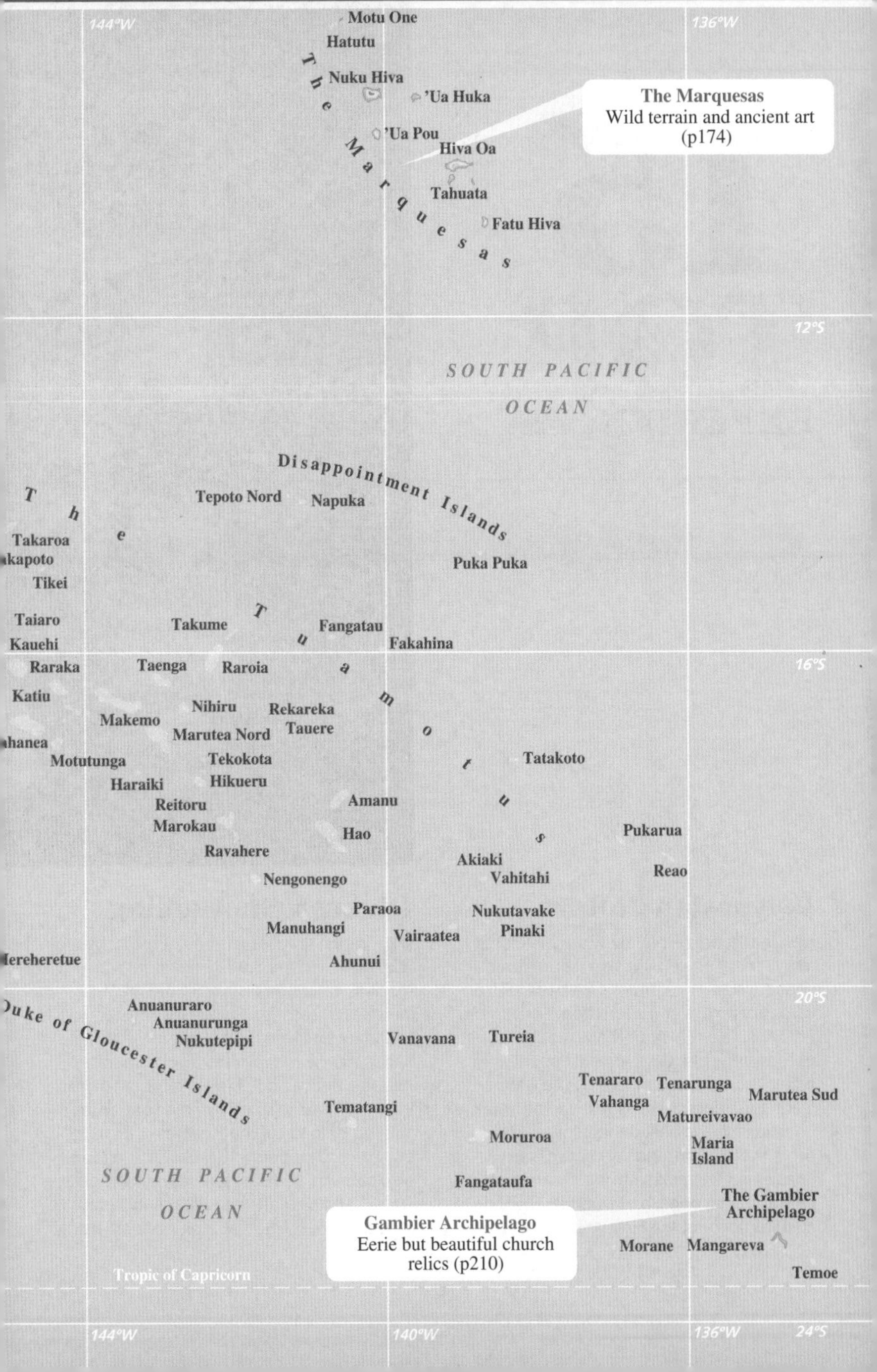
144°W
136°W
140°W
12°S
16°S
20°S
24°S
Motu One
Hatutu
The Marquesas
Nuku Hiva
'Ua Huka
'Ua Pou
Hiva Oa
Tahuata
Fatu Hiva
The Marquesas
Wild terrain and ancient art
(p174)
SOUTH PACIFIC
OCEAN
Disappointment Islands
Tepoto Nord
Napuka
Puka Puka
The Tuamotus
Takaroa
Tikei
Taiaro
Kauehi
Takume
Fangatau
Fakahina
Raraka
Taenga
Raroia
Katiu
Nihiru
Rekareka
Makemo
Tauere
Marutea Nord
Motutunga
Tekokota
Tatakoto
Haraiki
Hikueru
Reitoru
Amanu
Marokau
Hao
Pukarua
Ravahere
Akiaki
Reao
Vahitahi
Nengonengo
Paraoa
Nukutavake
Manuhangi
Pinaki
Vairaatea
Ahunui
Anuanuraro
Anuanurunga
Nukutepipi
Duke of Gloucester Islands
Vanavana
Tureia
Tenararo
Tenarunga
Vahanga
Marutea Sud
Matureivavao
Tematangi
Moruroa
Maria
Island
SOUTH PACIFIC
OCEAN
Fangataufa
The Gambier
Archipelago
Gambier Archipelago
Eerie but beautiful church
relics (p210)
Morane
Mangareva
Temoe
Tropic of Capricorn

15 TOP EXPERIENCES

Polynesian Culture

1 Gentle, unpretentiously sophisticated yet fiery, the Polynesian culture is as seductive as it is soothing. Sit back with a cold Hinano under a warm dome of stars to enjoy ukulele riffs or perhaps just the sound of the surf – free days are best spent picnicking on fish and taro by the water. During the annual Heiva festival the country goes full tilt: the best dancers wear little more than palm fronds and have warp-speed wiggling hips; outrigger-canoe racing ignites the lagoons; and traditional sports such as coconut husking go pro.

Diving & Snorkelling

2 French Polynesia is one of the richest realms in the South Pacific. Its warm, tropical waters hold some of the greatest varieties of sea life found in the region. Dream of encountering the beasts? You can mingle with grey reef sharks, manta rays, bottlenose dolphins and hammerhead sharks. Prefer smaller, technicolour critters? You'll spot loads of reef species, including stingrays, snappers and jacks. The lagoons also cater to avid snorkellers, with gin-clear waters and a smattering of healthy coral gardens around. See p31 for more on diving.

HOLGER LEUE/LONELY PLANET IMAGES ©

MICHAEL AW/LONELY PLANET IMAGES ©

Atoll Lagoons

3 Atolls are basically lagoons without the island. What little land mass there is peeks up only several metres above the surface and encircles lagoons so blue and thriving that high-island lagoons look meek in comparison. Best explored by boat, these watery landscapes hold empty white- and pink-sand beaches, sea-bird nesting grounds and some of the best spots in the world to dive in with a mask and snorkel. Rangiroa (p153) takes the crown as the world's third-largest atoll, while Fakarava's lagoon (p166) is a protected Unesco biosphere reserve. The lagoon on Fakarava

Bora Bora

4 As the plane begins to descend, a magical scene comes into view: a perfect Morse-code ring of *motu* (small islets), mop-topped with palms, separating the indigo of the ocean from the crisp palette of lagoon blues. Bora Bora (p126) is a hot favourite for honeymooners – but we feel certain you didn't come all this way merely to crack open a bottle of champagne. Hiking, diving, snorkelling and other adventure options are all readily available.

3

4

5

LINDA CHING/LONELY PLANET IMAGES ©

6

NIC BOTHMA/LONELY PLANET IMAGES ©

7

MERTEN SNIJDERS/LONELY PLANET IMAGES ©

Tahiti's Waterfall Valleys

5 Take an island with high mountains and 90-degree cliffs, douse it with tropical rainfall and give it a few million years to erode into magnificent forms – and what do you get? Waterfalls. Lots of them. You could walk up any river in Tahiti and find myriad cascades, but you're best sticking with known trails or going with a guide. Try the trodden (though near-empty) paths to Papenoo (p70), Fautaua (p69) or the Hitiaa lava tubes (p69). Waterfall at Pueu (p73), Tahiti Iti

Surfing

6 With warm, clear water, swell from all directions and innumerable breaks, it's no wonder that Polynesia has become a surf mecca. Beginners can paddle out to shore breaks, while more advanced surfers will be spoiled with hollow reef waves year-round. There are secret spots everywhere if you're willing to look. The fearsome wave at Teahupoo may be beyond many surfers' level, but watching the pros tackle it during the Billabong Pro is one of the greatest live sporting events you may ever get to see.

Mo'orea

7 Mo'orea (p77) is a tropical-island cliché brought to life. If you've been dreaming of a holiday-brochure turquoise lagoon, coral beaches, vertical peaks and lush landscapes, you'd be hard-pressed to find better than this gem of an island. Mo'orea has something for everyone. A startling variety of adventure options await: there are mountains to climb, coral gardens to snorkel along, scenic areas to quad bike, waves to surf and sloping reefs to dive. But if all you want to do is unwind, a couple of lovely expanses of coral sand beckon.

8

9

Huahine

8 Boasting some of the best beaches in the country and a snoozy Polynesian charm, Huahine (p98) is the perfect spot to recharge the batteries. If you've got energy to burn, there's a slew of activities available, from hiking in the lush interior to snorkelling fabulous coral gardens. Culture buffs will also love Maeva, one of the most extensive complexes of pre-European *marae* (traditional temples) in French Polynesia. Huahine is refreshingly void of bling and large-scale development. It's all about ecotravel, and this is why it's gaining in popularity. Marae Paepae Ofata (p100), Maeva

The Marquesas

9 Whether you believe in legends or not, this archipelago looks like something from the pages of a fairy tale. Think snaggle-toothed volcanic peaks, deep ravines, majestic waterfalls, secretive bays, and forests that could hold their own in a BBC documentary. The Marquesas (p174) also offer plenty of sites dating from pre-European times. Hiking, horse riding and diving will keep you busy. If you're short on time, book a cruise aboard the *Aranui*, a cargo boat and passenger vessel that serves the six inhabited islands of the archipelago. Arrival of the *Aranui* at Tahuata (p200)

RADIUS IMAGES/CORBIS ©

REINHARD DIRSCHERL/CORBIS ©

Maupiti

10 Bora Bora's discreet little sister, Maupiti (p143) is one of the most ravishing islands in French Polynesia and is already being talked of as a rising star of the region. Yet it still remains a hideaway where insiders come to revel in an unblemished tropical playground. Maupiti offers complete relaxation – there's only one road and virtually no cars, just bicycles. And when you want to play, there's plenty of scope for activities on and under the water, including kayaking, snorkelling and diving.

Whale-Watching

11 You put your snorkel gear on, slip into the water and when the bubbles clear and your eyes adjust, before you is a truly massive creature: a humpback whale. French Polynesia is an important breeding ground for humpback whales, which migrate to Polynesian waters between July and October. It's one of the best places in the world to see these magnificent creatures. They can be observed caring for new calves and engaging in elaborate mating rituals. The best areas to spot them are Mo'orea (p84), Tahiti (p66) and Rurutu (p206), where operators organise whale-watching trips.

MERTEN SNIJDERS/LONELY PLANET IMAGES ©

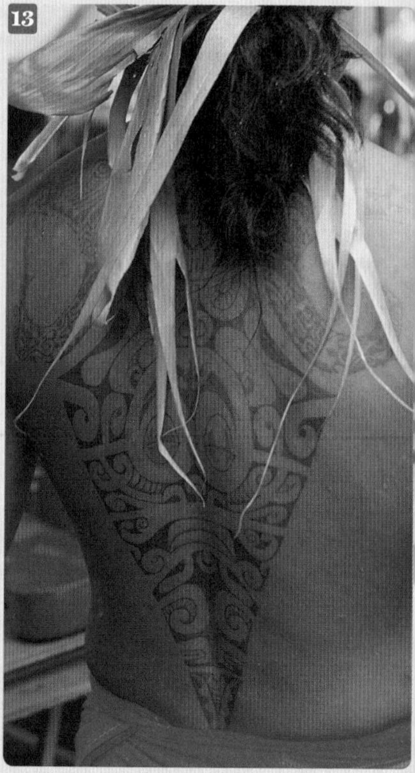

Marae

12 *Marae* are religious sites built from basalt blocks placed side by side and piled up. In pre-European times, they represented the equivalent of temples, and were places of worship, burial and human sacrifice. The most important *marae* in French Polynesia is Marae Taputapuatea (p112) on Ra'iatea, which has been extensively restored. Huahine and Mo'orea also have a slew of well-maintained *marae*. These archaeological sites are shrouded with a palpable aura and make for mind-boggling open-air museums.
Marae Anini (p101), Huahine

Tattoos

13 Both aesthetically beautiful and inexplicably raw, dark geometric patterns against bronzed skin have made a huge comeback all over Polynesia. The Marquesas are renowned for having perfected the art, and today ancient patterns are replicated or provide the inspiration for modern designs. In pre-European times, tattoos had great social significance and acted as a map of a person's social status and achievements. Today, they are simply for beautification and many a visitor leaves with an inked memory of Tahiti on their skin.

The Churches of the Gambier

14 French Polynesia's eeriest vestiges are churches, nunneries and other grand religious structures built from coral blocks in the late 1800s. Today, cracked, whitewashed churches with room for up to 1200 worshippers sit mutely, yet with an austere beauty, on islands with only a scattering of residents. They exist thanks to Father Honoré Laval, who history portrays as either an overzealous slave driver or a beacon of faith who inspired the islanders to build these amazing, yet out-of-place, European-style monuments.
Cathédrale Saint-Michel (p211), Mangareva

14

TONY WHEELER/LONELY PLANET IMAGES ©

Tahitian Pearl Farms

15 Forget diamonds, black pearls (p169) are a Tahitian gal's best friend. From silvery white to inky black and every colour in between, it's impossible not to get seduced by these sea gems' soothing hues. Don't miss visiting a farm, where you'll get to see how the oysters are raised and harvested, and maybe even get to see a technician performing the culturing operation (called a 'graft'). Afterwards, you'll surely get to drool over lustrous jewellery and hopefully get a great deal on a very special souvenir. Oyster grafting at a pearl farm

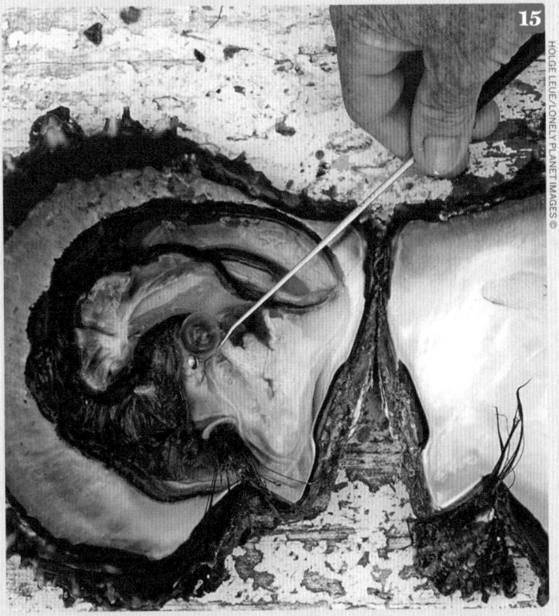

15

HOLGE LEUE/LONELY PLANET IMAGES ©

need to know

Currency

» *Cours de franc Pacifique* (CFP; Pacific franc)

Language

» French and Reo Maohi (Tahitian)

When to Go

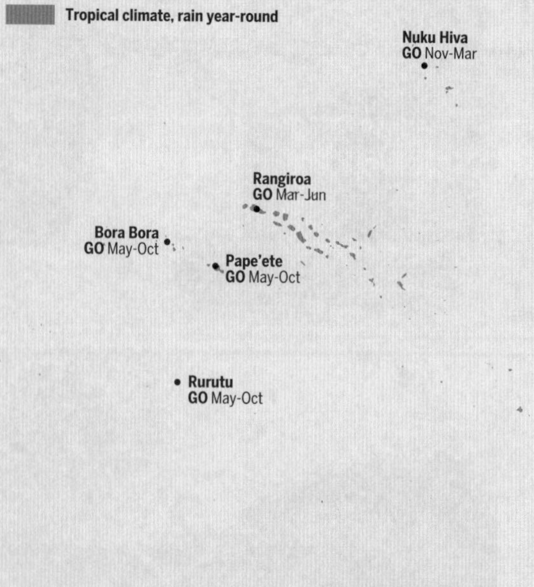

High Season
(Jun–Aug, Dec & Jan)

» June to August usually the coolest and driest months.

» December and January plenty of sun and cooling showers.

» Europeans, Americans and locals on holiday; book early.

Shoulder
(Feb, May, Sep)

» February is one of the hottest months, May and September are mild.

» Prices same as low season.

» Flights and accommodation can be hard to find; book in advance.

Low Season
(Mar & Apr, Oct & Nov)

» March and April are hot and rainy.

» Pleasant in October and November.

» Watch for frequent school holidays when interisland flights can be hard to book.

Your Daily Budget

Budget less than

12,000 CFP

» Room at basic family pension: 6000 CFP

» Baguette sandwich from grocer: 350 CFP

» Bicycle hire per day: 1500 CFP

Midrange

12,000–40,000 CFP

» Room at upscale pension or boutique hotel: 20,000 CFP

» Main dish at a local snack bar: 1000 CFP

» All-day lagoon tour with lunch: 7500 CFP

Top End over

40,000 CFP

» Overwater bungalow (Bora Bora): 80,000 CFP

» Dance show and buffet at a Tahitian resort: 8500 CFP

» Single dive: 8000 CFP

Money
» ATMs available on main islands only. Credit cards are accepted at hotels and restaurants on main islands, but not at family pensions or on remote islands.

Visas
» Most nationalities can stay one to three months without a visa.

Mobile Phones
» Local SIM cards can be used in unlocked GSM compatible phones. Other phones can be set to roaming.

Driving
» Drive on the right; steering wheel is on the left side of the car.

Websites
» **Tahiti Tourisme** (www.tahiti-tourisme.com) Official tourism website.

» **Lonely Planet** (www.lonelyplanet.com/tahiti-and-french-polynesia) Destination info, hotel bookings and more.

» **Haere Mai** (www.haere-mai.pf) Lists small hotels and pensions.

» **Tahiti Traveler** (www.thetahititraveler.com) Range of info, from history to local sights.

Exchange Rates

Australia	A$1	91 CFP
Canada	C$1	90 CFP
Euro zone	€1	119 CFP
Japan	¥100	112 CFP
New Zealand	NZ$1	71 CFP
UK	UK£1	145 CFP
US	US$1	90 CFP

For current exchange rates, see www.xe.com

Important Numbers
There are no area codes in French Polynesia so within the country numbers can be dialled as they're printed in this book.

Country code	☎689
International access code	☎00
Ambulance	☎15
Fire	☎120
Police	☎20

Arriving in Tahiti
» **Faa'a International Airport**

Hotel shuttle – Most hotels and pensions offer free or paid airport pick-up if you've prebooked.

Buses – Run about every half hour from 5am to 6pm and every hour from 6pm to 10pm.

Taxis – A taxi to downtown Pape'ete costs around 2000 CFP (2500 CFP between 8pm and 6am).

Car hire – Rental agencies inside the airport open for arriving flights if they have clients who have prebooked.

Packing
What to Bring
Most things are imported in French Polynesia and thus can be quite expensive; other items may not be available at all. Don't bring heavy clothes such as jeans, although you'll want long pants and a light sweater for evenings plus a dressier outfit if going to upscale restaurants or clubbing. Consider bringing the following from home: sunscreen, insect repellent, books in English, snorkelling gear, clothing (mostly lightweight), sunglasses/eye glasses, flip-flops, snacks such as energy or muesli bars, over-the-counter medications such as cold and flu medicine, batteries and duty-free alcohol.

What to Buy There
If you pack everything in the list above you won't need much more. Here's what you should buy in-country and not bring from home: *pareu* (sarong), plastic reef-walking sandals and mosquito coils.

if you like...

Diving, Snorkelling & Wildlife-Watching

Been searching for the world's most intense shade of aqua? Look no further. What's below the surface is even more spectacular: sharks, coral gardens, turtles, rays, dolphins, humpback whales, clouds of fish...

Rangiroa It's shark week! Or more like shark century. This is French Polynesia's fauna-heavy diving capital (p153)

Maupiti A manta ray cleaning station makes sightings likely, but human crowds are rare (p146)

Rurutu Spot humpbacks through air-clear water or breaching near your boat (p206)

Mo'orea Dolphins, whales, stingrays and sharks all star in a particularly stunning lagoon (p82)

Tahiti Whale-watching trips too crowded on Mo'orea? Marine mammals pass by Tahiti, too, but fewer people go out to watch them (p66)

Fakarava Dive in a Unesco biosphere reserve in and around the country's second largest lagoon (p167)

Luxury Pampering

Overwater bungalows were created then perfected in French Polynesia. Live *la vie en bleu* while lounging lagoon- or poolside with exotic cocktails, soaking in tropical flower–filled baths or getting your muscles soothed with hot volcanic stones.

Bora Bora The world capital of overwater-bungalow bliss and a full-throttle celebrity magnet (p126)

Taha'a Bora Bora's quiet counterpart offers glamour and luxe minus the hype (p110)

Mo'orea Chic decadence can be easy to access, kid-friendly and chock-full of activities (p77)

Tikehau Get your spa treatments in a remote paradise worthy of an adventure novel (p162)

Rangiroa The Kia Ora lets you lounge near town or whisks you to a Crusoe-chic private island (p158)

History & Archaeology

Spirituality has always been paramount to Polynesian people and the historical vestiges you'll find in the islands are testament to this. Stone temples and Europe-worthy churches are highlights.

Marae Taputapuatea, Ra'iatea Arguably the most important ancient Polynesian place of worship in the world (p112)

Opunohu Valley, Mo'orea Tumbled remains of archery platforms, dwellings and temples wend up a jungle hill (p86)

Cathedral & Churches, Gambier Archipelago In the 1880s, Father Laval lead islanders to build coral block churches that seat thousands (p210 and p210)

Kamuihei & Tahakia, Nuku Hiva Villages of stone rubble shaded by grand banyan trees (p183)

Iipona, Hiva Oa Five impressive stone *tiki* dominate this well-preserved site (p199)

Gauguin Tahiti's Gauguin Museum gives a taste of his work, but the artist's spirit lives near his tomb on Hiva Oa (p71 and p193)

Maeva, Huahine Walk along the lagoon and up the hill through the remains of this ancient village (p100)

HOLGER LEUE/LONELY PLANET IMAGES ©

» Basketry at Marché de Pape'ete (Pape'ete Market; p62), Tahiti

Hiking & Walking

Imagine waterfalls tumbling down fern-carpeted basalt cliffs, wild passionfruit vines draped over beach hibiscus trees, and dark caves, each with an ancient legend. Choose from short walks through botanical gardens to multiday treks far from the modern world.

Te Pari, Tahiti Coastal trail of waterfalls, caves, petroglyphs and leaping dolphins (p75)

Vaipahi Spring Gardens, Tahiti Stroll the waterfall gardens or trek up the hill through chestnut trees (p68)

Opunohu Valley Loop, Mo'orea From a lush valley, through archaeological sites to one of the most spectacular view points in the country (p85)

Temehani Plateau, Ra'iatea Hike this high plateau in search of the *tiare apetahi,* one of the planet's most rare flowers (p116)

Nuku Hiva An island with a myriad of spectacular treks along ridges, into waterfall valleys and along the coast (p180)

Art, Music & Dance

Hips that move like rippling water, men dancing in palm-leaf loincloths and percussion that stirs the primordial soul are reason enough to visit French Polynesia. Upping the ante are woodcarvings, basketry, local paintings and tattoo ink on bronzed skin.

Dancing and singing The Heiva is the country's biggest festival of dance, song and traditional sports. It's celebrated country-wide, but it's the grandest on Tahiti (p231)

Tattoos Marquesan designs are the most popular, but you'll find talented tattoo artists throughout the islands and their work displayed on many a tanned limb (p232)

Art galleries The islands have inspired painters since the time of Gauguin. The highest concentration of galleries are found on Tahiti (p64), Mo'orea and Bora Bora (p141)

Wood carving 'Ua Huka is the wood-carving capital although you can pick up finely worked pieces in most tourist areas (p185)

Basketry Pandanus hats, mats and bags from the Austral Islands are coveted throughout the country and can be found at the Pape'ete Market (p209)

Beaches

French Polynesia is home to svelte strips of white, pink and black sand that act as launching pads into the lagoons. Think intimate, palm-lined and pretty rather than flat or expansive.

Lagoon tours Get the most beaches for your buck with lagoon tours that explore remote coves accessible only by boat (p29)

Matira Beach, Bora Bora Chic enough to sport that designer bikini but laid back and spacious enough to bring the kids (p129)

Temae, Mo'orea One of the widest white-sand beaches in the country, fronted by a turquoise swimming pool of ocean (p79)

The Tuamotus Palm-covered rings of white and pink sand around sky-coloured lagoons (p151)

Motu Head to fringing islets (called *motu*) on high islands like Ra'iatea and Mo'orea for the best white sand (p113 and p77)

Black Sand Top spots include Pointe Vénus and around Tahiti's north coast to Tautira on Tahiti Iti (p71 and p73)

If you like... Tahitian pearls, see how they're made and buy them producer-direct at pearl farms in the Tuamotus (p154) or on Taha'a (p121) and Huahine (p101)

Surfing & Kitesurfing

The land of monster reef-breaking Teahupoo barrels also has softer beach waves, perfect for beginners; kitesurfers will find plenty of stretches of windy lagoon. Whatever your level, all you need are the guts to get out there.

Teahupoo, Tahiti The big one, the one you've seen photos of that made you gasp. Watch the pros surf it in August during the Billabong Pro (p74)

Papara, Tahiti A very powerful wave that breaks on sand consistently most of the year (p68)

Haapiti, Mo'orea The star of Mo'orea surf spots with powerful, deep waves over sand (p85)

Mo'orea's Lagoon Kitesurfers should fly their gear on the tradewind-catching lagoon in front of Temae or the Beachcomber Intercontinental Resort (p85)

Tubuai The windiest lagoon in the country offers an obstacle-free course of pure kitesurfing thrills – but you'll need your own gear (p207)

Getting Off the Beaten Path

With 118 islands and over 68% of the country's population on Tahiti, it's not hard to go 'Crusoe' in French Polynesia. Or, if you want company, head to small isles where Polynesian culture still reigns and welcomes are warm.

Ahe A coral atoll of nesting sea birds, pearl farms, lovely lodging and few visitors (p173)

Raivavae Rivals Bora Bora for beauty but has retained its taro farming and pandanus-weaving culture as well as its isolation (p208)

The Gambier Archipelago A stunning archipelago surrounded by a single lagoon and graced with eerie deserted churches. It's chilly and feels like the end of the world (p210)

'Ua Huka Gorge on mangoes, visit woodcarving studios and explore the hills on horseback – all with the locals (p185)

Taha'a Quietly sitting in the middle of the busy Society Islands, the wooded 'Vanilla Island' is one of the most laid-back places on the planet (p120)

Great Food & Drink

The Tahitian *hima'a* (earthen oven) is the pinnacle of Polynesian cooking, but in between these feasts savour local ingredients (fish, taro, fruits) prepared every which way. Try savoury vanilla sauces, Chinese specialities, gratins and some 1001 ways to eat coconut.

Roulottes Mobile food vans serve the cheapest eats and offer the most local atmosphere (found country-wide)

Ice-cold coconuts Bought from the roadside or ordered with a meal, nothing quenches island thirst better

Restaurant du Musée Gauguin, Tahiti Try the Sunday *ma'a Tahiti* special after working up an appetite strolling in the botanical gardens nearby (p71)

Mauarii, Huahine Traditional Tahitian food plus seafood dishes with a French twist (p108)

Villa Mahana, Bora Bora Polynesian fusion at its most chic and high-end (p139)

Baguettes, French cheese and wine Available in grocery stores in most major tourist areas, put together the perfect picnic for a tropical sunset

month by month

Top Events

1. **Heiva i Tahiti**, July
2. **Marquesas Arts Festival**, December
3. **Hawaiki Nui Canoe Race**, October
4. **Tahiti Billabong Pro**, August
5. **Miss Tahiti**, May or June

February

It's hot and it might be raining so tuck in and see a sure-to-impress documentary film or, if you're more masochistic, run a marathon. The rest of us will be cooling off in the water.

Chinese New Year

The date changes each year (it's based on the Chinese lunar calendar and is sometimes in January), but the two-week long celebrations always include dancing, martial-arts displays and fireworks. Head to the Kanti Chinese Temple (Ave Georges Clemenceau) in downtown Pape'ete for the most action.

Fifo Pacific International Documentary Film Festival

In early February comes this festival with screenings (many in English) of the year's best Pacific documentary films, from Australia to Hawaii. You can also catch the films at other times of the year with 'Travelling Fifo' (http://en.fifo-tahiti.com), around the islands.

International Mo'orea Marathon

This annual marathon tackles half of the island of Mo'orea. There is also a shorter 21km run and an 800m 'family run'. The race finishes at Temae Beach where runners can cool off in the lagoon. You can usually sign up just days before the race.

March

Arrival of the First Missionaries

On 5 March large religious festivities take place in churches all over the country to commemorate the arrival of the first protestant missionaries in 1797. Polynesian families piously and enthusiastically celebrate this arrival of Christianity. Head to Pointe Vénus where the landing is sometimes re-enacted.

May

Although the biggest festivals are in July, things softly kick off in May. Follow the rhythm of *toere* (traditional drums) to find people practising for the Heiva. The weather is mild and the tourist season has yet to begin.

Tu'aro Ma'ohi Traditional Sports Championship

This annual competition takes place at several venues around Tahiti and usually runs from late April to mid-June. Sports include javelin throwing, rock lifting, fruit carrying, outrigger canoeing, coconut-tree climbing and coconut husking. Look for info at the tourist office or at your hotel.

Tahiti Pearl Regatta

Sailboats, yachts and outrigger canoes from all over the world take part en masse in this fun regatta (www.tahitipearlregatta.org.pf) between Ra'iatea, Taha'a and Huahine. Although a sporting event, everyone takes plenty of time to relax on the white-sand islets dotting the lagoons.

Beauty Contests

Local beauty pageants for each district (plus Miss Dragon for Chinese

Tahitians and Miss Popa'a for European Tahitians) are held with great enthusiasm around the Society Islands in April and May, leading up to the bigger Miss Tahiti and Miss Heiva i Tahiti contests.

Matari'i i Raro

One of the most important dates on the Polynesian calendar in ancient times, the beginning of the dry period on 18 May is starting to be celebrated again, although something different happens every year. The wet season begins for Matari'i i Ni'a in November.

June

There's a lot going on in June as everyone prepares for festival month. Plenty of cultural activities are on offer, the weather is fine and the crowds haven't yet arrived.

Heiva Rima'i

From mid-June to mid-July artists from all over French Polynesia gather for this crafts fair at Salle Aora'i Tinihau (info ☎54 54 00) in Pape'ete. Expect jewellery, woven pandanus items, wooden sculptures and creative items made out of unusual materials (tin cans, plastic thread or who knows what).

Miss Tahiti

Tahiti has been known for its beautiful *vahine* for centuries and no one revels in this more than the women themselves. But the winner must have more than great looks – she must exemplify the Polynesian traditions this flashy show highlights. It's a cultural treat.

July

Here it is, festival month, and everywhere you look there are dance performances, music shows, parades and sports competitions. This is the most vibrant and busy time to visit, and the weather is usually cool and dry.

Heiva i Tahiti

Held in Pape'ete, French Polynesia's most important festival lasts an entire month and is so impressive it's almost worth timing your trip around. The best dancers and singers perform and there are parades and traditional sports competitions (see p60).

Heiva i Bora Bora

Bora Bora runs its Heiva festival, chock full of singing and dancing competitions, from the end of June to mid-July. This is a smaller but arguably more personable festival than the bigger hoopla happening on Tahiti.

Bastille Day

It's still widely celebrated and businesses close, but nowadays the French national holiday gets overshadowed by the much more lively Polynesian festivals going on around it. But don't let that stop you from buying a bottle of Bordeaux, a nice cheese and toasting *vive la France*.

Golf International Open

The best golfers in the Pacific come together at Atimaono on Tahiti to take part in this reputable competition (www.pga.org.au) at the Olivier Bréaud golf course. Amateur golfers can sometimes measure their skills against the international pros.

August

Early in the month is a great time to catch performances by winners of the Heiva i Tahiti dance competitions. The weather is often warm and dry and it's peak holiday season for European visitors.

Tahiti Billabong Pro

This is one of the biggest events in surfing because the wave at Teahupoo is as beautiful as it is scary. Including the trials, the event (www.billabongpro.com) spans about a month – you can get a boat ride to watch surfers bold the tube.

Miss Vahine Tane

To see the most gorgeous transvestites in the country, don't miss this vampy beauty pageant with its tears, outrageous dresses, sky-high heels and more than a few Adam's apples. It's usually on Bora Bora or Mo'orea and there's no official website; ask at your hotel.

October

There's a two-week school vacation mid-October so book your flights early and expect happy company from holidaying locals around the islands – especially at family pensions.

Stone-Fishing Contests

This is how Polynesians used to fish – herding fish with their canoes and stones. This traditional contest takes place on Bora Bora during the first half of October and you can find similar events on neighbouring Maupiti.

Hawaiki Nui Canoe Race

French Polynesia's major sporting event of the year, this is a three-day pirogue (canoe) race from Huahine to Ra'iatea, Taha'a and Bora Bora. Expect lots of people, ringside events on the beaches and a fun ambience (see www.hawaikinuivaa.pf, in French, and p230).

November

Pessimists call this the beginning of the rainy season, but Polynesians celebrate it as the 'season of abundance'. The fishing is great and most fruits start to come into season.

Matari'i i Ni'a

The 20th of November marks the beginning of the Polynesian 'season of abundance', which is essentially Polynesian New Year. It's a newly resurrected observance and there are no annual events yet – expect cultural ceremonies at *marae* (traditional temples) in Tahiti. Check at your hotel or pension.

Tattoonesia

Over 50 local and international tattoo artists come together to share their art and passion at this mid-November event (www.tattoonesia.com) at Aorai Tinihau in Pirae, Tahiti. Check out what's happening in the tattoo world, talk with the artists or get inked yourself.

December

French Polynesians are fervent about celebrating Christmas and this month is marked by heavy shopping and lots of church-going. It's a busy time for tourism, too, even though the wet season is taking hold.

Marquesas Arts Festival

This outrageously visceral arts festival celebrating Marquesan art and identity is held every four years; the next one is in 2015. Fortunately, there are usually 'mini' festivals in between and the next is scheduled for December 2013. See p191 for more.

Hura Tapairu

In an intimate setting at the Maison de la Culture on Pape'ete's waterfront, see up-and-coming traditional dance troupes give their all at this beautiful and inventive competition. It usually takes place during the first week of the month.

Salon Artisanal te Noera a te Rima'i

Where do Tahitians do their Christmas shopping? At this crafts fair of course. Find *tifaifai* (quilts), sculptures, handmade jewellery and plenty of plastic toys made in China. It's at Aorai Tinihau Centre in Pirae till 24 December.

itineraries

Whether you've got six days or 60, these itineraries provide a starting point for the trip of a lifetime. Want more inspiration? Head online to lonelyplanet.com/thorntree to chat with other travellers.

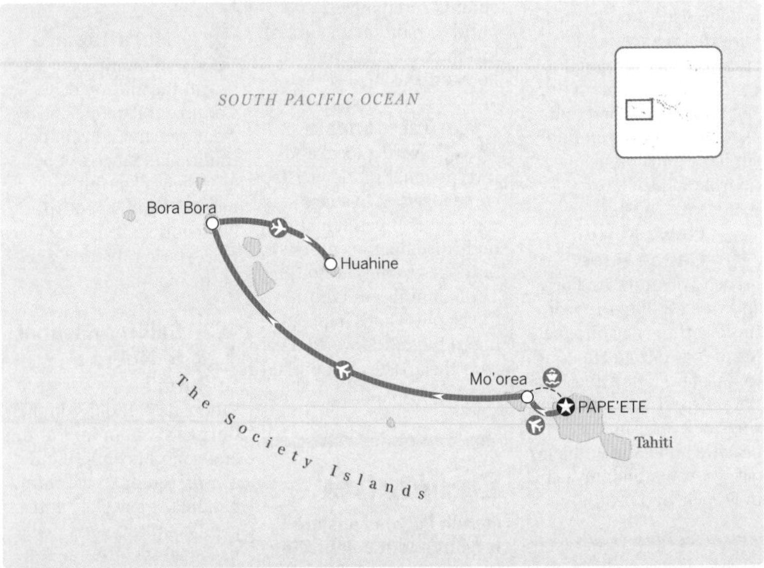

One week
A Glimpse of Paradise

From Pape'ete, fly or boat straight to **Mo'orea**, and stay for at least two nights. Mo'orea boasts soaring peaks, verdant hillsides and aqua waters, and is considered by many to be the most beautiful isle in the Society Islands. Cycle around magnificent Cook's Bay and Opunohu Bay, explore the island's archaeological sites or simply soak up the sun and splash around in the lagoon. From Mo'orea, fly to **Bora Bora**. Live it up for a night or more (depending on your budget) in an overwater bungalow or partake in a variety of water excursions on the vast, blue lagoon. Dine by candlelight, relax in a spa and look out for celebrities. From Bora Bora, it's a short flight to much more low-key **Huahine**, where you can end your holiday with two days of complete relaxation and a taste of authentic Polynesian culture. Go diving or snorkelling, take an island tour, and don't miss trying *ma'a Tahiti* (traditional-style food) at the restaurant Mauarii.

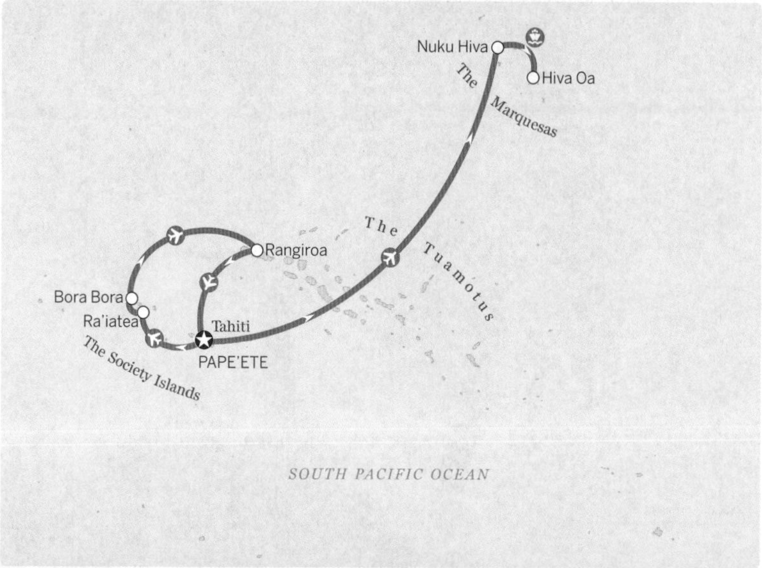

Two weeks or more

Polynesian Passage

Explore French Polynesia's myriad of welcoming cultures as well as its natural beauty. Start with a day or more on **Tahiti**, where you can take an island tour or hire a car to explore Marché de Pape'ete (Pape'ete Market) and the waterfalls, roadside caves and hidden beaches around the island. At night, catch a dance performance at one of the resorts or (if it's a Friday or Saturday) go out for a wild night in **Pape'ete**.

Next get on a plane to **Ra'iatea** to see the impressive Marae Taputapuatea, one of the most important spiritual sites of ancient Polynesia and hike up the Temehani Plateau in search of the *tiare apetahi,* one of the world's rarest flowers. Dive or snorkel the lagoon and be sure to take a picnic tour out to one of the island's fringing white-sand islets or kayak up Faaroa River, the only navigable river in French Polynesia. From here, take a short flight to **Bora Bora** to snorkel the lagoon, swoon at the island's square silhouette and live *la vida jet set* for a day or two. Then take a flight to **Rangiroa**, the largest coral atoll in the country. Dive with sharks, live in your swimsuit and quench your thirst with coconuts. Don't miss a tour of the immense lagoon to see pink-sand beaches and the surreally beautiful Lagon Bleu (Blue Lagoon), a lagoon within a lagoon. At sunset, watch dolphins frolic in Tiputa Pass.

Change cultures entirely when you fly on to the **Marquesas** (via Tahiti). Travelling here is like stepping back in time. You'll start in **Nuku Hiva**, where you can hike across windswept ridges into ancient volcanic craters before checking out the island's array of eerie archaeological sites, including Hikokua, Kamuihei and Tahakia. Follow Gauguin's trail to **Hiva Oa** to see the artist's tomb at Calvaire Cemetery and visit the Espace Cuturel Paul Gauguin. Don't miss the giant stone *tiki* (sacred statues) at Iipona and several other ancient sites on the island. Alternatively, you could visit all of the Marquesas islands by taking the *Aranui* cargo ship for one of the world's most unique cruises focusing on culture and archaeology.

PAUL KENNEDY/LONELY PLANET IMAGES ©

» (above) Stilt bungalows over the waters of Bora Bora (p126)
» (left) Cyclists on Mo'orea (p77)

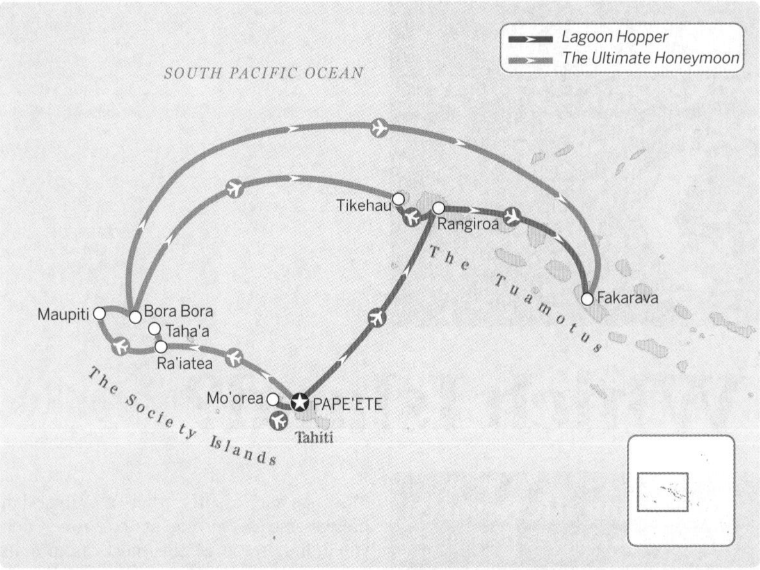

10 days

The Ultimate Honeymoon

The ultimate honeymoon skips the main islands and brings you to our favourite spots for privacy and romance. Fly to Ra'iatea from Pape'ete, then take a boat to a resort at one of **Taha'a's** *motu* (small islets), which look out over the turquoise lagoon and the awe-inspiring outline of Bora Bora. Kayak, take an island tour to visit pearl farms and vanilla plantations, and lounge in your own private paradise. Boat back to Ra'iatea from where you can catch a flight to **Maupiti**, a more isolated and rustic version of Bora Bora. Digs are Polynesian-style bungalows on the beach – nothing fancy, but perfect for snuggling. From Maupiti, take a boat or fly to Bora Bora where you can catch a flight to **Tikehau** to pamper yourselves at the secluded Tikehau Pearl Beach Resort, or to **Fakarava** for a more rustic and even more private experience at Raimiti. Virtually live in the glass-clear lagoon, dive, snorkel, frolic, and then dine on fabulous food and drink cocktails as the sun sets. Of course, you could pick just one of these islands and chill for a week or more.

10 days

Lagoon Hopper

French Polynesia is more of a lagoon destination than a beach destination, and the best lagoons are found in the Tuamotus. First, spend a day on **Tahiti**, followed by at least two nights on **Mo'orea** – see the previous itineraries for more details. Next it's time to explore the otherworldly atolls of the **Tuamotus**. Fly to **Rangiroa**, the biggest and most developed of the archipelago, and spend at least two days exploring the atoll's immense, mostly untouched, lagoon, or diving and snorkelling in its shark-filled passes. After exploring Rangiroa, spend a few days checking out the white-sand beaches and outrageously fauna-rich pass of the prettiest atoll in the Tuamotus, **Tikehau**. Alternatively you could visit the biosphere reserve of **Fakarava** with its two famous diving passes and pink-sand beaches. This itinerary can be done the most economically with an Air Tahiti Lagons Pass.

Which Island?

Best Romantic Resorts

Vahine Island (Taha'a)
La Pirogue (Taha'a)
Ninamu (Tikehau)
St Regis Resort (Bora Bora)
Maitai Lapita Village (Huahine)

Best Romantic Pensions

Raimiti (Fakarava)
Fare Pea Iti (Taha'a)
Fenua Mata'i'oa (Mo'orea)
Vanira Lodge (Tahiti)
Kuriri (Maupiti)

Best-Value Pensions

Maupiti Residence (Maupiti)
Rande's Shack (Huahine)
Pension Atger (Taha'a)
Sunset Hill Lodge (Bora Bora)
Temetiu Village (Hiva Oa)

Best-Value Overwater Bungalows

Le Maitai Bora Bora
Manihi Pearl Beach Resort
Sofitel Bora Bora Marara Beach Resort
Intercontinental Bora Bora Le Moana Resort
Hawaiki Nui Hotel (Ra'iatea)

Best for Families

Les Tipaniers (Mo'orea)
Intercontinental Moorea Resort & Spa
Four Seasons Resort Bora Bora
Sunset Beach Motel (Ra'iatea)

Most people assume that a Polynesian holiday means staying at a resort – and you'll find some of the most sumptuous in the world on these islands – but French Polynesia has a wide range of sleeping options, from camping upwards. The majority of French Polynesia's accommodation is in double-occupancy bungalows, either at a resort, a small hotel or a family-run pension (the French version of a bed and breakfast that doesn't necessarily include breakfast). Deciding where to stay will define the ex-perience you have in this country.

The Resort Experience

If you are ever going to pamper yourself silly, French Polynesia is a great place to do it. The luxury hotels often manage to blend their opulent bungalows into the natural setting. Many of the top hotels are on isolated *motu* (islets), and can only be reached by boat.

Resort Islands

While Bora Bora is undoubtedly French Polynesia's resort hotspot, its price tag is not for everyone. Here's the low-down on resort destinations around the country:

Tahiti

Most people stay at resorts on Tahiti as a stopover to farther-flung islands. Rooms are comfortable, there will inevitably be a

ACCOMMODATION PRICE RANGES

The following price ranges are used in this guide and refer to a double room or bungalow with bathroom in high season. Unless otherwise stated, the TVA (taxe sur la valeur ajoutée; value-added tax, 5%), a 5% government tax and the taxe de séjour (a daily tax of 50 CFP to 150 CFP per person) are included in the price.

» **$** less than 10,000 CFP

» **$$** 10,000–20,000 CFP

» **$$$** more than 20,000 CFP

stunning swimming pool and great restaurants, but the beach may be artificial and you'll be surrounded by suburban sprawl.

Mo'orea

Got kids? Mo'orea is the best family resort destination in the country although it also caters well to active honeymooners and seekers of good value. It's arguably as beautiful as Bora Bora, but the resorts have remained more low-key and thus lower-priced.

Huahine

Huahine has some fine, very laid-back resorts far from the jet-set. You'll find some overwater bungalows and lots of warm Polynesian charm.

Ra'iatea & Taha'a

Each island has one or more resorts that are far from the tourist hustle. Taha'a has resorts that rival the luxury of Bora Bora. Ra'iatea's resorts are unpretentious with a natural plantation or nautical feel to them. Both places have the advantage of letting you enjoy the perks of a fabulous resort while having the opportunity to explore a relatively untouristy Polynesian island.

Bora Bora

You'll pay more for less out here – a resort holiday isn't going to be much fun on this island if you have to worry about money. If you've got cash to burn, however, this is the Pacific's most opulent pyre. Beyond top-notch choices, there are midrange options near or on a main island beach.

The Tuamotus

Coral atolls are the ideal destination for divers, snorkellers and anyone who really wants to get away from it all. Rangiroa, Manihi and Tikehau all have sublime resorts. On Rangiroa, you'll be in the main village and between other hotels and houses unless you stay at Kia Ora Sauvage. The romantic resorts on Tikehau and Manihi are more isolated with their own private beaches and regular shuttle boats to explore the villages.

The Marquesas

The two resorts in the Marquesas (one on Nuku Hiva and one on Hiva Oa) are both hilltop retreats offering swimming pools and fine dining before guests hit the jungles and dirt roads via 4WD. The resorts are reasonably comfortable, but this is a destination for the outdoors, archaeology, history, culture and art – not the beach.

What to Expect

You can expect restaurants, bars, a swimming pool, a shop or two and a well organised activities desk. Glass-bottomed coffee tables, which look straight down into the lagoon, have become standard features of the overwater bungalows.

You'll be met at the airport by your resort representative and then be transferred to your resort – either by a waiting speedboat, airplane or van. From registration on you'll be given the choice to partake in organised activities or just chill and explore the island on your own.

Food & Drink

All resorts will have at least one restaurant that will serve a mix of Western, Polynesian, Asian and fusion specialties, usually prepared by an international chef. The bar will be stocked and a good wine selection will be available. Most of the bigger hotels put on a Polynesian dance performance, often with buffet meal, a few times a week. Breakfast is often a buffet and at other times meals will be à la carte, with more simple options like burgers and sandwiches available at lunch.

The Pension or Small Hotel Experience

Pensions are a godsend for travellers who baulk at the prices of the big hotels. These little establishments, generally family-run affairs, are great places to meet locals and other travellers. Upmarket versions can be private and have lots of amenities, but at the lower end of the scale, brace yourself for cold showers, lumpy pillows and thin walls, but lap up the charm and culture.

Think ahead in terms of money, as many pensions do not take credit cards.

Pension & Small-Hotel Islands

Pensions are found throughout French Polynesia and allow you to explore some very remote islands if you're up for an adventure.

Tahiti

There are small hotels and pensions all around Tahiti, from vaguely tacky waterfront business hotels to artistic French-run hilltop bungalows to surf lodges and rustic plywood huts only accessible by boat.

Mo'orea

Mo'orea is one of the few islands that has a handful of backpacker-style accommodation and camping. It also has some very homey local-run places that will treat you like family, some midrange bargains right on the beach and even some extremely high-end villas on private *motu*.

Huahine

Huahine is swarming with wonderful homey pensions, many beachfront, and is also home to Chez Guynette (p105), one of the best backpacker hangouts in the country.

Ra'iatea & Taha'a

Ra'iatea has some excellent choices on beaches and hilltops while Taha'a has mostly more chic, upmarket choices that include meals and activities.

Bora Bora

The pensions on Bora Bora don't give much bang for your buck and there are a scant few, so book in advance if you want to snag a good room. Fortunately, most are around Matira Point, one of the best beaches.

Maupiti

This is one of the world's most beautiful islands and you can choose to stay on a dreamy white-sand *motu* or the charming main island. Plus there are no resorts so it's a very low-key sort of traveller vibe.

The Tuamotus

Life on poor soil with little fresh water is a bit rough, but many higher-end places will buffer you from that – still you'll see firsthand how the locals live. Most places will be all-inclusive of meals.

The Marquesas

If you're staying outside of Nuku Hiva and Hiva Oa you'll have no choice but to stay at a pension. Choices range from bare bones to very comfortable and most places will include two or three meals per day in the price.

The Australs & Gambier

Rurutu has one relatively swanky hotel, while on the rest of these islands a pension will be the only option. Again, these range in type from a musty room in the back of grandma's house to professionally run bungalow operations offering plenty of tourist support and excursions.

CAMPING & HOSTELS

Camping options come and go, but generally it's a matter of pensions having areas where you can pitch your tent and offer use of their facilities; you'll pay anywhere from around 1200 CFP to 2500 CFP per person. You'll find camping on Tahiti, Mo'orea, Huahine, Ra'iatea, Bora Bora, Maupiti, Rangiroa, Tikehau and Mataiva. A scant number of guesthouses (on Tahiti, Mo'orea, Bora Bora, Rangiroa and Huahine) have dorm beds ranging from 2000 CFP to 3500 CFP per person per night. See the Sleeping sections in the destination chapters for more detail.

What to Expect

Some pensions on main islands may have air-con; many will be fan-cooled and provide mosquito nets and mosquito coils. Few have pools. All should have towels and linens. Most places will pick you up at the airport if you've arranged it in advance.

On the main islands some pensions are more like boutique hotels. On the more remote islands, however, you may encounter faulty plumbing, cold showers, unreliable electricity and a rustic set-up. If you need wi-fi or internet, check in advance to make sure your place will have it.

Expect to meet other travellers (often European), chat a bit with your host family, play with their kids and pet their dogs.

Food & Drink

Many pensions offer (and sometimes insist upon) half board (or *demi-pension*), which usually means breakfast and dinner eaten with the family and other guests. Full board means all meals are included. In many cases, the food is a mix of French, Chinese and Tahitian and, on less touristy islands, there might not be other eating options available anyway.

Activities

If you're staying at a pension on a remote island it's a good idea to organise activities before you go or at least to let your hosts know that you'll be interested in what's on offer. Resorts and upscale pensions will always have plenty of activities available for their guests or work with independent operators they know and trust.

Lagoon Tours

Lagoon tours are the best ways to see an island. Picnics are often included – this might mean *poisson cru* (raw fish in coconut milk) and other foods prepared for the day or it might mean a seafood barbeque on the beach. Whatever the case, cruising around the lagoon in a speed boat with a bunch of food and drink is the way most Polynesians like to spend their weekends so, even though you'll feel like a tourist, you'll actually be acting like a local.

The length and price of the tour will depend on where you're going, but you can expect a half day to cost 3000 CFP to 5000 CFP and a full day to cost 7000 CFP to 10,000 CFP. Resorts often run their own tours while there are also usually independent tours available – the latter will usually be cheaper and a more local experience.

TOP SPAS

- » Intercontinental Bora Bora Resort & Thalasso Spa
- » Intercontinental Moorea Resort & Spa
- » St Regis Resort (Bora Bora)
- » Hilton Bora Bora Nui Resort & Spa

Diving

Many resorts have dive centres and pensions will always hook you up with diving if it's available on the island. In fact, diving is such a big deal we've devoted a whole chapter to it; see p31 for details.

Spa Treatments

Almost all top-end resorts have a spa. Therapies make the most of the local bounty and can include luxuries like black-pearl and vanilla scrubs, coconut-based *monoi* massage oils, Polynesian healer–inspired remedies and baths full of fragrant tropical flowers. The best take advantage of the view – for example the Deep Ocean Spa at the Intercontinental Bora Bora Resort & Thalasso Spa lets you gaze at the island's iconic peak and look through glass floor panels at the fish while enjoying their signature sea-based treatments.

Some pensions work with local massage therapists who will come and give you a rub down onsite, but for a real spa experience you'll have to book something at a resort.

Water Sports

Most resorts have a water-sports centre (but not all, so make sure you check before booking). These vary enormously – some offer the most basic array of canoes and windsurfing, while others run the gauntlet from waterskiing to kiteboarding and wakeboarding. Only the biggest pensions will have water-sports centres, but even smaller mom-and-pop places may have old windsurfers or kayaks – ask in advance.

HOLIDAY RENTALS

Holiday rentals (private homes or rooms rented by an individual) are becoming more popular in French Polynesia, particularly on Mo'orea, although there are also some good options on Tahiti. These often self-catering options can be fun and economical for families or people travelling in larger groups who plan on staying in one place for more than a night or two.

We've listed our favourites under the sleeping headings in this book. To search further, good sites include the following:

» www.airbnb.com

» www.homeaway.com

» www.vrbo.com

Wildlife-Watching

Dive centres on many islands offer whale- and dolphin-watching – some of these places are affiliated with resorts. There are also plenty of independent dolphin- and whale-watching tours.

Planning & Choosing

Independent Travel

Outside of high season (June through August and mid-December through mid-January) you could arrive in French Polynesia without any idea of where you're going or what you're doing and have an amazing trip. During the seasonal rush, however, the better places will be booked so it's wise to plan in advance.

A good place to start planning your adventure is the website of **Air Tahiti** (www.airtahiti.com) to see where it flies, its schedules and its prices. If you've got lots of time and don't mind seriously roughing it, check the supply-ship schedules available daily in the *La Dêpeche* newspaper. See the Transport chapter for more details.

Package Tours

French Polynesia lends itself to the package tour. Given the high price of flights to the region, and the often astronomical price of accommodation once there, a package tour can work out to be a financial blessing. On the downside, package tours don't give much leeway to explore at will. Although most tours offer the opportunity to visit more than one island, you will have to prebook one hotel or pension for each destination before departure (meaning you can't swap resorts halfway through if you're not happy).

There's a variety of tour packages available from travel agents and online booking agencies in all Western countries. If you want more than a straightforward combo package, a good travel agent is essential – they can negotiate better prices at the larger hotels and handle Air Tahiti bookings for your domestic flights once in French Polynesia. In addition to the traditional travel operators, there are agencies that specialise in diving tours – these packages typically include flights, accommodation and diving excursions.

Where to Book a Package

A great list of packages available from several different agencies with departures from around the world is available on the **Air Tahiti Nui** (www.airtahitinui.com) website.

For stays in family pensions or small hotels you can book very economical packages from **Easy Tahiti** (www.easytahiti.com).

Note that most packages quote double occupancy pricing. Solo travellers have to pay a 'single-person supplement'. Extra people can usually share a room, but there's a charge for the extra bed, which varies enormously from resort to resort.

Diving

When to Go

There are regularly optimal diving conditions throughout the year, except when the trade wind blows, from June to August, producing choppy seas. Water temperatures range from a low of 26°C to a high of 29°C on most islands. You won't need anything more than a thin neoprene wetsuit.

Best for Certification

Tahiti
Mo'orea
Huahine
Bora Bora

Best Drift Dives

Tiputa Pass (Rangiroa)
Garuae Pass (Fakarava)

Best Manta-Ray Encounters

Anau (Bora Bora)
Manta Point (Maupiti)
La Ferme aux Mantas (Tikehau)
Tiputa Pass (Rangiroa)
Nuku Hiva (Marquesas)

Best Shark Encounters

Tapu (Bora Bora)
Tiputa Pass (Rangiroa)
Le Bleu (Rangiroa)
Tumakohua Pass (Fakarava)
Teavapiti Pass (Ra'iatea)

Island-by-Island Guide

From Fakarava in the Tuamotus to Hiva Oa in the Marquesas, you'll be spoilt for choice. Just as the individual islands have their distinct personalities, so too the dive sites have their own hallmarks. Just take your pick! All dive sites are mapped in the destination chapters.

Tahiti

Although less charismatic than other French Polynesian islands, Tahiti shouldn't be sneezed at, with about 20 lagoon and ocean sites between Arue and Pa'ea, plus the odd wreck. There's also superb diving off Tahiti Iti.

» **The Aquarium** Multihued tropicals flitting among coral boulders scattered on a sandy floor in less than 10m, as well as two minor wrecks (an old Cessna aircraft and a cargo boat), make this site exciting for beginners. Off Faa'a airport's runway.

» **The Cargo Ship & the Catalina** Another lagoon dive suitable for novices. It refers to a shipwreck and an aircraft wreck. Of particular interest is the *Catalina*, a twin-engine WWII flying boat that was scuttled in 1964. Its right wing tip rests on the seabed at 20m. Off the airport in Faa'a.

» **St Etienne Drop-Off** A perfect wall dive just outside the reef at Puna'auia.

» **The Spring** (La Source) A very atmospheric site featuring three towering coral mounts and a couple of freshwater springs bubbling up from the ocean floor. Off Puna'auia on the west coast.

DIVING IN TAHITI & FRENCH POLYNESIA – AN OVERVIEW

ISLAND	WRECK DIVES	FISH LIFE	SPECIAL FEATURES
Tahiti	+	+	Drop-offs, corals
Mo'orea	N/A	+	Water clarity, lemon sharks
Huahine	N/A	++	Shark dives, drift dives, corals
Ra'iatea & Taha'a	++	+++	Pristine dives, shark & drift dives, corals
Bora Bora	N/A	++	Shark dives, manta ray cleaning station
Maupiti	N/A	++	Manta ray cleaning station, corals, drop-offs
Rangiroa	N/A	+++	Shark dives, manta rays, drift dives
Tikehau	N/A	+++	Shark dives, manta ray cleaning station
Manihi	N/A	++	Manta ray cleaning station, easy dives
Fakarava	N/A	+++	Shark dives, manta rays, drift dives, corals
Makemo	N/A	++	Off the beaten track
Marquesas	N/A	+++	Hammerhead sharks, manta rays, plankton-filled waters

+ (average), ++ (good), +++ (very good)

» **Turtles' Plateau** As the name suggests, one or two curious turtles can be seen frolicking among divers. A pod of dolphins also frequents this site every morning. It's off Musée de Tahiti et des Îles on the west coast.

» **White Valley** You'll see whitetip and blacktip sharks as well as Napoleons and moray eels in about 20m. Off Pa'ea on the west coast.

» **Faults of Arue** On the north coast near Matavai Bay. This area features a good mix of gentle coral plateaus and steep drop-offs broken up by a series of fissures.

» **Marado** The best dive off Tahiti Iti. Renowned for its abundance of gorgonians that decorate a steep drop-off.

» **Hole in the Lagoon** (Le Trou du Lagon) Features a large circular basin inside the lagoon, off the south coast of Tahiti Iti.

Mo'orea

A perfect introduction to more challenging dive sites in the Tuamotus, Mo'orea offers easy, relaxed diving, with a good balance of reef dives and shark dives. Most diving is focused at the entrances to Cook's Bay and Opunohu Bay, and off the northwestern corner of the island. Unlike those in neighbouring Tahiti, the reefs here do not drop off steeply, but slope gently away in a series of canyons and valleys. Sadly, corals are in a bad shape due to the crown-of-thorns starfish.

» **Tiki** Because of the site's long history of fish feeding, there are gangs of blacktip, grey and lemon sharks. Off Hauru Point.

» **Opunohu Canyons/Eden Park** Famous for the many bulky lemon sharks (up to seven individuals) that regularly patrol the area, in about 20m. On the north coast.

» **Taotoi** Another favourite, on the north coast, with a pleasant seascape. Watch for eagle rays passing through a nearby channel.

» **Roses** Also on the north coast, seasoned divers might descend to 40m to hover over this gorgeous field of *Montipora* coral.

» **Vaiare Pass** This east-coast site is used by the dive centre based at the Sofitel Moorea la Ora Beach Resort. Lemon sharks and blacktip sharks are commonly seen patrolling around the pass.

» **Temae** Another east-coast site that's offered by the centre based at the Sofitel Moorea la Ora Beach Resort. On a sandy slope, conger eels wave in the current like some strange vegetation.

Huahine

If you want relaxed diving, Huahine will appeal to you. There are some superb reef dives off Fare, near the airport (to the north of the island), and off Huahine Iti (to the south).

» **Avapeihi (Fitii) Pass** A longstanding favourite, just a five-minute boat ride from Fare. The highlight of the site is the dazzling aggregation of barracudas, snappers, trevallies and grey reef sharks. The best opportunity to spot predators is during an outgoing current, when they patrol the pass in search of drifting lagoon fish. The only drawback is the slightly reduced visibility.

» **Faa Miti** Just before the airstrip, it features a series of atmospheric coral boulders laced with sand valleys at around 25m.

» **Araara Pass** Another well-respected dive site, off the southern tip of Huahine Iti. Turtles, sharks and barracudas.

Ra'iatea & Taha'a

Ra'iatea has the only real wreck dive in French Polynesia.

» **The Nordby** This 50m vessel that sank in August 1900 is easily accessible, right off the hotel Raiatea Hawaiki Nui, lying on her side on a sandy bottom, between 18m and 29m. Look for the resident fish that hide in the darker parts, including groupers, soldierfish, Moorish idols, lionfish, a couple of moray eels and crustaceans. Visibility is not the strong point of this dive.

» **Teavapiti Pass** As in all passes in French Polynesia, a strong tidal current runs through it, providing food for the little guys at the bottom of the food chain, who, in turn, attract middle- and upper-chain critters.

» **Miri Miri Pass** This pass off the western coast has lots of fish action and delicate bunches of purple *Distichopora* coral.

» **Roses** At about 40m, the seabed is blanketed with gorgeous *Montipora* coral formations. Off the northwestern coast, it's for advanced divers.

» **Mounts of Ceran** Off Taha'a, this site is renowned for its contoured topography and prolific fish life, including grey sharks, barracudas and trevallies.

» **Tiva Pass** Off Taha'a, this site offers a superb underwater terrain and a fine cast of reef fish and pelagics.

» **Octopus' Hole** (Le Trou de la Pieuvre) A spectacular blue hole that penetrates well into the reef. It's in the lagoon, to the southeast of Taha'a. The entrance is at 27m. For seasoned divers.

» **Tau Tau** Off Taha'a's west coast. A gently sloping reef with regular sightings of trevally, tuna, barracuda and Napoleon wrass. Visibility is top-notch.

» **Lagon Tau Tau** A superb dive inside Taha'a's lagoon – perfect for beginners. Features coral gardens and a small drop-off.

Bora Bora

Surprisingly, there are only four to five sites that are regularly offered on this magical island.

» **Anau** In the lagoon off Anau, this spot features a manta ray cleaning station in less than 20m. Visibility is average.

» **Tapu** Sharks are the major attraction – a result of regular fish feeding. Apart from blacktip reef

PRE-TRIP PREPARATION

» Make sure you possess a current diving-certification card (C-card) from a recognised scuba-diving instructional agency, and bring it with you. Dive operators will need to see it. It's a good idea to have your dive logbook with you as well.

» Remember to allow 24 hours after diving before you fly. Careful attention to flight times is necessary in French Polynesia because so much of the interisland transportation is by air.

» Divers with a C-card get a 15kg allowance on Air Tahiti flights.

THE FIRST TIME

Always fancied venturing underwater on a scuba dive? Now's your chance. French Polynesia is a perfect starting point for new divers, as the warm, turquoise water in the shallow lagoons is a forgiving training environment. Most resorts offer courses for beginners and employ experienced instructors, most of them competent in English.

Just about anyone in reasonably good health can sign up for an introductory dive (*baptême* in French), including children aged eight and over. It typically takes place in shallow (3m to 5m) water and lasts about 30 minutes. You're escorted by a divemaster.

If you choose to enrol in an Open Water course while in French Polynesia, count on it taking about three to four days, including classroom lectures and open-water training. Once you're certified, your C-card is valid permanently and recognised all over the world.

sharks, you'll certainly come across massive lemon sharks, usually found at around 25m. It's north of Motu Tapu.

» **Toopua & Toopua Iti** South of Teavanui Pass in the west of Bora Bora. Enjoy the channel where you can spot eagle rays, or explore the area's varied topography, with numerous canyons, gullies, corridors and swim-throughs.

» **Muri Muri** (The White Valley) At the northern apex of the ring of islets encircling Bora Bora. Strong currents and regular feedings in the past ensure a respectable crowd of sharks, as well as trevallies, tuna and turtles.

» **Haapiti** A relaxed dive along a sloping reef, with regular sightings of lemon sharks and blacktip reef sharks.

Maupiti

Maupiti has some remarkable lagoon dives, and some superb reef and wall dives along the east side of the island.

» **Manta Point** Maupiti's signature dive, in the lagoon, is aptly named. This cleaning station is visited by manta rays; small fish come out of the coral heads to scour the mantas of parasites, in less than 6m.

» **Nemo** Another lagoon dive, this is an easy site, with coral pinnacles scattered over a sandy floor in less than 6m.

» **Coral Garden** Also in the lagoon, with copious fish life and pinnacles blanketed in corals.

» **Faaapu** A hot-favourite reef dive; here the reef features a large circular basin at 12m and a succession of small sandy plateaus.

» **Grey's Hole** (Trou aux Gris) Nearby to Faaapu, Grey's Hole offers a range of terrain and varied marine life, including a great concentration of grey sharks at 50m.

Rangiroa

Rangiroa is the stuff of legend, and one of the most charismatic dive areas in the South Pacific. It's brimming with adrenaline-pumping dive sites, and opportunities to approach big stuff just offshore. The weak points include the rather dull coral formations.

» **Tiputa Pass** With its amazing drift dives and dense concentration of pelagics, Tiputa Pass is almost a spiritual experience. Incredible rides are guaranteed every time, as are bewildering numbers of grey reef sharks at the entrance of the pass. Eagle rays, manta rays, dolphins, tuna, trevallies and hammerheads are also regularly seen.

» **L'Eolienne** By outgoing current, L'Eolienne, along the outer reef east of Tiputa Pass, is regularly scheduled.

» **Avatoru Pass** This pass offers regular sightings of manta rays, as well as a few intimidating silvertips that are attracted by bait brought by the dive instructors.

» **The Aquarium** Located at Motu Nuhi Nuhi – a coral islet that stretches across Tiputa Pass just inside the lagoon – this is a favourite for novice divers, with a jumble of coral pinnacles providing a haven for a vast array of small critters in less than 10m.

» **Le Bleu** Some dive centres take divers out into the open ocean off Tiputa Pass. Then divers are positioned in about 15m of water, in the blue, while bait in a small cage is lowered in the midwater, attracting sharks from the depths. Thrilling!

» **Les Failles** Some dive centres organise day trips to Les Failles, Rangi's best-kept secret, at the southwestern edge of the atoll. Along the outer reef, a sheer drop-off sinks into the abyss. It's broken up by a series of fissures and overhangs festooned with gorgonians.

» (above) Shark feeding, Mo'orea (p32)
» (left) Manta ray, Fakarava (p36)

ERIC LE BORGNE

Eric Le Borgne is a dive instructor and an expert on marine life in French Polynesia. He works on Rurutu and Rangiroa.

What makes diving in French Polynesia so special? French Polynesia has no equivalent because big species, such as sharks, manta rays, turtles, barracudas and dolphins, are almost guaranteed, sometimes in one single dive. And most sites are suitable for novice divers.

Which islands do you particularly recommend? For diving fiends, the atolls of the Tuamotus are the highlights – try to combine at least three islands, such as Rangiroa, Fakarava and Tikehau. Novices can start their trip with more relaxed sites in the Society Islands, such as Mo'orea or Huahine.

Your favourite dive site? My favourite dive site is Tiputa Pass in Rangiroa. It's like visiting an underwater safari park. It's superior to the Cocos Island in Costa Rica or the Galapagos because it's so easy to get to the site – it's only a five-minute boat ride.

Other not-to-be-missed experiences? If you're travelling in French Polynesia between July and October, be sure to book a whale-watching trip. I suggest Rurutu in the Australs as the visibility is exceptional, but before getting there make sure the humpbacks are around – their presence is not guaranteed.

Tikehau

Although it's less charismatic than neighbouring Rangiroa, Tikehau has its fair share of underwater delights.

» **Tuheiava Pass** Most dives take place in or around Tikehau's only pass, about 30 minutes by boat from Tuherahera village. Grey sharks, silvertips, barracudas, trevallies and the usual reef species regularly cruise by.

» **Le Trou aux Requins** A steep drop-off south of Tuheiava Pass. It features a tunnel that descends well into the reef; the entrance is at 57m, but you don't need to go that deep to see a congregation of sharks that usually hang around the entrance. The reef is peppered with fissures, ledges and overhangs.

» **La Ferme aux Mantas** (Mantas' Farm) The only site inside the lagoon features a cleaning station where manta rays (usually three to five individuals) come to get scoured of parasites by little cleaner wrasses.

Manihi

Some 175km northeast of Rangiroa, Manihi has only one pass.

» **Tairapa Pass** The best dives are around the pass. With an outgoing current, you can dive the western exit of the pass at a place named Le Tombant Ouest or the eastern exit at Le Tombant Est, which both feature prolific fish life, including a few sharks, trevallies, barracudas and sea bream. Every year in May and June, masses of groupers come to breed here.

» **Le Cirque** This stunning site refers to an area in the lagoon at the exit of the pass. Visibility doesn't exceed 15m, but this site is famous for the regular manta-ray encounters in less than 20m of water.

» **La Faille** A large fissure in the reef north of the pass.

» **The Coral Garden** Near La Faille. A relaxed dive for beginners. Plenty of healthy corals and reef life.

Fakarava

A 40-minute plane hop from Rangiroa, Fakarava is one of the most fascinating atolls in the Tuamotus, with a true sense of wilderness and frontier diving. There are only two dive areas, Garuae Pass at the northern end of the atoll and Tumakohua Pass at the southern end. Fakarava shares the same characteristics as Rangiroa, with the added appeal of much healthier coral formations.

» **Garuae Pass** (Northern Pass) Swimming through the intense cobalt blue water towards the entrance of this gigantic pass is an unsurpassable experience. Expect to come across hunting sharks, numerous reef fish and, if you're lucky, manta rays. The dive usually finishes at Ali Baba Cavern, a large coral basin at 15m, replete with schooling fish. When the tide is going out, you dive along the outer reef at Ohotu, away from the current. Here you can find some really healthy coral gardens.

» **Pufana (The Red Buoy)** This easy site inside the lagoon is great for brushing up your skills before tackling Garuae Pass.

» **Tumakohua Pass** (Southern Pass) At the southern end of the atoll. At the entrance of the pass, you'll see a profusion of small and large reef fish, including bigeyes and marbled groupers (they breed here in July). Dozens of grey reef sharks (up to 200 individuals on one single dive!) regularly pass by the right side of the pass, at 28m. Other attractions include white-sand gullies, where whitetip sharks usually lie, as well as healthy coral formations in the shallows at the end of the dive.

Makemo

Makemo is still a secret, word-of-mouth destination for divers. If you venture this far in the central Tuamotus, you'll be rewarded with pristine sites.

» **Arikitamiro Pass** A five-minute boat ride from the village. Sharks, Napoleon wrasses, barracudas, tuna, groupers and the whole gamut of tropicals can be spotted here.

» **Tapuhiria Pass** This second pass is well worth the 90-minute boat ride from the village, with lots of fish action during tidal changes and a surreal atmosphere due to the remoteness of the site.

» **Pohue Point** A virgin tract of reef about 45 minutes from the village.

The Marquesas

A three-hour flight from Tahiti, the Marquesas open up a whole new world of diving. The main highlight is the dramatic seascape, with numerous drop-offs, caverns, arches and ledges, giving the sites a peculiarly sculpted look and an eerie atmosphere. To top it all off, the environment is still unspoiled. However, don't expect gin-clear waters. Since the Marquesas are devoid of any protective barrier reefs, the water is thick with plankton and visibility doesn't exceed 10m to 15m. You should also be prepared to cope with sometimes-difficult conditions to get to the sites. Diving is available on Nuku Hiva and Hiva Oa.

» **Sentinelle aux Marteaux** (Nuku Hiva) At the entrance of Taiohae Bay, this is a great spot to see hammerheads. Sadly, visibility usually doesn't exceed 10m.

» **Tikapo Point** (Nuku Hiva) Off Tikapo Point, to the southeast of Nuku Hiva, this is a sensational site packed with fish action. Expect strong currents, though. For advanced divers.

» **Motumano Point** (Nuku Hiva) Off the southwestern coast of the island, this site is known for its concentration of manta rays, eagle rays and sharks.

» **Matateiko Point** (Nuku Hiva) The furthest site from Taiohae, this is another point jutting out into the ocean. The varied underwater terrain and the currents act as magnets for a host of pelagics, including sharks and rays.

Dive Centres

There are about 30 professional dive centres in French Polynesia. They are open year-round, most of them every day. All are land-based and many of them are attached to a hotel. See the individual island chapters for specific operators. You can expect the following from the dive centres:

» They offer a whole range of services and products, such as introductory dives (for children aged eight years and over, and adults), Nitrox

RESPONSIBLE DIVING

The French Polynesian islands and atolls are ecologically vulnerable. By following these guidelines while diving, you can help preserve the ecology and beauty of the reefs:

» Encourage dive operators in their efforts to establish permanent moorings at appropriate dive sites.

» Practise and maintain proper buoyancy control.

» Avoid touching living marine organisms with your body and equipment.

» Take great care in underwater caves, as your air bubbles can damage fragile organisms.

» Minimise your disturbance of marine animals.

» Take home all your rubbish and any litter you may find as well.

» Never stand on corals, even if they look solid and robust.

dives, night dives, exploratory dives and certification programs. They typically offer two to four dives a day.

» All are affiliated to one or more internationally recognised certifying agencies (PADI, NAUI, CMAS, SSI).

» All require you to have a dive medical certificate if you enrol in a certification course, which they can arrange (about 3000 CFP).

» In general, equipment is well maintained, facilities are well equipped and staff are friendly, knowledgeable and can speak English.

» Most offer free pick-up from, and drop off to, your accommodation.

» Almost all accept credit cards.

Live-Aboards

Only two live-aboards operate in French Polynesia: **Aqua Polynésie** (www.aquatiki.com) and **Niyati Plongée** (www.niyati-plongee.com). Aqua Polynésie specialises in the Tuamotus while Niyati Plongée offers trips to the Society Islands.

Costs

Diving in French Polynesia is fairly expensive; expect to pay about 6000 CFP to 8500 CFP for a single dive. However, there are multi-dive packages, which per dive come much cheaper. Prices include equipment rental, so you don't need to bring all your gear.

Topdive (www.topdive.com) has its own interisland pass that can be used in Tahiti, Mo'orea, Bora Bora, Fakarava, Tikehau, Manihi and Rangiroa. Another good-value pass is Te Moana Pass, an interisland dive pass that's accepted in 11 dive shops in French Polynesia. Purchase it at any of the participating dive shops.

Recompression Chamber

There's one recompression chamber in Pape'ete, Tahiti, at the Centre Hospitalier du Taaone. See also Diving Hazards, p241.

Travel with Children

Best Regions for Kids

Mo'orea
The best beaches, dolphin- and whale-watching, horse riding, dive centres catering to kids and lots of amenities.

Huahine
A true Polynesian cultural experience, plus soft, white beaches and places to swim and snorkel. Enjoy a history lesson by taking an island tour and strolling the Maeva archaeology site.

Bora Bora
The lagoon is like a giant swimming pool and resorts will cater to your every need, including babysitting. Biking the island is a good family outing.

Tahiti
Great for teens, with lively beaches, dances and a surf scene. Hike, surf, horse ride and find dive centres with kids programs.

Rangiroa
For water- and beach-loving families wanting to dive, snorkel and watch dolphins frolicking at sunset.

French Polynesia for Kids

French Polynesia is a water playground for all ages. But beyond sun and swimming it's also a place of gentle culture and adventures to caves and waterfalls.

Water Activities

Diving, Snorkelling & Swimming

Babies and toddlers will be happy on a soft beach and perhaps with a hermit crab to hassle. For slightly older children, any place with a shallow sandy bottom is a great place to learn to swim. Seasoned swimmers can cruise around the lagoon in areas free of current and boat traffic.

Once kids are comfortable in a mask and snorkel, it can be hard to get them out of the water. Just be sure that they don't touch or walk on coral, both for their safety and for the preservation of the underwater environment. If no one touches anything, there are few dangers beyond sunburn.

Many dive centres offer 'Bubble Maker' courses for children eight years and up, where kids take their first breaths under water. Good swimmers over nine can enrol in Junior PADI Open Water courses, and in some cases can even get school credit for it (see www.padi.com).

Wildlife Watching

Dolphin- and whale-watching will thrill kids, but if it's rough out, the unpleasantness of seasickness may outweigh the excitement of seeing marine mammals.

BEACH & SHALLOW-WATER CRITTERS

Wear plastic or protective sandals when playing in the water to guard against stonefish – fish that look exactly like a piece of rock or coral and have poisonous spines that can potentially ruin your trip.

What you're more likely to see are black or beige sea cucumbers in the shallows that can be picked up safely. Be gentle! Hermit crab races make for hours of fun and if you find an empty shell suitable for a hermit crab home, try putting it in a container with the right sized hermit crab to see if he/she will come out to trade shells. They are surprisingly fashion conscious. Then, most importantly, put the newly dressed crab back where you found it.

Another option is to visit the Intercontinental Moorea Resort & Spa where you can pay for an in-water 'dolphin encounter'. Nonpaying guests aren't technically allowed past the resort's restaurant area, but you can ask permission to watch the dolphins. The mammals were either born in captivity or are retired US Navy dolphins, and the centre has plenty of accreditation behind it; still, seeing these beautiful creatures in captivity can be a bit sad.

Surfing & Boogie Boarding

It can be hard to find a board in French Polynesia, but some hotels and pensions have them for guests. Boogie boards are often on sale in local shops; if you can buy one, you'll make a local kid's year by leaving it with them when you leave. The best beach breaks are found almost exclusively on Tahiti and Mo'orea. Surf lessons are available on Tahiti (see p73).

Landlubbers

Hiking & Canyoneering

Over-eights will love Tahiti's interior, which is chock-a-block with waterfalls, many with icy pools to swim in. There are also plenty of dark caves (these can be scary so take it slow). For older kid adventure, hire a canyoneering guide to take your family rappelling down steep river valleys.

Archaeology

French Polynesian archaeological sites are fun for kids because there is tons of open space, you can climb on almost anything and the surrounding jungles often hold discoveries like wild passionfruit. Remember the mosquito repellent.

Horse Riding & Biking

There are several places for trail riding on Tahiti, Mo'orea, Huahine and in the Marquesas. In general the routes go through hilly regions and plantations and are geared to all ages.

Bicycles can be rented on most islands and, other than on Tahiti, traffic is light. Child-sized bicycles can be hard to find, however.

Eating Out

French Polynesian food is rarely spicy and, although children's portions are virtually unheard of, it's easy to find kid-friendly dishes on most menus. Don't expect booster seats or high chairs, but do expect a welcoming atmosphere in most eateries. Tahitian food is traditionally eaten with the fingers; kids will love digging into dishes like *chevrettes* (freshwater shrimp), *brochettes* (shish kebabs of meat or fish) or *poisson cru* (fish in coconut milk). Western-style food is also widely available.

For babies, jarred baby food and infant formula can be found even in remote areas. Polynesians love children; don't be afraid to ask for assistance in finding certain foods or cooking facilities.

The water is safe to drink in Pape'ete and other select areas of Tahiti, on Bora Bora and on Tubuai, but you may like to buy bottled water anyway. On the other islands you will all be dependent on bottled or filtered water.

Teen Nightlife

It's normal in French Polynesia for whole families to party together; teens are welcome, and usually show up in numbers at any sort of local dance performance or show.

In Pape'ete, discotheques like Mana Rock are swarming with high-schoolers. Be warned that alcohol flows freely and it's a meat-market atmosphere.

Children's Highlights

Beach Yourself

» **Swimming & Splashing** Temae Beach (Mo'orea) is like a giant, calm swimming pool; Matira Beach (Bora Bora) has gorgeous white sand and shallow swimming; black-sand Pointe

Vénus (Tahiti) is popular with local families; Fare (Huahine) is a mellow, white beach with swimming and snorkelling in front.

» **Surfing** Teahupoo (Tahiti) has a great beach break at the river mouth that's swarming with local kids; Papenoo (Tahiti) is where the island learns to surf thanks to the line-up of easy waves; Pueu (Tahiti) can get big, but it's on sand and is popular with boogie boarders.

» **Snorkelling** Plop in almost anywhere in the lagoon in the Tuamotus, but be prepared to see (near-harmless) sharks; Temae Beach and Hauru Point on Mo'orea offer easy, shallow snorkelling; Ra'iatea's *motu* are the best spots to see fish; plunge in from Fare Beach on Huahine for some beautiful undersea life; sandy Bora Bora doesn't have a lot to see underwater, but it's a good spot for beginners; the *motu* of Maupiti are better for confident swimmers, with plenty of fish and corals.

A History Lesson

» **Archaeology** Taputapuatea (Ra'iatea) is so big it's as good to run around as it is to learn from; the *tiki* (sacred statues) at Iipona (the Marquesas) will make older kids feel like Indiana Jones; look for wild passionfruit around Marae Titiroa (Mo'orea).

» **European & American Contact** Pointe Vénus (Tahiti), where Cook first landed, and Cook's Bay (Mo'orea); Bora Bora's WWII guns for war chitchat; the Gambier for European-style churches looking out of place in Polynesia.

» **Museums** Musée de Tahiti et des Îles on Tahiti has great history displays plus it's right on the beach; Tahiti's Musée Gauguin has a reproduction of the painter's house and the botanical gardens next door; older kids who know the *Mutiny on the Bounty* story will appreciate seeing how the author lived at the House of James Norman Hall, also on Tahiti; Espace Culturel Paul Gauguin, on Hiva Oa in the Marquesas, has a life-sized replica of Gauguin's house and Jacques Brel's airplane among other fun exhibits.

Budding Naturalists

» **Caves** Mara'a Grotto (Tahiti) is set in a lush, fairytale-like park; at Vaipoiri (Tahiti) the brave can swim to the back of a pitch-black cave and let their eyes adjust to the light; Hitiaa Lava Tubes (Tahiti) is best for older kids who can swim and hike well (guides often provide wetsuits for the cold water); Rurutu has tons of easy-access caves full of stalactites and stalagmites.

» **Gardens** Tahiti's botanical gardens is one of the best places for kids on the island with plenty of space to run around, vines to swing on and ducks and two Galapagos turtles to ogle; also on Tahiti, Vaipahi Spring Gardens is a lovely space with a waterfall and lots of room to move.

» **Waterfalls** At Faarumai Waterfalls (Tahiti) look for star fruit along the way and crane your head to see the tops of these incredibly high falls; Vaipahi Spring Gardens (Tahiti) has a beautiful landscaped area around its waterfall.

WHAT TO PACK

All ages need the usual suspects: sunscreen (expensive in French Polynesia), insect repellent and rain gear.

Babies & Toddlers

» A folding pushchair is practical for most areas of this guide, while a baby carrier is a better option if you plan on hiking or exploring archaeological sites.

» A portable changing mat, handwash gel etc (baby-changing facilities are a rarity).

» Nappies (diapers) are available but are pricey (about 2000 CFP for 38 nappies).

Six to 12 years

» Binoculars for young explorers to zoom in on wildlife, surfers riding reef-breaking waves etc.

» A camera to inject newfound fun into 'boring' grown-up sights and walks.

» Field guides to Polynesian flora and fauna.

Teens

» A French phrasebook.

» Mask, snorkel and flippers.

» A copy of *Mutiny on the Bounty.*

» **Dolphin- & Whale-Watching** Mo'orea has heaps of boats available; Tahiti is less popular, so you can avoid the crowds; Rurutu is better for older kids who are confident snorkelling.

Planning

Where to Stay

Choosing the right place to stay in French Polynesia is important. The majority of French Polynesia's lodgings will cater to children, but some are geared more towards families than others. Some resorts offer kids clubs and babysitting, while family pensions are usually a great place for your children to play with local kids!

Discounts

The **Carte Famille** (Family Card; 2000 CFP) entitles you to significant reductions on some flights (see p249 for details). At hotels and guesthouses, children under 12 generally pay only 50% of the adult rate; very young children usually stay for free.

regions at a glance

French Polynesia is made up of five archipelagos, each with a different culture, language and topography. Linked by their history and European colonisation, the islands within these archipelagos hold even more variations between them – you could spend a lifetime exploring the nuances. The Society Islands hold the places most of us have heard of – Tahiti, Mo'orea, Bora Bora and so on – while we've narrowed down other lesser-known destinations by archipelago name.

Unless you have unlimited time and money, you'll only scratch the surface of this island territory. You'll get a much deeper appreciation for the place, however, by veering off the beaten path, even if it's just for a few days.

Tahiti

Hiking ✓✓✓
Surfing ✓✓✓
Culture ✓✓

Waterfall Valleys

Tahiti is riddled with spring-fed rivers that, over hundreds of thousands of years, have carved mystical fern-carpeted valleys. Explore them on foot or scale the towering waterfalls and lava tubes with a professional canyoneering guide.

The Teahupoo Monster

Don't surf? Get in a taxi boat and watch the pros get gobbled into this wave's cavernous tube from so close you can see their facial expressions. Surf? Then you'd better have balls the size of watermelons.

Dance Spectacular

Watch the locals wiggle at warp speed at traditional dance performances then get your own groove on at Pape'ete's raucous clubs.

p48

Mo'orea

Hiking ✓✓✓
Diving ✓✓
Surfing ✓✓✓

Pineapples to Peaks

Hike or horse ride through jungle-encircled pineapple plantations to viewpoints of peaks carved so intricately by time that they look like they might break off in a strong wind.

Dolphins, Whales & Stingrays

Take a dolphin- or whale-watching tour or get into the lagoon to swim with rubbery stingrays and friendly, snack-seeking reef sharks.

Breaks & Trade Winds

Surf one of the country's better beach breaks at Haapiti and meet friendly locals in the surf. Otherwise, let your kite be towed over stretches of blue lagoon by heady trade winds past white-sand beaches and palm-fringed shores.

p77

Huahine

Archaeology ✓✓
Culture ✓✓
Diving ✓✓

Ancient Village

Stroll the remains of Maeva, a seaside village that was once the seat of royalty on Huahine. Explore the waterfront temples then scramble up the hillside to find crumbling stone vestiges in the bush.

Lost in Time

Slip into island time in Fare, the somniferous capital of Huahine. Fishing boats come in, fishing boats go out, women in flowered clothing buy groceries and, if you're lucky, the cargo ship may be unloading the island's supplies.

Relax Underwater

Low-key diving, snorkelling and beaches are a Huahine speciality. Expect lots of fish, stretches of sand and mellow conditions, great for novices.

p98

Ra'iatea & Taha'a

Archaeology ✓✓✓
Hiking ✓✓
Diving ✓✓

The Big One

You'll feel an unavoidable spiritual buzz at Marae Taputapuatea. Once a meeting place for Polynesians throughout the Pacific, this *marae* (traditional temple) is still one of the most important and well-preserved ancient temples of its kind.

Rare Flower

The *tiare apetahi* is a delicate five-petalled flower resembling a woman's hand that only grows on the Temahani Plateau in Ra'iatea. To see it you'll have to make a challenging hike to the summit and hope for good luck – sightings aren't guaranteed.

What a Wreck

Ra'iatea is home to the *Norby,* the only real diveable wreck in French Polynesia. Expect fish and corals but not great visibility.

p110

Bora Bora

Resorts ✓✓✓
Diving ✓
Hiking ✓

Glamorous Life

Welcome to over-the-water bungalow heaven where drinks are served with a view and pampering is on your tab. Top dining, luxury lagoon tours and sparkling white sands complete the package.

Every Shade of Blue

Bora Bora's sandy-bottom lagoon reflects the sky in so many hues it changes the definition of the word blue. There's not much coral unless you head out to the fringing reef, but it's as safe as a swimming pool, perfect for lapping and lounging.

View From Above

Hike the interior with a guide through deserted forests. If you want to sweat, make the challenging climb up Mt Pahia, the island's signature square peak.

p126

Maupiti

Diving ✓✓
Culture ✓
Hiking ✓

Gentle Mantas

Watch manta rays as small fish come and nibble off their parasites, all in 6m of clear water. Snorkelling off the fringing islets is also fantastic.

Ia Ora Na

Maupiti is a place where everyone still waves hello as you stroll or pedal by. Islanders are busy tending their hibiscus, gossiping or making crafts to sell from their homes or at the community craft shop.

Summits

There are two peaks to climb: Mt Hotu Paraoa and Mt Teurafaatiu. Both offer splendid views over the turquoise lagoon, and on clear days you'll spot Bora Bora.

p143

The Tuamotus

Diving ✓✓✓
Culture ✓✓
Pearls ✓✓✓

Live Large

The current-filled passes are where you'll see the big stuff: sharks, manta rays, eels and giant tuna – and you don't even need a dive bottle to do it. Otherwise take it easy with plenty of fish (and some mellow reef sharks) inside the lagoon.

Desert-Island People

People of the Tuamotus, called Paumotu, are some of the hardiest people on earth, collecting rain water for drinking, farming sandy soil and mastering everything that has to do with coconuts.

Gems of the Lagoon

Tahitian pearls seem to capture the liquid reflections of the Tuamotus lagoons. Check out how they're farmed and buy something special.

p151

The Marquesas

Archaeology ✓✓✓
Culture ✓✓✓
Hiking ✓✓✓

Land of the Lost

Stone tikis, temple platforms and the foundations for ancient homes fill the jungles. Often covered in moss and shaded by giant banyan trees, these sites feel like something out of Tomb Raider.

Wood & Tattoos

The most revered wood carvers and tattoo artists live here, where these arts were perfected. Admire Virgin Mary statues in churches, visit carvers' workshops and, for the ultimate souvenir, get an authentic Marquesan tattoo from a master.

Crater Walks

Hike ridges to waterfall valleys and empty beaches or through lush jungles to archaeological sites. Horseback is a local mode of transport and you may find yourself riding with a wooden saddle.

p174

The Australs & the Gambier Archipelago

Culture ✓✓✓
Kitesurfing ✓
History ✓✓✓

Polynesian Feast

On Raivavae, Rapa and Rimatara most families eat traditional Polynesian food including lots of taro and tuna. Tubuai is the primary fruit and vegetable producer in the country and you'll see bananas growing alongside peach trees. Perhaps it's the good food that fuels the renowned pandanus basket, mat and hat weaving.

Windy Lagoon

Kitesurfers rejoice! Tubuai gets an average of 300 days of wind per year on its cerulean lagoon.

Churches

A coral cathedral, plus nine other churches, towers and nunneries dot this archipelago with an eerie splendour. The buildings were built under the direction of Father Laval in the 1800s. Today they sit near-empty and are scarcely able to be kept up by the residents of the islands.

p203

Every listing is recommended by our authors, and their favourite places are listed first

Look out for these icons:

TOP CHOICE	Our author's top recommendation
(green leaf icon)	A green or sustainable option
FREE	No payment required

See the Index for a full list of destinations covered in this book.

On the Road

Tahiti

POP 185,000

Includes »

Best Places to Stay

» Vanira Lodge (p75)
» Fare Suisse (p58)
» Le Méridien Tahiti (p66)
» Green Room Villa (p75)
» Intercontinental Resort Tahiti (p58)

Best Places to Eat

» Place To'ata Snacks (p59)
» Place Vaiete Roulottes (p61)
» Le Lotus (p60)
» Blue Banana (p67)
» La Plage de Maui (p76)

Why Go?

While Tahiti isn't the white-sand island of your holiday brochure, it is the heart of French Polynesia, and it would be a shame to bypass it. Waterfall-laden, shadowy mountains; unpretentiously beautiful black-sand beaches; and a distinctly Polynesian buzz make Tahiti a gem in its own right.

While exploring the lively backstreets and strolling the waterfront of the pint-sized capital Pape'ete is a must, it's the outdoor action and cultural offerings that woo visitors to extend their stay. Explore the mystical, mountainous interior on a 4WD tour, learn to dive in the translucent lagoon, wander flabbergasted amid archaeological sites, and from July to October go whale-watching or hike across the fecund interior. In July catch the country's most spectacular festival, the percussion and dance-heavy Heiva. And don't miss Tahiti Iti – this peninsula on the southeast of Tahiti, so far only known to surfers, is one of the hidden gems of French Polynesia.

When to Go

Tahiti enjoys a year-round tropical climate, but it's most popular during the dry season, from May to October. The weather is cooler and you can expect sun and clear skies – perfect for outdoor activities, including hiking. The rainy season begins in November and continues until the end of April, with frequent heavy showers and occasional storms. The island has a rather busy social calendar year-round, but in July Pape'ete is in full swing with the Heiva. Diving and surfing are popular year-round; the whale-watching season runs from July to October.

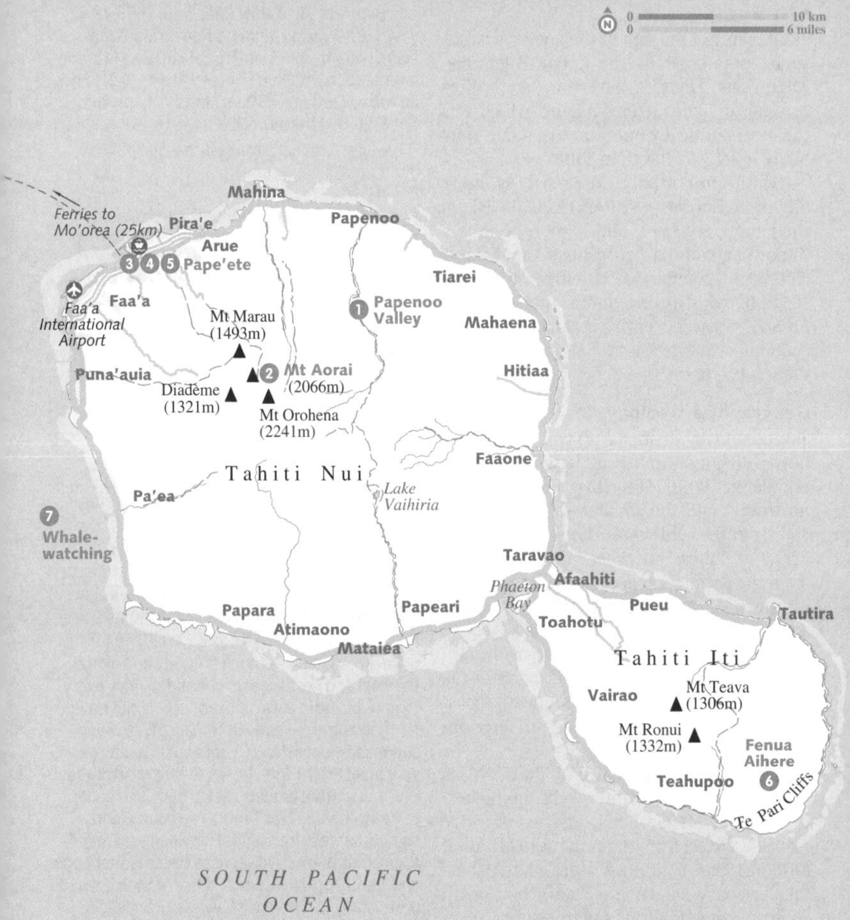

Tahiti Highlights

1 Exploring by 4WD the lush and craggy interior along the **Papenoo Valley** (p70)

2 Huffing to the top of **Mt Aorai** (p69) for the sensational views

3 Catching local vibes while eating at the **roulottes** (mobile food vans; p61) on the waterfront in Pape'ete

4 Sipping an ice-cold coconut while perusing the colourful **Marché de Pape'ete** (p54)

5 Watching the best of the best shake their hips at the Heiva festival's **dance competitions** (p60) in Pape'ete

6 Taking a boat excursion past the road's end at Teahupoo to visit the remote **Fenua Aihere** (p75)

7 Witnessing 30-tonne humpbacks on a **whale-watching trip** (p66)

History

Tahiti was not the first of the Society Islands to be populated in the Great Polynesian Migrations. Legends have the first settlers arriving in Tahiti from Ra'iatea, which was the most politically important island despite being much smaller than Tahiti.

Tahiti's importance increased as more and more European visitors made the island their preferred base, and it soon became a minor pawn in the European colonial game.

Tahiti's population is currently about 185,000, constituting more than 70% of French Polynesia's entire population. It's the economic, cultural and political centre of French Polynesia.

Geography & Geology

Tahiti is neatly divided into two circles connected by an isthmus: the larger and more populated Tahiti Nui (Big Tahiti) to the northwest and the smaller Tahiti Iti (Little Tahiti) to the southeast. The narrow coastal fringe of Tahiti Nui, where the vast majority of the population is concentrated, sweeps rapidly inwards and upwards to a jumble of soaring, green-clad mountain peaks.

A fringing reef encloses a narrow lagoon around much of the island, but parts of the coast, particularly along the north coast from Mahina through Papenoo to Tiarei, are unprotected.

The mountainous centre of Tahiti Nui is effectively one huge crater, with the highest peak being Mt Orohena (2241m). A ridge runs northwest from the summit to Mt Aorai (2066m), and continues south to the spectacular rocky Diadème (1321m) then north to Mt Marau (1493m). A number of valleys run down to the coast from the mountains, the most impressive being the wide Papenoo Valley to the north. Tahiti Iti has its highest point at Mt Ronui (1332m).

ℹ Getting There & Away

AIR

Faa'a International Airport (PPT; ☎86 60 61; www.tahiti-aeroport.pf) is the aviation centre of French Polynesia. All international flights arrive here, and Air Tahiti flights to the other islands leave from here. Flights within each archipelago hop from one island to the next, but most connections between archipelagos are via Faa'a(pronounced fa-ah-ah).

For international flights to and from Tahiti, see p246; for general information about air travel within French Polynesia, see p248; and for connections to/from an island group or an individual island, see the relevant chapter or section.

In Pape'ete, **Air Tahiti** (Map p56; ☎86 42 42, 47 44 00; www.airtahiti.pf; Rue du Maréchal Foch; ⏰8am-5pm Mon-Fri, 8-11am Sat) is at the intersection with Rue Edouard Ahnne. It also has an **office** (⏰6am-4.30pm Mon-Fri, 6am-4pm Sat & Sun) at the airport.

For international airline offices, see p246.

Boat

All passenger boats to other islands moor at the **Gare Maritime** (Map p56; Blvd Pomare) in Pape'ete. The numerous cargo ships to the different archipelagos work from the Motu Uta port zone, to the north of the city.

See p249 for general information on inter-island ships, and the individual island chapters or sections for specific information on travel to/from those destinations.

ℹ Getting Around

BUS

French Polynesia's once-famous *le trucks* have now mostly gone to bus heaven. The 'real' air-con buses (still often referred to as *le trucks*) now, in theory, only stop at designated stops (with blue signs) and run to a timetable, but in reality the routes haven't changed and the drivers will usually stop if you wave them down.

Weekdays, buses around Pape'ete and along the west and north coasts operate roughly every 15 minutes from dawn until about 5.30pm except for the Pape'ete–Faa'a–Outumaoro line, which supposedly operates 24 hours but in reality gets very quiet after 10pm. Buses to Taravao run about every hour from around 5am to 5pm, and buses to/from Teahupoo or Tautira run hourly (and sometimes less frequently) between 5am and 10am, plus one or two services towards Teahupoo and Tautira only in the afternoon. At the weekend, particularly on Sunday, services are far less frequent. Fares for the shortest trips, say from Pape'ete to a little beyond the airport, start from 140 CFP (80 CFP for children and students); this fare rises to 250 CFP after 6pm. Outside this area, the prices are less clear. Out to about 20km from Pape'ete the fare will go up in stages to around 300 CFP; getting to Tahiti Iti costs 500 CFP.

Tahiti's buses have their route number and the final destination clearly marked. There are basically three routes: greater Pape'ete, which is handy for the Pape'ete–Faa'a airport trip (catch this along Rue du Général de Gaulle); the east coast (catch this along Blvd Pomare); and the west coast (catch this along Rue du Maréchal Foch and Rue du Général de Gaulle). Both the east- and west-coast buses can be taken to reach Tahiti Iti.

CAR

Driving on Tahiti is quite straightforward and, although accident statistics are not encouraging, the traffic is fairly light once you get away from Pape'ete. Apart from on the Route de Dégagement Ouest (RDO) freeway out of Pape'ete to the west, the traffic saunters along at an island pace. As always, beware of children wandering on the road, and prepare yourself for a rather casual approach to overtaking. Don't leave anything in view in your car and always lock up; hire cars all have big orange stickers on them, which can act like a thief magnet.

For the price you'll be paying, you may be unpleasantly surprised by the standard of hire cars. Rates start at about 10,000 CFP per day. Prices drop after three days.

Most car-hire companies on Tahiti are based at Faa'a airport and stay open until the last departure. They can deliver vehicles to hotels and pensions on the west coast. Some companies also have desks at the bigger hotels.

Avis Pacificar (☎85 02 84; www.avis-tahiti.com; Faa'a airport) Also has a branch in Taravao.

Daniel Rent-a-Car (☎82 30 04, 81 96 32; daniel.location@mail.pf; Faa'a airport)

Europcar (☎86 61 96; www.europcarpolynesie.com; Faa'a airport)

Hertz (☎82 55 86; Faa'a airport)

Tahiti Auto Center (Map p52; ☎82 33 33; www.tahitiautocenter.pf; PK20.2, Pa'ea; ⏲7.30am-4.30pm Mon-Fri, 8-11.30am Sat) Had the cheapest published rates at the time of writing, but cheaper vehicles need to be booked well in advance. No delivery to the airport.

Tahiti Rent-a-Car (☎81 94 00; Faa'a airport)

HITCHING

Hitching in Tahiti is relatively easy and you'll see both locals and *popaa* (Westerners) standing on the tarmac with their thumbs in the air. Still, hitching is never entirely safe and while French Polynesia has low crime levels, solo women in particular could still encounter problems and should always use common sense. Avoid hitching on Friday and Saturday nights, when the roads are filled with alarmingly intoxicated drivers.

PAPE'ETE

Metropolis this is not. Pape'ete is really just a medium-sized town (by Western standards) of moulding architecture with a lively port, lots of traffic and plenty of smiling faces to pull you through it all. You'll either get its compact chaos and colourful clutter or you'll run quickly from its grimy edges and lack of gorgeous vistas. Sip a cappuccino at a Parisian-style sidewalk cafe, shop the vibrant market for everything and anything (from pearls to bright *pareu* – sarongs) or dine at a *roulotte* (mobile food van) in the balmy evening.

THE PK

The *point kilométrique* (PK; kilometre point) markers start at zero in Pape'ete and increase in both a clockwise and an anticlockwise direction around Tahiti Nui until they meet at Taravao, the town at the isthmus that connects Tahiti Nui with Tahiti Iti. Taravao is 54km from Pape'ete clockwise (via the east coast) and 60km anticlockwise (via the west coast). The counting starts again on Tahiti Iti, where the markers only go as far as the sealed road – remarkably, there's no road along the easternmost coast.

History

Translated from Tahitian, Pape'ete's name literally means 'basket of water'. Historians theorise that this name is probably a reference to the springs where water was once collected.

In 1769, when James Cook anchored in Matavai Bay, there was no settlement in Pape'ete. Towards the end of the 18th century European visitors realised the value of its sheltered bay and easy access through the reef. London Missionary Society (LMS) missionaries arrived in Pape'ete in 1824 and the young Queen Pomare became a regular visitor to the growing town, which gradually swelled to become a religious and political centre.

Visiting whaling ships made Pape'ete an increasingly important port, and it was selected as the administrative headquarters for the new French protectorate in 1843. Chinese merchants and shopkeepers also started to trickle into Pape'ete, but at the beginning of the 20th century the population was still less than 5000. A disastrous cyclone in 1906 and a German naval bombardment in 1914 took a toll, but during WWII the population reached 10,000 and by the early 1960s it was over 20,000. The last few decades have seen the almost total destruction of the charming old colonial heart of Pape'ete.

Tahiti

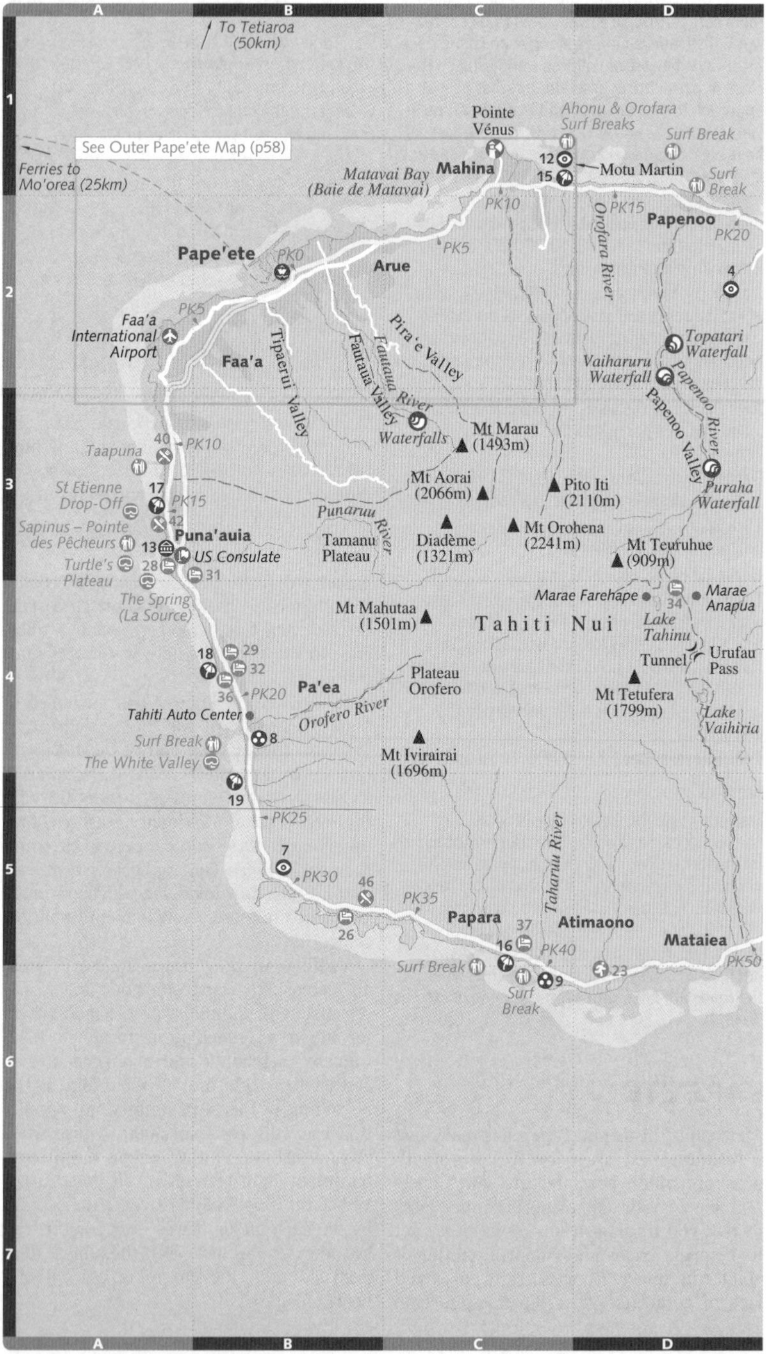

A
B
C
D
1
2
3
4
5
6
7
To Tetiaroa (50km)
See Outer Pape'ete Map (p58)
Ferries to Mo'orea (25km)
Pointe Vénus
Ahonu & Orofara Surf Breaks
Surf Break
12
15
Motu Martin
Matavai Bay (Baie de Matavai)
Mahina
PK10
PK15
Orofara River
Papenoo
PK20
4
Pape'ete
PK0
PK5
Arue
Faa'a International Airport
Faa'a
Tipaerui Valley
Fautaua Valley
Fautaua River
Pira'e Valley
Waterfalls
Topatari Waterfall
Vaiharuru Waterfall
Papenoo Valley
Papenoo River
Puraha Waterfall
Mt Marau (1493m)
Mt Aorai (2066m)
Pito Iti (2110m)
Diadème (1321m)
Mt Orohena (2241m)
Mt Teuruhue (909m)
40
Taapuna
17
St Etienne Drop-Off
42
Sapinus – Pointe des Pêcheurs
Puna'auia
13
US Consulate
Turtle's Plateau
28
31
The Spring (La Source)
Punaruu River
Tamanu Plateau
Marae Farehape
34
Marae Anapua
Lake Tahinu
Tunnel
Urufau Pass
Mt Mahutaa (1501m)
Tahiti Nui
18
29
32
36
Pa'ea
Plateau Orofero
Mt Tetufera (1799m)
Lake Vaihiria
Tahiti Auto Center
Orofero River
8
Surf Break
The White Valley
Mt Ivirairai (1696m)
19
PK25
7
PK30
46
PK35
26
Papara
Taharuu River
37
Atimaono
16
PK40
Mataiea
PK50
23
9
Surf Break

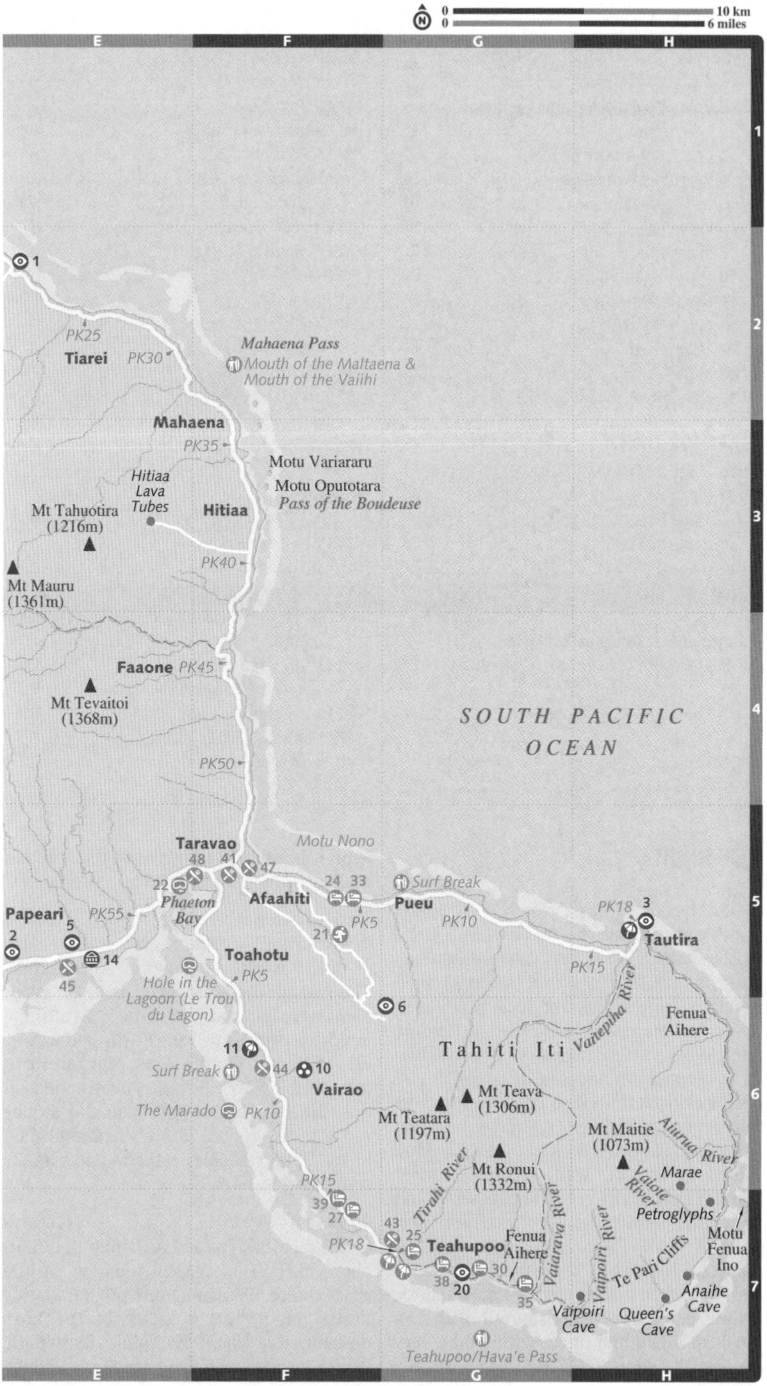
0 10 km
0 6 miles
SOUTH PACIFIC OCEAN
Tiarei
PK25
PK30
Mahaena Pass
Mouth of the Maltaena & Mouth of the Vaiihi
Mahaena
PK35
Motu Variararu
Motu Oputotara
Pass of the Boudeuse
Hitiaa Lava Tubes
Hitiaa
Mt Tahuotira (1216m)
PK40
Mt Mauru (1361m)
Faaone
PK45
Mt Tevaitoi (1368m)
PK50
Taravao
Motu Nono
Surf Break
Phaeton Bay
Afaahiti
Pueu
PK5
PK10
PK18
Tautira
Papeari
PK55
Toahotu
PK15
Hole in the Lagoon (Le Trou du Lagon)
Vaitepiha River
Fenua Aihere
Tahiti Iti
Surf Break
Vairao
The Marado
Mt Teava (1306m)
Mt Teatara (1197m)
Mt Maitie (1073m)
Aiurua River
Mt Ronui (1332m)
Tirahi River
Vaiote River
Marae
Petroglyphs
Vaiarava River
Vaipoiri River
Motu Fenua Ino
Teahupoo
Fenua Aihere
Te Pari Cliffs
Anaihe Cave
Vaipoiri Cave
Queen's Cave
Teahupoo/Hava'e Pass
TAHITI

Tahiti

Sights

1 Arahoho Blowhole ... E2
2 Bain de Vaima & Vaipahi Spring Gardens ... E5
3 Boenechea's Grave ... H5
4 Faarumai Waterfalls ... D2
5 Jardins Botaniques ... E5
6 Lookout ... G6
7 Mara'a Grotto ... B5
8 Marae Arahurahu ... B4
9 Marae Mahaiatea ... C6
10 Marae Nuutere ... F6
11 Maui Beach ... F6
12 Motu Martin ... C1
13 Musée de Tahiti et des Îles ... A3
14 Musée Gauguin ... E5
15 Plage de Hitimahana ... C1
16 Plage de Taharuu (Papara) ... C5
17 Plage de Toaroto ... A3
Plage du Mahana Park ... (see 18)
18 Plage du PK18 ... B4
19 Plage du PK23.5 ... B5
20 Teahupoo ... G7

Activities, Courses & Tours

21 L'Amour de la Nature à Cheval ... F5
22 Tahiti Iti Diving ... E5
23 Terrain de Golf Olivier Breaud ... D6

Sleeping

24 Chez Maïté ... F5
25 Green Room Villa ... G7
26 Hiti Moana Villa ... B5
27 La Vague Bleue ... F7
28 Le Méridien Tahiti ... A3
29 Le Relais Fenua ... B4
Manava Suite Resort Tahiti ... (see 40)
Motu Martin ... (see 12)
30 Pension Bonjouir ... G7
31 Pension de la Plage ... A4
32 Pension Te Miti ... B4
33 Punatea Village ... F5
34 Relais de la Maroto ... D4
35 Reva ... G7
36 Taaroa Lodge ... B4
37 Taharuu Lodge ... C5
38 Te Pari Village ... G7
39 Vanira Lodge ... F7

Eating

40 Blue Banana ... A3
41 Chez Loula & Remy ... F5
42 Coco's Restaurant ... A3
43 Hinareva ... G7
44 La Plage de Maui ... G6
Le Carré ... (see 28)
Le Club House ... (see 23)
45 Restaurant du Musée Gauguin ... B5
46 Restaurant Nuutere ... B5
47 Taumatai ... F5
48 Terre-Mer ... F5

Sights

TOP CHOICE **Marché de Pape'ete** MARKET

(Pape'ete Market; Map p56; cnr Rue Colette & Rue du 22 Septembre; 7am-5pm Mon-Fri, 4-9am Sun) Load up on colourful *pareu* (sarongs), shell necklaces, woven hats and local produce at the famed Marché de Pape'ete – a Pape'ete must. It covers the whole block between Rue du 22 Septembre and Rue F Cardella, just one block back from Blvd Pomare. The most fun time to visit is early Sunday morning when local residents flock in as early as 4am. Dotted among the fruit, vegetables, meat and fish downstairs are little patisseries and lunchtime hawkers selling takeaway portions of *ma'a Tahiti* (traditional Tahitian food). Grab an ice-cold coconut at the door and then stroll upstairs to the knick-knacks, a local cafeteria-style restaurant with live music at lunchtime (most days) and a very good tattoo shop. Fish from other islands is on sale early in the day but the Tahitian catch does not appear until late afternoon.

Cathédrale Notre-Dame CATHEDRAL

(Map p56) Taking pride of place in the centre of town is the Cathédrale Notre-Dame. The cathedral's story began in 1856, when plans were hatched for it to be built of stone imported from Australia, with a doorway carved out of granite from Mangareva in the Gambier Archipelago. Construction on the cathedral began, but then the money ran out; the original edifice was demolished in 1867, and a smaller cathedral was finally completed in 1875.

Temple de Paofai CHURCH

(off Map p56; Blvd Pomare) Although the Catholic cathedral is placed squarely in the town centre, Tahiti remains predominantly Protestant, a lasting legacy of the LMS missionaries. The large pink Temple de Paofai makes a colourful scene on Sunday morning, when it is bursting at the seams with a devout congregation dressed in white and belting out rousing *himene* (hymns). The church is on the site of the first Protestant church in Pape'ete, which was built in 1818.

Jardins de Paofai GARDENS
(off Map p56; Blvd Pomare) Thanks to lots of effort by the image-conscious local government, Pape'ete's waterfront has received a major facelift over the last few years, as testified by these trimmed public gardens near Place To'ata. You'll find paved walking paths that meander past blooming planter boxes and the occasional tree. While the traffic still buzzes by, it's an almost relaxing place for a stroll. As you walk east there are racing pirogues (outrigger canoes) lined up on the pebbly shore. Local teams can be seen practising some afternoons and every Saturday morning.

Musée de la Perle MUSEUM
(Pearl Museum; off Map p56; ☎46 15 54; www.robertwan.com; Blvd Pomare; admission free; ⏲9am-5pm Mon-Sat) This pearl museum was created by pearl magnate Robert Wan with aims of luring visitors into his glamorous shop. It's a worthwhile, small and modern museum that covers all facets of the pearl-cultivating business. Explanations of the displays are in English, and ogling Monsieur Wan's gorgeous, albeit uncommonly pricey, jewellery collection is almost as fun as the museum.

Chinese Temple TEMPLE
(off Map p56; cnr Ave Georges Clémenceau & Ave du Commandant Chessé) You'll be impressed by the massive proportions of the vividly colourful Chinese temple, also known as 'Kanti de Mamao'. It's a 10-minute stroll east from the cathedral.

Parc Bougainville PARK
(Bougainville Park; Map p56; Blvd Pomare) A great spot to just chill out, Parc Bougainville is a tropical oasis in the middle of the city. Lush and cool, it's fronted by a 1909 bust of the great French navigator.

Place To'ata SQUARE
(To'ata Sq; off Map p56) This square is an evolving multi-use development project on Pape'ete's western edge. The far end of the square is home to a 5000-seat pavilion, which is the scene of the July Heiva festivities; it also hosts rock concerts throughout the year.

Place Vaiete SQUARE
(Vaiete Sq; Map p56) Place Vaiete is home to multiple *roulottes* and occasional live-music performances at night but is quite peaceful during the day. There are plenty of public benches along here where you can sit and watch the world go by.

Administrative District NEIGHBOURHOOD
(Map p56) The **Territorial Assembly** and other government buildings occupy Place Tarahoi, the former site of the Pomare palace. The termite-riddled 1883 palace was razed in 1960, but you can get an idea of what it looked like from the modern *mairie* (town hall), a few blocks east, which is built in a similar style. On Rue du Général de Gaulle, the assembly building is fronted by a **memorial to Pouvana'a a Oopa**, the late

TAHITI IN...

Two Days

Spend the first day exploring colourful Pape'ete, making sure to spend some time shopping at the famous **Marché de Pape'ete** (Pape'ete Market) and the pearl boutiques along the main drag. Have dinner at the **roulottes**, Pape'ete's legendary mobile food vans on Place Vaiete. After dinner, catch a dance performance and sip a cocktail at one of the stylish resorts, or opt for a night of dancing in Pape'ete's cacophonous **bars**. Head out of town on day two, and explore the island on your own. Spend the night at the fantastic **Vanira Lodge**, the most creative pension in Tahiti.

Five Days

Follow the two-day itinerary then spend day three on a boat tour to Tahiti Iti's **Fenua Aihere** and **Te Pari**. On day four take a **hiking excursion** to the island's interior or just plop yourself on a **beach** somewhere with mask, fins and a snorkel. The last day could be spent on the ocean, either **diving** or on a **whale-watching tour**.

Central Pape'ete

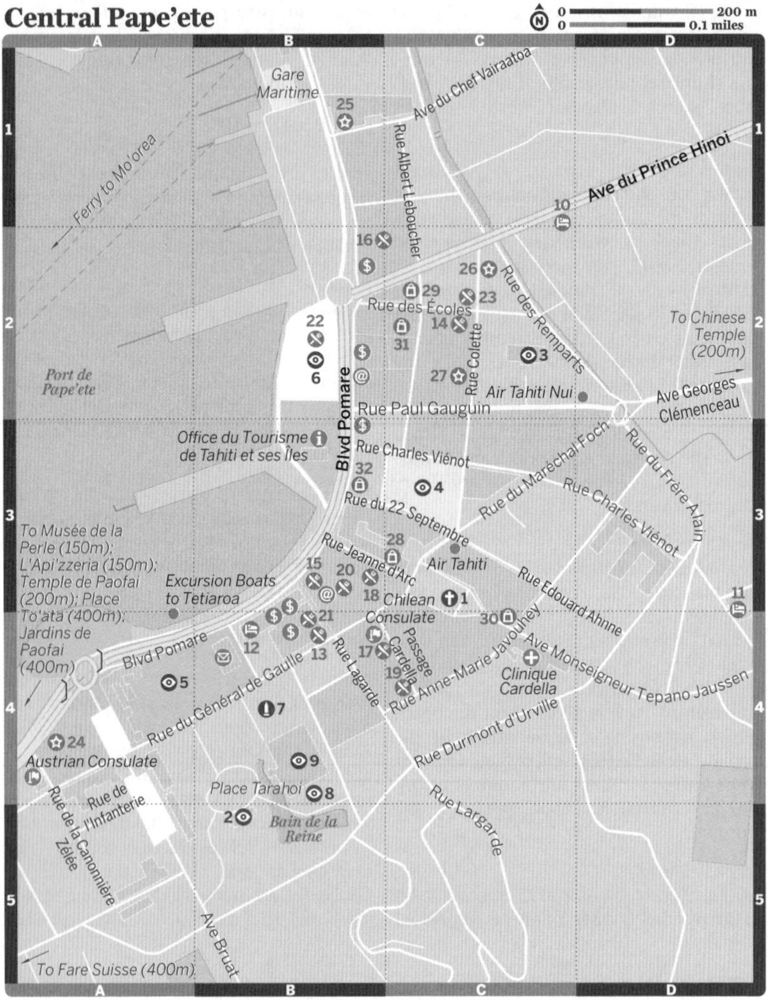

pro-independence figure of heroic proportions. The **High Commissioner's Residence** that stands to one side of the assembly building replaced the 1843 Palace of the Governor (those pesky termites again). A more recent addition is the **Presidential Palace**, an imposing building used by the president.

Mairie de Pape'ete BUILDING

(Town Hall; Map p56; Rue Paul Gauguin) Pape'ete's *mairie* is two blocks back from Blvd Pomare and a block north of Marché de Pape'ete. It was completed in 1990, in vague imitation of the old queen's palace.

House of James Norman Hall MUSEUM

(Map p58; adult/child 600 CFP/free; ⌚9am-4pm Mon-Sat) Towards the outer edge of Pape'ete's urban sprawl in Arue is this lovely little replica of *Mutiny on the Bounty* co-author James Norman Hall's house. The house is in a shady garden and is decorated with Hall's original c 1920s furniture plus heaps of photos and memorabilia.

Central Pape'ete

Sights

1 Cathédrale Notre-Dame C3
2 High Commissioner's Residence B5
3 Mairie de Pape'ete C2
4 Marché de Pape'ete C3
5 Parc Bougainville A4
6 Place Vaiete B2
7 Pouvana'a a Oopa Memorial B4
8 Presidential Palace B4
9 Territorial Assembly B4

Sleeping

10 Hotel Tahiti Nui C1
11 Teamo Pension D3
12 Tiare Tahiti B4

Eating

13 La Terrasse Api B4
14 Le Mandarin C2
15 Le Rétro B3
16 Les 3 Brasseurs B2
17 L'O à la Bouche B4
18 L'Oasis B3
19 Lou Pescadou C4
20 Morrison's Café B3
21 Patachoux B4
22 Place Vaiete Roulottes B2
23 Restaurant Jimmy C2

Drinking

Le Rétro .... (see 15)
Les 3 Brasseurs .... (see 16)
Morrison's Café .... (see 20)

Entertainment

24 Club 106 .... A4
25 Le Paradise Night B1
Les 3 Brasseurs .... (see 16)
Morrison's Café .... (see 20)
26 Royal Kikiriri C2
27 Ute Ute C2

Shopping

Efraima & Simeon Huuti .... (see 4)
28 Galerie Winkler C3
Ganesha .... (see 20)
29 Mana'O Tattoo C2
Marché de Pape'ete .... (see 4)
30 Odyssey C4
31 Tahiti Vanilla Market C2
32 Te Mana B3

Pointe du Taharaa – One Tree Hill LOOKOUT
(Map p58; PK8.1) At the top of the hill at around PK8, pull off to the lagoon side of the road and park in the lot that once belonged to Tahiti's very upmarket Hyatt Regency. From this crumbling site of the abandoned hotel you'll get sublime views of Matavai Bay all the way to Pape'ete, including the silhouette of Mo'orea in the distance. One Tree Hill was named by Captain Cook who used a tree here (now gone) as a landmark. The hotel has been closed since 1998.

Plage Lafayette BEACH
(Map p58; PK7) On the edge of Matavai Bay, this wide curve of sparkling black sand is great for a dip. It never gets crowded. The eastern side is framed by steep sheltering cliffs. Public access is via a path just next to Radisson Plaza Resort (there's a sign).

Tombeau du Roi Pomare V TOMB
(Map p58; PK4.7) In Arue, on the water's edge, signposted and just a short detour off the coastal road, is the tomb of the last of the Pomare family. The Tomb of Pomare V looks like a stubby lighthouse made of coral boulders. It was actually built in 1879 for Queen Pomare IV, who died in 1877 after 50 years in power. Her ungrateful son, Pomare V, had her remains exhumed a few years later and when he died in 1891 it became his tomb.

Activities

Scuba Tek Tahiti DIVING, WHALE WATCHING
(Map p58; ☎42 23 55; www.scubatek-tahiti.com; PK4, Arue) This small dive shop on the eastern outskirts of Pape'ete has the cheapest rates in French Polynesia. A single dive or an introductory dive costs 4800 CFP, and a five/10-dive package is 21,000/38,000 CFP. It specialises in dive sites between Arue and Faa'a and has whale-watching tours in season.

Sleeping

Central Pape'ete is not the place to stay if you're looking for tranquillity or anything resembling a tourist brochure; the options on the outskirts of town offer more palm-fringed, beachlike choices.

Outer Pape'ete

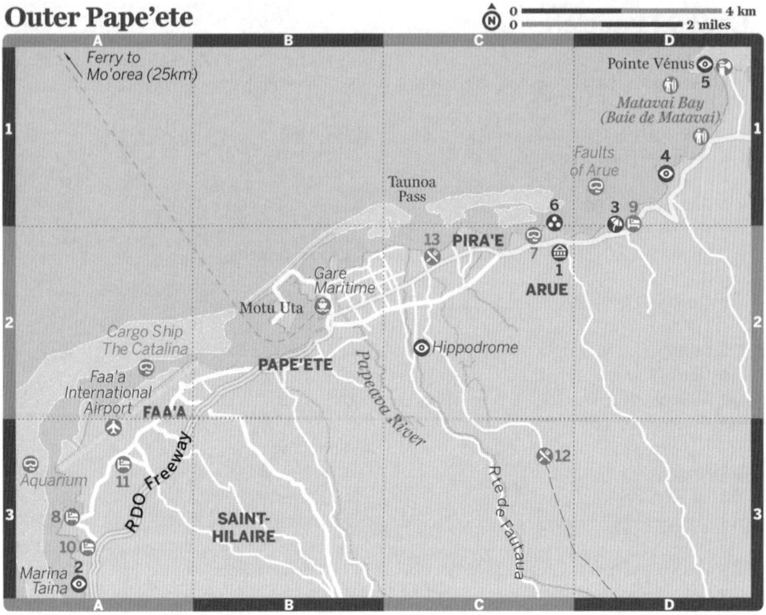

TOP CHOICE **Intercontinental Resort Tahiti** RESORT $$$

(Map p58; ☎86 51 10; www.tahitiresorts.intercontinental.com; PK8, Faa'a; r & bungalow d from 25,000 CFP; ❄📶🏊) Hands down, this is the best luxury resort on the island. The Intercontinental is as posh as Tahiti gets. Marble bathrooms, plush canopies and Mo'orea views from private balconies are standard both in the rooms and romantic overwater bungalows, which range from smallish to quite spacious. The two swimming pools are fabulous (one features a slick, cascading horizon) and the water-sports centre is the best on the island. On the downside, the beach here is artificial (it's made from imported white sand) and the lagoon is not nearly as translucent or dreamy as ones that you'll find on other islands.

Fare Suisse GUESTHOUSE $$

(off Map p56; ☎42 00 30; www.fare-suisse.com; Rue des Poilus Tahitiens; d 10,200 CFP; ❄📶) Getting rave reviews from our readers, this guesthouse is in a spotless and stylish cement home in a quiet area not far from the centre of town. The tiled rooms are simple but nicely decorated with bamboo furniture, and are bright and airy. The best thing about this place is the owner Beni, who picks guests up free of charge at the airport, lets folks store their luggage and creates a super-pleasant atmosphere with his helpfulness. Great for solo travellers who want to be close to the action or for island-hoppers on overnight layovers. Breakfast is an extra 1200 CFP.

Sofitel Tahiti Maeva Beach Resort RESORT $$

(Map p58; ☎86 66 00; www.accorhotels.com; PK8, Faa'a; d from 15,000 CFP; ❄📶🏊) Look at the rates! This resort is one of the better deals on the island, provided you keep your expectations in check. The '70s-style exterior could use a facelift, but rooms are comfortable enough. The pool is ordinary, but the semi-manmade beach with Mo'orea smack dab in the distance really makes you feel you are on a tropical holiday, especially at sunset. Le Sakura restaurant serves the best Japanese food this side of Hawaii.

Radisson Plaza Resort Tahiti RESORT $$

(Map p58; ☎48 88 88; www.radisson.com/tahiti; PK7, Arue; d from 15,000 CFP; ❄📶🏊) East of Pape'ete is this elegant hotel on a black-sand beach lined with almond trees and fronted with Mo'orea views. The exterior of the hotel looks like a common apartment block but once you enter the minimalist-chic lobby things get much better. Nearly all the dark but tastefully designed rooms

Outer Pape'ete

Sights

1 House of James Norman Hall C2
2 Marina Taina A3
3 Plage Lafayette D1
4 Pointe du Taharaa D1
5 Pointe Vénus D1
6 Tombeau du Roi Pomare V C1

Activities, Courses & Tours

Eleuthera Plongée ....(see 2)
Fluid Dive Centre ....(see 2)
7 Scuba Tek Tahiti C2
Topdive ....(see 8)

Sleeping

8 Intercontinental Resort Tahiti A3
9 Radisson Plaza Resort Tahiti D1
10 Sofitel Tahiti Maeva Beach Resort A3
11 Tahiti Airport Motel A3

Eating

Casa Bianca ....(see 2)
12 Le Belvédère C3
Le Lotus ....(see 8)
13 Le Royal Tahitien C2
Le Sakura ....(see 10)
Pink Coconut ....(see 2)
Quai des Îles ....(see 2)

Entertainment

Le Royal Tahitien ....(see 13)

have a sea view; angle for one located on the upper floors for the most privacy. Staff are particularly friendly and there's a less ostentatious vibe here than at Tahiti's other high-end resorts.

Hotel Tahiti Nui HOTEL **$$**
(Map p56; ☎46 38 99; www.hoteltahitinui.com; Ave du Prince Hinoi; d from 18,600 CFP; ❄🏊📶) Attractive primarily to business travellers, the Tahiti Nui is a modernish hotel right in the heart of Pape'ete and close to the waterfront. There's a pool, a restaurant and a business centre. Don't expect dollops of atmosphere; the rooms have no Polynesian character but are serviceable and tidy.

Tiare Tahiti HOTEL **$$**
(Map p56; ☎50 01 00; hoteltiaretahiti@mail.pf; Blvd Pomare; d from 15,500 CFP; ❄) This clean hotel overlooks the water in the hub of Pape'ete, but sadly is afflicted by the traffic noise. A somewhat kitschy favourite with tour groups, it has 38 simply furnished, motel-like rooms that are overpriced; the cheaper ones are at the back and lack views but are quieter. There are special deals for late check-out. Breakfast costs 1500 CFP.

Tahiti Airport Motel HOTEL **$$**
(Map p58; ☎50 40 00; www.tahitiairportmotel.com; PK5.5, Faa'a; d/q incl breakfast 14,000/22,000 CFP; ❄📶) Right across from Faa'a International Airport, this would appear to be the most convenient place to stay for a quick stopover, but there's no shuttle so you have to drag your luggage across the parking lot then up the short but sometimes muddy hill. A two-minute taxi ride here costs 1000 CFP. Rooms are impersonal but crisp and comfortable, with TVs and fridges.

Teamo Pension GUESTHOUSE **$**
(Map p56; ☎42 47 26; www.teamoguesthouse.com; Rue du Pont-Neuf; dm 2600 CFP, d with shared bathroom 6600 CFP, d 7600-8600 CFP; ❄📶) This place is a little depressing and the boxy rooms are in need of a serious freshen-up, but the location is the saving grace – it's in a quiet area not far from the waterfront. The dearer rooms have private bathrooms and air-con while the dorm room has six beds. The shared kitchen is a plus.

Eating

Whatever you think of the capital, you're sure to have memorable eating experiences here. You can skip from French to Polynesian to Chinese and back again via Italian and Vietnamese – you couldn't possibly tire of the cuisines in Pape'ete.

Ma'a Tahiti is often served as a special on Fridays at many budget and midrange places.

Self-catering is a breeze in Pape'ete. The market has fresh fish, fruit and vegies, and there's no shortage of supermarkets.

TOP CHOICE **Place To'ata Snacks** POLYNESIAN **$$**
(Place To'ata; mains 1300-2700 CFP; ⏲lunch & dinner) What a find! This cluster of open-air *snacks* (snack bars) with outdoor seating – Vaimiti, Chez Jimmy, Mado, Moeata, Toa Sushi – near Place To'ata are a great place to chill with regulars and savour the most authentic and best-value food in town (but no alcohol is served). From *poisson cru* (raw fish) and burgers to crêpes and sushi, each joint has its specialities. If you want a recommendation, go for the *poisson cru à la javanaise* (raw fish with a spicy sauce) served at Chez Jimmy or the crêpes concocted at Vaimiti. The setting

DON'T MISS

THE HEIVA

If your visit is in July, extend your stay on Tahiti for the hugely popular Heiva, French Polynesia's premier festival, which is held at various venues in and near Pape'ete. It lasts about four weeks from late June to late July and is so impressive that it's almost worth timing your trip around it. Expect a series of music, dance, cultural and sporting contests. See p231.

is simple; think plastic chairs under the shade of trees – so Pape'ete. Opening hours vary but there are usually at least two or three places serving lunch from 11am to 1.30pm and dinner from 6am to 10pm. Cash only.

TOP CHOICE Le Lotus FUSION $$$

(Map p58; ☎86 51 25; Intercontinental Resort Tahiti, PK8, Faa'a; mains 2000-4500 CFP; ⊙lunch & dinner) Inside the Intercontinental Resort Tahiti, this uber-romantic restaurant on the edge of the lagoon is perfect for a special night out and a good excuse to put on your best, but still casual, outfit. Flickering candles, a breezy terrace and the gentle lap of waves will rekindle the faintest romantic flame. The food is suitably refined; flavourful French and Polynesian favourites are whipped into eye-pleasing concoctions. Make sure you arrive before sunset to watch Mo'orea bathed in a pink glow.

L'O à la Bouche FRENCH, POLYNESIAN $$

(Map p56; ☎45 29 76; Passage Cardella; mains 1600-3700 CFP; ⊙lunch Mon-Fri, dinner Mon-Sat) This handsome French restaurant is a perennial favourite with locals and tourists in the know. French-style dishes take inspiration from the tropics and are imaginatively prepared and beautifully presented. The wine cellar is good too.

L'Oasis POLYNESIAN, FRENCH $$

(Map p56; ☎45 45 01; Centre Vaima; mains 1600-2500 CFP; ⊙6am-3pm Mon-Sat) There's no contest about the most popular lunch spot in Pape'ete – this place is always busy, but you won't have to wait long for a table on the breezy terrace. The range of daily specials on offer – mostly French dishes prepared with local ingredients – is well priced and filled with subtle flavours.

Le Sakura JAPANESE $$$

(Map p58; ☎86 66 00; Sofitel Tahiti Maeva Beach Resort, PK8, Faa'a; mains 3500-7000 CFP; ⊙dinner Tue-Sat) It's tucked away in an unlikely location at the Sofitel Tahiti Maeva Beach Resort, but this tiny Japanese teppanyaki grill restaurant is packed nightly with as many locals as tourists – reserve in advance. You eat at the bar while friendly chefs theatrically grill your choice of meats, fish and vegies right in front of you on an iron griddle. There's also good sushi.

Patachoux CAFETERIA $

(Map p56; ☎83 72 82; Rue Lagarde; mains 600-1200 CFP; ⊙6am-4pm Mon-Sat) Takeaway sandwiches here are the deluxe version – fresh wholemeal or French bread stuffed with gourmet meats, fish and/or salads. Otherwise sit at the outdoor patio (on a lively pedestrian-only street) and order from an ever-changing menu of salads and fresh fish with international flair. Desserts like fruit tarts, mysterious creamy French pastries and a divine chocolate fondant from the bakery window are not to be missed.

Lou Pescadou ITALIAN $$

(Map p56; ☎43 74 26; Rue Anne-Marie Javouhey; mains 1200-2700 CFP; ⊙Tue-Sat) A Pape'ete institution, this cheery restaurant has hearty pasta and wood-fired pizza dishes. It's authentic Italian, right down to the red-and-white check tablecloths and carafes of red wine. Service is fast and there are lots of vegie options. Be sure to check out the quirky cartoons on the walls.

L'Api'zzeria ITALIAN $$

(off Map p56; ☎42 98 30; Blvd Pomare; mains 1200-3000 CFP; ⊙11am-10pm Mon-Sat) This semi-outdoor venture is often packed, the service is efficient and it's one of the few spots in town where you can get served an off-hour meal at say, 4pm. The wood-fired, thin-crust pizzas are dependably good, as are the pastas, meat grills and salads. Unfortunately, it's set on a busy thoroughfare and isn't very peaceful.

Les 3 Brasseurs BRASSERIE $$

(Map p56; ☎50 60 25; Blvd Pomare; mains 1800-2500 CFP; ⊙lunch & dinner) You can't miss the colourful facade of this lively brasserie in front of the Gare Maritime. It might feel weird to sit down for *flammekueche* (an Alsatian pizza-like dish) and *choucroute* (sauerkraut) in the middle of the Pacific, but go with the flow – the fare is reasonably priced and well prepared. You'll also find daily specials as well as more mainstream dishes on the menu, which is laid out like a French newspaper. Oh, and it stays open late (an exception in Pape'ete).

Restaurant Jimmy ASIAN $$
(Map p56; ☎43 63 32; Rue Colette; mains 1600-3000 CFP; ⊙lunch & dinner Mon-Sat) Choose from Thai, Vietnamese or Chinese at this dimly lit local favourite. Thai mains are far from authentic but the rest of the menu is quite good. Try the *bo bun* salad, a delicious creation of green salad, thin noodles and either grilled beef or chicken or Vietnamese spring rolls on top.

La Terrasse Api POLYNESIAN, FRENCH $$
(Map p56; ☎43 01 98; Rue Lagarde; mains 1800-2400 CFP; ⊙breakfast & lunch Mon-Sat) You'll find all the usual Polynesian favourites and a sprinkling of French dishes served in hearty portions in this busy restaurant right in the centre. The *plat du jour* (daily special) is good value.

Le Rétro BISTRO $$
(Map p56; ☎50 60 25; Blvd Pomare; mains 1800-2500 CFP; ⊙lunch & dinner) After an extensive renovation, this Pape'ete icon now features trendy furnishings and a hip outdoor terrace overlooking the busy boulevard. The wide-ranging menu covers enough territory to please most palates, from burgers and sandwiches to fish grills and salads. Alas, the traffic noise mars the experience a bit.

Le Mandarin CHINESE $$
(Map p56; ☎50 33 90; Rue des Écoles; mains 1600-3500 CFP; ⊙11.30am-1.30pm & 6.30-9.30pm) This well-established restaurant serves an exquisite selection of authentic Chinese dishes – those in the know claim that the Peking roasted duck is among the very best this side of the Pacific. The decor is suitably refined.

Le Royal Tahitien POLYNESIAN $$
(Map p58; ☎50 40 40; PK3.1, Pira'e; mains 1500-3500 CFP; ⊙lunch & dinner) Le Royal Tahitien (affectionately dubbed 'RT') is a perennial fave with locals, despite the c 1975 *tiki*-tacky decor. The setting is delightfully chilled-out – the vast, open-air dining room overlooks the lagoon. The food is simple and done without fanfare or flair, but the view is serene and the staff and customers are convivial and relaxed. It's about 3km east of Pape'ete in Pira'e.

Morrison's Café FRENCH, POLYNESIAN $$
(Map p56; ☎42 78 61; Centre Vaima; mains 1600-2800 CFP; ⊙lunch Tue-Fri, dinner Wed-Sat) By far the trendiest spot in town, this casually elegant eatery on a rooftop is a delightful escape from the main drag. Savour well-prepared fish and meat dishes as well as salads and pastas. It stays open late Fridays and Saturdays.

Le Belvédère FRENCH $$
(Map p58; ☎42 73 44; Pira'e; mains 2000-3500 CFP; ⊙lunch & dinner Wed-Mon) The views over Pape'ete are fantastic, particularly at sunset. Fondues are the speciality at this fine-dining restaurant, which is perched 600m above the city in Pira'e. If you drive, take the first right after the Hamuta Total petrol station. The 7km road to the restaurant is steep, winding and rugged towards the top.

Drinking

After a stay on other islands, where nightlife is just about nonexistent, Pape'ete could almost pass itself off as a city of wild abandon.

Most restaurants at Marina Taina (p67) double as bars, so you can bar-hop on weekends for a low-key night out.

Top-end hotel bars are a focus of Pape'ete social life, especially on Friday and Saturday evenings. It's more fun than it might sound,

DON'T MISS

PLACE VAIETE ROULOTTES

The country's famous **roulottes** (Map p56; Place Vaiete; mains from 900 CFP; ⊙dinner) – literally 'caravans' in French, these are mobile food vans – tick all the right boxes: they're a wondrous gastronomic pleasure, a great way to catch local vibes and represent tremendous value. These little stalls sizzle, fry and grill up a storm every evening from around 6pm; things don't quieten down until well into the night. There are dozens of *roulottes* to choose from. Punters sit on stools along either side of the van or on plastic chairs scattered around each *roulotte*. Squeeze in next to that guy devouring his steak and chips and that woman relishing her chow mein. Get good thin-crust pizzas or everything else from grilled fish to sashimi. Finish your meal with a Nutella-and-banana waffle and... enough! We're drooling on the page! Live music enhances the scene most weekend nights. Cash only.

pulling in a range of locals, residents and tourists. Consider the bars at the Radisson Plaza Resort, the Intercontinental Resort Tahiti, the Sofitel Tahiti Maeva Beach Resort, the Manava Suite Resort and Le Méridien Tahiti.

Morrison's Café BAR
(Map p56; ☎42 78 61; ⏲Tue-Sat) Upstairs in the Vaima Centre is this popular spot for a drink. There's a pleasant, loungey feel.

Les 3 Brasseurs PUB
(Map p56; Blvd Pomare; ⏲daily) This congenial brewpub has excellent microbrewed beer on tap and a constant stream of locals and tourists wanting to sample it. Cover bands perform here at the weekend and you can also chow on some good French-style pub grub for lunch and dinner.

Le Rétro BAR
(Map p56; ☎42 86 83; Blvd Pomare; ⏲daily) Le Rétro is full of attitude and atmosphere and is a great place to watch the world go by while sipping an espresso. It also serves a great selection of cocktails and juices.

☆ Entertainment

Dance performances

Tahiti is a good island for tapping your toes along to some of the best Polynesian dance and music groups, many of which appear several times a week in the big hotels. Those worried about cheesy, touristy performances can rest assured these groups are very professional and are enjoyed every bit as much by locals as by wide-eyed visitors. When held in the luxury hotels, these performances are often accompanied by a buffet (which usually costs around 9000 CFP), although parking yourself at the bar and ordering a drink will sometimes suffice. Check with the hotel reception desks at the Radisson Plaza Resort, Intercontinental Resort Tahiti, Le Méridien Tahiti and Sofitel Tahiti Maeva Beach Resort about their programs and entrance policies.

Live Music

Ute Ute LIVE MUSIC
(Map p56; Rue Colette; ⏲Mon-Sat) Meaning 'red hot' in Tahitian, it's exactly what Ute Ute is right now. Decor is city lounge–style red and black and the coolest DJs and live bands play here at weekends.

Morrison's Café LIVE MUSIC
(Map p56; Vaima Centre; ⏲Tue-Sat) Rock, electro, jazz and blues groups play several times a week and occasionally foreign DJs stop by for a spin.

> **WHAT'S ON?**
>
> For up-to-date listings of live-music gigs, DJ clubs, dance shows and cultural events, pick up of copy of *What's On* at the tourist office. Also check the website www.tahiti-agenda.com.

Le Royal Tahitien LIVE MUSIC
(Map p58; PK3.1, Pira'e; ⏲Fri & Sat) Local musicians perform on Friday and Saturday evenings and the place can really rock with locals.

Les 3 Brasseurs LIVE MUSIC
(Map p56; Blvd Pomare; ⏲daily) Cover bands regularly perform here at the weekend.

Nightclubs

From the Tahitian waltz to electronic music, it's all here. Dress codes are enforced and men in shorts or flip-flops will be turned away; women can get away with wearing as little as they like. Admission for men is between 1500 CFP and 2000 CFP (usually including a drink), but women can usually get in for free. Clubs typically close around 3am or 4am.

Le Paradise Night NIGHTCLUB
(Map p56; Blvd Pomare; ⏲Wed-Sat) This is the classic, slightly kitsch Pape'ete bar-disco playing international tunes. It attracts a mixed crowd of Polynesians and French.

Royal Kikiriri NIGHTCLUB, BAR
(Map p56; Rue Colette; ⏲Thu-Sat) A local favourite, the Royal Kikiriri showcases live music with its namesake band on weekends. Just about everyone gets asked to dance and you'll soon be swaying your hips in local foxtrot or *tamure* (Tahitian dance) style. It's at its liveliest on Friday.

Club 106 NIGHTCLUB
(Map p56; Blvd Pomare; ⏲Thu-Sat) The crowd is mostly on the other side of 30 and dances to '80s hits.

Shopping

In Pape'ete you can buy products from all over French Polynesia, including clothes, pearls and more pearls.

Marché de Pape'ete MARKET
(Map p56; cnr Rue Colette & Rue du 22 Septembre; ⏲9am-4pm Mon-Fri, 9am-noon Sat) Upstairs in the Marché de Pape'ete you can wander for

ages among the handicrafts. Wooden salad servers, fabric, wonderful homemade *monoi* (fragrant coconut oil), *pareu,* jewellery and even mother-of-pearl love-heart key rings can be purchased here. Watch out, though – anything that seems to be mass-produced probably is, in China, Indonesia or the Philippines.

Tahiti Vanilla Market FOOD, BEAUTY

(Map p56; Rue Émile Martin; ⏲9am-5pm Mon-Fri) For a truly great-smelling shopping experience, check out this boutique. Nearly everything in the shop is made from local vanilla; you can get whole pods, plus vanilla-infused honey, scented coconut cooking oil, incense, soaps and much more.

Te Mana CLOTHING

(Map p56; www.temana.com; Blvd Pomare; ⏲8am-5pm Mon-Fri, 8am-4pm Sat) Get glammed up at this trendsetting boutique stocking island-made shirts, T-shirts, dresses and accessories. Inspired from traditional designs, the pieces are transformed into sprightly contemporary looks.

Odyssey MUSIC

(Map p56; off Rue Edouard Ahnne; ⏲9am-5pm Mon-Sat) This music shop has a decent selection of CDs by local artists; you can listen before you buy.

Ganesha HANDICRAFTS

(Map p56; ☎43 04 18; www.ganeshatahiti.com; Vaima Centre; ⏲9am-5.30pm Mon-Fri, 9am-noon & 2-5.30pm Sat) This high-end boutique sells all kinds of quality arts and crafts from French Polynesia and other Pacific islands.

Mana'O Tattoo TATTOOS

(Map p56; ☎42 45 00; www.manaotattoo.com; 43 Rue Albert Leboucher; ⏲by appointment) So you really don't want to forget your trip to Tahiti? This shop has many styles available,

HOW TO BUY A PEARL

There are so many jewellery shops and pearl specialists in Pape'ete that you have to be careful not to trip over them. Look around before buying a pearl, and consider purchasing it here and getting it set at home (this will probably work out cheaper and ensures you get exactly what you want). Depending on the quality, you can buy a single pearl for around 10,000 CFP (cheaper if you don't mind imperfections and much more expensive for something really outrageous); for a decent-quality ring you are looking at anywhere from 60,000 CFP. Also bear in mind that there are numerous pearl shops and pearl farms on the outer islands, so don't rush into purchasing.

When shopping around look out for these qualities:

» **Shape** Pearls come in various shapes, from perfectly round or teardrop shaped (the two most expensive) to misshapen globs. Many pearls have rings etched around them (called *circlé*) that increase their artistic value but decrease their price.

» **Size** Tahitian pearls start at around 7mm and go up from there (the biggest Tahitian pearl ever recorded is 25mm). The bigger they are, the pricier they are.

» **Colour** From black to white to everything in between. Look for greens, pinks, silvers, golds, blues and purples. What you like is up to you.

» **Surface Quality** Dimples, scrapes, cloudy spots and other imperfections decrease a pearl's value. A dull white spot anywhere means the pearl is of very low quality, so don't buy it.

» **Lustre** How shiny is it? A high-quality pearl has a near liquid-looking surface.

» **Nacre Thickness** This refers to the thickness of the layer of mother of pearl on top of the nucleus inside. Nacre wears away eventually so if the layer is too thin you'll be left with dull patches on your pearl, especially if you wear it a lot. The only way to determine nacre thickness is with an x-ray, so in many cases you simply can't know. Use common sense: if you buy cheap pearls in the 1000 CFP bin of shops, you're probably getting a thin-skinned pearl.

But the most important factor is do you like the pearl? Many people try so hard to determine how much a pearl is worth that they forget to take into account their own tastes. If you love it, buy it.

DON'T MISS

HANDICRAFTS FAIRS

A few handicrafts fairs (Salons de l'Artisanat) featuring the work of artisans from across French Polynesia are held several times a year in Pape'ete. Check out the weeklong Salons de l'Artisanat in February and October that are hosted at the Territorial Assembly, as well as the Heiva des Artisans from late June to late July in Pira'e.

including traditional Polynesian designs as well as some more creative motifs.

Efraima & Simeon Huuti TATTOOS
(Map p56; ☎70 36 34; Marché de Pape'ete; ⌚by appointment) This popular studio in the Marché de Pape'ete (upstairs) is run by two brothers who are originally from the Marquesas. They create traditional-style black-ink tattoos and have good credentials.

Galerie des Tropiques ART GALLERY
(☎41 05 00; Place To'ata) This highly reputable gallery has works from established artists, such as Christian Deloffre and Gotz, as well as works from emerging painters or sculptors.

Galerie Winkler ART GALLERY
(Map p56; ☎42 81 77; Rue Jeanne d'Arc) This gallery near the cathedral has an interesting mix of etchings, paintings and crockery. It's a great place to buy works from local artists, both well known and emerging.

Information

Emergency

Ambulance (☎15)

Police (☎17)

Internet Access

Business Center (Faa'a International Airport; per hr 1000 CFP; ⌚8am-6pm & 8-10pm Mon-Fri, 8am-noon Sat & Sun) In the domestic area of the terminal.

Cybernesia (Vaima Centre; per hr 720 CFP; ⌚8.30am-5pm Mon-Fri, 9am-1pm Sat)

Maison de la Presse (Blvd Pomare; per hr 600 CFP; ⌚8am-6pm Mon-Fri, 8.30am-1pm & 4.30-6pm Sat)

Medical Services

Clinique Cardella (Map p56; ☎42 04 25; Rue Anne-Marie Javouhey; ⌚24hr) Private clinic behind the cathedral.

Centre Hospitalier du Taaone (☎48 62 62, 24hr emergencies 42 01 01; Pira'e) The biggest hospital in French Polynesia, with good facilities and a range of medical specialities.

Money

There are banks (Banque Socredo, Banque de Tahiti and Banque de Polynésie) and ATMs scattered around Pape'ete and its suburbs. Banque Socredo has a branch at Faa'a airport, where there's also an ATM. See p243 for general information on banks and changing money.

The following branches have ATMs:

Banque de Polynésie (Blvd Pomare; ⌚7.45am-3.30pm Mon-Thu, 7.45am-2.30pm Fri)

Banque de Tahiti (Blvd Pomare; ⌚8-11.45am & 1.30-4.30pm Mon-Fri, 8-11.30am Sat)

Banque Socredo (Blvd Pomare; ⌚8-11.45am & 2-5pm Mon-Fri)

Broadway (Blvd Pomare; ⌚7.30am-11pm Mon-Wed, 7am-1am Thu-Sat, 8am-11pm Sun) Small bureau de change with longer opening hours next door to Les 3 Brasseurs. No commission on currency exchange but the rates offered are slightly lower than what you'll get at banks.

Post

Post office (OPT; www.opt.pf; Blvd Pomare; ⌚7.30am-5pm Mon-Fri, 7.30-11am Sat) Pape'ete's main post office is next to Parc Bougainville.

Tourist Information

Office du Tourisme de Tahiti et ses Îles (Tourist Office; Map p56; ☎50 40 30; www.tahiti-tourisme.com; Fare Manihini, Blvd Pomare; ⌚7.30am-5.30pm Mon-Fri, 8am-4pm Sat, 8am-noon Sun) Has information on all of French Polynesia. Although Mo'orea and Bora Bora have tourist offices, the more remote islands don't, so if you have any queries, ask here.

Getting Around

There aren't any city buses but Pape'ete can easily be covered on foot.

To/From the Airport

The taxi drive to central Pape'ete will set you back 2000 CFP during the day and 2500 CFP at night (8pm to 6am).

If you arrive at a reasonable time of the day, you'll be able to catch any bus going towards town from the airport (northeast bound or to your left as you leave the airport), which will take you straight to the centre of Pape'ete in about 15 minutes for a flat fare of 140 CFP during the day and 250 CFP after 6pm. Walk straight across the car park outside the airport, up the steps to street level and across the road to hail a city-bound bus.

From Pape'ete to the airport, take a bus heading to Faa'a and Outumaoro – the destination will be clearly posted on the front – from along Rue du Général de Gaulle.

Taxi

All the big hotels have taxi ranks, and there are plenty of taxis in central Pape'ete. Any trip of a reasonable length will approximate a day's car hire, so if you want wheels you may as well hire them.

AROUND TAHITI NUI

It's another world outside of Pape'ete; the sea is a deep blue, the jagged, green mountains frame the sky and cars putter along at 50km/h. While many people just zip around the 120km circuit of Tahiti Nui taking everything in from their car windows, it's better to do as the locals do by taking it slow, stopping often and soaking in the incredible lushness. And smile, because this is paradise.

West Coast

Tahiti Nui's west coast is busier and much more touristy than the island's eastern side. It has the greatest concentration of places to stay outside Pape'ete, plus many of the museums and major sights. The chic suburb of Puna'auia, which stretches from around PK10 to PK18, has an excellent restaurant scene and Tahiti's best beaches (though this is not saying a lot). The most expensive homes on Tahiti are found along this stretch of coast, along the beach and high above the coast to better enjoy the breathtaking views across to Mo'orea.

Sights

Listings here follow the coastal road around from Pape'ete.

Marina Taina MARINA

(Map p58; PK9) The elegant Marina Taina is a trendy spot featuring restaurants, bars, two diving centres and, of course, lots of yachts.

TOP CHOICE **Musée de Tahiti et des Îles** MUSEUM

(Museum of Tahiti & its Islands; Map p52; ☎54 84 36; PK15.1; admission 800 CFP; ⌚9.30am-5.30pm Tue-Sun) Only 15km from Pape'ete along the west coast, this excellent museum, in Puna'auia, is divided into four sections:

WORTH A TRIP

TETIAROA

Bought by Marlon Brando in 1965 after he filmed *Mutiny on the Bounty* and fell in love with his Tahitian co-star Tarita Teriipia, the stunning atoll of Tetiaroa, 59km north of Tahiti, is in the process of major change. While Brando was alive, the atoll remained a bird preserve and housed only one small pension where visitors could live like Robinson Crusoe in paradise. Brando, a pioneer in ecotourism, always made it clear that he wished the island to remain preserved and that any development would have to be ecologically sound as well as aesthetically conforming to the atoll. Brando died in 2004 and by 2005 his estate executors had sold the rights to development to a major property developer in Tahiti. At the time of writing, a luxury ecoresort – to be called **The Brando** (www.brandohotel.com) – was being constructed on the island; it should be open by 2014.

At the time of writing the only way to get to the island was by charter yacht, a few of which line up along the Pape'ete waterfront advertising lovely day trips to the atoll.

Blue Island (☎77 94 10; www.ablueisland.com) Monohull. Arranges two-day/one-night trips to the atoll for 19,500 CFP (night on board). The crossing takes about 4¼ hours and there are two or three outings per week.

L'Escapade (☎72 85 31; www.tahiti-charter-catamaran.com) Catamaran. It costs 13,000 CFP and includes breakfast and lunch on board. Duration of the crossing is about 3¾ hours and there are two or three outings per week.

Vehia (☎71 53 15; www.vehiatetiaroa.com) Motorised catamaran. Has about three weekly outings (13,000 CFP, including picnic). The crossing takes about 2½ hours.

geography and natural history; pre-European culture; the European era; and outdoor exhibits. It's in a large garden and if you get tired of history, culture and art, you can wander out to the water's edge to watch the surfers at one of Tahiti's most popular breaks.

Plage de Toaroto BEACH
(Map p52; PK15.4) This narrow stretch of white coral sand is suitable for swimming and has public facilities.

Plage du PK18 BEACH
(Map p52; PK18) Beloved by locals, Plage du PK18 is a stunning beach to sun yourself on, but not that great for swimming or snorkelling due to the shallow water. The sands can get jammed on weekends, but that's part of the scene.

Plage du Mahana Park BEACH
(Map p52; PK18.5) Plage du Mahana Park has calm waters and a snorkelling reef close to shore. On weekends there are kayaks for hire.

Marae Arahurahu ARCHAEOLOGICAL SITE
(Map p52; PK22.5) Whether or not you believe in the powers of the *tiki* (sacred statue), it's hard to deny there is an amazing energy radiating from Marae Arahurahu in the Pa'ea district. Tranquil, huge and beautifully maintained, the *marae* (traditional temple) is undoubtedly the best-looking one on the island and even rivals those on other islands.

Plage du PK23.5 BEACH
(Map p52; PK23.5) This rather wide (by Tahiti standards) beach is popular with families and has public facilities. The colour of the sand? White-gray.

Mara'a Grotto CAVE
(Map p52; PK28.5) Lush gardens, overhung caverns, crystal-clear pools and ferny grottoes are all standard features at gorgeous Mara'a Grotto. The fairy-tale park is found along the coastal road, and a manicured path runs throughout.

Activities

Diving & Whale-Watching

There are some excellent diving opportunities to be had in Tahiti. For details about sites see p31. Most dive shops lead whale-watching tours between July and October when humpbacks swim near the coasts. Half-day trips cost from 8000 CFP per person. Dolphin-watching tours run year-round and are slightly cheaper.

TAHITI FOR CHILDREN

Travelling with children is extremely easy in Tahiti. They'll love having dinner at the *roulottes* (mobile food vans) in Pape'ete, and families are welcome in most restaurants and *snacks* (snack bars) around the island. Most beaches on Tahiti are safe and suitable for children. With the kids in tow, it's also great fun exploring the walking paths winding through the Jardins Botantiques on the south coast, past ponds and palms, eels, crabs, ducks and chickens.

Between July and October, whale-watching is a great activity for families. Children over eight can also try an introductory dive with any of Tahiti's dive centres.

Eleuthera Plongée DIVING, WHALE-WATCHING
(Map p58; ☎42 49 29, 77 65 68; www.dive-tahiti.com; Marina Taina, PK9) A big outfit that also leads whale-watching excursions. It charges 7900/14,100 CFP for a single/two-tank dive, 7600 CFP for an introductory dive and 35,000/60,000 CFP for a five-/10-dive package. Nitrox dives are also offered.

Fluid Dive Centre DIVING, WHALE-WATCHING
(Map p58; ☎85 41 46, 70 83 75; www.fluidtahiti.com; Marina Taina, PK9) Fluid is known for friendly service and small groups. It offers introductory dives (10,000 CFP), single dives (7000 CFP) and two-tank dives (12,600 CFP), as well as 10-dive packages (48,000 CFP).

Topdive DIVING, WHALE-WATCHING
(Map p58; ☎53 34 96; www.topdive.com; Intercontinental Tahiti Resort, PK8) This large and efficient operation offers a full range of dives, from Nitrox dives to introductory dives (8000 CFP). Six- and 10-dive packages are 43,000/70,000 CFP.

Sleeping

There are a number of places to stay along the west coast, particularly around Puna'auia. Compared with Pape'ete these places offer much more of a beach-holiday type of experience.

Le Méridien Tahiti RESORT $$$
(Map p52; ☎47 07 07; www.lemeridien-tahiti.com; PK15; d from 35,000 CFP; ❄@🛜🏊) Le Méridien has truly lovely grounds dotted with lily ponds and fronted by a natural white-sand

beach that has Mo'orea views – if you want a resort where you can swim in the lagoon this is your best bet. The overwater bungalows are stylishly built with hard woods and natural materials and most rooms have recently been spruced up. We found the service here outstanding and the waterfront Carré restaurant has a great reputation.

Manava Suite Resort Tahiti RESORT $$
(Map p52; ☎47 31 00; www.spmhotels.com/resort/tahiti; PK10.8; d from 18,000 CFP;) Le Manava is a good choice – combining friendly informality with some class and style. It lacks a beach but sports the biggest infinity pool on Tahiti. It has smartly finished suites and studios with clean lines, ample space and heaps of amenities. All have minikitchens, but if you don't fancy self-catering, opt for the on-site restaurant, which enjoys a good reputation. Many rooms have a view of Mo'orea. Good value.

Pension Te Miti PENSION $
(Map p52; ☎58 48 61; www.pensiontemiti.com; PK18.6; dm with breakfast 2500 CFP, d with shared bathroom 6600-7600 CFP;) Run by a young, friendly French couple, this lively place has a low-key backpacker vibe and is deservedly popular with budgeteers. It's on the mountain side of the main road in Pa'ea, about 200m from the beach. Digs are in two four-bed dorms as well as seven fan-cooled rooms. They're all very simple and the property feels a tad compact, but there's a good social vibe going on. Also has an equipped communal kitchen, a few bicycles for guests' use and a laundry service (1000 CFP); 24-hour airport transfers are available for 1500 CFP per person (1800 CFP at night).

Taaroa Lodge GUESTHOUSE $
(Map p52; ☎58 39 21; www.taaroalodge.com; PK18.2; dm 2800 CFP, d 6000 CFP, bungalows 10,000 CFP) Right on the waterfront, Taaroa Lodge features three categories of accommodation options. If funds are short, opt for a bed in the dorm. The room downstairs is a bit sombre but acceptable. The two individual bungalows in the garden represent better value and have lovely views of Mo'orea. There are kitchen facilities and a friendly atmosphere. Kayaks are free, and the nearest public beach is a two-minute walk away. The lodge is owned by Ralph Stanford, a former longboard surfing champion of Tahiti and France.

Pension de la Plage PENSION $
(Map p52; ☎45 56 12; www.pensiondelaplage.com; PK15.4; s/d from 8500/9000 CFP;) Just across the road from Plage de Toaroto, this impeccably maintained place offers comfortable motel-style rooms in several gardenside buildings around a swimming pool. Each has tile floors and giant windows; some have kitchenettes. There's a bit of street noise but nothing to lose sleep over. Breakfast is available for 1000 CFP, dinner for 2600 CFP. Snorkel gear is complimentary.

Le Relais Fenua STUDIOS $$
(Map p52; ☎45 01 98, 77 25 45; www.relaisfenua.fr; PK18.25; studios d 9500-12,000 CFP;) A great option in Pa'ea, with seven clean and spacious studios with TVs set around a little swimming pool. It's close to the main road, so expect some traffic noise during the day. Plage de Mahana Park is stumbling distance away, and there are a few affordable eating options just around the corner. Breakfast costs 1000 CFP per person; prices go down by 10% after three nights.

Eating & Drinking

Besides the following finer restaurants, there are plenty of tasty *roulottes* that open up along the roadside at night. All of the following restaurants have a bar section and stay open late on weekends.

TOP CHOICE **Blue Banana** FRENCH, POLYNESIAN $$
(Map p52; ☎41 22 24; http://bluebanana-tahiti.com; PK11.2; mains 1500-3500 CFP; lunch Tue-Sun, dinner Mon-Sat) Success has done nothing to dull the buzz at Blue Banana, a hip lagoonside restaurant in Puna'auia. The food is as good as the ambience – feast on innovative French and Polynesian dishes (small portions but artistically presented) and fine French vintages from the air-conditioned cellar. Pizzas also grace the menu. Make sure you ask for a table out on the pontoon and arrive early enough to sip a drink and watch the sun set over Mo'orea. Reservations are recommended on weekends.

Le Carré FRENCH, POLYNESIAN $$
(Map p52; ☎47 07 23; Le Méridien Tahiti, PK15; mains 2000-3800 CFP; lunch & dinner) Dining at this stylish eatery is a treat. At night it's a romantic spot to enjoy well-prepared local seafood and Western dishes with a Tahitian twist. It's inside Le Méridien Tahiti, close to the beach.

Pink Coconut FRENCH $$
(Map p58; ☎41 22 23; www.tahitipinkcoconut.com; PK9, Marina Taina; mains 1800-3600 CFP; ⊙lunch & dinner Mon-Sat) We love this lively spot located right on Marina Taina with great views of stylish yachts at anchor. Dine on French-inspired fare with a contemporary twist. At night it's candlelit and there's live music and dancing on the weekends.

Quai des Îles FRENCH, CREOLE $$
(Map p58; ☎81 02 38; PK9, Marina Taina; mains 2000-3600 CFP; ⊙lunch & dinner Tue-Sun) Creole, French and Polynesian dishes populate the menu of this well-regarded restaurant, just next door to Pink Coconut. On Friday nights it has live music to soothe the soul (salsa, anyone?). On Sunday it lays on an excellent Tahitian brunch (3800 CFP).

Casa Bianca ITALIAN $$
(Map p58; ☎43 91 35; PK9, Marina Taina; mains 1300-2700 CFP; ⊙lunch & dinner) If pasta offerings or pizzas make your stomach quiver with excitement, opt for this perky eatery with an outdoor dining area overlooking the marina. Come for the good fun, good mix of people, hearty dishes and wicked cocktails. Carnivores, don't miss out on *veau á la broche* (veal cooked on a spit) on Friday evenings.

Coco's Restaurant FRENCH $$$
(Map p52; ☎58 21 08; PK16; mains 2900-6400CFP; ⊙lunch Tue-Sun, dinner Tue-Sat) Dine in a gorgeous, open plantation-style house bordered by a tropical garden that's framed by coconut trees and looks out to Mo'orea. The fine food is very French, with lots of seafood options. Arguably Tahiti's swankiest and most romantic option.

South Coast

Moving further away from Pape'ete, the coastline from the village of Pa'ea to Taravao is much more quiet than the west coast from which it continues. Here you'll find a few interesting sights as well as some decent places to sleep and eat.

Sights

The following sights are listed in an anticlockwise direction.

Plage de Taharuu (Papara) BEACH
(Map p52; PK39) Everybody loves Plage de Taharuu – locals taking the kids for a swim, tourists on day trips from Pape'ete and surfers catching some great waves. This gently curving black-sand beach is long, broad and fairly protected. It usually has some good swimming conditions. Feeling peckish? There's a *snack* right on the beach.

Marae Mahaiatea ARCHAEOLOGICAL SITE
(Map p52; PK39.2) Just east of the village of Papara, the Marae Mahaiatea was the most magnificent *marae* on Tahiti at the time of Cook's first visit (according to Cook it measured 80m by 27m at its base, rising in 11 great steps to a height of 13m). Today the crumbling remains of the *marae* are still impressive for their sheer size.

Coming from Pape'ete, take the first turn towards the sea past the PK39 sign. Follow the road about half a kilometre all the way towards the coast. In the middle of the carpark area are the hidden massive remains of the *marae*.

Mataiea VILLAGE
(Map p52; PK48-PK45) Between 1891 and 1893, Gauguin lived in Mataiea where he produced works including *Two Women on the Beach, Woman with a Mango* and *Ia Orana Maria – Hail Mary*. The village has two notable buildings – the **church of St John the Baptist** (1857) and the quirky **Protestant chapel**, which looks vaguely like a Hindu temple.

Bain de Vaima & Vaipahi Spring Gardens BOTANICAL GARDENS, WALKS
(Map p52; PK49) Vaima Pool is where locals come from all over to bathe in the icy but exceptionally clear waters that are thought to have healing properties. Unfortunately, there are so many visitors here on weekends and holidays that the 'clean' pools can get filled with rubbish.

The Vaipahi Spring Gardens further along is a beautifully landscaped garden with a magnificent natural waterfall. There's a small network of **hiking trails** that lead from a signpost with a map up to more waterfalls and forests of *mape* (chestnut) and pine trees. The longest loop takes a little over two hours to walk if you're in reasonable shape – some parts are pretty steep!

Jardins Botaniques BOTANICAL GARDENS
(Map p52; PK51; admission 600 CFP; ⊙9am-5pm) Tahiti's Jardins Botaniques and Musée Gauguin share an entrance road and car park at PK51.2. The 137-hectare Jardins Botaniques has walking paths that wind their way through the garden past ponds, palms

DON'T MISS

HIKING & CANYONING ON TAHITI

Hiking

Tahiti's interior is home to some of the most exquisite – and challenging – hikes in French Polynesia.

Fautaua Valley Trail One of the most pleasant and accessible walks on Tahiti, on the east coast. The easy 4km walk to the Fachoda (Tearape) Bridge takes about an hour. Then comes a rather steep climb, and after about 45 minutes you reach a superb viewpoint over Fautaua Waterfall. Another half an hour takes you to the summit of the waterfall, a prime swimming spot. In theory, the Fautaua Valley trail doesn't require a guide, but we suggest hiring one. You'll need an access permit (adult/child 600/150 CFP).

Mt Aorai The third-highest peak on Tahiti (2066m) and its ascent is one of the island's classic climbs. The path, starting at Le Belvédère restaurant (p61), is clearly visible and well maintained, so you don't need a guide, but we suggest hiring one for safety reasons. It takes at least 4½ hours of steady walking to reach the top. It's possible to summit the peak and return in a day, but start at dawn because the summit tends to be covered in cloud after 11am. A better option is to spend the night in one of two simple shelters on the route. Each accommodates about 20 walkers, has electricity and is equipped with aluminium cisterns that are usually filled with drinkable rain water.

Lava Tubes At Hitiaa on the east coast, these lava tubes are elongated tunnels formed by the cooling and rapid hardening of lava. A river runs through the giant, wormlike caves so that hiking through them actually means lots of swimming in cold water. The hike can only be attempted when there's little or no chance of rain (you wouldn't want to be here during a flash flood) and it's imperative to have a guide. You'll need a good torch (flashlight) and waterproof shoes for the three-hour hike/swim. Wetsuits are provided. The hike is suitable for all levels; children over 12 are welcome if they can swim. It's less than 15 minutes' walk from the parking area to the first tube, at 750m, which is around 100m long. The second tube is 300m long with two waterfalls. The third tube is the longest and darkest and, at about 100m in, it divides: the left fork continues about 300m to an exit, while the right fork leads to a large cave, complete with lake and waterfall.

OTHER HIKES & GUIDES

There are also plenty of other hikes on the island. Most trails require a guide as there's no waymark and it's easy to get lost. For a DIY hike, consider the trail from the Vaipahi Spring Gardens.

We recommend the following guides:

Mato-Nui Excursions (☎78 95 47) Mato leads hiking excursions and camping trips.

Polynesian Adventure (☎43 25 95, 77 24 37; http://polynesianadv.ex-flash.com/) Offers all kinds of hikes on the island.

Tahiti Evasion (☎56 48 77; www.tahitievasion.com; all-day hikes per person from 5500 CFP) One of the most reputable operators in the country.

Tahiti Reva Trek (☎74 77 20; www.tahitirevatrek.com in French) Run by a female guide who has lots of experience and offers a wide range of hikes for all levels.

Canyoning

Canyoning (rappelling down waterfalls) is an even more exhilarating way to explore the interior. Tahiti's canyoning hot spots are found in various valleys. All are atmospheric; you can expect various jumps, leaps in natural pools and jaw-dropping rappelling. Plan on 10,000 CFP to 12,000 CFP per person, including gear and transfers. All canyoning outings are led by a qualified instructor. Contact **Rando Pacific** (☎70 56 18; www.randopacific.com) and **Mato Nui Excursions** (☎78 95 47).

WORTH A TRIP

INLAND THRILLS

Archaeological remains, mossy, velvet-green mountains and sensational vistas await you in Tahiti Nui's lush (and uninhabited) interior.

Papenoo to the Relais de la Maroto

The 18km route from **Papenoo** on the north coast to the Relais de la Maroto follows the wide Papenoo Valley, the only valley to cut right through the volcanic interior of Tahiti. In Papenoo, the turn-off is just past PK17. The Papenoo River is the largest on Tahiti. When Christianity began to spread along the coastal regions, the Papenoo Valley became a last refuge for those faithful to the ancient Polynesian religion, and until 1846 it was also a shelter for the Tahitian rebel forces that opposed the French takeover. There are several waterfalls along the valley, including the **Topatari Waterfall**, the **Vaiharuru Waterfall** and, further, the **Puraha Waterfall**. Between the Vaiharuru Waterfall and the Puraha Waterfall lies the **Marae Vaitoare**, a well-preserved sacred site. Then the track reaches the Relais de la Maroto.

Around the Relais de la Maroto

The **Relais de la Maroto** (Map p52; ☎57 90 29; d 7000-10,000 CFP, bungalows d 13,000 CFP; mains 1400-2800 CFP) is the only place to stay and eat, smack in the lush heart of the island. It was originally built as accommodation quarters for workers on the hydroelectricity project that began in 1980. Under new ownership, it's sprucing up. The rooms and bungalows are simple yet tidy and offer sensational mountain views. The restaurant is a great spot to break the journey.

The restored **Marae Farehape** site is almost directly below the ridge line on which the Relais de la Maroto perches; you can see an archery platform from where arrows were shot up the valley. Another archaeological site, **Marae Anapua**, has also been beautifully restored and is worth a gander.

From Relais de la Maroto to Mataiea

From Relais de la Maroto, the track makes a very steep and winding climb to a pass and a 200m-long **tunnel**, at a height of about 800m, before plunging down to **Lake Vaihiria** (450m). Most tours stop here before returning via the same route; at the time of research the road was closed further down the valley due to a barricade built by the area's residents. Legal proceedings were under way to ensure that the road would remain accessible both to visitors and Tahiti's hydroelectric company workers. Check when you're on Tahiti.

Tours

The best way to explore the area is to join a 4WD tour. Specialised 4WD operators do the Papenoo-to-Vaihiria route regularly. Full-day trips cost 6500 CFP; children under 10 are half-price and hotel pick-up is included. You'll stop at Relais de la Maroto for lunch (not included). The following are a few favourite operators:

Tahiti Safari Expeditions (☎42 14 15, 77 80 76; www.tahiti-safari.com) This is the biggest operator, with reliable standards.

Patrick Adventure (☎83 29 29, 79 08 09; patrickadventure@mail.pf) An experienced operator.

Ciao Tahiti (☎81 03 17, 73 73 97; www.ciaotahiti.com, in French) A fairly recent operation with good credentials.

Tahiti Aventures (☎29 01 60; www.tahiti-aventures.net) Offers something different: guided ATV tours in the Papenoo Valley.

and a superb *mape* forest. The gardens were founded in 1919 by an American, Harrison Smith, who introduced many plants to Tahiti including the large southeast Asian pomelo known on Tahiti as *pamplemousse,* the French word for grapefruit. Unfortunately, Smith also introduced one or two botanical disasters that Tahiti could well have done without, including the Miconia calvescens, which has caused serious damage to other plants. Mosquitoes in the gardens can be fierce.

Musée Gauguin MUSEUM
(Gauguin Museum; Map p52; ☎57 10 58; PK51; admission 300 CFP; ⏰9am-5pm) The Musée Gauguin is no great shakes; if you expect any original works by Gauguin, you'll leave disappointed. Much of the text about Gauguin and his life is in English, though, and the natural setting is lovely. The museum gardens are home to three superb **tiki** from Raivavae in the Australs. *Tiki* do not like to be moved, and there are colourful stories about what happened to the men who moved these *tiki* here (they apparently died 'mysteriously' within weeks of the move).

Activities

Terrain de Golf Olivier Breaud GOLF
(Map p52; ☎57 43 41; PK42, Atimaono; 9/18 holes 2500/6100 CFP; ⏰8am-6pm) Located at Atimaono, this beautiful 18-hole, par 72 course, with some rather difficult par 3s, occupies a pleasant estate that was the site of the 1860s Terre Eugénie cotton plantation. Chinese workers were shipped in to supplant unwilling Polynesians, and descendants of the Chinese immigrants still live on the island today. There's a clubhouse here and a good restaurant.

Sleeping

Taharuu Lodge GUESTHOUSE $
(Map p52; ☎74 79 32; PK39; s/d with shared bathroom 5000/7000 CFP; wi-fi) This traveller-savvy haven occupies a functional building amid tropical gardens. Location is ace – Plage de Taharuu is just across the road. The eight rooms are spartan but clean and have good mattresses. The outside ablution block is in top nick and has hot-water showers. There are surfboards and bikes available for rent, a fully equipped kitchen for self-catering and a vast lounge area. There's free fruit on offer and if you're preparing your own food you'll find several shops nearby. Perfect for wallet-conscious travellers.

Hiti Moana Villa BUNGALOWS $$
(Map p52; ☎57 93 93; www.hitimoanavilla.com; PK32; bungalow d from 10,500 CFP; wi-fi, pool) Eight bungalows, including four with kitchenettes, set around a well-tended garden make this lagoonside complex in Papara a pleasant option, despite the fact only two bungalows have direct sea views. The catch? Some cop a bit of road noise. No beach, but there is a pontoon for swimming and a small pool. Kayaks are available. No meals are served except breakfast (900 CFP), but there's a small supermarket nearby.

Eating

Le Club House POLYNESIAN $$
(Map p52; ☎57 40 32; PK42, Atimaono; mains 1900-2200 CFP; ⏰8am-7pm) At the Atimaono golf course, this is a good find and you don't have to be a golfer to eat here. If you have a weakness for ultrafresh fish, Le Club House is the place to indulge (check out the day's catch). Tables overlook the golf course and a small lake. It also has a small swimming pool that can be used.

Restaurant du Musée Gauguin POLYNESIAN $$
(Map p52; ☎51 13 80; PK50.5; mains 1800-2500 CFP; ⏰lunch Tue-Sun) The Restaurant du Musée Gauguin is actually not attached to the museum at all – it's about 800m to the west, in a great setting on the lagoon. The menu is eclectic, with an emphasis on seafood. On Sundays there's a full authentic *ma'a Tahiti* for 3500 CFP.

Restaurant Nuutere FRENCH $$
(Map p52; ☎57 41 15; PK32.5; mains 2000-5400 CFP; ⏰Wed-Mon) You won't be able to miss the extravagantly painted facade at this great little restaurant. French specialities, cooked with local ingredients and some odd imported ones like ostrich or crocodile, are served in an intimate dining room. Don't expect fast service.

East Coast

The east coast is the quietest and most isolated section of Tahiti Nui. From lava tubes to waterfalls and a blowhole, it has some seriously great natural attractions. The road winds between cliffs and sea, and the views, deep into valleys and out along the reefless, jagged coast, are simply stunning. Sleeping and eating options are limited on this coast, but it's a must-see for a day trip.

Sights

Listings here follow the coastal road around from Pape'ete.

Pointe Vénus & Matavai Bay HISTORIC SITE
(Map p58; PK10) Part of Captain Cook's mission on his three-month sojourn in 1769 was to

record the transit of Venus across the face of the sun in an attempt to calculate the distance between the sun and the earth. Pointe Vénus, the promontory that marks the eastern end of Matavai Bay, was the site of Cook's observatory.

Today Pointe Vénus is a popular beach stop. There are shady trees, a stretch of lawn, a black-sand **beach**, a couple of souvenir shops and an impressive **lighthouse** (1867). The beach is crowded on weekends; however, midweek you'll have it all to yourself. It's also a popular centre for local **outrigger-canoe racing clubs** – no doubt you'll see outrigger-canoe teams training for race events. There is no sign to Pointe Vénus from the main road; just turn off at the VenuStar Supermarket in Mahina around PK10. It's about 1.5km from the road to the car park near the end of the point.

There is a **memorial** here to the first LMS Protestant missionaries, who made their landfall at Pointe Vénus on 4 March 1797.

Plage de Hitimahana & Motu Martin BEACH, ISLET

(Map p52; PK11) The black-sand Plage de Hitimahana is exposed to the prevailing winds, which makes it an excellent kitesurfing and windsurfing spot. Just offshore lies **Motu Martin** (☎77 63 71; www.motu-martin.com), an islet where you can relax and picnic (by reservation). Transfers from Pointe Vénus cost 2000 CFP per person return. Kayaks are available for free. It's also possible to stay overnight here.

Papenoo VILLAGE

(Map p52; PK17) There's a popular surf break just before the headland that signals the start of the small village of Papenoo. A long bridge crosses the Papenoo River at the far end of the village, and the 4WD route up the Papenoo Valley, cutting through the ancient crater rim to Relais de la Maroto, starts up the west side of the river. See p70 for more information about this magnificent route.

Arahoho Blowhole NATURAL SITE

(Map p52; PK22) When the swell is big enough, huge sprays of water shoot out from the *trou du souffleur* (blowhole) by the road just before Tiarei at PK22, coming from Pape'ete. The blowhole is on the corner and there's a car park just beyond it. When the waves are right, the blow can be extremely strong.

Just past the blowhole is a fine sliver of black-sand **beach**, ideal for a picnic pause. There are sometimes fruit vendors here.

Faarumai Waterfalls WATERFALL

(Map p52; PK22.1) Through the village of Tiarei where the road swoops around a black-sand beach, you'll see a sign on the mountain side of the road for the exceedingly high Faarumai Waterfalls. Unfortunately you can't swim here anymore since a tourist was hit on the head by a falling rock, so bring mosquito repellent and just enjoy the view. It's a couple of hundred metres through a forest of *mape* trees to **Vaimahutu**, the first of the waterfalls. Another 20-minute stroll leads to the other two falls, **Haamarere Iti** and **Haamarere Rahi**, which stand almost side by side. You technically aren't supposed to swim here either, but many people do.

Taravao VILLAGE

(Map p52; PK54) Strategically situated at the narrow isthmus connecting Tahiti Nui with Tahiti Iti, the town of Taravao has been a military base on and off since 1844, when the first French fort was established. The original fort was intended to forestall Tahitian guerrilla forces opposed to the French takeover from mounting operations against Tahiti Nui from Tahiti Iti. Today the Faratea Port, on the northeastern side of the isthmus, is being built to shift commercial sea trade from Pape'ete (which is getting gussied up for tourists) to Taravao.

Although there is little of interest in the town, it does have shops, banks, petrol stations and a number of small restaurants.

Sleeping & Eating

There is almost nowhere to stay on the east coast. Heading east out of Pape'ete, there are not many restaurants until you reach Taravao, although there are a few little *snacks*.

Motu Martin BUNGALOWS $$

(Map p52; ☎77 63 71; www.motu-martin.com; PK11; bungalows d with shared bathrooms from 10,000 CFP) In search of an escape? Consider renting a bungalow on this tiny *motu* that lies just offshore. The four units are simply built but clean, spacious (they can sleep up to eight people) and wonderfully quiet. No food is served but each bungalow comes equipped with a kitchen. Bonus: free kayaks. This place is surprisingly green, running on solar and wind power. Call ahead to arrange boat transfers from Pointe Vénus.

Taumatai FRENCH, POLYNESIAN **$$**
(Map p52; ☎57 13 59; Taravao; mains 1700-3000 CFP; ⊙lunch & dinner Tue-Sat, lunch Sun) Grab a terrace table at this delightful little place in Taravao, right across the street from Chez Loula and Remy. It serves the town's best French and Tahitian food in an elegant garden setting. The restaurant is hidden behind a stone wall so it's a little hard to find.

Chez Loula & Remy FRENCH **$$**
(Map p52; ☎57 74 99; Taravao; mains 1700-4200 CFP; ⊙lunch daily, dinner Mon, Tue & Thu-Sat) This family-run place in Taravao on the Tautira road serves an excellent array of French-style grilled meats and fish in boozy, congenial environs.

Terre-Mer POLYNESIAN **$$**
(Map p52; ☎57 08 57; PK58.8; mains 1400-2900 CFP; ⊙lunch Tue-Sun, dinner Wed-Sat) This reputable eatery could hardly be better situated: the dining deck is right on the seashore. At night it's a romantic spot to enjoy succulent local seafood and meat dishes with a Tahitian twist.

TAHITI ITI

Traditional Polynesian villages, beaches, archaeological sites and caves are all part of the alluring charm of Tahiti Iti. Unpretentious and beautiful, the smaller loop of Tahiti's figure eight quietly attracts independent, outdoorsy folk looking for a more authentic glimpse of Polynesia. More commonly called the Presqu'île, Tahiti Iti has made a bit of a name for itself in recent years thanks to the promotion of its famous wave at Teahupoo. But even though it has become famous because of surfing, there's much more to do in Tahiti Iti than ride the waves. Exceptional walks and abundant lack of commercialism are perks.

From Taravao on Tahiti Nui, roads run along the north and south coasts of Tahiti Iti. The central road into the Tahiti Iti plateau commences a short distance along a back road that links the north-coast road with the south-coast road.

Sights

The best way to explore Tahiti Iti is to drive to the ends of both the north- and south-coast roads.

NORTH-COAST ROAD

The coastal road from Taravao runs through Afaahiti to Pueu, past steep hills and numerous waterfalls, to the road's end at Tautira.

This stretch of coast is one of the least visited areas on the island, though historically things were different. In 1772 the Spanish captain Boenechea, who was leading the first missionary expedition to French Polynesia (see the boxed text, p224), anchored his ship *Aguilla* about 10km beyond Tautira; Cook landed here in 1774; and many years later, in 1886, the writer Robert Louis Stevenson spent two months here. The landings of French Catholic missionaries at Tautira eventually led to the French takeover of Tahiti and the end of the Protestant monopoly.

The black-sand beach at PK6 in Pueu is good for boogie-boarding or surfing but can be rough for swimming.

SURFING ON TAHITI

Polynesia is the birthplace of surfing, and Tahiti offers some fabulous beginner breaks, particularly at Papenoo and other beach breaks along the east coast. More advanced surfers can head to the Papara shore break and the reef breaks at Sapinus and Taapuna along the west coast and the big and small Vairao passes at Tahiti Iti. Tahiti's most famous and radical wave is at Hava'e Pass in Teahupoo on Tahiti Iti where there's a big international surf contest held each August. In general the west-coast waves break the biggest between May and October, while the east coast is best from November to April – waves are fickle, so this isn't set in stone.

To paddle out for your first time or hone your skills, contact the following outfits:

Tura'i Mataare Surf School (☎41 91 37; www.tahitisurfschool.info) Courses are run by a qualified instructor and include equipment, transport to the different surfing spots and insurance.

École Surf Iti Nui (☎73 14 21) In Tahiti Iti, qualified and superfriendly Doumé runs this small, low-key outfit – classes go to spots around Tahiti Nui as well as Tahiti Iti and transport, equipment and insurance are included.

The sealed road ends at Tautira, but you can bump along for another kilometre or two before the road becomes impassable to vehicles. A walking track leads round the coast for another 10km or so before reaching the Te Pari Cliffs.

Tautira (Map p52) itself is a lovely village and unique on Tahiti as it's not clustered along one main road but has many small residential lanes that criss-cross the town in a near grid. There's a sweeping **black-sand beach** at the edge of town; it's often empty and offers good swimming. You can also visit **Boenechea's grave** in front of the Catholic church in the centre of town.

Offshore close to Afaahiti is the stunning white-sand **Motu Nono** (Map p52), a popular picnic spot for locals and tourist excursions.

INLAND

There are two routes that climb to an inland **lookout** and can be combined to make a loop. In Afaahiti, at PK2.5, you'll find the turn-off by looking out for the equestrian-centre signpost. The 7km road climbs through green fields, some home to very un-Tahitian-looking herds of cows, to the little, covered lookout. The alternative route turns off the south-coast road at PK1.3 (turn inland at the grain factory, pass the high school and its football field then take a right at the stop sign). It meets the first route where the road forks, from where it's a short walk to the viewpoint. There are superb vistas across the isthmus of Taravao to the towering bulk of Tahiti Nui.

SOUTH-COAST ROAD

The south-coast road runs by beaches and bays before abruptly stopping at the Tirahi River at PK18.

A picturesque strip of white sand, **Maui Beach** (Map p52; PK8, Vairao) gets packed and noisy on weekends, but is peaceful during the week. It's right on the road but has shallow swimming, perfect for children, as well as deeper swimming and snorkelling off the reef.

A signposted turn-off at PK9.5 leads a short distance inland to the rarely visited remains of **Marae Nuutere** (Map p52), restored in 1994. There are three paved yards known as *tohua* (meeting places) with *ahu* (altars) at the end of them.

Starting at PK15 **Teahupoo** is world famous among surfing circles for its monster wave. It's also an obvious launching pad for the Te Pari Cliffs. At Teahupoo's Tirahi River, park then cross the footbridge. From here it's a lovely five-minute walk through a shaded residential area and past lily ponds to a public **beach** with black sand and a few shady almond trees. It's safe for swimming and suitable for kids.

Activities

Diving

Very few divers know that there's fantastic diving on Tahiti Iti. Most sites are scattered along the south coast, between Taravao and Teahupoo. You can expect pristine sites and fabulous drop-offs. For more information, see p31.

There's only one centre that offers dives to the area.

Tahiti Iti Diving DIVING
(Map p52; ☎42 25 33, 71 80 77; www.tahiti-iti-diving.com; PK58.1; ⌚Tue-Sun) This well-run dive shop is based near Taravao on Tahiti Nui but runs dive trips to Tahiti Iti. It charges 5800 CFP for an introductory dive or single dive and 48,000 CFP for a 10-dive package. Cash only.

Boat Excursions

Probably the most fun you can have in a day on Tahiti Iti is by taking a boat excursion, which invariably includes a picnic lunch, a visit to Vaipoiri Cave and, if the weather permits, Te Pari. All pensions in the area can arrange excursions.

Teahupoo Excursions BOAT EXCURSIONS
(☎75 11 98; half-/full day 5000/9000 CFP) This is the most professional independent boat operator, and it's run by contagiously happy

DON'T MISS

TAHITI BILLABONG PRO

Held at Teahupoo every August, the famous Billabong Pro surfing contest attracts the industry's best riders and draws surf fans and media from around the world. Until the early 2000s, the Teahupoo wave was only known to local surfers. It now ranks as one of the most powerful waves on the planet – on a par with Jaws in Hawaii. Teahupoo (dubbed 'Choopes') is a left that breaks over a very shallow reef, producing a perfect barrel. In the 2011 contest, the waves exceeded 8m.

WORTH A TRIP

EXPLORING THE FENUA AIHERE

A soggy but pretty 8km walk along the coast from the Teahupoo footbridge through several rivers brings you to **Vaipoiri Cave**. This coast, which is accessible only by boat or on foot, is called the **Fenua Aihere**, which literally means 'the bush country'. Although this walk is popular, there are a few aggressive unchained dogs along the way, making it a bit stressful. Boat excursions also go to Vaipoiri Cave.

From Vaipoiri Cave you can continue another 1.5km along the coast till you reach the **Te Pari Cliffs**. At this point the reef ends and the coastline becomes steep and gets pounded by waves when there's swell. It's possible to hike the entire 8km of this precarious coast dotted with archaeological treasures, wild passion fruit, waterfalls and caves, but you can only do it in good weather and if the swell isn't too big. Near the Vaiote River are some interesting **petroglyphs** inscribed on coastal boulders and a series of **marae** inland in the valley. There are fewer growling dogs along this trail and plenty of rivers and waterfalls waiting to be explored.

On the northern half of Tahiti Iti towards Tautira, the coastline continues along from the Te Pari Cliffs another 10km or so through a second **Fenua Aihere**, till the paved road begins once again at Tautira village.

A guide is highly recommended both for safety and to help you discover all the very hidden gems found mostly off the trail. It takes two days to hike from Teahupoo to Tautira and camp is usually made in an airy and open beachside cave. Most guides also offer one-day hikes on a section of the coast, in combination with a boat transfer. It's an unforgettable experience. For a list of professional guides see the Hiking & Canyoning on Tahiti boxed text, p69.

Michael. He organises à la carte tours or will shuttle folks out to the Teahupoo wave to watch surfing or to surf for 1000 CFP per person.

Tahiti Iti Tour BOAT EXCURSIONS
(☎75 55 66; www.tahitiititourandsurf.pf; half-/full day 5000/9000 CFP) A reputable operator that can organise anything that involves a boat.

Surfing

See the boxed text, p73, for information on Tahiti Iti's world-famous surf breaks.

Hiking

By far the best hike on Tahiti Iti is along the coast from Teahupoo to Tautira. Another popular hike is the cross-island trek from Tautira to Teahupoo (or conversely), which requires two days.

Horse Riding

L'Amour de la Nature à Cheval HORSE RIDING
(Map p52; ☎73 84 43; http://lamournatcheval.onlc.fr, in French; PK2.5, Taravao; rides from 2000 CFP) This equestrian centre offers guided rides to rarely visited points on the plateau with stunning views. It's best to reserve a few days in advance; there are no set hours.

Sleeping

TOP CHOICE **Vanira Lodge** BUNGALOW $$
(Map p52; ☎57 70 18; www.vaniralodge.com; PK15, Teahupoo; bungalows d/q 13,000/17,000 CFP;) Our favourite pension in Tahiti, this place is up a steep driveway on a miniplateau with vast views of the lagoon, surf, village and myriad island colours. The nine bungalows are fabulously eclectic and are all built from some combination of bamboo, thatch, rustic planks of wood, glass, adobe, coral and rock. One of the bungalows has an earth roof that's bursting with flowers. Cosy nooks, hand-carved furniture, airy mezzanines and alfresco kitchens (in the five family-size bungalows that sleep four) are nice touches. There's tons of open space for kids as well as a little lily pond, a pool and fruit trees. Breakfast costs 1400 CFP, but you're on your own for other meals (Plage de Maui restaurant can deliver to your bungalow). Bikes, kayaks and snorkel gear are available for rent. You'll need a car if you stay here.

Green Room Villa VILLA $$
(Map p52; www.greenroomvilla.com; PK18, Teahupoo; house from 30,000 CFP;) Rent this exquisite four-bedroom house for a romantic getaway or bring up to seven other people

(eight total) for a family or surfing get-together. The main house is octagonal-shaped with a huge covered wooden deck, tons of windows, teak flooring, brightly painted walls and a fully equipped kitchen. At the bottom half of the large, fruit-tree covered garden is the 'honeymoon bungalow' that's perched on stilts over a pond filled with purple water lilies. While this is the most private sleeping option and the only room with air-con, there is only an outdoor jungle shower adjacent to the bungalow and no toilet, although there may be one installed in the future. The quiet, private property is a five-minute walk to Teahupoo's beach and a minute's walk to a river bathing pool. Note that the owners require a credit-card damage deposit and there's a three-day minimum stay.

La Vague Bleue BUNGALOW **$$**
(Map p52; ☎57 23 23, 30 70 73; www.net-pf.com/lavaguebleue/; PK16, Teahupoo; bungalows d 10,000-12,000 CFP; 📶) The outwardly attractive bungalows here might be a little past their prime on the inside, but they are clean, and the location, on a quiet property opening on to the lagoon, is appealing. Sadly, the bungalows are tightly packed and only one unit boasts lagoon views. Meals are available on request (from 1500 CFP) and tours to Vaipoiri Cave can be arranged. Kayaks and bikes are complimentary. Cash only.

Te Pari Village BUNGALOW **$$**
(Map p52; ☎42 59 12; bungalows full board per person 11,000 CFP) Ten minutes by boat from the Teahupoo pier, this option is in the middle of a magnificent coconut- and fruit-tree grove beside the lagoon and oozes tranquillity. The handful of simple wooden bungalows make a circle around tall red ginger flowers and the main eating area is a big Polynesian meeting hall–style building. Prices include one excursion to Vaipoiri Cave and transfers from Teahupoo. Cash only.

Pension Bonjouir PENSION **$**
(Map p52; ☎77 89 69, 57 02 15; www.bonjouir.com; r 8000 CFP, bungalows from 13,000 CFP; @) Bonjouir is a nature-lover's paradise – it's surrounded by walks to waterfalls, swimming holes and caves and fronted by the clear lagoon – but it's far from being perfect. Some travellers have complained of being charged for 'extras' they thought were free, so be clear with your hosts what the rates cover. Digs are in rooms or bungalows; they're quite basic but have Tahitian flair. You'll need to take the shuttle boat from the dock at PK17 in Teahupoo (2200 CFP return). Bring mosquito repellent even though all the beds have nets. Half board is 5000 CFP and a few bungalows have their own kitchens. There's a young, fun and convivial vibe. Various activities can be organised. Cash only.

Reva PENSION **$$**
(Map p52; ☎57 92 16, 77 14 28; www.reva-teahupoo.com; bungalows full board per person 13,000 CFP) A place of easy bliss, Reva is another isolated place that's accessible by boat from Teahupoo. It takes full advantage of the waterfront property, with a long pontoon jutting out over the lagoon – great for swimming. There are four well-designed bungalows scattered amid lush gardens. Various activities can be arranged. Electricity is generated from solar power. Prices include transfers from Teahupoo. Cash only.

Punatea Village BUNGALOWS **$**
(Map p52; ☎57 71 00, 77 20 31; www.punatea.com; PK4.7, Afaahiti; d with shared bathroom 6000 CFP, bungalow d 9600 CFP; ❄) Four stand-alone bungalows and five tiny rooms in a verdant property opening onto the lagoon. There's a small artificial beach. No meal service.

Chez Maïté B&B **$**
(Map p52; ☎57 18 24; www.chez-maithe.com; PK4.5, Afaahiti; d 7500-8500 CFP) Accommodation here consists of two rooms on the ground floor of the owner's house. One room has air-conditioning, the other is a bit dank. Great for families, with a communal kitchen and access to a small swimming area. Cash only.

Eating

La Plage de Maui POLYNESIAN **$$**
(Map p52; ☎74 71 74; PK7.6, Vairao; mains 1600-2700 CFP; ⊙10am-5pm) On the beach of the same name, this place looks like a shack inside and out, but the food is Polynesian haute cuisine. The meals are expensive, but tasty, and the position overlooking the lagoon is sublime. There are also cheaper burgers and such for the kids. Cash only.

Hinerava POLYNESIAN **$$**
(Map p52; ☎57 60 84; PK18, Teahupoo; mains 1200-2200 CFP; ⊙lunch & dinner Tue-Sun) At the end of the road in Teahupoo, this place serves good food. You can dine outside or inside in the air-con. There's a great selection of fish, meats and burger plates every day, *ma'a Tahiti* (2500 CFP) all day on Sundays, and daily specials on other days of the week.

Mo'orea

POP 16,000

Includes »

Best Places to Stay

- » Résidence Linareva (p91)
- » Green Lodge (p92)
- » Sofitel Moorea la Ora Beach Resort (p92)
- » Tehuarupe (p91)
- » Legends Resort Moorea (p89)

Best Places to Eat

- » Le K (p95)
- » Coco Beach (p95)
- » Le Mayflower (p94)
- » Snack Mahana (p94)
- » Crêperie Toatea (p93)

Why Go?

Mo'orea is so beautiful you'll be rubbing your eyes at your first glimpse of it from Tahiti. The loveliness of the island intensifies as you draw nearer. That turquoise lagoon that you were sure was Photoshopped in the brochure? It's better in real life. As you admire the near-vertical emerald cliffs, you'll wonder if you are the luckiest person in the world. The short answer is: yes.

Mo'orea has a healthy selection of top-end resorts, but it is also host to a good choice of smaller hotels and pensions (guesthouses). There are pretty white-sand beaches, but nothing big and sweeping. The drawcard is the limpid, warm water of the vibrant lagoon. Frolic with rays and sharks, snorkel or dive through schools of fish in translucent waters, savour the brilliant sunsets, and just chill. If you need more action, learn to kitesurf, take a hike, go on a whale- or dolphin-watching tour, hire a bike or a kayak, or go horse riding. Whatever the experience, there's only one word to describe Mo'orea: divine!

When to Go

Like Tahiti, Mo'orea enjoys a year-round tropical climate. November to April are the wetter months. From May to October it's usually much drier – perfect for outdoor activities. July and August are fairly windy. Diving and surfing are popular year-round; the whale-watching season runs from July to October.

History

The island's ancient name was Eimeo (sometimes spelled Aimeho). Some say that Mo'orea, which means 'yellow lizard', was the name of one of the island's ruling families, while others attribute this name to an image seen by a high priest while visiting the island.

Mo'orea was heavily populated before the Europeans arrived on its idyllic doorstep. Samuel Wallis was the first European to sight the island (1767); he was soon followed by Louis-Antoine de Bougainville (1768) and James Cook (1769). The missionaries arrived on the scene in the early 1800s and made themselves at home, soon establishing their headquarters on the island. As elsewhere, European diseases and the introduction of weapons and alcohol had a disastrous effect on the population of Mo'orea, which declined during the 19th century.

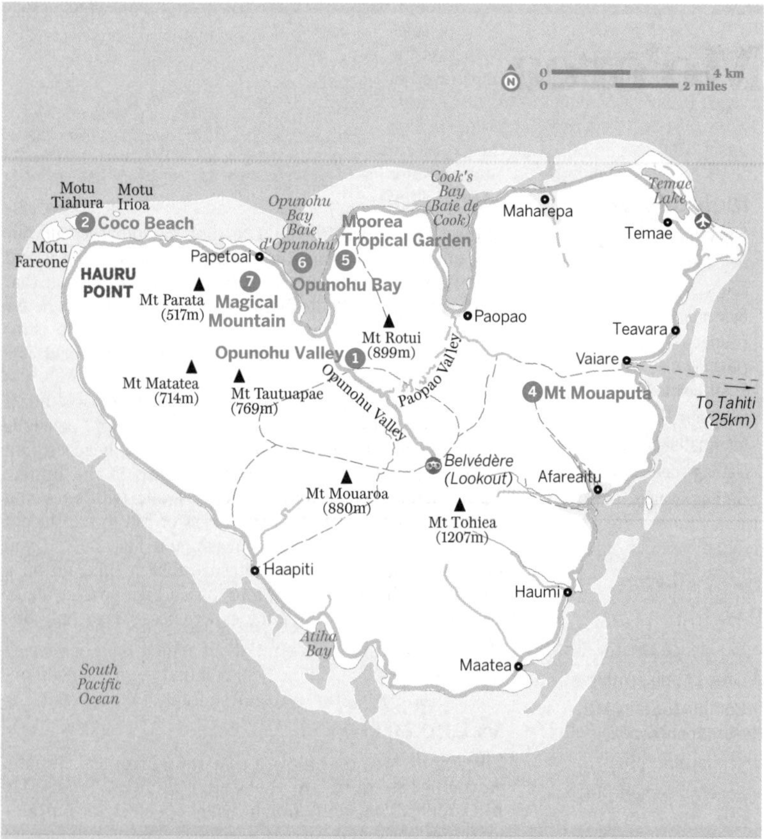

Mo'orea Highlights

1. Getting lost in **Opunohu Valley** (p86), with its ancient *marae* (traditional temples), breathtaking vistas and hidden walking paths
2. Paddling to Motu Tiahura from Hauru Point for lunch at **Coco Beach** (p95)
3. Sighting and maybe swimming with **whales and dolphins** (p84) from July to October
4. Taking an unforgettable hike to **Mt Mouaputa** (p86)
5. Sampling tropical delights at **Moorea Tropical Garden** (p85)
6. Diving amid a concentration of lemon sharks in **Opunohu Bay** (p82)
7. Savouring fabulous lagoon vistas from the **Magical Mountain lookout** (p80)

Copra and vanilla were important crops in the past, but these days Mo'orea is the pineapple-growing centre of French Polynesia. Tourism is the other major industry, but Mo'orea saw its economic bottom begin to fall out in 2008.

Sights

The following circuit starts near the airport and moves in an anticlockwise direction, following the northern PK markers.

Teavaro & Temae Beaches BEACH

(Map p80; PK1 to PK0) The best beaches on the east coast, and the widest perhaps in all of French Polynesia, stretch from Teavaro round to the airport. The Sofitel Moorea Ia Ora Beach Resort occupies Teavaro Beach, where there's good snorkelling in the shallow water and out on the lagoon side of the fringing reef. The public section of Teavaro Beach, just north of the Sofitel, is usually referred to as Temae Beach. It gets crowded on weekends.

A road on the lagoon side of the runway extends around **Temae Lake**, which is now home to the Moorea Green Pearl Golf Course, but the route is cut off so it is not possible to rejoin the main coastal road, or to reach the airport or the entrance to the golf course.

Toatea Lookout LOOKOUT

(Map p80; PK0.6) This spot really fits the picture-postcard ideal. Atop the hill north of the Sofitel Moorea Ia Ora Beach Resort, this lookout affords dazzling views of the hotel, the lagoon mottled with coral formations, the barrier reef and Tahiti in the background.

Maison Blanche HISTORIC BUILDING

(Map p83; PK5) One notable sight in the village of Maharepa is the Maison Blanche, on the mountain side of the road. This early-20th-century building is a fine example of a *fare vanira,* a plantation house from Mo'orea's vanilla-boom era. Located near the Moorea Pearl Resort & Spa, the Maison Blanche is now a souvenir shop. It has a fairly typical selection of *pareu* (sarongs) and Balinese woodcarvings.

TOP CHOICE **Cook's Bay** NATURAL SITE

(PK6 to PK11) The spectacular Cook's Bay is something of a misnomer because Cook actually anchored in Opunohu Bay. With Mt Rotui as a backdrop, Cook's Bay is a lovely stretch of water. There's no real centre to Cook's Bay; shops, restaurants and hotels are simply dotted along the road.

At the base of Cook's Bay is the sleepy village of **Paopao** (Map p83). There's the **old fish market** and a few shops here. Even though the fish market is no more, you can still see the mural painted by Mo'orea-based artist François Ravello.

Settlements are creeping up the Paopao Valley but the main activity is still agriculture, with many hectares of pineapple plantations. The road inland from Paopao and Cook's Bay meets the Opunohu Valley road, just before the agricultural college and the walking track up to Three Coconut Trees Pass (see p85).

FREE **Distillerie et Usine de Jus de Fruits de Moorea** DISTILLERY, FACTORY

(Map p80; ☎55 20 00; www.manuteatahiti.com; PK11; ⊙8.30am-4.30pm Mon-Thu, 8.30am-3pm Fri, 9am-4pm Sat) About 300m inland from the coastal road, this juice-processing factory and distillery is well worth a stop. It produces various juices and alcoholic beverages, including yummy liqueurs and a devilish 'Tahitian punch'. The tasting of liqueurs and juices is free. Tours are available at 9am and 2pm from Monday to Thursday and last about 40 minutes. The gift shop sells drinks, jams, honey and souvenirs.

Ta'ahiamanu (Mareto) Beach BEACH

(Map p80; PK14) At last, a public beach! Ta'ahiamanu (Mareto) Beach is one of the few public access beaches on the island. This narrow stretch of white sand is a popular spot for both tourists and locals on weekends. Fear not, you'll find plenty of room to stretch without bumping anyone else's beach towel. Despite the lack of facilities, it's ideal for splashing about, sunbathing or picnicking. Snorkellers will find plenty of coral and marine life right in front of the beach.

TOP CHOICE **Opunohu Bay** NATURAL SITE

(Map p80; PK14 to PK18) Magnificent Opunohu Bay feels wonderfully fresh and isolated.

PK MARKERS

Adhering to French Polynesian logic, the *point kilométrique* (PK; kilometre point) markers start at PK0 at the airport and go around the coast in both clockwise and anticlockwise directions; they meet at Haapiti, which is at PK24 along the southern (clockwise) route and at PK37 along the northern (anticlockwise) route.

Mo'orea

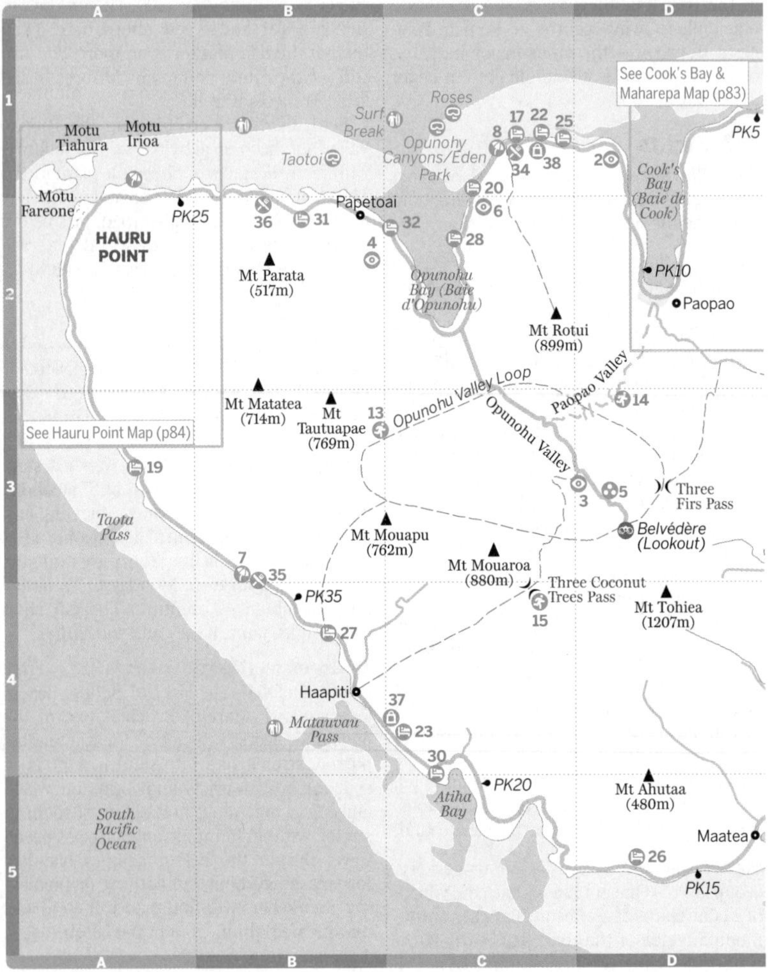

The coastal road rounds Mt Rotui, and at about PK14 turns inland along the eastern side of Opunohu Bay. There is less development along here than around Cook's Bay, and it's one of the more tranquil and eye-catching spots on the island. Most of the Polynesian scenes in the 1984 movie *Bounty* were shot on Opunohu Bay.

At PK18, a road turns off inland along the Opunohu Valley to the valley *marae* and the *belvédère* (lookout) – see p86.

Magical Mountain LOOKOUT

(Map p80; PK21; admission 300 CFP) At PK21, a cement road veers inland and makes a very steep climb to a lookout called 'Magical Mountain', at a height of 209m. Hold on to your hat and lift your jaw off the floor as you approach the viewpoint – the view over the northern part of the island and the lagoon is mesmerising. The access road is private, so permission must be obtained before entering the property; contact the owners who live in the house at the entrance of the property. Should you decide to walk to the look-

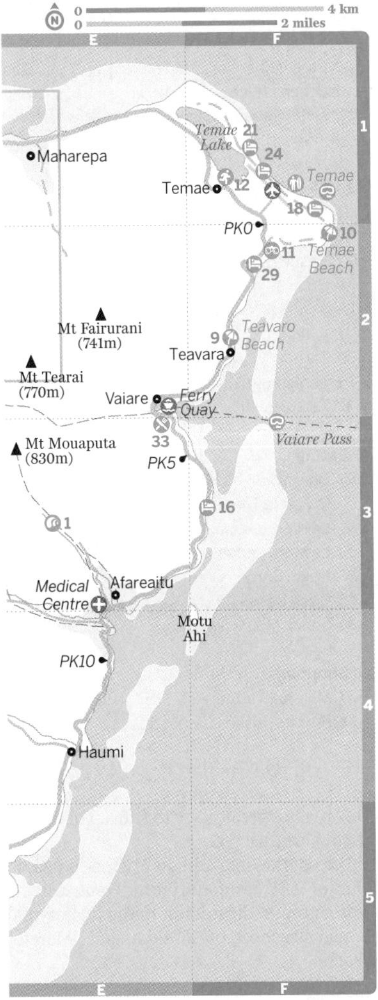

out, start early before it gets too hot. Your best bet is to join an ATV tour (p87).

Papetoai VILLAGE

(Map p80; PK22) A busy little village with a post office and a number of restaurants, Papetoai was established as the Pacific headquarters of the London Missionary Society (LMS) in 1811. In the 1870s the missionaries constructed an octagonal **church** at Papetoai; today this is the oldest standing European building in the South Pacific. As was often the case, the missionaries deliberately built this church atop an old *marae*.

Hauru Point NATURAL SITE

(Map p84; PK25 to PK30) The coastal road rounds Hauru Point, the northwestern corner of the island, between PK25 and PK30. This is one of the island's major tourist enclaves, although it has seen better days – a number of shops, restaurants and hotels have closed since 2008. The tourist strip starts with the Intercontinental Moorea Resort & Spa at about PK25, and finishes at around PK31.

Unlike Cook's Bay, Hauru Point has a beach. Though narrow, it's pretty spectacular with turquoise water and good snorkelling. Immediately offshore are **Motu Tiahura** and **Motu Fareone**, attractive little islets so close to the shore you can easily swim out to them and enjoy fine snorkelling on the way. A little further east is the tiny **Motu Irioa**. Remember that the actual *motu* (islets) are private (although the littoral areas aren't).

Painapo Beach BEACH

(Map p80; PK33) You can't miss the huge (though falling apart) statue of a tattooed man holding a club at the entrance of this private property overlooking a lovely strip of white sand. In theory, there's an access fee to get to the beach – ask around.

Haapiti VILLAGE

(Map p80; PK37) The largest village on the west coast, Haapiti is home to the huge twin-towered Catholic **Église de la Sainte Famille**, which is made of coral and lime. The **Protestant Temple** is another notable building; it's at PK23.5, on the lagoon side of the road.

Atiha Bay NATURAL SITE

(Map p80; PK18) Mo'orea's lazy west-coast atmosphere continues right round to Atiha Bay (Baie d'Atiha), a quiet fishing village that also attracts surfers.

Afareaitu VILLAGE

(Map p80; PK10) Afareaitu is the island's administrative centre. There are two **waterfalls** that are worth a gander (although they are but feeble trickles in winter). Ask locals for directions.

Vaiare VILLAGE

(Map p80; PK4) The constant toing and froing of ferry boats and high-speed catamarans at the ferry quay, the busy market scene and the cars, taxis and *le trucks* (buses) shuttling visitors around render the 100m or so near the dock area the busiest patch of real estate on Mo'orea.

Mo'orea

Sights

1	Afareaitu Waterfalls	E3
2	Distillerie et Usine de Jus de Fruits de Moorea	D1
3	Lycée Agricole (Agricultural College)	D3
4	Magical Mountain	B2
	Marae Afareaito	(see 5)
	Marae Ah-o-Mahine	(see 5)
5	Marae Titiroa	D3
6	Moorea Tropical Garden	C2
7	Painapo Beach	B3
8	Ta'ahiamanu (Mareto) Beach	C1
9	Teavaro Beach	F2
10	Temae Beach	F2
11	Toatea Lookout	F2

Activities, Courses & Tours

	Ia Ora Diving	(see 29)
12	Moorea Green Pearl	F1
13	Opunohu Valley Loop	B3
14	Ranch Opunohu Valley	D3
15	Three Coconut Trees Pass	C4

Sleeping

16	Atuana Lodge	F3
17	Fare Junette	C1
18	Fare Maeva	F1
19	Fare Pole	A3
20	Fare Vaihere	C1
21	Green Lodge	F1
22	Hilton Moorea Lagoon Resort & Spa	C1
23	Mark's Place Moorea	C4
24	Moorea Golf Lodge	F1
25	Motu Iti	C1
26	Pension Aute	D5
27	Résidence Linareva	B4
28	Robinson Cove	C2
29	Sofitel Moorea Ia Ora Beach Resort	F2
30	Tarariki Village	C4
31	Tehuarupe	B2
32	Tipaniers Iti	C2

Eating

33	Champion-TOA	E3
	Crêperie Toatea	(see 22)
	Le K	(see 29)
	Le Motu Lodge	(see 24)
34	Lilikoi Garden Café	C1
35	Pizza Daniel	B3
36	Snack Mahana	B2

Shopping

37	Mo'orea Tattoo	C4
38	Purotu Tattoo	C1

Activities

It is wise to book activities as soon as you arrive on the island; contact organisers directly or check with your hotel or guesthouse.

Diving & Snorkelling

Mo'orea is one of French Polynesia's main underwater playgrounds, which is no surprise considering its high visibility and clean waters. The underwater scenery is every bit the equal of what's on land: you can dive sloping reefs and go nose-to-nose with sharks – especially lemon sharks – rays and numerous reef species. Most dive operators are concentrated to the northwest of the island. As a result, most diving is focused along the north coast, especially between Hauru Point and Opunohu Bay. And if you don't already know how to dive, Mo'orea is a great place to learn. For details about sites, see p32.

For snorkelling, join an organised lagoon tour or DIY around Hauru Point and its *motu*, around the interior of the reef beyond Temae Beach or off Ta'ahiamanu (Mareto) Beach.

Topdive DIVING
(Map p84; ☎56 31 44; www.topdive.com) This well established dive shop at Intercontinental Moorea Resort & Spa offers the full range of scuba activities, with Nitrox dives at no extra cost. It also arranges shark dives involving shark-feeding demonstrations. Note that this practice is controversial as these encounters are artificial and may disrupt natural behaviour patterns. It charges 8000 CFP for an introductory dive, 8000 CFP for a single dive and 43,000/70,000 CFP for a six-/10-dive package.

Ia Ora Diving DIVING
(Map p80; ☎56 35 78) Due to its location (at Sofitel Ia Ora Moorea Beach Resort) on the northeastern corner of the island, Ia Ora specialises in dive sites along the east coast. Count on 7500 CFP for an introductory dive and 7200 CFP for a single dive.

Moorea Blue Diving DIVING
(Map p83; ☎55 17 04; www.mooreabluediving.com) At Moorea Pearl Resort & Spa, this hotel dive shop gets good reviews. An introductory dive costs 7500 CFP, a single dive is 6900 CFP and five-/10-dive packages are 33,000/60,000 CFP.

Moorea Fun Dive DIVING
(Map p84; ☎56 40 38; www.moorea-fundive.com; PK26.7) This small, family-run operation at Hauru Point, on the beach, offers knowledgeable and personal service. If you've never been diving before, these are the people to see. An introductory dive costs 7100 CFP, a single dive is 6400 CFP and six-/10-dive packages are 33,000/52,000 CFP.

Scubapiti DIVING
(Map p84; ☎56 20 38, 78 03 52; www.scubapiti.com) At Les Tipaniers. The only dive centre that has never engaged in shark-feeding. Goes out with small groups. Introductory dives are 6500 CFP, single dives cost 6100 CFP. Prices drop by about 10% for more than two dives.

Undersea Walks

Aqua Blue UNDERSEA WALKS
(Map p84; ☎56 53 53, 73 24 40; http://contact.aquablue.free.fr; trips 7500 CFP) If you want to experience diving but aren't quite sure it's for you, try this outfit at the Intercontinental Moorea Resort & Spa. It offers an excursion in which you walk along the sea bed wearing a weighted helmet with air pumped into it. Since you actually walk on the bottom, you don't even need to be able to swim.

Lagoon Excursions

The best way to discover Mo'orea's magnificent lagoon is by joining a lagoon excursion. Tours typically visit the two bays, stop to feed the sharks, feed and swim with the rays at a spot off the Intercontinental Moorea Resort & Spa, and picnic and snorkel on Motu Fareone. Plenty of operators are available for day-long tours that usually include lunch and cost around 8000 CFP; check at your accommodation or contact the following operators.

Cook's Bay & Maharepa

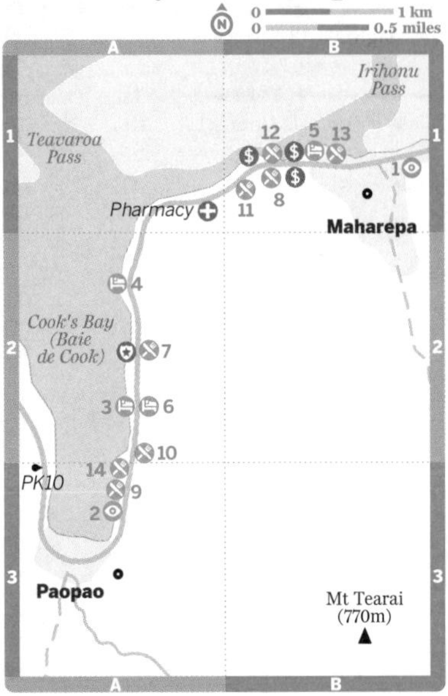

Cook's Bay & Maharepa

Sights
- 1 Maison Blanche ... B1
- 2 Old Fish Market ... A3

Activities, Courses & Tours
- Moorea Blue Diving ... (see 5)

Sleeping
- 3 Club Bali Hai ... A2
- 4 Kaveka ... A2
- 5 Moorea Pearl Resort & Spa ... B1
- 6 Motel Albert ... A2

Eating
- 7 Allo Pizza ... A2
- 8 Caraméline ... B1
- 9 Chez Jean-Pierre ... A3
- L'Ananas Bleu ... (see 3)
- 10 Le Martinez ... A2
- 11 Le Rudy's ... B1
- 12 Le Sud ... B1
- 13 Pukalani ... B1
- 14 Te Honu Iti - Chez Roger ... A3

Hauru Point

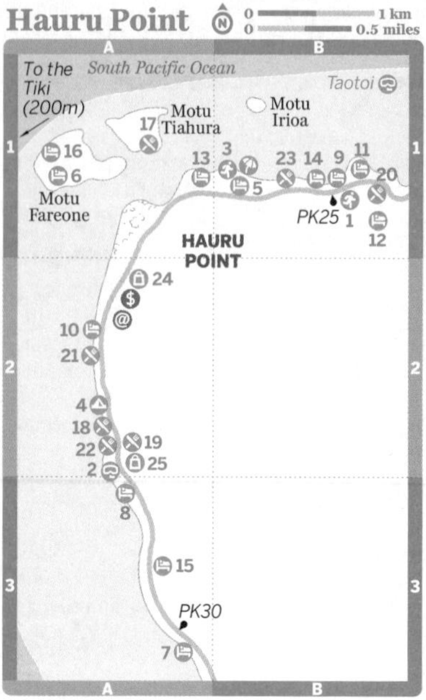

Hauru Point

Activities, Courses & Tours

- Aqua Blue .... (see 11)
- 1 ATV Moorea Tours B1
- Moorea Dolphin Center .... (see 11)
- 2 Moorea Fun Dive A2
- 3 Moorea Loca Boat B1
- Scubapiti .... (see 13)
- Tip Nautic .... (see 13)
- Topdive .... (see 11)

Sleeping

- 4 Camping Nelson A2
- 5 Domloc B1
- 6 Dream Island A1
- 7 Fare Manuia A3
- 8 Fare Miti A3
- 9 Fenua Mata'i'oa B1
- 10 Hotel Hibiscus A2
- 11 Intercontinental Moorea Resort & Spa B1
- 12 Legends Resort B1
- 13 Les Tipaniers A1
- 14 Taoa Here Beach House B1
- 15 Tapu Lodge A3
- 16 Villa Corallina A1

Eating

- 17 Coco Beach A1
- 18 Coco d'Isle A2
- 19 La Paillotte A2
- 20 La Villa des Sens B1
- 21 Le Mayflower A2
- Le Sunset .... (see 10)
- Legends Gourmet .... (see 12)
- Les Tipaniers .... (see 13)
- 22 PKO A2
- 23 Vina – Chez Serge B1

Shopping

- 24 Le Petit Village A2
- 25 Taniera Tattoo A2

Tip Nautic BOAT TOUR
(☎78 76 73) At Les Tipaniers. No shark or ray feeding.

Manu BOAT TOUR
(☎79 03 28) Uses a catamaran. No shark or ray feeding.

Moorea Boat Tours BOAT TOUR
(☎56 28 44, 78 68 86; www.mooreaboattours.com) A popular operator.

What to do Moorea Tours BOAT TOUR
(☎56 57 66; www.hirotour.com) Standard tours that include shark and ray feeding.

Moorea Loca Boat BOATING
(Map p84; ☎78 13 39; 2/4/8hr incl fuel 7000/9000/11,000 CFP) This outfit right on the beach beside Les Tipaniers rents outboard-powered boats – an ideal way to explore the lagoon and small *motu*. No licence is required. Also has pedal boats.

Whale- & Dolphin-Watching

This activity has exploded in recent years. You can count on finding dolphins year-round, but it's the whales, who migrate to Mo'orea from July to October, who draw in the crowds. A face-to-face encounter with these gentle sea mammals is the kind of mind-blowing 'whoa' experience you'll remember for the rest of your days. If you're lucky you'll get to swim with the mammals, but just seeing them in the water is a real thrill – trips cost 8000 CFP and kids under 12 are half price. Most dive centres run whale-watching trips, or you can contact the following outfits.

Dr Michael Poole WHALE- & DOLPHIN-WATCHING
(☎56 23 22; www.drmichaelpoole.com) A world specialist on South Pacific marine mammals and an advocate for their protection, Dr Poole began the first whale-watching tours and continues to lead the best ones available.

Moorea

Deep Blue WHALE- & DOLPHIN-WATCHING
(☎76 37 27; www.moorea-deepblue.com) A former dive instructor runs small-group whale- and dolphin-watching trips with environmental awareness and with minimal impact on the animals.

Moorea Dolphin Expedition WHALE- & DOLPHIN-WATCHING
(☎78 42 42; www.moorea-dolphin-expedition.com) Whale- and dolphin-watching trips as well as ray and shark feeding demonstrations.

Moorea Dolphin Center DOLPHIN ENCOUNTERS
(Map p84; ☎55 19 48; www.mooreadolphincenter.com; Intercontinental Moorea Resort & Spa) If you want a calmer environment in which to commune with dolphins (or if you just get way too seasick to brave the boat!), try for a 'shallow-water encounter' (from 16,000 CFP) with captive dolphins in an enclosure at the Intercontinental Moorea Resort & Spa. The program has received accreditation from the Alliance of Marine Mammal Parks, an international organisation that promotes quality control for the care of captive sea mammals. That said, the practice is not without controversy. For more information about the global industry of dolphin captivity, check www.thecovemovie.com.

Surfing

The island's excellent surfing waves are for experienced to advanced surfers. The most popular spot is Haapiti (May to October), which has the regularity and strength of reef waves with the security of a beach wave; plus it's pretty deep at the take-off point. Other spots include Temae (year-round, depending on the winds), which is a difficult right-hander at a recess in the reef; Paopao (Cook's Bay) and Opunohu Bay (November to April) in a magnificent setting; and the expert-only left-hander at Intercontinental Moorea Resort & Spa (June to October), near the hotel's beach.

Kitesurfing

With an easterly wind blowing much of the time, and its shallow waters protected by the barrier reef, kitesurfing has become very popular on Mo'orea and on windy days you'll see dozens of kites whipping across the lagoon in front of the Intercontinental Moorea Resort & Spa. If you want to give it a go contact **Lakana Fly** (☎70 96 71), which offers beginner to advanced kitesurfing lessons for ages nine and up (two-hour course 3000 CFP).

Hiking

Exhilarating hikes of varying difficulty tackle the lush inland area. Most trails are infrequently used and poorly marked, so it's necessary to use a guide. For a DIY hike, consider the trails at the Lyćee Agricole (p86).

Vaiare to Paopao HIKING
(Map p80) This interesting and reasonably easy walk takes about two hours, starting from Vaiare and climbing to the ridge between Mt Tearai (770m) and Mt Mouaputa (830m) before dropping down into the valley and emerging at Paopao on Cook's Bay.

Three Coconut Trees Pass HIKING
(Map p80) This climb is hard work, but the pay-off is superb views from the ridge between Mt Mouaroa (880m) and Mt Tohiea (1207m). There are no longer three coconut trees up here – two were blown down in an early 1980s cyclone.

Opunohu Valley Loop HIKING
(Map p80) This one-day walk starts at Three Coconut Trees Pass then continues on. Follow the ridgeline through undergrowth of *purau* (hibiscus) and *mape* until you get to the *belvédère* (about 1½ hours). From there, it's about 45 minutes to Three Firs Pass, with superb views of Cook's Bay and Opunohu Bay as you face the ridge of Mt Rotui. The last stage is the return to the agricultural college, about 1¾ hours. After a steep descent you come to the basin of the caldera.

DON'T MISS

MOOREA TROPICAL GARDEN

At PK16, a secondary road turns off inland and leads to **Moorea Tropical Garden** (Map p80; ☎70 53 63; ⌚8am-5pm Mon-Sat, 8am-3pm Sun). This delightfully peaceful property perched on a small plateau is heaven on earth for the sweet-toothed, who can sample (and buy) homemade organic jams and delicious ice creams; there are lots of original flavours, such as *noni* and *uru* (breadfruit). Freshly squeezed juices are also on offer. If you happen to be there on Friday, don't miss out on the Polynesian lunch menu (2000 CFP). Needless to say, the lagoon views are fantastic.

DON'T MISS

PAOPAO & OPUNOHU VALLEYS

From Mo'orea's two great bays, valleys sweep inland, meeting south of the coastal bulk of Mt Rotui. In the pre-European era the valleys were densely populated and the Opunohu Valley was dotted with *marae* (traditional temples), some of which have been restored and maintained. All *marae* seem to attract mosquitoes and these are no exception!

Lycée Agricole

A small *fare* at the **Lycée Agricole** (Agricultural College; Map p80; ⌚8am-4.30pm Mon-Thu, 8am-3.30pm Fri, 9am-2.30pm Sat) sells jams in local flavours and, on occasion, ice cream. If you've got itchy feet, there's a small network of **walking trails** that lead through the estate, in the basin of the caldera. These are detailed in leaflets that are available at the *fare*. The longest loop takes a little over two hours to walk. The trails are well maintained and marked.

From the college, the road continues inland and up to the *marae* sites and finally to the *belvédère* (lookout) on the slopes of Mt Tohiea (1207m).

Archaeological Sites

The Opunohu Valley has some of the most important and numerous *marae* in French Polynesia. Unusually, you can walk to them along marked tracks and there are explanatory panels in French and English. The complex comprises a range of partially restored remains including family and communal *marae* as well as dwellings, archery platforms and other structures.

It's believed the valley was continuously inhabited for six centuries, and the oldest surviving structures date from the 13th century. This agricultural community reached its apogee in the 17th and 18th centuries. The first excavations date from 1925. In 1960, Roger Green carried out the most complete research on the area, and 500 structures have been inventoried. See p219 for more information on *marae*. Past the agricultural college, the valley road comes to a parking area beside the huge **Marae Titiroa** (Map p80), on the edge of a dense forest of magnificent *mape* (chestnut) trees. From the *marae* a walking track leads to the *tohua* (council platform), and two smaller *marae*.

From there the track continues to the **Marae Ahu-o-Mahine**, a more recent *marae* of round stones with an imposing three-stepped *ahu* (altar).

A short distance along the road from Marae Titiroa is **Marae Afareaito**. The large *marae* has a small, raised-terrace *ahu*, and back rests that were used by the priests. It is flanked by two crescent-shaped archery platforms.

Belvédère

Beyond Marae Afareaito the road continues to climb steeply, winding its way up to the **belvédère**. This lookout offers superb views of Mt Rotui, which splits the two bays, and back to the towering mountains that rise in the centre of the island and which once formed the southern rim of the ancient crater.

Mt Mouaputa HIKING
(Map p80) If you're really fit, you can try the arduous climb up to Mt Mouaputa (830m), one of Mo'orea's iconic summits. It's a six- to seven-hour hard-going return hike from Afareaitu, with some difficult uphill scrambles, but the 360-degree panorama at the summit is worth the effort.

Mt Rotui HIKING
(Map p80) Another strenuous but scenic hike, the Mt Rotui (899m) climb starts from near Moorea Pearl Resort & Spa. You walk almost all the way along a ridge (no shade). It's steep, but the reward is a tremendous view of the island. Allow roughly six hours there and back.

GUIDED HIKES

Not everyone grooves to guided hikes, but the geology, flora and fauna of this lovely island pop vividly when described by the experts. They usually charge between 5500 CFP and 13,000 CFP depending on the outing. Note that a minimum of two to four people is usually required. Some recommended companies: **Hiking Discovery** (☎70 73 31); **Moorea Hiking** (☎56 16 48, 79 41 54; meretmontagne@mail.pf); **Polynesian Adventure** (☎43 25 95, 77 24 37; www.polynesianadv.com); and **Tahiti Evasion** (☎70 56 18; www.tahitievasion.com).

Horse Riding

Ranch Opunohu Valley HORSE RIDING
(Map p80; ☎56 28 55, 78 42 47; 2hr rides 5000 CFP; ⏰by reservation) Two-hour guided rides into the island's interior are available mornings and afternoons. The ranch is up in the Paopao Valley (it's signposted).

ATV

ATV Moorea Tours ATV TOURS
(Map p84; ☎70 73 45; www.atvmoorea.com; PK24.6; tours per ATV from 12,000 CFP) Double-seater ATV 4WD buggies are a fun but expensive way to see some rugged interior areas near the Lycée Agricole and the Magical Mountain; 2½-hour and 3½-hour guided tours are available and include several stops. A driving licence is required.

Kayak

The translucent waters of the lagoon are as inviting for kayakers as they are for divers and snorkellers. Many places to stay offer free kayaks for guests' use.

Tip Nautic KAYAKING
(Map p84; ☎78 76 73; single/double/triple kayak per hr 500/1000/1500 CFP) This reputable outfit based on the beach at Les Tipaniers rents out various kayaks that are in tip-top shape. The beach here is the optimal launching pad to get to Motu Fareone and Motu Tiahura.

Golf

Moorea Green Pearl GOLF
(Map p80; ☎56 27 32; www.mooreagolf-resort.com; Temaie; 9/18 holes 6000/10,000 CFP) This 18-hole course is in full, scorching sun. The mountain behind is low and weedy and there's not much of a view of the sea but the lake is pretty enough. There's a clubhouse, a small pro shop and bistro dining. Lessons are available.

Tours

Several operators organise island tours aboard open 4WDs. There are complete tours of the island with visits to the archaeological sites in the Opunohu Valley, stops at the *belvédère* and visits to pineapple and vanilla plantations and the fruit-juice factory. The three-hour tours cost around 6000 CFP per person and are good value if you don't want to hire a car. Some recommended companies: **Inner Island Safari Tours** (☎56 20 09, 72 84 87); **What to do Moorea Tours** (☎56 57 66; www.hirotour.com); and **Julienne Safari Tours** (☎56 48 87, 78 65 40).

Sleeping

Aaah, Mo'orea. There's no traffic (but plenty of roaring mosquitoes) and even the budget accommodation options have lovely garden settings.

Most accommodation is concentrated on the eastern side of Cook's Bay and around Hauru Point. Both these centres are very spread out; if you're staying at one end and want to eat at the other, it's not a case of just wandering a few steps along the road, although many restaurants will arrange to pick you up.

Unless otherwise noted all places take credit cards.

COOK'S BAY

Magnificent Cook's Bay does not have any beach, and so is the quieter, less touristy sister to Hauru Point.

Club Bali Hai RESORT **$$**
(Map p83; ☎56 13 68; www.clubbalihai.com; PK8; r & bungalows d from 16,000 CFP; ❄@📶🏊) Just across from Motel Albert, Club Bali Hai sits on the eastern shore of Cook's Bay with a picture-postcard view of Mt Rotui. One of Mo'orea's few mid-price accommodation options, it has a range of spick-and-span rooms in a two-storey, motel-like building as well as an assortment of local-style bungalows, including a handful of overwater units that are among the least expensive in French Polynesia. The upper-floor rooms have spectacular views. The decor is nothing special, but the setting and the relaxed feel more than make up for the slightly dated sense of style. White sand has been brought in to form a sunbathing patch along the shore, and there's superb snorkelling a few fin-strokes away. A tiny swimming pool and a restaurant over the water round off the offerings. Frequent online promotional deals provide real value.

Moorea Pearl Resort & Spa RESORT **$$$**
(Map p83; ☎55 17 50; www.pearlresorts.com; PK5; bungalows d from 30,000 CFP; ❄📶🏊) The infinity pool here is the island's best. The artificial, white-sand beach is smaller than those at other resorts, but the Pearl's vibe is more

MO'OREA FOR CHILDREN

Don't hesitate to bring the whole family, as Mo'orea is particularly kid friendly. Some highlights:

» Petting rays and approaching unaggressive blacktip sharks and colourful fish on a lagoon tour (p83)

» Splashing about on Temae Beach (p79)

» Spotting dolphins and humpback whales (p84)

» Experiencing a 'shallow-water encounter' with captive dolphins (p85)

» Taking an introductory dive in the shallow waters of the lagoon (p82)

» Walking along the seabed (p83)

» Enjoying an ice cream at Moorea Tropical Garden (p85)

» Clip-clopping amid volcanic landscapes (p87)

» Riding an ATV – on the passenger seat (p87)

intimate and relaxed. If you opt for an over-the-water bungalow, take a premium one as these are over deeper, clearer water. It also prides itself on its deluxe garden bungalows, which come with a private pool. Facilities include a restaurant, a spa and a dive centre.

Kaveka BUNGALOWS **$$**

(Map p83; ☎56 50 50; www.hotel-kaveka-moorea.com; PK7.3; bungalows d from 14,000 CFP;) This is not the place to come for style or swank, but if you're in search of a restful, budget-friendly spot, look no further. American-owned Kaveka has been around for years; although its 30 bungalows are showing their age a tad, they still have traditional island charms, such as thatched roofs extending over front porches and bamboo furnishings. Note that the cheaper units are fan-cooled. There's also a restaurant and bar on stilts over the water, which offer prime sunset-watching. The beach here is minimal (a breakwater fronts most of the property), but you can swim or snorkel off a wooden pier that extends over the lagoon to a magnificent drop-off.

Motel Albert BUNGALOWS **$**

(Map p83; ☎56 12 76; www.ile-tropicale.com/motelalbert; PK8; studios 6500-7600 CFP, bungalows q 11,000 CFP;) A good budget choice, this modest place has a handful of serviceable bungalows with open terraces, as well as a row of uninspiring studios with mini terraces closed in with mosquito screens. They're all pretty tired – but not bad value considering the price and location. It's on the mountain side of the road in a lush garden, and the views of the ragged mountains across Cook's Bay are nothing short of spectacular. All options have kitchens and there's a minimum stay of two nights. Cash only.

COOK'S BAY TO HAURU POINT

Hilton Moorea Lagoon Resort & Spa RESORT **$$$**

(Map p80; ☎55 11 11; www.hilton.com/worldwide; PK14; bungalows d from 38,000 CFP;) A lovely choice where we encountered bright, helpful service and lots of very happy guests; this is really one of Mo'orea's best resorts. The beach here is particularly attractive (with top snorkelling) and the activities desk is great – both of these aspects are important since the hotel is quite isolated from the main areas of the island. Of the 103 guest units, 54 are built over the water and come with the requisite glass floor panels for fish-viewing and decks with steps down into the clear, waist-deep water. The garden bungalows have their own (small) plunge pool but are tightly packed together. Amenities include a water-sports centre, a dive shop, a pool, a spa, a gym, two bars and two restaurants, including Crêperie Toatea.

Tipaniers Iti BUNGALOWS **$**

(Map p80; ☎56 12 67; www.lestipaniers.com; PK21; bungalows d/q 9000/10,000 CFP) Depending on your perspective, you'll find Tipaniers Iti either quiet or isolated. Looking out over spectacular Opunohu Bay, it consists of a handful of bungalows that are identical to those at the larger Les Tipaniers at Hauru Point. There's an over-the-water dock for lounging, but no beach. Guests can participate in the other hotel's activities, and a free shuttle runs to Les Tipaniers at Hauru Point in the evening.

Motu Iti BUNGALOWS, DORM $

(Map p80; ☎55 05 20, 74 43 38; www.pensionmotuiti.com; dm 1700 CFP, bungalows d 10,500-12,000 CFP; @) A good bet for unfussy travellers, despite the odd layout of the compound. The five bungalows are tightly packed together on a small property overlooking the lagoon. Nothing is fancy but it all feels very proper, in a chilled-out setting. Be sure to book one of the three sea-facing bungalows (the garden units have blocked views). The dorm is airy (but not very social) with a view of the sea, and the waterfront restaurant serves reasonably priced food. Swimming is not that tempting, with very shallow waters and a profusion of algae – hard-core beach-hounds may be disappointed, but they can make use of kayaks to get to more appealing spots on the lagoon.

Fare Vaihere BUNGALOWS $$

(Map p80; ☎56 19 19; www.farevaihere.com; PK15.5; bungalows d incl breakfast 19,000 CFP;) Sitting on the eastern shore of Opunohu Bay, Faire Vaihere consists of four bungalows resting in a leafy plot. The casual atmosphere and quiet waterfront location make this the kind of place where you quickly lose track of the days. The bungalows are nothing special (and for the price, you'd expect air-conditioning), but are well kitted out; book in to the 'Badamier', which is right on the water. The owner is a dive instructor who readily dispenses expert opinions about local snorkel and dive trips and is always at the ready with restaurant suggestions. There's no beach, but snorkelling is excellent off the pontoon. Meals are prepared to order (3900 CFP). Bikes and kayaks are complimentary. Rack rates are a tad overpriced, but specials are available in low season (stay four nights, pay for three).

Fare Junette BUNGALOWS $$

(Map p80; ☎71 61 91; farejunettemoorea@gmail.com; PK14; bungalows 12,000-14,000 CFP;) Two self-contained bungalows share an outside shower (with hot water) and open onto a small patch of white sand. They're very simple, but well priced. There's one kayak for guests' use.

HAURU POINT

Legends Resort Moorea VILLAS $$$

(Map p84; ☎55 15 15; www.legendsresortvillas.com; PK24.8; villas from 45,000 CFP;) A new concept for Mo'orea, this upscale property combines the luxury of a resort with the practicality of a rental property. Each modern villa has gorgeous views over the lagoon (the resort is on a hill), its own kitchen and laundry area, plus a private jacuzzi on the generous terrace. It's perfect for families as villas can sleep between four to six people, but also great for couples since the villas offer a high degree of privacy. You're not near the beach, but a free shuttle service is available to a private *motu* where you can do the Mo'orea thing and lounge on the sand. It also features a spa, an infinity-edge swimming pool, a gym, a gourmet deli and a restaurant.

Les Tipaniers RESORT $$

(Map p84; ☎56 12 67; www.lestipaniers.com; PK25; d 8500 CFP, bungalows d 15,500-17,000 CFP;) It's a bustling hub of activity on this lovely knuckle of beach jutting out towards a coral-laden stretch of lagoon. Scattered amid a flowery garden, the 22 bungalows aren't going to win any architectural awards but are big, practical (most have kitchens and one to two bedrooms) and clean. Budget tip: it also harbours four cheaper rooms (book well ahead). Les Tipaniers is a great spot for families and friends, but not private enough for a honeymoon. The resort also features two restaurants (half-board is optional), a bar, a dive shop and a small water-sports centre. Free bikes and kayaks.

Intercontinental Moorea Resort & Spa RESORT $$$

(Map p84; ☎55 19 19; www.tahitiresorts.intercontinental.com; PK25; r & bungalows d from 28,000 CFP;) Spread over more than 4 hectares along the seashore, Mo'orea's biggest resort features a host of facilities and amenities, including two pools, two restaurants, two bars, a well-respected spa, a water-sports centre, a full dive shop, a marine-turtle rehabilitation centre and a dolphin centre. Choose your accommodation wisely and this hodgepodge of a hotel with a laid-back vibe can be a sweet deal. Pick a garden bungalow with plunge pool or a unit that sits on a small artificial island with a terrace over the water. Avoid the dim, impersonal hotel rooms in the curving two-storey motel-style wing. Due to its position on the northwest corner of the island, it gets plenty of natural light from sunrise to sunset. With its varied accommodation options, it's appropriate for couples and families alike, though some guests have found the service a bit lackadaisical and the meals uninspired. It's a member of Earthcheck (www.earthcheck.org).

Fare Miti BUNGALOWS $$

(Map p84; ☎56 57 42, 21 65 59; www.moorea faremiti.com; PK27.5; bungalows q 13,000-15,000 CFP; @📶) Deservedly popular and occupying a thin but picturesque stretch of sand lapped by azure waters (with a small *motu* as a backdrop), Fare Miti is a real anti-resort and it gets our vote. With only eight few-frills-but-functional bungalows (that can sleep up to four people) and a friendly relaxed atmosphere, this is a great place to veg out on the beach in a low-key environment. The best choice and most expensive unit – bungalow 5 – is right on the beach; bungalows 4 and 6 offer great lagoon views, while the others are back in the garden. Kayaks and snorkel gear are available for hire. It's all within walking distance of shops and restaurants. Don't fancy eating out? Order a meal and have it delivered to your bungalow.

Taoa Here Beach House BUNGALOWS $$

(Map p84; ☎56 13 30; www.taoahere.com; Village Tiahura, PK25; bungalows d incl breakfast from 17,000 CFP; 📶👪) This upscale option offers three smartly finished bungalows built from quality materials, including local hardwoods and volcanic stones. 'Painapo' is partly built on stilts and has a lovely terrace facing the lagoon, while 'Tipanier' and 'Tiare' are large enough to accommodate a small troop. They're all self-contained and geared for families looking for a quiet spot that overlooks the sea, although there is not really a beach here. Kayaks and bikes are free.

Fenua Mata'i'oa VILLAS $$$

(Map p84; ☎55 00 25; www.fenua-mataioa.com; Village Tiahura, PK25; ste 25,000-40,000 CFP; ❄@📶) After something extra-special? An atmosphere of dream-like tranquillity wafts over this superb property with a spiffing water frontage. Here you'll go giddy over the exuberant, ever-so-slightly OTT interior, which blends Mediterranean and Asian touches. Resting in leafy grounds, the four suites are dripping with paintings, pillows, silks and antiques. If you don't want to budge by evening time, opt for half board (10,000 CFP). Pure bliss for honeymooners who are after some serious cosseting and privacy. The only downside is that although Fenua Mata'i'oa has lagoon access, there's no beach.

Domloc VILLAS $$

(Map p84; ☎72 75 80; www.domlocpolynesie.com; PK25; bungalows from 12,000 CFP; ❄📶) Domloc is actually a time-share vacation club, but it's run like a hotel – a cool hotel indeed, with nine well-appointed villas of varying sizes and shapes. They're closely packed but are buffered by lush gardens. The beach is just a few steps away from the property; it's usually busy with kitesurfers on weekends. Prices fluctuate wildly according to seasons and school holidays.

Fare Manuia BUNGALOWS $

(Map p84; ☎56 26 17; PK30; bungalows q 12,000 CFP; 👪) A good deal for friends or families. Seven bungalows are spaced out in a growing garden by a sunny stretch of beach. All have bathrooms with hot water, kitchens, TVs and large verandas. They're showing their age and furnishings are seriously dated but get the job done. There's one kayak that can be rented. There's a two-night minimum stay. Cash only.

Tapu Lodge APARTMENTS $$

(Map p84; ☎55 20 55; www.tapulodge.com; PK 28; d/q 13,000/22,000 CFP; 📶) These digs offer something different, with a cluster of well-appointed, light-drenched, spacious A-framed villas poised on a greenery-cloaked hillside. Needless to say, there are stupendous views from the terrace. They're close enough to the action of Hauru Point but far enough away to be quiet, with beach access across the road. The welcoming management offers free trips out to the *motu* and rates are discounted for longer stays (except during school holidays). Minimum stay of two nights.

Hotel Hibiscus HOTEL $$

(Map p84; ☎56 12 20; www.hotel-hibiscus.pf; PK 27; d & bungalows from 15,000 CFP; ❄📶🏊) The best part of this venture is the grounds, covered in swaying palms, expansive lawns and tropical flowers and highlighted by a skinny stretch of white sand. The 29 functional thatched-roof bungalows, although they won't knock your socks off, are tidy enough, and some units have terraces that command a turquoise lagoon vista; try for bungalows No 1–3, 7–8 or 11–13. There's also an undistinguished motel-like building with 12 bland, fairly identical-looking rooms without much island flavour, but they may be an option if air-conditioning is important to you. The on-site restaurant overlooks the beach.

Camping Nelson CAMPGROUND, BUNGALOWS $

(Map p84; ☎56 15 18; www.camping-nelson.pf; PK27; campsites per person 1500 CFP, dm/d with shared bathroom from 1800/4300 CFP, bungalows d from 6300 CFP; @) A long-time budget favourite – an easy distinction given the lack of competitors – Camping Nelson boasts a spiffing lagoon frontage in a green location (but no shade to speak of). Pitch your tent on the grassy plot within earshot of the gentle surf, or choose one of the slightly claustrophobic cabins. If you're flushed with cash, opt for the pricier 'Aito' bungalow, which is at the water's edge, catching cool breezes and salty scents. A handful of more comfortable bungalows, with private bathrooms, were under construction at the time of writing. Precious perks include a kitchen for guests' use, hot water in the shared bathrooms and internet access. Prices are valid for a minimum stay of two nights; add an extra 20% if you stay only one night.

HAAPITI TO VAIARE

TOP CHOICE **Résidence Linareva** BUNGALOWS $$
(Map p80; ☎55 05 65; www.linareva.com; PK34.5; studios & bungalows d from 16,000 CFP; ❄@📶) Run by a couple of former dive instructors, Résidence Linareva has a great reputation and a wide variety of well-furnished bungalows in a lush garden by the lagoon. Bicycles, kayaks and snorkelling equipment are all provided free of charge. Meals come in for warm praise, with an emphasis on organic ingredients (breakfast from 1600 CFP, dinner 3800 CFP). No beach, but there's great swimming and snorkelling off the long pontoon jutting out over the lagoon. If you don't mind the isolated location, it's a great place to stay.

Tehuarupe BUNGALOWS $$
(Map p80; ☎56 57 33; www.moorea-paradise.com; PK 22.2; bungalows d 12,000 CFP; 📶🏊) On the mountain side of the road, these sea-view bungalows are a home away from home, with lovingly finished interiors, wooden decks, vast beds and tastefully chosen furniture. They're spacious and the kitchens are probably better equipped than the one you've got back home. Expect a bit of road noise during the day. The catch? They're not on the lagoon (though within hopping distance of the sea). There's no beach nearby, but guests are provided with free kayaks to paddle to coral gardens, or they can chill by the small pool. There's a green touch: rainwater is recycled and there's a waste management policy.

Atuana Lodge B&B $$
(Map p80; ☎56 36 03; www.atuanalodge.com; PK6.3; bungalow d 15,000 CFP, half board per person 10,000 CFP; ❄📶) Concealed behind a rather dull wall is this peach of a place run by a French-Tahitian couple. The two rooms in the owners' house are immaculate; try for the one upstairs, which has a better lagoon view. There's also a self-contained bungalow that is popular with do-it-yourself types. What's missing? A 'real' beach. However, free kayaks offer adequate compensation. And mercifully, you can order a meal if you don't fancy cooking. Transfers to/from the ferry quay are free. Cash only.

Fare Pole BUNGALOWS $$
(Map p84; ☎56 59 17; www.farepolemoorea.com; PK30.6; bungalows 13,200 CFP; 📶) Fare Pole is a bit isolated, but that's part of its appeal. Three *fare* are ideally positioned on a skinny stretch of white sand and offer killer views over the turquoise water. Here the lagoon is shallow, which makes it safe for young children. Adults can kayak to superb coral gardens closer to the barrier reef. A good deal for independent travellers, but you'll need wheels.

Mark's Place Moorea BUNGALOWS $$
(Map p80; ☎56 43 02, 78 93 65; www.marksplacemoorea.com; PK23.5; bungalows s/d from 6000/8000 CFP; @📶) The open, lush garden and creative, smartly finished bungalows – it helps that the American owner is a carpenter – make this a good option on Mo'orea, but we've heard the odd grumble about variable service. No two units are alike, but they are all equipped to a high standard and competitively priced. It's away from the beach and just about everything else besides the Haapiti surf break, but bike and kayak hire (1000 CFP per day) makes getting around less of a chore. There's a minimum stay of two nights.

Tarariki Village BUNGALOWS $
(Map p80; ☎55 21 05, 77 95 91; pensiontarariki@mail.pf; PK21.9; d with shared bathroom 4500 CFP, bungalows d 5500 CFP) Most guests here are young, unfussy surfers lured by the proximity of the Haapiti surf break. Tarariki has miniature, Spartan cabins with two beds and a bathroom (cold water only), and two ultra-basic rooms in a barrackslike building. In the middle of the property is a large *fare potee* (open dining area), which is used as a communal kitchen. Sunbathing is top-notch but swimming is average, with very shallow waters and algae. Kayaks are free and there's a grocery store 200m away. Minimum stay of two nights. Cash only.

VILLA RENTALS

For groups, families or long-term stays, renting a villa or house is a good bet, and this is a growing business on Mo'orea. Villas are great because you have room to stretch out, do your own cooking and enjoy plenty of privacy. These properties range from affordable units to lavish villas. A minimum stay of three nights is usually required. Check the following:

Abritel (www.abritel.fr)

Dream Island (Map p80; www.dream-island.com)

Fare Temehau (http://faretemehau.tahiti-moorea.com)

Robinson's Cove (Map p80; www.robinsoncove.com)

Sejour en Polynésie (www.sejour-en-polynesie.com)

Villa Corallina (Map p80; www.villa-corallina.com)

Pension Aute BUNGALOWS **$$**
(Map p80; ☎56 45 19, 78 23 34; www.pensionaute.com; PK16.4; bungalows 11,000-13,000 CFP;) This abode with a green ethos (it uses solar power) has an amazing position on the wild southern side of the island and a variety of spacious bungalows for three to six people. They're all set in exotic garden areas and are very well equipped (they even have washing machines and TVs), tidy and comfy. Families will love this: Pension Aute has a child-friendly beach, with safe swimming and a few beach toys. It's quite far from the 'action' but car and scooter hire makes it easier to get around. Prices drop by 10% for longer stays. Minimum stay of two nights.

TEMAE

TOP CHOICE **Green Lodge** INN **$$**
(Map p80; ☎56 31 00, 77 62 26; www.greenlodge.pf; d incl breakfast from 16,000 CFP, bungalows d incl breakfast from 18,500 CFP;) This relaxing cocoon with a boutique feel is great for couples looking to get away from the resort scene. It offers all the luxuries of the fancy resorts but with enough intimacy and local flavour to remind you that you're still in Polynesia. The well-designed, sensitively furnished bungalows come with all mod cons and orbit around an alluring pool and a nicely laid out tropical garden. If you've never tried golf, this is your chance; the owner is a golf instructor. Evening meals are available on request (4000 CFP). The beach here is nice for sunbathing, less so for swimming; Temae Beach is a five-minute walk away. Bikes are free.

Sofitel Moorea la Ora Beach Resort RESORT **$$$**
(Map p80; ☎55 12 12; www.sofitel-frenchpolynesia.com; bungalows d from 35,000 CFP;) This excellent, modern Polynesian resort sports 114 units, including 39 opulent overwater bungalows. It's on the best beach on the island and the service is beyond anything else we found on Mo'orea. Some of the 'modern touches' (bright-orange tables and digitalised Gauguin bedheads) may not be to everybody's taste, but overall the hotel is elegant and relaxing. The list of facilities is prolific, with two restaurants, a wonderful spa, a small pool and a reputable diving centre. It's the only resort facing Tahiti, whose cloud-capped summits form a picture-postcard backdrop. This also means that it gets less sunshine in the afternoon.

Fare Maeva BUNGALOWS **$**
(Map p80; ☎74 10 14; www.faremaevamoorea.com; bungalows d 10,200 CFP) A good deal for chill-seekers. This charming, isolated place is dominated by coconut trees and coral gravel. All the tidy, tastefully done-out bungalows have a bathroom with hot water, a kitchen and beach access (but, for swimming, head to Temae Beach, which is 500m away). No meal service, but there's a grocery store nearby. Booking online gets you the best deal. Cash only.

Moorea Golf Lodge BUNGALOWS **$$**
(Map p80; ☎55 08 55; www.mooreagolflodge.pf; bungalows d from 14,500 CFP;) This haven of peace sits on a quiet strip of beach (walk five minutes to the better main beach) and is only 100m from the golf course. The four pine bungalows resemble Swiss chalets and are very large (sleeping up to six people) and airy. All have equipped kitchens, but there's an on-site restaurant if you don't fancy cooking. Hint: try for the 'Bora Bora' or the 'Mangareva', which are more expensive but offer unimpeded ocean views.

Eating

Beach loungers beware: with all the rich, exquisite food available at Mo'orea's restaurants, you'll be packing on some extra kilos. Cook's Bay and Hauru Point are the dining epicentres.

Most places close around 9pm and accept credit cards unless otherwise noted. Many of the restaurants will pick you up for free or for a nominal fee if you call them.

Self-catering on Mo'orea can save you heaps of cash and many places to stay have little kitchens. There are quite a few supermarkets and smaller shops around the island where you can buy fresh baguettes and basic supplies. However, it's not as easy as you'd hope to find fresh produce in Mo'orea's shops beyond lettuce and sad-looking tomatoes. Your best bet for local fruit is at roadside stands that pop up along the southwest coast between PK30 and PK35.

MAHAREPA TO HAURU POINT

Crêperie Toatea CREPERIE **$$**

(Map p80; ☎55 11 11; Hilton Moorea Lagoon Resort & Spa, PK14; mains 1300-3400 CFP; ⏲dinner) Crêperie Toatea will leave you a drooling mess. Here you can dine on lip-smackingly good crêpes prepared to order by an Alsatian chef. How does Crêpe Aka (a pancake with maple syrup, pecan nuts and a scoop of Tonga-bean ice cream) sound? Another draw is the setting – it's inside the Hilton Moorea, on the pontoon that leads to the overwater bungalows (nonguests are welcome). At night the water is lit up so you can watch rays and blacktip sharks swim below. Pricey, but well worth it for the experience. It's such a shame that service is so slow.

Lilikoi Garden Café POLYNESIAN **$**

(Map p80; ☎29 61 41; PK13.5; mains 1100-1900 CFP; ⏲breakfast & lunch daily, dinner Fri) Lilikoi Garden Café is that easy-to-miss 'secret spot' that locals like to recommend. Not your average *roulotte* (food van operating as a snack bar), it's painted in vivid colours and positioned in lush tropical gardens. Foodwise, it serves meals made with locally sourced ingredients. It also has a takeaway counter.

Pukalani POLYNESIAN **$**

(Map p83; ☎28 89 54; Maharepa; mains 1000-1500 CFP; ⏲dinner) For basic fare like chow mein, raw fish or sashimi at unbeatable prices, you can't do better than this family-run *snack* (snack bar) slightly set back from the main road in Maharepa.

Allo Pizza PIZZERIA **$$**

(Map p83; ☎56 18 22; Cook's Bay; mains 1400-1900 CFP; ⏲11am-2pm & 5-9pm) Despite its unpromising location across the road from the *gendarmerie* (police station), this is a great place to taste wood-fired pizzas dense enough to drown grandpa's dentures. There's also a fine selection of salads and steaks as well as a limited dessert menu – titillate your tastebuds with the unusual 'banana pizza' or a homemade chocolate mousse. Takeaway is available.

L'Ananas Bleu POLYNESIAN **$$**

(Map p83; ☎56 13 68; Club Bali Hai, PK8; mains 1600-2200 CFP; ⏲lunch daily, dinner Wed) On the water in the Club Bali Hai, this hotel restaurant serves snacks and light lunches, but it's the setting that's the pull here, more than the food – the views of Cook's Bay are divine. Catch the dance show and seafood barbecue Wednesday nights at 6.30pm.

Caraméline SNACK **$**

(Map p83; ☎56 15 88; Maharepa; breakfasts from 1100 CFP, mains 900-2100 CFP; ⏲7am-4pm) Get all-day American-, French- or Tahitian-style breakfasts, burgers, pizzas, salads, ice-cream treats and more at this affordable and popular cafe. Don't miss the French-style coffee, pastries and crêpes.

Le Sud INTERNATIONAL **$$**

(Map p83; ☎56 42 95; Maharepa; mains 1600-3000 CFP; ⏲lunch Tue-Sat, dinner Mon-Sat) The airy French-plantation decor is inviting, despite the unassuming location on the main road. The menu lurches between Mediterranean, Polynesian and Italian, but has a lightness of touch missing from many of its nearby peers. The lunch specials are good value.

Chez Jean-Pierre CHINESE **$$**

(Map p83; ☎56 18 51; Cook's Bay; mains 1500-2500 CFP; ⏲lunch Mon, lunch & dinner Tue, Thu, Fri & Sun, dinner Sat) This very Chinese place offers tofu and other vegetarian dishes on its extensive menu. The setting is frustratingly bland (think a vast, tiled room in a modernish building), but you can order takeaway.

Le Rudy's FRENCH, POLYNESIAN **$$$**

(Map p83; ☎56 58 00; Maharepa; mains 2000-4500 CFP) This white hacienda-style building on the mountain side of the road is quite popular with American visitors staying at nearby luxury resorts and looking for a special night out. Dig into well-executed meat and fish dishes and wash it down with a glass of wine.

Te Honu Iti – Chez Roger FRENCH $$
(Map p83; ☎56 19 84; Cook's Bay; mains 1700-3500 CFP; ⏰lunch Tue-Sat, dinner Mon-Sat) Te Honu Iti has seen better days and we've heard mixed reports about the food and service but the setting is magical. The terrace of this place sits over the water, with a perfect view of Mo'orea's iconic shark-toothed summits. It specialises in French-influenced dishes (which are mostly prepared with local ingredients).

Le Martinez FRENCH $$
(Map p83; ☎56 17 71; Cook's Bay; mains 1700-3500 CFP; ⏰lunch & dinner Wed-Mon) The food is nothing spectacular, and somewhat pricey, but there's a good choice ranging from salads and *tartares* to grilled dishes and pastas.

HAURU POINT

TOP CHOICE **Le Mayflower** FRENCH, INTERNATIONAL $$$
(Map p84; ☎56 53 59; PK27; mains 1900-3300 CFP; ⏰lunch Tue, Thu & Fri, dinner Tue-Sun) The G-spot for local gourmands. The adept French chef is a true alchemist, judging from the ambitious menu on offer. Everything here is special, but a personal recommendation is the duck breast served in a mango sauce. The signature dish? Lobster ravioli. If only it had beach frontage, life would be perfect.

TOP CHOICE **Snack Mahana** POLYNESIAN $$
(Map p80; ☎56 41 70; PK23.2; mains 1500-2100 CFP; ⏰11am-3pm Mon-Sat) In a sublime location overlooking the turquoise lagoon, breezy Mahana is a heart-stealing open-air *snack*. Linger over burgers, a plate of grilled *mahi mahi* (dorado) or tuna sashimi while savouring the lagoon views. Light years away from the glitz usually associated with French Polynesia, it can't get more mellow than this. So Mo'orea. Cash only.

PKO JAPANESE $$$
(Map p84; ☎22 84 01; www.pkomoorea.com; PK27.3; mains 1900-3300 CFP; ⏰lunch & dinner Tue-Sun) Another dash of culinary flair in cosy surrounds (wooden floors, tropical plants, tapa-adorned walls and teak furniture), the PKO offers delectable Japanese-inspired dishes with a twist.

Legends Gourmet DELI $$
(Map p84; ☎55 15 05; PK24.8; mains 1500-2300 CFP; ⏰breakfast & lunch) In a terrific hilltop setting above Haura Point, this lovely gourmet deli is part of the eponymous Legends Resort (but nonguests are welcome). The supremely relaxing surrounds and good food make this a winner (though portions are a bit small). The outdoor dining area opens onto an infinity pool with sensational island and lagoon views. And yes, you're allowed to take a dip. Bang for your buck.

La Villa des Sens INTERNATIONAL $$$
(Map p84; ☎55 15 15; PK24.8; mains 2600-3600 CFP; ⏰dinner Wed-Sun) This upscale restaurant was designed with couples in mind – the widely spaced tables, attentive service, dim lighting and strong design-led interior create a suitably romantic atmosphere. The international cuisine is first class and always popular, with an inventive mix of local ingredients and European flair. Alas, no views to speak of.

Les Tipaniers FRENCH, POLYNESIAN $$
(Map p84; ☎56 12 67; PK25; mains 1100-2600 CFP; ⏰lunch & dinner) Lunch is served at the **Beach Restaurant** (⏰lunch daily) which, as the name suggests, has a fabulous beach frontage. After a morning spent paddling across the lagoon, re-energise with a copious salad, a juicy burger or a plate of spag. Dinner is at the less well located but elegant roadside restaurant, where Italian and French-inspired dishes feature prominently on the menu. Dim lighting contributes to romantic dining under a natural thatched roof.

Vina – Chez Serge POLYNESIAN $$
(Map p84; ☎56 13 17; PK24; mains 1400-2000 CFP; ⏰lunch & dinner) With cement floors, bananas hanging in the foyer and a goat out the back, this homey place has character as well as good, well-priced food. Try the specialty shrimp coconut curry or, for a real treat, show up for the Sunday all-you-can-eat *ma'a Tahiti* (traditional Tahitian food) banquet (3800 CFP) at noon. Voluminous sandwiches, too.

Le Sunset POLYNESIAN, FRENCH $$
(Map p84; ☎55 12 20; PK27; mains 1000-3500 CFP; ⏰lunch & dinner) This eatery in the Hibiscus hotel has a great beachside setting; the terrace offers front-row seats for the sunset and there is occasionally live music on Friday and Saturday evenings. From pizzas and salads to burgers and satisfying grilled meats, the menu covers enough territory to please most palates. The Sunday Tahitian brunch (3000 CFP) is a steal.

Coco d'Isle POLYNESIAN, FRENCH **$$**
(Map p84; ☎56 59 07; PK27; mains 1400-2600 CFP; ⌚dinner Mon-Sat) Don't be discouraged by the modest exterior and the unspectacular location on the main road. The cool sand floor – delicious between your toes – is a nice touch, although the plastic chairs mar the experience a bit. The food is a crowd-pleasing mix of steaks, fish dishes, salads and pizzas.

La Paillotte ROULOTTE **$**
(Map p84; ☎56 48 49; PK27.3; mains 400-1300 CFP; ⌚lunch & dinner) This popular *roulotte* is worth visiting for its good, cheap and wholesome snacks and mains, including pancakes, grilled chicken and voluminous sandwiches. Take your plunder to the beach or grab a (plastic) table in the lil' garden beside the *roulotte*.

MOTU TIAHURA

TOP CHOICE **Coco Beach** POLYNESIAN **$$**
(Map p84; ☎72 57 26; Motu Tiahura; mains 1000-2200 CFP; ⌚lunch Wed, Thu, Sat & Sun, daily during school holidays) This friendly eatery with a casual atmosphere has an idyllic setting on Motu Tiahura (also known as Motu Moea) that is guaranteed to help you switch to 'relax' mode. The choice is limited and prices are a bit inflated, but the food is fresh and tasty. Budget tip: the excellent fish burger is just 1400 CFP. Take a dip (or swim back to whence you came) once you've digested your meal – this is the life! You can get a boat over to the *motu* (700 CFP per person return) from the mainland – call ahead. Cash only.

HAAPITI TO TEMAE

TOP CHOICE **Le K** POLYNESIAN, INTERNATIONAL **$$$**
(Map p80; ☎56 39 95; Sofitel Moorea la Ora Beach Resort, Temae; mains 2100-3900 CFP; dinner Mon-Wed & Fri-Sat) Ah, Le K. One of Mo'orea's most prestigious venues at the time of writing, it offers the intoxicating mix of fine dining, romantic atmosphere and the feel of sand between your toes. Flickering candles, soft music, carved wooden tables and chairs, a soaring thatched-roof ceiling and an attentive service make it a real date-pleaser. Order cocktails, clink glasses and fall in love. No alchemy? There's always the delicious food, which is best described as 'modern French and modern Polynesian', and the magical atmosphere at night. Reservations here are essential.

Le Motu Lodge CHINESE, POLYNESIAN **$$**
(Map p80; ☎55 08 55; Temae; mains 1100-2000 CFP; ⌚lunch & dinner) Dining options are scarce in the Temae area, but this family-run eatery, part of Moorea Golf Lodge, is a delight. The menu offers plenty of Chinese classics and Polynesian staples at affordable prices. The lush garden setting makes for a relaxed atmosphere but there are no direct lagoon views.

Pizza Daniel PIZZERIA **$$**
(Map p80; ☎56 39 95; PK34; pizzas 1300-1500 CFP; ⌚closed Thu) Locals swear this little shack serves the best pizza on Mo'orea, but we think Allo Pizza is a serious contender. Pull up a stool, order the thin-crust tuna pizza (with fresh tuna – delicious!), chat with the owner, and then check out the eels in the adjacent stream.

Champion-TOA SUPERMARKET
(Map p80; ⌚8am-7pm Mon-Sat, 6am-noon Sun) Champion-Toa is the biggest supermarket on the island. It's about 500m south of the quay in Vaiare.

Drinking & Entertainment

Mo'orea is more the place to pay off a sleep debt than to kick up your heels. A boozy dinner and a dance performance is about as lively as things get. The big hotels have bars where all are welcome to whet their palates with a predinner drink, and some restaurants host occasional live music.

A couple of times a week (usually on Wednesday and Saturday evenings) the bigger hotels organise Polynesian music and dance performances by local groups. These performances tend to be of a very high standard, so it's worth trying to catch one. Call the hotels for dates and times.

Shopping

There are two small shopping centres on the island. The shopping centre in Maharepa has a few shops and some banks. Le Petit Village (Map p84) at Hauru Point has various shops and souvenir outlets, a bank, a supermarket and a bookshop/newsagency.

The coastal road is littered with places selling *pareu* (some of them hand-painted), T-shirts, Balinese woodcarvings and other curios. There are also a number of places dotted around the island where artists display their work. Keep an eye out for signs along the coastal road.

MO'OREA'S TATTOO ARTISTS

Unfortunately Mo'orea's two most famous resident tattoo artists, Chimé and Roonui, have left to ink different pastures. Our guess is they'll return some day, so ask around. Luckily there is still James Samuela from **Moorea Tattoo** (Map p80; ☎76 42 60; www.mooreatattoo.com; PK32), as well as **Taniera Tattoo** (Map p84; ☎56 16 98, 24 10 62; PK27.3) and **Purotu Tattoo** (Map p80; ☎77 79 42, 56 49 00; www.purotu.com; PK18). They're all highly experienced and talented.

Although no pearl farms are located on Mo'orea (no matter what anyone tells you), a number of places around the island specialise in black pearls. Prices are generally the same as on Tahiti, but you'll have to shop around. Often the smaller, less glamorous shops have the best deals while the bigger places have a greater variety of jewellery designs.

Information

Many hotels and pensions have wi-fi access. There's a medical centre in Afareaitu, and several private doctors and two pharmacies. The Banque Socredo across from the quay at Vaiare has an ATM. There are banks and ATMs clustered around the small shopping centre in Maharepa near PK6. In Le Petit Village (the Hauru Point shopping centre) there is a Banque de Polynésie and an ATM. Mo'orea has a post office in Maharepa and another in Papetoai, just before Hauru Point.

Magic Photo (☎56 59 59; PK26.5, Hauru Point; per hr 540 CFP; ⏲8am-6pm Mon-Sat; wi-fi) Internet and wi-fi access.

Mo'orea Tourist Bureau (☎56 29 09; ferry quay, Vaiare; ⏲8am-1pm Mon-Sat) Has a small kiosk at the ferry quay. Mildly helpful.

Tiki@Net (☎31 39 72; Le Petit Village shopping centre, Hauru Point; per hr 500 CFP; ⏲8am-5pm Mon, 8am-6pm Tue-Sat; wi-fi) Internet and wi-fi access.

Getting There & Away

There's less than 20km of blue Pacific between Tahiti and Mo'orea, and getting from one island to the other is simplicity itself.

Air

Air Tahiti (☎86 42 42; www.airtahiti.pf) flies between Mo'orea and Pape'ete (4200 CFP one way), Bora Bora (19,000 CFP one way, daily), Huahine (14,000 CFP one way, three weekly) and Ra'iatea (14,000 CFP one way, three weekly).

Boat

It's a breezy ride between Tahiti and Mo'orea. At the Gare Maritime in Pape'ete you can hop on one of the high-speed ferries and be on Mo'orea in less than half an hour. First departures in the morning are usually around 6am; the last trips are around 4.30pm or 5.30pm. All fares are about 1450 CFP each way (child 900 CFP). You can buy tickets at the ticket counter on the quay just a few minutes before departure. If you are bringing a car (from 3100 CFP) it's best to book in advance.

Aremiti 5 (☎50 57 91, 56 31 10; www.aremiti.pf) This catamaran jets to and from Mo'orea in about 35 minutes, five to seven times daily.

Aremiti Ferry (☎50 57 91, 56 31 10; www.aremiti.pf) Runs two to four times daily and takes about 75 minutes to cross.

Getting Around

The coastal road is about 60km. Getting around Mo'orea without a car or bicycle is not that easy. Distances aren't great but are often a bit too far to walk. Bear in mind that many of the restaurants will pick you up for free or for a nominal fee if you call them. Hitching is never entirely safe but if you use good judgment it can be a decent way to get around Mo'orea – watch out particularly for drunk drivers.

To/From the Airport & Quay

All ferries dock at the quay in Vaiare. Buses (400 CFP) meet all *Aremiti 5* arrivals and departures but not the *Aremiti* ferry. From the quay, one bus heads south and the other north and completes the island circuit, dropping you off wherever you and everyone else on board needs to stop. Mo'orea's taxis are notoriously expensive: from the airport to the Intercontinental Moorea Resort & Spa will cost about 4500 CFP.

The airport is in the island's northeastern corner. Most hotels offer airport transfers.

Bicycle & Scooter

Bikes can be hired or are sometimes offered for free by many hotels and pensions.

Albert Rent-a-Car (☎56 19 28, 56 33 75) Has scooters (6000 CFP for 24 hours).

Europcar (☎56 34 00, 56 28 64; www.europcarpolynesie.com) Bikes for 1700 CFP for 24 hours.

Magic Photo (☎56 59 59; PK26.5, Hauru Point) Has mountain bikes (1200 CFP for eight hours).

Rent a Bike – Rent a Scooter (☎71 11 09) Bikes 1600 CFP for 24 hours; scooters 5500 CFP for 24 hours.

Bus

In theory, there's a bus service but it's notoriously unreliable.

Car

On Mo'orea having your own wheels is very useful but expensive. Car-hire operators can be found at the Vaiare ferry quay and at some of the major hotels. Generally, you'll pay from around 9500 CFP per day including liability insurance and unlimited kilometres. Try booking online for cheaper rates. There are petrol stations located near the Vaiare ferry quay, close to the airport, beside Cook's Bay and at Le Petit Village on Hauru Point.

Albert Rent-a-Car (☎56 19 28, 56 33 75) This place has prices that are generally a bit lower than the international companies. Has three outlets around the island and can deliver to your hotel.

Avis (☎56 32 61, 56 32 68; www.avis-tahiti.com) At the ferry quay at Vaiare, Intercontinental Moorea Resort & Spa and Club Bali Hai.

Europcar (☎56 34 00, 56 28 64; www.europcarpolynesie.com) At Le Petit Village shopping centre (Hauru Point) and the ferry quay at Vaiare.

Huahine

POP 5741

Includes »

Best Places to Stay

» Maitai Lapita Village (p104)

» Au Motu Mahare (p106)

» Rande's Shack (p105)

» Fare Ie Fare (p105)

Best Places to Eat

» Chez Tara (p108)

» New Te Marara (p107)

» Mauarii (p108)

Why Go?

Huahine is actually two islands. Huahine Nui (Big Huahine), to the north, is home to the bustling little village of Fare and most of the main tourist and administrative facilities. Rugged and isolated Huahine Iti (Little Huahine), to the south, offers the islands' best beaches, azure lagoons and a serene, get-away-from-it-all atmosphere.

Huahine is immaculately tropical and effortlessly Polynesian. Lush and scarcely developed, this is an island to visit for extreme calm, communing with nature and a genuine taste of culture. You'll find one of the largest and best-maintained *marae* (traditional temple) complexes in the country and a few empty beaches, but if you're looking for a party, head elsewhere. It's a fantastic choice for families or honeymooners looking for quiet, romantic evenings. The aim of the game on Huahine is to relax – but visitors who move deeper into the island will find opportunities for diving, surfing, snorkelling and horse riding.

When to Go

July through to September is the dry and sunny high season – perfect for outdoor activities, especially hiking. In July the Heiva cultural festival (see p231) is a prime time to be on the island for some spontaneous fun. May, June, October and November are good shoulder-season months for decent weather. French Polynesia's biggest sporting event, Hawaiki Nui canoe race (p230), starts on Huahine in early November. Diving and surfing are popular year-round.

History

Europeans first arrived here in 1769, when James Cook and company landed on Huahine's shores. Polynesians inhabited the island for thousands of years before the *popaa* (Europeans) arrived: archaeological excavations to the north of Fare reveal some of the earliest traces of settlement in the Society Islands. Despite a hostile reception from the native inhabitants, Cook returned to Huahine twice, in 1774 and 1777. In 1808 a group of London Missionary Society (LMS) missionaries moved to Huahine to escape the turmoil on Tahiti. They remained for only a year but returned in 1818 to further the spread of Christianity in the region. Huahine supported the Pomare royal family in the struggle against the French, and there were a number of clashes between 1846 and 1888, before French rule was eventually accepted. Although the French kicked the English Protestant missionaries out, the island remains predominantly Protestant.

Sights

HUAHINE NUI

The following 60km circuit of the larger island starts in Fare and goes around the island in a clockwise direction.

Fare — TOWN, BEACH

A visit to tiny Fare almost feels like stepping back in time, so perfectly does it capture the image of a sleepy South Seas port. There's not a lot to do, but that's part of Fare's appeal. Check out the colourful little waterside market and the few creative boutiques, sign up for a dive or hire a ramshackle bicycle and just pedal around a bit.

You'll find a good stretch of coral sand **beach** on the northern outskirts of town (follow the coastline from New Te Marara restaurant). It's great for sunbathing and swimming, and offers excellent sunset vistas. The wide, super-clear lagoon here drops off quickly, providing some truly great snorkelling amid stunning coral and dense fish populations.

Fare looks out over Haamene Bay, which has two passes to the sea: the northern Avamoa Pass is the main entry point for inter-island shipping, while the Avapeihi Pass (Fitii Pass) to the south is a great diving site.

Lake Fauna Nui — LAKE

The shallow expanse of Lake Fauna Nui (also known as Lake Maeva) is in fact an inlet

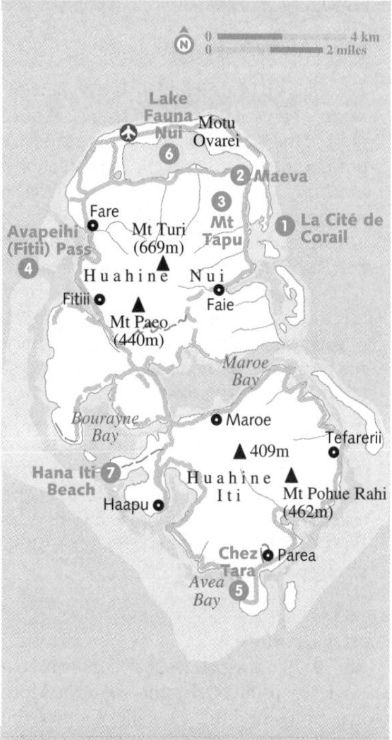

Huahine Highlights

1. Snorkelling over colourful fish and coral at **La Cité de Corail** (p101)
2. Taking the uphill *marae* walk at **Maeva** (p100)
3. Hiking **Mt Tapu** (p104) for panoramic views over the island and lagoon
4. Diving in the **Avapeihi (Fitii) Pass** (p101)
5. Feasting on Tahitian specialities at **Chez Tara** (p108)
6. **Horse riding** (p104) around Lake Fauna Nui
7. Hiring a dinghy and finding your own slice of paradise at **Hana Iti Beach** (p101)

from the sea. The land to the north of this is known as Motu Ovarei.

About 2km north of Fare the main sealed road runs along the inland side of Lake Fauna Nui. It's also possible to turn off to the airport and take the road on the ocean side of the lake and then return to the main part of the island by the bridge at Maeva village.

DON'T MISS

MARAE WALK

This walk up **Matairea Hill** is a high point for anyone interested in archaeology. A signpost on the Fare side of Maeva, about 200m west from the Fare Potee, points to the start of the hiking trail. You'll go past a **fortification wall**, which was built during the pre-European era, probably as protection against the warlike Bora Bora tribes, before reaching **Marae Tefano**, draped up the hillside. There's a massive banyan tree overwhelming one end of the *ahu* (altar).

Further on, a trail branches off to the left and runs slightly downhill to **Marae Matairea Rahi**. Once the principal *marae* at Maeva, where the most important island chief sat on his throne at major ceremonies, it was superseded by Marae Manunu, on the *motu* below. Also surviving are the foundations of a *fare atua* (god house), where images of gods were guarded day and night. Retrace your steps to the main trail and continue to the turn-off to **Marae Paepae Ofata**, a steep climb above the main trail but worth the effort. The *marae* is like a large platform perched on the edge of the hill, with fine views down the hillside and across Motu Papiti to the outer lagoon, and down to the mouth of Lake Fauna Nui. Return to the main path, which drops steeply down to the road.

Given the lack of signboards and proper waymarks, it makes sense to hire a guide. Contact American anthropologist Paul Atallah, from **Island Ecotours** (☎71 30 83; www.islandecotours.net) – a more knowledgeable person you'd be hard-pressed to find. Count on 5000 CFP for the tour (about three hours). Take some drinking water as well as strong insect repellent.

Gallery Umatatea ART GALLERY
(☎68 70 79; www.polynesiapaintings.com) On an isolated property by the road on Motu Ovarei, you'll find this art gallery, where the exotic paintings of the highly respected artist Melanie Dupre are on display and prints are on sale. The gallery is open when the artist is home.

Maeva VILLAGE
Prior to European influence, Maeva village, about 7km east of Fare, was the seat of royal power on the island. It's mostly famous for its concentration of pre-European **archaeological sites**, including a host of **marae** scattered along the shoreline and also up the slopes of Matairea Hill. Excavations and restoration of the site commenced in 1923; nearly 30 *marae* have since been located, more than half of which have been restored. The exceptional density of *marae* on the hillside has led to a theory that it was entirely inhabited by nobility and the families of the chiefs.

Situated on the water's edge on the Fare side of Maeva, the **fare potee** is a replica of an open traditional house. Around the site are 10 or more *marae,* some of which may date back to the 16th century. Flagstones cover a wide expanse of land along the shoreline.

In the village, look for the **Maison de la Vanille** (☎28 96 43; ⌚8am-4pm Mon-Sat), a family-run outfit that sells sweet-scented vanilla pods.

Beside the bridge coming off Motu Ovarei are a number of V-shaped **fish traps**, made from rocks. They have been here for centuries and some are still in use. The tips of the Vs point towards the ocean, the long stone arms emerging above the water level. As the fish are pulled towards the sea by the ebb tide they become trapped in the circular basin at the point of the V, where they are easily caught, usually by net or harpoon.

Marae Manunu ARCHAEOLOGICAL SITE
Marae Manunu stands on the *motu,* across the bridge from the main Maeva complex. The massive structure is 2m high, 40m long and nearly 7m wide. It features a two-stepped *ahu* (altar) platform. (The only other such platform in the Leeward Islands is at Marae Anini, the community *marae* of Huahine Iti.) This *marae* was primarily dedicated to Tane, Huahine's own god of war and fishing.

La Cité de Corail BEACH
If solitude is what you're seeking, head for this secluded beach at the southern tip of Motu Ovarei, just off the now defunct Sofitel. It features shade trees, white sand, calm waters and healthy coral gardens a few finstrokes away.

FREE **Huahine Nui Pearls & Pottery** PEARL FARM
(☎78 30 20; www.huahine-pearlfarm.com; ⏲10am-4pm Mon-Sat, 10am-noon Sun) Peter Owen, the owner, is a potter as well as a pearl farmer and his work is shown in Pape'ete's galleries. His studio is on his pearl farm in the middle of the lagoon. From Faie a ferry departs for the studio every 15 minutes from 10am to 4pm. Upon arrival you'll be given a demonstration of pearl farming and have an opportunity to browse the collection of pearls inside the shop – they're particularly well priced.

Faie VILLAGE
The coast road turns inland beside narrow Faie Bay to the village of Faie. Huahine's famous **blue-eyed eels** can be seen in the river downstream of the bridge – buy a can of sardines at the store here and handfeed them if you're brave enough. Inland from Faie it's a steep climb to the **belvédère** (lookout) on the slopes of Mt Turi. From this high point, the road drops even more steeply to the shores of Maroe Bay.

Fitii VILLAGE
Just before completing the Huahine Nui circuit, the road passes through the Fitii district. This is an important agricultural area in the shadow of Mt Paeo (440m), where taro, vanilla and other crops are grown.

HUAHINE ITI

Maroe VILLAGE
Dotted with the reminders of the god Hiro's splitting of the island in two, the village of Maroe sits on the southern side of **Maroe Bay**. You can spot the marks left by Hiro's paddle, the imprint of his finger, and even his rocky phallus.

Tefarerii VILLAGE
From here the coast road skirts across the mouth of a number of shallow inlets, looking across to Motu Murimahora, before coming to Tefarerii (House of the Kings). A century ago this small village was the home of Huahine's most powerful family. Today the inhabitants devote their time to fishing and growing watermelons and other produce on the nearby *motu*.

Marae Anini ARCHAEOLOGICAL SITE
Right on the southern tip of Huahine Iti, Marae Anini was a community *marae* made of massive coral blocks. The comparatively recent construction was dedicated to 'Oro (the god of war) and Hiro (the god of thieves and sailors). There's a signpost from the coast road.

Beside Marae Anini, **Anini Beach** is a lovely spot for a picnic. It's also great for sunbathing and swimming – a shallow reef close to shore makes for calm, protected waters.

Avea Bay BAY, BEACH
Some of the best beaches around Huahine are on the southern peninsula and along the western shore around Avea Bay. The lagoon here is very wide and good for swimming. The best beach is at Relais Mahana (p107). Further on, the road comes to a junction: left leads to the little village of Haapu; to the right, the road soon brings you back to the bridge and the completion of the island circuit.

Activities

Diving & Snorkelling

Huahine has three scuba centres offering magnificent dives for all experience levels. Just offshore from Fare, the **Avapeihi Pass (Fitii Pass)** is the most sought-after site, with dense fish action at all times. For more information on diving off Huahine, see p33. Snorkelling is no less impressive. On the east coast, near the visitor car park at the now defunct Sofitel, you'll find **La Cité de Corail**, which offers superb snorkelling among coral pinnacles and rich marine life only a few metres offshore. **Motu Topati**, at the entrance to Maroe Bay, and **Motu Vaiorea**, at the entrance to Bourayne Bay, are magnificent sites for snorkelling that are accessible by boat.

Mahana Dive DIVING
(☎73 07 17; www.mahanadive.com) This outfit in Fare is run by English-speaking Annie and

WORTH A TRIP

HANA ITI BEACH

Here's a secret, only known to locals (whisper it softly): the beach of the former Hana Iti Hotel. This dreamlike cove lapped by lapis-lazuli waters offers a nice patch of sand backed by lush hills, with a row of palm trees leaning over the shore. There's no access road; get there by kayak or hire a dinghy from Huahine Lagoon (p103). No licence required. Fuel costs extra.

Huahine

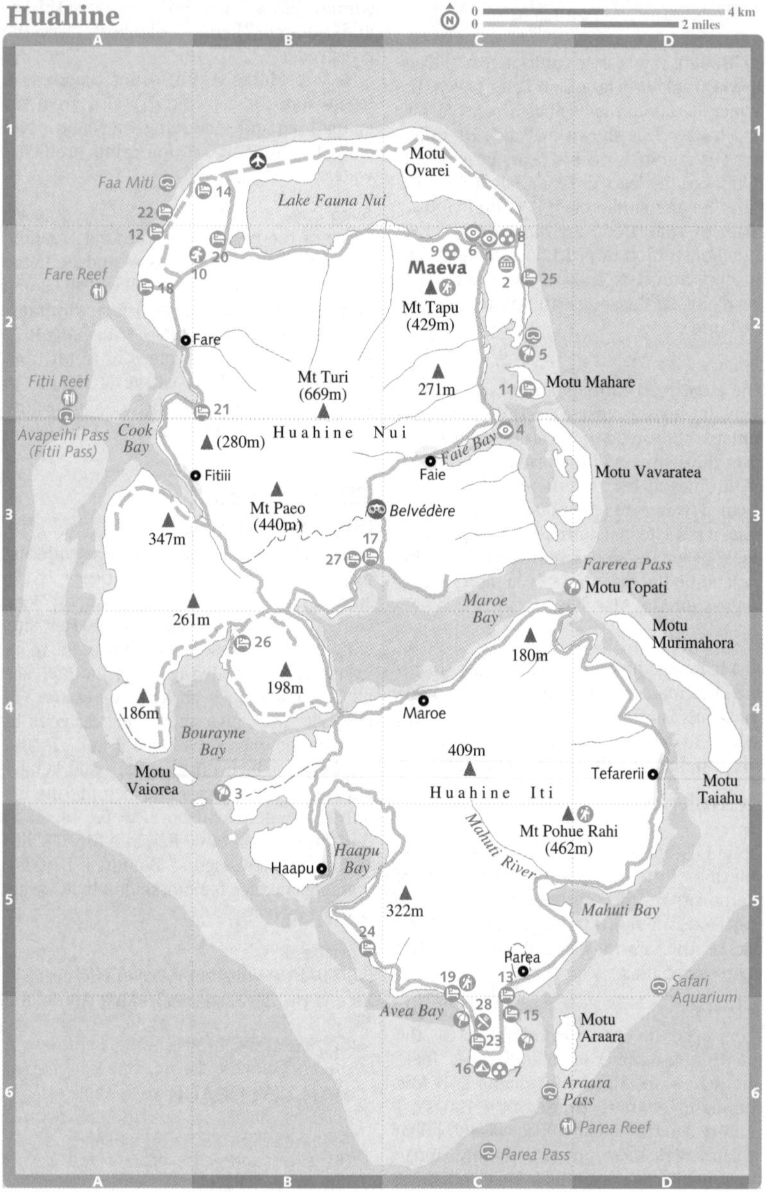

offers hands-on beginner dives as well as a slew of personalised trips for experienced divers. It charges 7000 CFP for an introductory dive, 6200 CFP for a single dive and 23,200 CFP for a four-dive package.

Pacific Blue Adventure DIVING
(☎68 87 21; www.divehuahine.com; ⌚Mon-Sat) A friendly centre on the quay at Fare. Same prices as Mahana Dive.

Huahine

Heremiti Dive DIVING, SNORKELLING
(☎27 90 57, 68 86 49; www.heremitidive.com) At Mauarii on Huahine Iti. It costs 7000 CFP for an introductory dive, 6500 CFP for a single dive and 22,000 CFP for a four-dive package. Also organises dedicated snorkelling trips (6500 CFP).

Lagoon Excursions

The lagoon around Huahine is one of those picture-perfect azure visions for which French Polynesia is famous, but to truly experience paradise you'll need to set sail for an untouched *motu* – the beaches are isolated and fantastic.

Various lagoon tours are offered on Huahine, with stops for snorkelling, swimming, fish or shark feeding, a pearl-farm visit and a *motu* picnic. Departures are at around 9am or 10am, returning towards 4pm. A minimum number of participants is required, so book ahead.

Poetaina Cruises BOAT TOUR
(☎60 60 06; www.poetaina.com; tours from 9800 CFP) This family-run company offers information and very friendly lagoon tours that include a *motu* picnic, a visit to a pearl farm, and French Polynesian song and dance performances. No shark feeding.

Huahine Nautique BOAT TOUR
(☎68 83 15; www.huahine-nautique.com; tours from 8500 CFP) Offers outrigger-canoe trips that include a picnic on the lagoon, stops for snorkelling and shark feeding, and also the chance to learn about the island's history.

Huahine Lagoon BOATING
(☎68 70 00; 2-/4hr boat hire 5000/7000 CFP) To explore the lagoon and *motu* on your own, head to this outfit at the end of the main street in Fare. It hires out boats with outboard motors (no licence required). Nautical maps are provided but you have to pay for fuel. There are no set hours, so just stop by and see if it's open.

Saling Huahine Voile SAILING
(☎68 72 49, 23 23 79; www.tahitisailingcharter.com; half-/full day tours from 7500/12,500 CFP) Offers half-/full day trips aboard a monohull along Huahine's west coast. The itinerary is flexible.

Water Sports

Huahine provides opportunities to dip a paddle around the quiet lagoon. You can steer to Hana Iti Beach (p101), Motu Araara or any other *motu*, but bear in mind that many of the *motu* belong to local families: don't treat the land as yours to explore without permission. Most places to stay either hire out or offer free sea kayaks for guests' use.

Huahine Lagoon KAYAKING
(☎68 70 00) In Fare, hires out kayaks for 4000 CFP per day.

Guillaume Chastagnol WATER SPORTS
(☎25 62 62) Those seeking kitesurfing instruction or gear hire can contact Guillaume. Make reservations a few days in advance for lessons.

HUAHINE'S TOP SURF SPOTS

Huahine has some of the best and most consistent surf in French Polynesia, with left and right reef breaks best tackled by experienced surfers. Local surfers can be very possessive, however, so be sure to be courteous in the waves, smile and say 'hi', don't show up in a big group and, especially, don't bring a camera. If you're cool and friendly, that's how you'll be treated too.

The following spots have good surf all year round:

Fare Reef break Northwest of Huahine Nui. The left here attracts the big names of world surfing. The right is also pretty good.

Fitii Reef break Northwest of Huahine Nui. As with the left at Fare, this one is best when a southwest swell is running.

Parea Reef break South of Huahine Iti. Beautiful waves as long as the trade winds aren't blowing.

Horse Riding

La Petite Ferme HORSE RIDING

(☎68 82 98; lapetiteferme@mail.pf; 2hr trips from 7500 CFP) To see the island from the back of a horse, head to this equestrian centre on the main road between Fare and the airport. The two-hour ride along the beach, through coconut plantations and around the shore of Lake Fauna Nui is truly enchanting. Longer excursions include an all-day ride (18,000 CFP), during which you'll visit a vanilla plantation, and stop for a picnic lunch and snorkelling. The horses are suitable for all levels as well as for children. Transfers are extra (1500 CFP per person).

Hiking

There are no clearly marked trails on Huahine and the occasional paths in the interior grow over quickly if they're not maintained (which is usually the case) so DIY hikes are limited. The *marae* walk (p100) at Maeva is the most interesting option (although we suggest hiring a guide who can explain the cultural significance of the archaeological sites). Other walks require a guide.

Mt Pohue Rahi WALKING

Mt Pohue Rahi (462m) on Huahine Iti offers sublime views of rolling mountains and the nearby lagoon. About four hours, moderate.

Avea Bay WALKING

A short circuit walk around Avea Bay. Easy.

Mt Tapu WALKING

Walk to the top of Mt Tapu (429m) on Huahine Nui for seriously breathtaking views of the island. About four hours, moderate.

Huahine Randonnée HIKING

(☎73 53 45; teriitetumu@mail.pf; Camping Hiva Plage; half-day hikes per person 4500 CFP) Professional guide Terii Tetumu has limited English skills but is extremely friendly and competent. He offers hikes to the tops of either Mt Tapu on Huahine Nui or Mt Pohue Rahi on Huahine Iti, as well as a walk on Matairea Hill and around Avea Bay.

Tours

A few 4WD tours offer a good overview of the island. They typically start in the morning or early afternoon and take three hours, and a minimum number of participants (usually two) may be required. The tours cover the principal places of interest, including villages, archaeological sites, viewpoints, plantations, fish parks and handicraft outlets. None of the following have offices, but they'll pick you up from your hotel. All charge from 5000 CFP.

Island Ecotours 4WD TOURS, WALKING TOURS

(☎68 81 69, 71 30 83; www.islandecotours.net) Owner Paul Atallah is an American anthropologist who specialises in highly interesting guided walks on Matairea Hills, with a focus on history and archaeology.

Huahine Land 4WD TOURS

(☎68 89 21) This American-run outfit has an excellent reputation and offers a bit of everything.

Sleeping

FARE & AROUND

The places listed here are either right in town or a few kilometres to the north or south.

TOP CHOICE **Maitai Lapita Village** RESORT $$$

(☎68 80 80; www.hotelmaitai.com; bungalows d from 27,000 CFP; ❄🛜🏊) Opened in 2011, the

Maitai is not just another luxury resort. No fancy overwater units here, but an array of creatively designed bungalows around a small lake complete with waterlilies. All units mimic *fare va'a* (outrigger-canoe huts). They're not just posh and huge, they also blend into the environment. The on-site restaurant serves fine food at reasonable prices and the small beach is perfect for swimming. It's ecofriendly: there's a solar-powered energy system, some of the food is grown organically and green waste is composted.

Rande's Shack BUNGALOW **$$**
(68 86 27; randesshack@mail.pf; bungalows 10,000-15,000 CFP;) Great for families and a long-time surfer favourite. American expat Rande and his lovely Tahitian wife give a warm welcome and offer two great-value self-catering beachside houses, the larger of which sleeps up to six people. While the houses are nothing fancy, they're spotless, well maintained and ideally located on a small beach perfect for swimming and snorkelling, just a few minutes walk from Fare. Bikes and kayaks are complimentary. Airport transfers are 600 CFP (one way).

Fare Ie Fare LUXURY CAMPING **$$**
(60 63 77; www.tahitisafari.com; tents d incl breakfast 16,500 CFP;) By far the most unusual sleeping option on Huahine, this good find offers two giant African-themed luxury safari tents. Spacious and airy, the tents are uniquely decorated and comfortable, featuring wooden floors, creative artwork and large beds with fluffy quilts. Right on a good swimming beach, the place has a funky, self-catering, gnarled-wood kitchen, and free snorkels, masks, kayaks and bicycles. There's also a sister set-up, Fare Ie Parea, on Huahine Iti. Airport transfers are free.

Chez Guynette GUESTHOUSE **$**
(68 83 75; www.pension-guynette-huahine.com; dm 1800 CFP, s/d with shared bathroom 4900/5900 CFP) This excellent-value place right in the centre of Fare – it's in front of the quay – offers seven simple but comfortable rooms with fans and bathrooms (with hot water). The eight-bed dorm is spacious and clean (though not at all private), there's a big communal kitchen and the terrace restaurant has the best people-watching this side of Pape'ete. The French owners are friendly and helpful. Airport transfers are 500 CFP per person (one way) and breakfast costs 800 CFP. Minimum stay of two nights.

Meherio PENSION **$**
(60 75 71, 60 61 35; meherio.huahine@mail.pf; s/d incl breakfast 8500/10,600 CFP;) A reliable abode, on the northern outskirts of Fare. Room exteriors are woven bamboo, interiors have lots of colourful local fabrics, there are plenty of plant-filled common areas and you're a stone's throw from Fare's nicest beach and snorkelling. The atmosphere is more convivial than intimate. Bikes and kayaks are free for guests. Meals are available on request. Airport transfers are free.

Motel Vanille BUNGALOW **$$**
(68 71 77; www.motelvanille.com; bungalows d 10,700 CFP;) It's not really a 'motel' at all, but a casual property with five fairly uninspiring local-style bungalows with bathrooms (hot water), mosquito screens and small verandahs, set around a small swimming pool. They're all well kept, if somewhat close together. Bicycles are available for guests' use – a precious perk, given it's not on the beach. Half-board is an additional 3500 CFP per person and the restaurant here is quite good. Look for deals on the website. Airport transfers are free.

Fare Maeva BUNGALOW **$$**
(68 75 53; www.fare-maeva.com; d/bungalows d 7500/12,800 CFP;) On a coral rock beach (not good for swimming), this place has 10 elementary bungalows sleeping two to four people, all with kitchens, private bathrooms (with hot water) and mosquito screens. Each bungalow is surrounded by manicured flowering shrubs. It also rents out five adjoining rooms that are smaller, less expensive versions of the bungalows. There's a room-plus-car deal from 14,600 CFP per day for two people. The on-site restaurant is no great shakes and we didn't find the small pool *that* inviting. Although the airport is a mere two-minute drive away, transfers cost a whopping 1000 CFP per person return.

Poetaina PENSION **$**
(60 60 06; www.poetaina.com; d incl breakfast from 9000 CFP;) The white cement house doesn't contain one whit of soul or Polynesian character, but inside you'll find big, clean rooms, a kitchen for self-catering and an upper-level dining terrace. The cheapest rooms share bathrooms and don't have air-con. The swimming pool is a joke.

Enite PENSION $

(☎68 82 37; martial.enite@mail.pf; d with shared bathrooms 6200 CFP, d half board per person 6900 CFP; 📶) This modest venue is worth considering for its ace location – a tranquil property five minutes' walk to the beach while being spitting distance from the main drag. Offers eight well-kept if soulless rooms.

AROUND HUAHINE NUI

TOP CHOICE **Au Motu Mahare** BUNGALOW $

(☎77 76 97; www.aumotumahare.blogspot.com; bungalows d/tr 8000/9900 CFP) Look at the homepage on the website; it's truly like this. Run by a French-English couple (no language barrier here), this lovely retreat on a peaceful *motu* has two handsomely designed bungalows that were built using local materials in authentic Polynesian style (cold-water showers). They're dotted around a huge coconut grove. Solar panels provide the electricity and rainwater is recycled. Luxury it ain't, but it has charm in spades. Best of all, there are lovely swimming and snorkelling spots just offshore and the *motu* is edged with white-sand beaches. No meals are served but there's an impeccable communal kitchen, and the friendly owners will happily drive you to Fare to stock up on essentials. Free kayaks and free airport transfers. Just one grumble: mosquitoes enjoy the place, too – bring strong insect repellent. Cash only.

Tifaifai & Café B&B $

(☎77 07 74; uguen05@yahoo.fr; s/d incl breakfast 5500/7500 CFP; 📶) Isolated out on Motu Ovarei, this is a place for a back-to-nature escape. Run by the affable Flora, it exudes low-key vibes and features two rooms in the owner's house. They're threadbare but fit the bill for shoestringers. The house overlooks a stretch of coral-and-sand beach which isn't swimmable but La Cité de Corail (p100) is a short walk away. There's a communal kitchen; if you don't fancy cooking, you can order dinner (2000 CFP). Free airport transfers. Cash only.

Tupuna BUNGALOW $$

(☎68 70 36, 79 07 94; www.pensiontupuna.com; bungalows d incl breakfast 8000-12,000 CFP; 📶) This venue offers something different. On an isolated property, the four rustic Polynesian-style bungalows, each with a private hot-water bathroom, are located in a lush tropical garden bursting with all sorts of exotic trees. Mostly organic meals (dinner 3500 CFP) are served family-style; kayaks and snorkelling equipment are free. Note that there's no beach and the waters are murky at low tide; for a dip, you'll need to paddle to the Hana Iti Beach (p101). Airport transfers are 1500 CFP. Cash only.

For longer-term villa rental for couples to bigger groups, including use of a car and a boat, contact these companies. Both are on the murky north shore of Maroe Bay and prices go down for longer stays.

Villas Bougainville VILLA $$

(☎60 60 30; www.villas-bougainville.com; villas from 21,000 CFP; ❄📶) Has four villas. There is a minimum stay of three nights. Airport transfers are free.

Huahine Vacances VILLA $$

(☎68 73 63; www.huahinevacances.pf; villas from 21,000 CFP; 📶) Has three villas. Airport transfers are free.

> **HUAHINE NUI OR HUAHINE ITI?**
>
> Staying near Fare means easy access to facilities. Huahine Iti's beaches do put Huahine Nui's to shame, but if you choose to stay on this side of the island and don't have a car, you'll have to rely on hitchhiking or your legs to get around. That said, most lodging options on Huahine Iti have on-site restaurants or guest kitchens and offer free bikes and kayaks for their clients.

HUAHINE ITI

The (marginally) smaller island has several ideally situated places.

Mauarii PENSION $

(☎68 86 49; www.mauarii.com; bungalows d incl breakfast 9200 CFP; @📶👪) Mauarii is in a fabulous beachside location, has tons of character and one of the island's most respected restaurants – but some travellers have complained that it tries so hard to exude shabby chic it sacrifices comfort. There are several different room-and-bungalow options, some fancier than others, but all crafted from local materials and enhanced with creative touches. There's an on-site dive shop and free use of kayaks. Airport transfers cost 2000 CFP per person return.

Fare Ie Parea LUXURY CAMPING $$

(☎60 63 77; www.tahitisafari.com; tents d incl breakfast from 16,500 CFP) The beach here is about on par with the Fare location but it's much quieter over this side. Manager Marguerite is charming, helpful and adds some Polynesian flair. The four tents are the same style as those at Fare Ie Fare and are well spaced out in a neat garden. Free bikes and kayaks, and free airport transfers. Cash only.

Hiva Plage CAMPGROUND, GUESTHOUSE $

(☎68 89 50, 73 53 45; teriitetumu@mail.pf; campsites s/d 1300/1800 CFP, s/d with shared bathrooms 2800/5000 CFP; wi-fi) Run by friendly Terii Tetumu, who is also a licensed hiking guide, and his French wife, this place is a dependable bet for budgeteers. The relaxed, family atmosphere in a green location (but no shade to speak of) and the proximity of the seashore make this the kind of place where you quickly lose track of the days. Pitch your tent on the grassy plot, within earshot of the lapping wavelets, or choose one of the basic rooms in a separate house; they feel a tad claustrophobic but fit the bill for a night or two. Precious perks include a kitchen for guests' use, surfboard, scooter and tent hire, wi-fi access, laundry service and complimentary bikes and kayaks. If you don't fancy cooking, meals are available on request (from 1500 CFP). Airport transfers are 2000 CFP per person return. Cash only.

Relais Mahana RESORT $$$

(☎68 81 54; www.relaismahana.com; bungalows d 23,000-34,000 CFP; @ wi-fi pool) This upscale hotel is on what's arguably the best beach on Huahine, and there's a sensational coral garden just offshore. Bungalow interiors are tastefully decorated with local art in soothing muted colours and all bathrooms (except in the rooms) have indoor-outdoor showers in private minigardens. Not all units have sea views, though. Prices are very high for what you get and we've heard a few complaints about poor service, but this is an indisputably lovely spot. The food at the on-site restaurant is fairly bland – luckily the very good restaurants at Mauarii and Chez Tara are a short walk away. Airport transfers are 4200 CFP per person return.

Te Nahe Toetoe Parea PENSION, CAMPGROUND $

(☎68 71 43; www.pensionarmelle.com; campsites per person 1100 CFP, bungalows d 7500-8500 CFP) The four local-style bungalows are right on a skinny strip of white sand; from your bed you can see the glinting waters of the lagoon. Standards of cleanliness seem to fluctuate and the welcome could be warmer, but the location is hard to beat. You can also pitch a tent on a little plot of sand squashed between the road and the beach. The communal kitchen is in serious need of a makeover, though.

Chez Tara BUNGALOW $

(☎68 78 45; bungalow d incl breakfast 12,000 CFP) Next to the eponymous restaurant, this place has a wonderfully rustic bungalow overlooking the beach. Free kayaks.

Hiva One PENSION $$

(☎90 01 83; www.hivaone.com; bungalows d incl breakfast 15,600 CFP; wi-fi) Three simple bungalows facing a lovely bay fringed with a coral and sand beach lapped by turquoise waters. There's a communal kitchen. Free kayaks.

Eating & Drinking

FARE & AROUND

Once you've left Fare there aren't too many places to eat, apart from the hotels and a few scattered, inexpensive *snack* (snack bars).

TOP CHOICE **New Te Marara** RESTAURANT $$

(☎68 70 81; mains 1600-2400 CFP; ⊙lunch & dinner Mon-Sat) In a great location right on the lagoon, this lively restaurant is a favourite local watering hole and the best place to eat around Fare. With polished oyster shells nailed to the walls and coloured lights strewn from the thatched ceiling, it has a beach-bar vibe and cooks a mean shrimp curry. The menu is meat- and seafood-based, portions are generous and dishes come with a choice of starch or vegetable on the side. Linger over a fruity cocktail as the sun sinks low on the horizon or get rowdy over a few pitchers with friends old and new after the dinner crowd heads home.

Chez Guynette SNACK $

(☎68 83 75; mains 800-1500 CFP; ⊙breakfast & lunch Thu-Tue) Fare's best coffee plus fresh fruit juices, breakfast dishes and light meals are served on a lively open-air terrace. The tuna steak and the skewered *mahi mahi* (dorado) certainly won our heart. Brilliant value.

Le Mahi Mahi RESTAURANT $

(mains 1100-2200 CFP; ⊙lunch Tue-Sun, dinner Tue-Sat) Right in downtown Fare, this surf-style eatery has a live lobster tank (a meal of them is 3500 CFP) and a stunning mural on the wall of the namesake fish. The menu

DON'T MISS

CHEZ TARA

Thank God for this place, in Avea Bay! One of Huahine's unexpected gems, **Chez Tara** (☎68 78 45; mains 1300-3800 CFP; ⏲lunch & dinner) is easily the best place on the island to sample Tahitian specialities. Head here on Sundays for its legendary *ma'a Tahiti* (traditional Tahitian food, served buffet-style; 3500 CFP) served at lunchtime, which should satisfy all but the hungriest of visitors. It's in a great location, right on the lagoon. Bookings essential.

is creative with dishes such as duck breast with pineapple, plenty of seafood, an excellent fish burger, a great pastry counter, cocktails from 900 CFP and a good wine list.

Roulottes FOOD VANS $
(mains 1000-1500 CFP; ⏲lunch & dinner) The quayside *roulottes* (food vans) are Huahine's best bargain for cheap eats. Huge portions of fish, chicken, burgers, steaks and chips are the order of the day, but there are also pizzas, crêpes and ice cream.

Les Dauphins RESTAURANT $$
(☎68 89 01; mains 1600-2400 CFP; ⏲lunch & dinner Tue-Sun) This unassuming place located on the outskirts of Fare serves traditional Polynesian-French food and is popular with locals. There's a terrace but no views to speak of.

Super Fare Nui – Super U SUPERMARKET $
(⏲6am-6.30pm Mon-Sat, 6-11.30am Sun) If you're preparing your own meals, head to this well-stocked supermarket opposite the waterfront.

Market MARKET $
(⏲Mon-Sat) For organic fruits and vegetables, as well as fresh fish, nothing can beat the market on the waterfront.

HUAHINE ITI

TOP CHOICE **Mauarii** RESTAURANT $$
(☎68 86 49; mains 1500-4500 CFP; ⏲lunch & dinner) Not only is this one of the only places in French Polynesia where you can consistently order *ma'a Tahiti* (traditional Tahitian food) à la carte, but it's also one of the only places you'll find the absolutely delectable local crab on the menu (from 3500 CFP – but worth it). It's also a terrific place for hearty sandwiches (600 CFP). The setting is in a Polynesian-style hut overlooking an expanse of turquoise water. Definitely reserve here on the weekends, when there is occasional entertainment at night.

Tenahe – Relais Mahana RESTAURANT $$
(☎68 81 54; mains 1800-3100 CFP; ⏲lunch & dinner) At this hotel the food is no great shakes and the decor feels old-fashioned but the setting is lovely, right on the beach.

Information

The following are all in Fare, where you'll also find private doctors and a pharmacy. Visiting yachties can obtain water from Pacific Blue Adventure (p102), on the quay.

Ao Api New World (per hr 900 CFP; ⏲8.30am-7pm Mon-Fri) Internet access with a view of Fare's port. It's upstairs.

Banque de Tahiti (⏲8.15am-noon & 1-3.30pm Mon-Fri) Currency exchange and ATM.

Banque Socredo (⏲7.30-11am & 1.30-4pm Mon-Fri) Currency exchange and ATM.

Comité du Tourisme (Tourist office; ☎68 78 81; ⏲9am-2pm Mon-Fri) On Fare's main street.

Post office (OPT; ⏲7am-3pm Mon-Thu, 7am-2pm Fri, 7.30-8am Sat) Internet and wi-fi access (with the Manaspot network).

Getting There & Away

Huahine, the first of the Leeward Islands, is 170km west of Tahiti and 35km east of Ra'iatea and Taha'a.

Air

Air Tahiti (☎68 77 02, 86 42 42; www.airtahiti.pf; ⏲7.30-11.30am & 1.30-4.30pm Mon-Fri, 8-11.30am Sat) has an office on the main street in Fare. Destinations include Pape'ete (12,600 CFP, 35 minutes, four to five daily), Ra'iatea (7100 CFP, 15 minutes, daily), Bora Bora (9500 CFP, 20 minutes, daily) and Mo'orea (14,000 CFP, 30 minutes, daily).

Boat

The passenger boat **Aremiti 4** (☎50 57 57; www.aremiti.pf) runs once a week between Pape'ete and Bora Bora (9500 CFP), stopping at Ra'iatea and Huahine en route. It generally departs on Friday and returns on Sunday.

Two cargo ships, the *Hawaiki Nui* and the *Taporo*, make two trips a week between Pape'ete and Bora Bora (via Huahine, Ra'iatea and Taha'a), leaving Pape'ete on Tuesday and Thursday around 4pm. Note that it's pretty difficult for tourists to get passage aboard the *Taporo* as it's usually booked out by locals. See p250 for more information.

Getting Around

To/From the Airport

Huahine's airport is 2.5km north of Fare. Pensions and hotels will arrange taxi transfers (sometimes included in the tariff). It costs from 500 CFP to go to Fare and 1500 CFP to get to the south of the island.

Bicycle & Scooter

You can hire bicycles from Europcar or Huahine Lagoon (p103) for about 2000 CFP a day. For scooters, check with Europcar, which charges 6200 CFP for 24 hours.

Car

A sealed road follows the coast all the way around both islands. Huahine's car-hire operators will deliver directly to the airport or to your hotel. Public rates are exorbitant – about 9500 CFP to 12,600 CFP per day – but discounts are available if you book through your hotel or pension. There are two petrol stations in Fare.

Avis-Pacificar (☎68 73 34)

Europcar (☎68 82 59; kake@mail.pf)

Fare Maeva (☎68 75 53; www.fare-maeva.com)

Ra'iatea & Taha'a

Includes »

Best Places to Stay

» Sunset Beach Motel (p118)
» Raiatea Lodge (p118)
» Opoa Beach Hotel (p117)
» Titaina (p123)
» Vahine Island Private Island Resort (p124)
» La Pirogue (p124)

Best Places to Eat

» Opoa Beach Hotel (p118)
» Tahaa Maitai (p124)
» La Pirogue (p125)
» Chez Louise (p125)

Why Go?

Ra'iatea and Taha'a are encircled by a common lagoon, but here you get two very different islands for the price of one. Ra'iatea is high, imposing and fiercely independent, has the second biggest town in French Polynesia after Pape'ete and is considered by many to be the spiritual seat of the Polynesian Triangle. Taha'a, on the other hand, has graceful low hills, is famous only for its sweet-scented vanilla and is arguably the quietest of the Society Islands. Neither island gets many tourists, making them the ideal place to explore a mysterious and wild-feeling Polynesia.

The islands have very few beaches. Fortunately the reef is dotted with *motu,* white-sand gems that can fulfil anyone's dreams of a palm-fringed, blue-lagoon paradise. Within the vast lagoon itself is a never-ending aquarium perfect for diving, snorkelling, kayaking or just splashing around. On land, the mountains, particularly on Ra'iatea, make you want to strap on your hiking boots in search of breezy vistas, waterfalls and one of the world's rarest flowers, the *tiare apetahi.*

When to Go

The dry winter period from May to October is the best time to go; the weather is cooler and there is much less rainfall during this time – perfect for outdoor activities, especially hiking. In July both islands are in full swing with the Heiva cultural festivities, including dancing contests. The Hawaiki Nui canoe race (p230) in early November is another highly colourful event. Diving is popular year-round.

RA'IATEA

POP 3568

Ra'iatea is the second largest of the Society Islands after Tahiti and also the second most important economic centre, but its lack of beaches has left it relatively off the tourist radar. What dominates here are the high, steep mountains and the vast, reef-fringed lagoon – the combination of the two are quite awe-striking and can make you forget that there's no beach. The capital, Uturoa, is the only town of significance; explore the rest of the island and you'll find an intensely calm, back-to-nature reality.

Ra'iatea was home to Marae Taputapuatea, the most important traditional temple in Polynesia, which many believe still exudes power today. What is undeniable is that the island emanates a hard-to-pinpoint, mysterious energy that you won't feel anywhere else in French Polynesia.

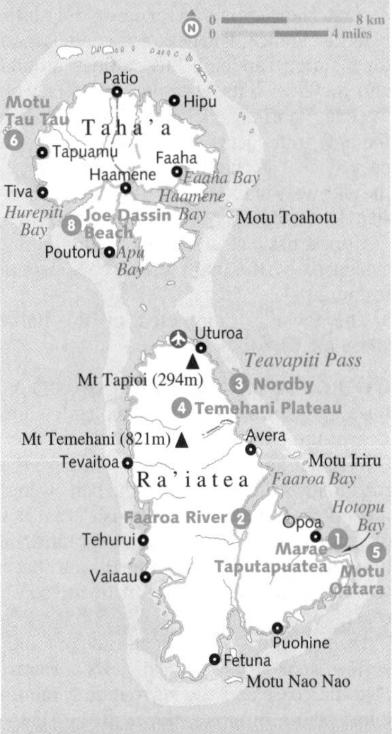

Ra'iatea & Taha'a Highlights

1. Feeling the power of **Marae Taputapuatea** (p112), one of Polynesia's greatest spiritual centres
2. Kayaking to *motu* in either lagoon or up **Faaroa River** (p113), the country's only navigable waterway
3. Diving the **Nordby** (p113), a superb wreck very close to shore
4. Taking an unforgettable hike to **Temehani Plateau** (p116) and looking for the *tiare apetahi*, one of the world's rarest flowers
5. Absorbing the silence on the deserted **Motu Oatara** (p112) and snorkelling in crystal-clear waters
6. Spending a day on Taha'a with an island tour, stopping at **Motu Tau Tau** (p121) for a bout of snorkelling
7. Learning how vanilla is prepared and purchasing a sweet-scented vanilla pod at a **vanilla farm** (p121)
8. Unwinding on blissful **Joe Dassin Beach** (p121), Taha'a's hidden gem

History

Ra'iatea, known as Havai'iki Nui in ancient times, is the cultural, religious and historic centre of the Society Islands. According to legend, Ra'iatea and Taha'a were the first islands far to the northwest to be settled, probably by people from Samoa.

Cook first came to the island on the *Endeavour* in 1769, when he anchored off Opoa. He returned in 1774 during his second Pacific voyage, and in 1777 he made a prolonged visit before sailing to Hawaii on his last voyage.

Protestant missionaries came to Ra'iatea in 1818 and from here continued to Rarotonga in the Cook Islands in 1823 and to Samoa in 1830. Following the French takeover of Tahiti in 1842 was a long period of instability and fierce Ra'iatean resistance. It was not until 1888 that the French attempted a real takeover of the island, and in 1897 troops were sent to put down the final Polynesian rebellion.

Sights

We recommend hiring a vehicle and driving the 98km sealed-road circuit around Ra'iatea. Exploring the island this way gives you the opportunity to experience not only its wild natural beauty but also its relaxed atmosphere.

The following sights are listed clockwise around the island.

UTUROA

At first glance you'd never guess this little place is French Polynesia's second largest town (after Pape'ete), but wander around and you'll catch its feisty buzz, especially on weekday mornings, when you'll experience the only traffic jams outside of Tahiti. For a peek at local life, nothing beats immersion in the alleyways of the **covered market** (⏰6am-4pm Mon-Fri, 6am-noon Sat), right in the centre.

Uturoa has a strong Chinese community, evidenced by the many Chinese shops and restaurants.

The town is dominated by the bulky 294m **Mt Tapioi**.

UTUROA TO MARAE TAPUTAPUATEA

Bustling Uturoa blends seamlessly into **Avera**, the site of the final battle between the French and local rebels. From here the road follows the contours of the narrow and magnificent **Faaroa Bay**. The islet that lies offshore is **Motu Iriru**. After going round the base of the bay and crossing Faaroa River, you reach the inland turn-off to the south coast.

From the turn-off, the road runs to a **belvédère** (lookout), with great views of Faaroa Bay, the coast and the surrounding mountains, before dropping down to the south-coast road.

If you don't take the turn-off to the south coast, the road winds around the lush south coast of Faaroa Bay and through the village of **Opoa** to Marae Taputapuatea. Next to the *marae* (traditional temple) there's a small artificial **beach** that makes for a great picnic spot.

MOTU OATARA

The glassy waters around Motu Oatara, just across from Opoa village, are excellent for snorkelling. This idyllic, deserted islet also harbours a small colony of sea birds. It can be visited on excursion tours or reached by kayak from Opoa Beach Hotel or Oviri Lodge.

MARAE TAPUTAPUATEA TO TEVAITOA

The stretch of road from Marae Taputapuatea to Tevaitoa is the most remote part of Ra'iatea and it's here you'll really get a glimpse of the old spirit of the island. The road wriggles along the coast past agriculture and mucky beaches backed by blue lagoon. Shortly after going past PK41 look for the modest **Musée du Coquillage** (Shell Museum; ☎60 04 70; admission 600 CFP; ⏰by reservation), which hosts a private collection of about 2500 sea shells. Between PK42 and PK44, there's a long stretch where the steep green mountainsides are streaked with **waterfalls** during the wetter months of the year. Past the village of **Puohine**, the majestic **Faatemu Bay** comes into view. The road follows the coast before reaching the village of **Fetuna**. During WWII, when the US military occupied Bora Bora, a landing strip was constructed here. **Motu Nao Nao**, just across from Fetuna, has a pleasant beach but it's private.

DON'T MISS

MARAE TAPUTAPUATEA

The most important *marae* (traditional temple) in French Polynesia, sprawling Marae Taputapuatea dates from the 17th century. It's dedicated to 'Oro, the god of war who dominated 18th-century Polynesian religious beliefs.

Despite its relatively short history, this *marae* assumed great importance in the Polynesian religion. Any *marae* constructed on other islands had to incorporate one of Taputapuatea's stones as a symbol of allegiance and spiritual lineage. This was the centre of spiritual power in Polynesia when the first Europeans arrived, and its influence was international: *ari'i* (chiefs) from all over the Maohi (Polynesian) world, including the Australs, the Cook Islands and New Zealand, came here for important ceremonies.

The main part of the site is a large paved platform with a long *ahu* (altar) stretching down one side. At the very end of the cape is the smaller **Marae Tauraa**, a *tapu* (taboo) enclosure with a tall 'stone of investiture', where young *ari'i* were enthroned. The lagoon-side **Marae Hauviri** also has an upright stone, and the whole site is made of pieces of coral.

The well-restored *marae* complex is an imposing sight, but unfortunately there is little information for visitors beyond some signboards that explain what a *marae* is, with nothing specific about Taputapuatea.

The sparsely inhabited coast continues all the way along to **Tevaitoa**, with vistas over the lagoon and some particularly large *motu* quite close to shore. In the middle of the village of Tevaitoa you'll find the island's oldest Protestant church, an architectural curiosity built smack on top of the magnificent **Marae Tainuu**. Behind the church, the walls of the *marae* stretch for just over 50m, with some of the massive upright stones standing more than 4m high.

TEVAITOA TO UTUROA

You'll find the megabucks **Apooiti Marina** between Tevaitoa and Uturoa. With a few shops, yacht charter companies, a restaurant, a bar and a diving centre, it's a pleasant place to stop for a sunset cocktail or early dinner. From the marina the road passes by the airport before circling back to Uturoa.

Activities

Diving & Snorkelling

There are about 15 dive sites along the east and west coasts and around Taha'a. Highlights include the superb Teavapiti Pass and the *Nordby,* the only real wreck dive in French Polynesia. For more information, see p33.

Ra'iatea has two diving centres. Both companies provide transport from your hotel.

Hemisphere Sub DIVING
(☎66 12 49, 72 19 52; www.hemispheresub.com) This operation based at the Apooiti Marina has excellent gear and a well-trained and friendly staff. It offers dives on the east and west coasts as well as around Taha'a. It charges 7000 CFP for an introductory dive, 6200 CFP for a single dive, 11,700 CFP for a two-tank dive and 29,000 CFP for a five-dive package. Nitrox dives can also be arranged. The centre also has a base at the Hawaiki Nui Hotel – ask for package room-and-scuba deals at the resort.

Te Mara Nui DIVING
(☎66 11 88, 72 60 19; www.temaranui.pf) This small outfit offers personalised service and charges 6200 CFP for an introductory dive, 6000 CFP for a single dive and 37,000 CFP for a certification course.

Sailing

Ra'iatea's central position in the Society Islands, and its fine lagoon, have helped make it the yacht-charter centre of French Polynesia. Most operations will offer whatever a customer demands and prepare fully stocked and equipped boats. Bare-boat charter rates vary seasonally (July to August is the high season). The following Ra'iatea-based companies are recommended.

Charter Tane SAILING
(☎73 96 90; http://chartertane.free.fr) This small operation offers crewed cruises in the Lee ward Islands. Also specialises in cruises within Ra'iatea and Taha'a's common lagoon.

Dream Yacht Charter SAILING
(☎66 18 80; www.dreamyachtcharter.com) Offers catamaran and monohull cruises in the Leeward Islands.

Moorings SAILING
(☎66 35 93; www.moorings.com) This international outfitter has about 20 monohulls and catamarans on offer for custom-crewed or bareboat cruises in the Leeward Islands.

Sunsail SAILING
(☎60 04 85; www.sunsailtahiti.com) Operates a variety of bare-boat charters and crewed cruises in the Leeward Islands and the Tuamotu Islands. A skipper is mandatory for the Tuamotus. Offers monohulls and catamarans.

Tahiti Yacht Charter SAILING
(☎66 28 86; www.tahitiyachtcharter.com) Has catamarans and monohulls.

Kayaking

Lagon Aventure KAYAKING
(☎79 26 27; www.lagonaventures.com) For something unique, sign on with enthusiastic Gwen, who leads kayak tours (half/full day 5000/8000 CFP) not only to the dreamy *motu,* but also up the jungle-clad Faaroa River – a real adventure. Kayak rentals are also available (3000 CFP per two hours).

SWIMMING & SNORKELLING

Ra'iatea has no beaches besides rare, skinny strips of sand – a hotel or guesthouse pontoon is your best bet for chilling or snorkelling. The reef *motu,* however, have splendid beaches and even more snorkelling. The most scenic include **Motu Iriru** to the east, **Motu Miri Miri** to the west, **Motu Oatara** to the southeast, and **Motu Nao Nao** to the south. Ask at your accommodation about joining a lagoon tour or arranging boat transfers to a *motu*.

Ra'iatea & Taha'a

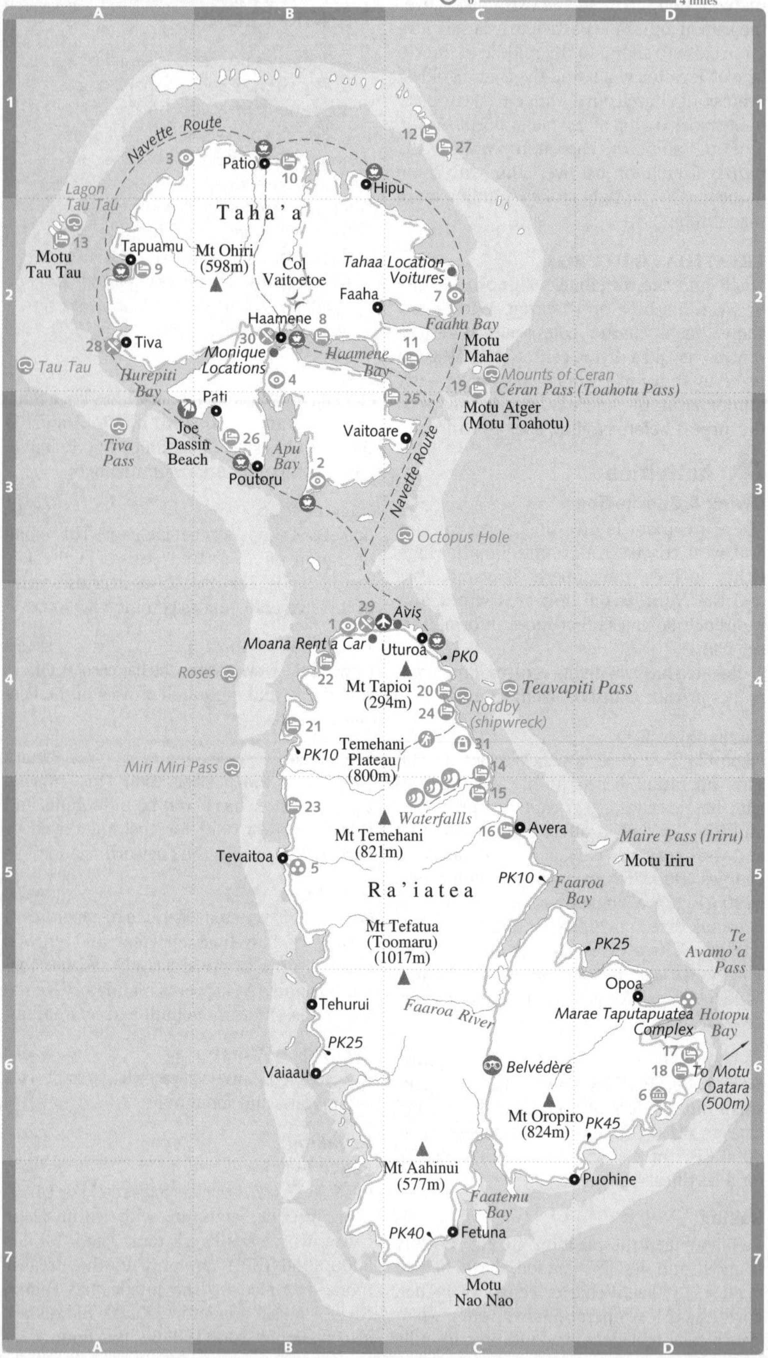

0 8 km
0 4 miles
Navette Route
Patio
Hipu
Lagon Tau Tau
Taha'a
Motu Tau Tau
Tapuamu
Mt Ohiri (598m)
Col Vaitoetoe
Tahaa Location Voitures
Faaha
Haamene
Faaha Bay
Tiva
Monique Locations
Haamene Bay
Motu Mahae
Tau Tau
Hurepiti Bay
Mounts of Ceran
Céran Pass (Toahotu Pass)
Pati
Motu Atger (Motu Toahotu)
Joe Dassin Beach
Vaitoare
Tiva Pass
Apu Bay
Poutoru
Navette Route
Octopus Hole
Avis
Moana Rent a Car
Uturoa
PK0
Roses
Mt Tapioi (294m)
Teavapiti Pass
Nordby (shipwreck)
Temehani Plateau (800m)
PK10
Miri Miri Pass
Waterfallls
Mt Temehani (821m)
Avera
Maire Pass (Iriru)
Tevaitoa
Motu Iriru
PK10
Faaroa Bay
Ra'iatea
Mt Tefatua (Toomaru) (1017m)
PK25
Te Avamo'a Pass
Opoa
Tehurui
Faaroa River
Marae Taputapuatea Complex
Hotopu Bay
PK25
Belvédère
To Motu Oatara (500m)
Vaiaau
Mt Oropiro (824m)
PK45
Mt Aahinui (577m)
Puohine
Faatemu Bay
PK40
Fetuna
Motu Nao Nao

Ra'iatea & Taha'a

Sights

1	Apooiti Marina	B4
2	Ferme Perlière Champon	B3
	Foundation Hibiscus	(see 11)
3	Love Here	A1
4	Maison de la Vanille	B2
5	Marae Tainuu	B5
6	Musée du Coquillage	D6
7	Vallée de la Vanille	C2

Activities, Courses & Tours

	Hemisphere Sub	(see 20)
	Hemisphere Sub	(see 1)
	Temehani	(see 23)

Sleeping

8	Chez Edwin & Jacqueline	B2
	Chez Louise	(see 28)
9	Chez Pascal	A2
10	Fare Pea Iti	B1
11	Hibiscus	C2
12	La Pirogue	C1
13	Le Taha'a Private Island & Spa	A2
14	Les 3 Cascades	C4
15	Manava	C5
16	Opeha	C5
17	Opoa Beach Hotel	D6
18	Oviri Lodge	D6
19	Pension Atger	C2
20	Raiatea Hawaiki Nui	C4
21	Raiatea Lodge	B4
22	Sunset Beach Motel	B4
23	Temehani	B5
24	Tepua	C4
25	Tiare Breeze	C3
26	Titaina	B3
27	Vahine Island Private Island Resort	C1

Eating

28	Chez Louise	A2
	La Pirogue	(see 12)
	La Plage	(see 13)
	La Voile d'Or	(see 1)
29	Le Napoli	B4
	Le Nordby	(see 20)
	L'Hibiscus	(see 11)
	Opoa Beach Hotel	(see 17)
	Raiatea Lodge	(see 21)
30	Tahaa Maitai	B2

Shopping

31	Tahi Perles	C4

Water Sports

Raiatea Windsurfing WATER SPORTS
(☎20 76 69; www.raiateawindsurfing.com) The windswept lagoon between Ra'iatea and Taha'a makes windsurfing hounds go ga-ga. Want to have a go? Contact this professional venture that runs courses and hires out gear, including SUP (stand-up paddle) boards.

Raiatea Sup Discovery TOUR
(☎78 81 72; cedrictahiti@yahoo.com; tours 5000 CFP) Stand-up paddle boarding is an eco-friendly way to commune with the natural environment. This outfit offers guided SUP tours up the Faaroa River – it's fun, safe and easy to boot. The outing lasts about three hours. It specialises in small groups (maximum four people), so you're guaranteed personalised attention.

Lagoon Excursions

Boat tours are very popular in Ra'iatea and we definitely recommend doing one during your stay. Most tours actually spend the majority of their time on the island of Taha'a, but most companies are based on Ra'iatea and pick up from the pier in Uturoa; see p122 for a list of operators.

Two companies run dedicated trips on Ra'iatea:

Temehani BOAT TOUR
(☎66 12 88, 77 54 87; www.vacances-tahiti.com) Half/full day trips aboard a monohull cost 7500/9500 CFP. The itinerary is flexible.

Arii Moana Tours BOAT TOUR
(☎79 69 72) The only operator that offers full-day tours of Ra'iatea that include snorkelling and swimming stops and a visit to Marae Taputapuatea (9000 CFP, including lunch).

Tours

Book early as a minimum of two to four people are required for these tours.

TOP CHOICE **Trucky Tour** BUS TOUR
(☎78 23 36, 75 66 02; full-day tour per person 5000 CFP) Christian is passionate about Ra'iatea and dispenses lots of interesting information during this minibus tour.

DON'T MISS

HIKING ON RA'IATEA

Ra'iatea has the usual assortment of water-based activities, but it also offers plenty of great hiking opportunities in its mountainous interior.

» **Temehani Plateau** A very scenic hike. Starting from the coastal road south of Uturoa (near PK6) a dirt track leads through a pine forest to the 800m-high Temehani Plateau, which affords fantastic island views. The highlight of the hike is the rare *tiare apetahi* (p117), a white gardenia endemic to Ra'iatea. About seven hours return. Moderate.

» **Les Trois Cascades** (Three Waterfalls) This hike takes you past three waterfalls. It's an easy stroll to the first (the smallest), which has a great swimming hole, but the trail climbs steeply from here, with some tricky scrambles. After passing the second waterfall, the trail follows the riverbed through a bamboo forest. The third waterfall is the most splendid – a 40m beauty with a fabulous swimming hole at its basin. About four hours return. Moderate.

» **Sentier de Faaroa** An easy loop in a vast forest near Faaroa Bay. About three hours return. Suitable for families.

» **Mt Tapioi** Bulky Mt Tapioi (294m) affords sensational views of the lagoon between Ra'iatea and Taha'a. You don't need a guide to climb up it – just follow the dirt track that starts between the post office and the *gendarmerie* (police station) in Uturoa. Count on two hours return. Beware of dogs.

With the exception of the walk to Mt Tapioi, a guide is required. **Thierry Laroche** (☎66 20 32, 77 91 23; raiatearando@mail.pf) is a reputable guide who's very knowledgeable about local flora. He charges 4000 CFP per person (8000 CFP for Temehani Plateau). Prices include transfers and snacks.

Raiatea Discovery 4WD TOUR
(☎66 24 16, 78 33 25; half-day tour per person 4500 CFP) Covers the highlights of the east coast, including Marae Taputapuatea and Faaroa Bay.

Manava Tours TOUR
(☎66 28 26; half-day tour 5000 CFP) Based at Manava pension, this operator offers a 'combo' tour that takes in Marae Taputapuatea, a pirogue (outrigger canoe) trip up the Faaroa River and a swimming stop on Motu Iriru.

Sleeping

UTUROA & AROUND

Hawaiki Nui Hotel RESORT **$$**
(☎60 05 00; www.hawaikinuihotel.com; PK2; r/bungalows d from 15,000/20,000 CFP; ❄📶🏊) This small complex on the outskirts of Uturoa has suffered in recent years from a lack of maintenance, but at the time of research enthusiastic new managers were working to get the place back into shape. It consists of several different accommodation options, including plain rooms, garden bungalows, 'semi-lagoon' (read: partially over water) bungalows and over-the-water units. Its location, wedged between the road and the lagoon (no beach), isn't exactly stunning, but there is outrageous snorkelling in front and you can paddle free kayaks out to the white-sand *motu* across the lagoon. Amenities include a restaurant, a bar and a dive shop. Good deals can usually be found online.

Tepua PENSION **$**
(☎66 33 00; www.pension-tepua.com; PK2.5; dm/s/d with shared bathroom 2500/5000/7500 CFP, bungalows d 10,000-13,000 CFP; @📶🏊) A good base for budget travellers. The four rooms are bare and the partition walls are thin, but they're clean and colourfully decorated, the shared bathrooms have hot showers, and the 12-bed dorm is spartan and compact but kept clean. For more privacy, opt for one of the bungalows. Adding to the laid-back ambience are the communal kitchen, TV lounge, tiny pool and pontoon over the lagoon. The property feels a tad cramped, but in this location, for this price, you won't hear anyone complaining. Bike and kayak hire is available. Airport transfers are 1000 CFP return.

Hinano Api HOTEL $

(☎66 13 13, 70 82 40; www.hotel-hinano-tahiti.com; s/d 6700/7800 CFP; ❄📶) This motel-like venture right in the centre of Uturoa has as much character as a newly paved footpath but it's an acceptable fall-back. The 10 rooms feel quite bare but are roomy and well scrubbed, and come with air-con (add 1000 CFP). Some rooms are more luminous than others, so ask to see a few before committing. Perks include bike hire, wi-fi access, laundry service and breakfast (600 CFP).

EAST COAST

TOP CHOICE **Opoa Beach Hotel** RESORT $$$

(☎60 05 10; www.hotel-raiatea.com; PK37; bungalows d from 25,000 CFP; 📶🏊) This small resort with a boutique feel is one of Ra'iatea's top hotels, and it's easy to understand why. An effortless tropical charm pervades the collection of cottages set amid beautifully landscaped gardens. From the outside, the white facades and blue tin roofs lack the wow factor, but each one is artistically decorated with local materials and teak furnishings. It's intimate and friendly, and appeals to couples looking for creature comforts and style without an exorbitant price tag. The pool is smallish and the beach is skinny but there's great swimming off the long pontoon jutting out over the lagoon; or ask for a boat transfer to Motu Oatara just offshore. Note that there's no air-con, which may be an issue in humid periods between December and March. Opoa Beach Hotel restaurant is also highly respected. As it's isolated, you'll definitely need your own wheels if you plan to leave the property.

Oviri Lodge BUNGALOWS $$

(☎66 30 51, 79 53 96; www.ovirilodge.com; PK35.2; bungalows d 14,000 CFP; 📶) Oviri Lodge offers guests the chance to escape and unplug in two hand-crafted treehouse-style villas positioned in the velvety emerald hills above Hotopu Bay. Very 'Me Tarzan, you Jane'. With wooden furnishings and modern amenities, they represent a nicely judged balance between comfort, rustic charm and tropical atmosphere. There's no beach, but what this place lacks in sunbathing opportunities it makes up for in ample snorkelling opportunities off the shore; you can also grab a free kayak to get to nearby Motu Oatara. Note that there's no meal service (except breakfast, 1500 CFP) and you'll need your own transport because it's about as remote as it gets.

Manava PENSION $

(☎66 28 26; www.manavapension.com; PK6; d with shared bathroom 5000 CFP, bungalows d 8500 CFP; 📶) This is a friendly, well-managed place with four spacious bungalows, all with kitchens and private bathrooms (hot water), dotting a tropical garden. If you're scratching the pennies, opt for one of two adjoining rooms that share bathrooms (hot water) and a communal kitchen; they show some wear but fit the bill for a night or two. There's a bit of road noise but nothing to lose sleep over. No meals are served except breakfast (800 CFP), but there's a *roulotte* (food van operating as a snack bar) down the road and the owners can drive you to various *snacks* (snack bars) in Uturoa for dinner. Fancy swimming and snorkelling? Ask to be dropped off on nearby Motu Iriru (1500 CFP, minimum four people). Excursions to Marae Taputapuatea and Faaroa River are also available. Airport transfers are free.

Les 3 Cascades PENSION $

(☎66 10 90; www.pensionles3cascades.com; PK6; s/d with shared bathroom 4500/5500 CFP, bungalows d 7000-8000 CFP; 📶) Laid-back Les 3 Cascades has four spartan but clean rooms opening on to an airy communal area with a guest kitchen. The two free-standing bungalows offer more comfort and privacy. Meals can be prepared on request (breakfast 900 CFP, dinner 2200 CFP) – a definite plus, especially given the lack of restaurants nearby. No beach, but the owner can drop you off on Motu Iriru (3000 CFP for two people return). He also runs reputable boat tours to Taha'a (L'Excursion Bleue, p122). Airport transfers are free for a minimum stay of two nights.

TIARE APETAHI: A RARE FLOWER ON A STRANGE ISLAND

Ra'iatea is home to one of the world's rarest flowers, the *tiare apetahi*. The endemic species is only found on the Temehani Plateau and although attempts have been made, it simply won't grow elsewhere. The petals close at night then open at dawn with a whisper of a crackle. You should be able to see the flower on a guided hike – but note that it is strictly protected, so no picking.

Opeha PENSION $$

(☎66 19 48; www.pensionopeha.pf; PK10.5; bungalows d incl breakfast 10,000 CFP; ❄📶) A crisp and compact waterfront abode, Opeha has a handful of very white, very clean, kitchen-equipped bungalows, lined up in a row in a tiny, immaculate property. They're charmless but well proportioned and perfectly serviceable, and prices include a copious breakfast, kayaks and bikes. Despite a pontoon over the water, the area is not really suitable for swimming; for a dip, paddle to Motu Iriru. The owners run their own lagoon tours, which come recommended. Airport transfers are 1000 CFP per person return. Cash only.

WEST COAST

TOP CHOICE Sunset Beach Motel BUNGALOWS, CAMPGROUND $$

(☎66 33 47; www.sunset-raiatea.pf; PK5; campsites per person 1300 CFP, bungalows s/d 11,000/12,000 CFP; 📶👪) The location (on an expansive coconut plantation fronting the lagoon) alone would make this one of Ra'iatea's best options, but the 22 bungalows – which are perhaps better described as small homes – make this one of the best deals in the islands. It's a particularly great find for families as the kitchen-equipped bungalows comfortably sleep four and they're well spaced out. Bikes, snorkelling equipment and airport transfers are free. A grassy, shady plot is set aside for campers, who have their own ablution block and kitchen. One proviso: the name is a bit misleading as there is no beach, but you can swim in the lagoon from the fantastic pontoon. No meals are served except breakfast (1200 CFP), but you'll find a few *snacks* and grocery stores down the road, and the friendly owners will happily drive you to Uturoa to stock up on essentials. Brilliant value.

Raiatea Lodge HOTEL $$

(☎66 20 00; www.raiateahotel.com; PK8.8; s 14,000 CFP, d 16,500-20,000 CFP; ❄📶🏊) Raiatea Lodge pays elegant homage to colonial architecture, with a two-storey plantation-style building sitting quietly at the back of a coconut plantation. It attracts holidaymakers looking for comfortable rooms and amenities, including a restaurant, a bar and a pool. The Superior rooms feature handsomely designed bathrooms and contemporary furnishings, while the standard ones are more ordinary. Add 4000 CFP (up to four people) for return airport transfers. Bikes, snorkelling gear and kayaks are free and English is spoken. No beach, but you can paddle to Motu Miri Miri.

Temehani B&B $$

(☎66 12 88, 77 54 87; www.vacances-tahiti.com; PK11.3; s incl breakfast 8000-11,000 CFP, d incl breakfast 9000-12,000 CFP; 📶) This mellow B&B is just a 10-minute drive from Uturoa, but feels a million miles away. It has only three guest rooms in total, in the owner's waterfront home – two with shared bathrooms, and one with private bathroom and lagoon views. They are all decorated with handmade bedspreads and plenty of wood. Excellent French-Polynesian dinners (2800 CFP) can be taken family-style. There's not really a beach, but you can paddle free kayaks out to a scenic sandbar offshore or to Motu Miri Miri. The owners also organise reputable lagoon tours aboard a monohull (p122) and you can borrow the free bicycles to get to and from Uturoa. Airport transfers are free. Cash only.

Eating & Drinking

Uturoa has several well-stocked supermarkets, open Monday to Saturday and some on Sunday morning. They include the Champion on the seafront and Leogite and Liaut on the main street. For fruit and vegies, head to the covered market.

TOP CHOICE Opoa Beach Hotel HOTEL RESTAURANT $$$

(☎60 05 10; PK37; set menu 5000 CFP; ⊙dinner by reservation) At the Opoa Beach Hotel, this is Ra'iatea's most glamorous dinner spot. The chef earns raves for her high-flying creative dishes combining fresh produce and spices. The menu changes daily. The decor is elegant and the tables are well spaced out and candlelit, which is perfect for a tête-à-tête. Hotel guests have priority, so reserve early.

Raiatea Lodge HOTEL RESTAURANT $$$

(☎66 20 00; PK8.8; mains 2200-2900 CFP; ⊙lunch & dinner) For refined dining, opt for the Raiatea Lodge's on-site restaurant. The semi-outdoor Zen-style setting is superb and is a great place for a drink as well as a meal. There's sure to be a dish on the extensive menu that suits your palate, but be sure to leave room for dessert.

Le Nordby HOTEL RESTAURANT $$

(☎60 05 00; mains 1500-3000 CFP; ⊙breakfast, lunch & dinner) Got the post-dive munchies? After diving the *Nordby,* the wreck, head to the Nordby, the restaurant inside the Hawaiki Nui Hotel, and order a killer *mahi mahi* (dorado) burger or a salad. The desserts are equally good and the place has great water views. The convivial bar serves good cocktails for about 900 CFP. It stages Polynesian dance performances and live music on weekends – call for details.

Brasserie Maraamu BISTRO **$$**
(66 46 54; mains 1300-2200 CFP; breakfast & dinner Mon-Fri, lunch Mon-Sat) This popular joint serves huge plates of reasonably priced food including a handful of tofu-based vegetarian options as well as steaks, poultry and fish. Hinano beer is on tap and breakfasts range from American eggs to Tahitian *poisson cru* (a raw fish dish) and *firifiri* (doughnuts).

Le Napoli ITALIAN, PIZZERIA **$$**
(66 10 77; www.pizzerialenapoli.com; Uturoa; mains 1400-2400 CFP; lunch Tue-Fri, dinner Tue-Sun) In a reed hut decorated with loads of flowers, this congenial pizzeria near the Avis agency offers a long list of Italian dishes including pasta, wood-fired pizzas and meat and fish specials.

La Voile d'Or FRENCH, TAHITIAN **$$**
(66 12 97; Apooiti Marina; mains 1500-2500 CFP; lunch & dinner) One reason to dine in this casual eatery right on the waterfront at the far end of Apooiti Marina is the romantic view of Taha'a and Bora Bora. Food-wise, the French and Tahitian dishes on offer are rather ordinary but reasonably priced. And, joy of joys, it's open on Sunday.

Shopping

Central Market SOUVENIRS
(5.30am-5pm Mon-Sat & 5am-9am Sun) The upstairs section of the market has various souvenir outlets. Vanilla pods are also sold here.

Galerie Anuanua ARTS & CRAFTS
(66 12 66; www.galerie-anuanua.com) This place features works by island craftspeople, including sculptures, pottery, paintings and mother-of-pearl objects.

La Palme d'Or JEWELLERY, GIFTS
(60 07 85) Has a good selection of pearls, and also sells vanilla pods.

Arii Creation CLOTHING
(66 35 54) Sells a wide variety of clothes and T-shirts.

> **PICNIC**
>
> Bring a picnic if you're travelling around the island as there is virtually nowhere along the way to buy lunch. You can pick up cheap baguette sandwiches at small local shops around the island, but do so before noon when most close for siesta.

Te Fare SOUVENIRS
(66 17 17) Has clothes, paintings, jewellery, wooden handicrafts and decorative trinkets.

Tahi Perles JEWELLERY
(60 20 20; PK4.1) A family-run pearl farm, a few kilometres south of Uturoa. Has loose and mounted pearls.

Information

The following places are all found within Uturoa.

Banque de Polynésie (8.15am-noon & 1-3.30pm Mon-Fri) Currency exchange and ATM.

Banque de Tahiti (8.15am-noon & 1-3.30pm Mon-Fri) Currency exchange and ATM.

Hospital (60 08 01) Opposite the post office; offers emergency services.

ITS (per hr 1000 CFP; 8am-noon & 1-5pm Mon-Fri, 8-11.30am Sat) Internet access. Inside the *gare maritime* (boat terminal).

Post office (OPT; 8am-12.30pm & 2-4pm Mon-Fri, 8-10am Sat) North of the centre, towards the airport. Internet and wi-fi access (with the Manaspot network). Has an ATM.

Raiatea visitors information centre (60 07 77; 8am-4pm Mon-Fri) In the *gare maritime*. It's also open on weekends when visiting cruise ships are in port.

Socredo (8.15am-noon & 1-3.30pm Mon-Fri) Currency exchange and ATM.

Getting There & Away

Ra'iatea is 220km northwest of Tahiti and 40km southeast of Bora Bora.

Air

Air Tahiti (60 04 44, 86 42 42; www.airtahiti.pf; 7.30-11.30am & 1.30-3.30pm Mon-Fri, 7.30-11.30am Sat) has an airport office. The airline operates direct flights from Tahiti (14,200 CFP, 40 minutes, seven to eight daily) with connections via Mo'orea (14,000 CFP) and Huahine (7100 CFP). There are also direct flights to Bora Bora (7800 CFP, 20 minutes, daily) and Maupiti (8500 CFP, 20 minutes, three weekly).

Boat

Ra'iatea is separated from Taha'a by a 3km-wide channel.

TAHA'A The *navette* (shuttle boat) services on the **Te Haere Maru** (☎65 61 33) run between Uturoa and various stops on Taha'a – Apu, Poutoru, Tiva, Tapuamu, Patio, Hipu and Haamene – twice a day, at 5.30am and 11.30am. From Taha'a, they leave at 9.30am and 3.30pm. There is no service on Saturday afternoon or Sunday. It takes less than 15 minutes to get from Uturoa to Apu, the closest stop on Taha'a (but almost one hour to Patio); the one-way fare is 650 CFP. You can buy tickets on board.

There is also a **taxi-boat service** (☎79 62 01) between the two islands, which operates daily. It costs 6600 CFP to go to southern Taha'a and 12,600 CFP to get to the north of the island (prices are for two people). You can be picked up at the airport or any of the accessible pontoons. Advance booking (24 hours) is required.

OTHER ISLANDS The passenger boat **Aremiti 4** (☎50 57 57; www.aremiti.pf) runs once a week between Pape'ete and Bora Bora, stopping at Ra'iatea en route. It generally departs on Friday and returns on Sunday. Pape'ete–Ra'iatea costs 6300 CFP, while Ra'iatea–Bora Bora is 5250 CFP one way.

The **Maupiti Express** (☎67 66 69; www.maupitiexpress.com) travels between Bora Bora, Taha'a and Ra'iatea. Three days a week it departs from Vaitape (Bora Bora) at 7am, arriving at Taha'a (Poutoru) at 8.30am and at Uturoa at 8.45am. It leaves Uturoa on the same days at 4pm, stopping at Taha'a (Poutoru) and arriving back at Bora Bora at 6pm. The one-way/return fare is 4000/5000 CFP; it costs 500 CFP to go from Ra'iatea to Taha'a.

The cargo ships *Taporo* and *Hawaiki Nui* also make a stop at Ra'iatea; see p250.

Getting Around

A sealed road hugs the coast all the way around the island. *Point kilométrique* (PK; kilometre point) distances start in Uturoa near the *gendarmerie* (police station) and then run south to Faatemu Bay. The options for getting around are to hire a car or hitchhike. Hitchhiking appears to be fairly accepted here because of the low-key tourism and lack of public transport. However, remember that there are always dangers associated with hitching.

To/From the Airport

The airport, which also serves Taha'a, is on the northern tip of the island. There are taxis at the airport; the 3km trip into Uturoa costs 1500 CFP. Most island accommodation will pick you up if you have booked (although there may be a charge).

Bicycle & Scooter

Avis (☎66 34 06; avis.raiatea.loc@mail.pf) hires out bicycles/scooters for 3500/6500 CFP for 24 hours. Some hotels and guesthouses hire out bicycles.

Boat

Avis (☎66 34 06; avis.raiatea.loc@mail.pf) hires out small boats with outboard motors for 10,200/12,200 CFP for eight/24 hours; they're the perfect way to explore the lagoon, and no boat licence is required.

Car

Avis (☎66 34 06; avis.raiatea.loc@mail.pf) The head office is on the edge of Uturoa towards the airport; there's also a desk at the airport. An economy car costs 10,000 CFP for 24 hours.

Hertz (☎66 35 35; hertz.raiatea@mail.pf) Has a desk just outside the airport and charges 11,500 CFP per day for an economy car.

Moana Rent a Car (☎75 08 30; www.moanarentacar.com) This family-run venture near the airport charges 8300 CFP per day for an economy car.

Taxi

There's a **taxi stand** by the market. Taxis can also be found at the airport, but even the shortest trips don't cost less than 1300 CFP.

TAHA'A

POP 4845

If a refuge from the troubles of the world is what you seek, look no further. Even the nicest spots are nearly deserted; for the ultimate do-nothing vacation it's a place that's hard to beat. Roughly orchid-shaped, the island runs on one of the most pleasant things French Polynesia has to offer: vanilla. This befits the subtle and sweet personality of Taha'a, where smiles are as common as hibiscus flowers and the scent of vanilla wafts through the air. For tourists, the main draw is the string of sandy *motu* to the north of the island where the silhouette of Bora Bora sits so close you could almost believe you were in the high-rolling neighbour's lagoon.

A sealed coast road encircles most of the island, but traffic is very light and there is no public transport. Taha'a's easily navigable lagoon and safe anchorages make it a favourite for visiting yachties and day-trippers from Ra'iatea.

Sights

A 70km sealed road winds around the island and the population is concentrated in eight villages on the coast. Tapuamu has the main quay, Patio is the main town, and Haamene is where the roads around the southern and northern parts of the island meet, forming a figure eight. Apu Bay to the south, Haamene Bay to the east and Hurepiti Bay to the west offer sheltered anchorages. The following sights are listed clockwise around the island.

FROM VAITOARE TO HAAMENE

Starting from the village of Vaitoare, the road follows the coast around Apu Bay. At the top of the bay there's a turn-off south to **Poutoru** and **Pati**, a delightful hamlet that really feels like the end of the line; then the main road leaves the coast and climbs up and over to the larger village of **Haamene**.

Ferme Perlière Champon PEARL FARM
(☎65 66 26; www.championperles.com; ⏰8am-4pm) This well-run pearl farm/shop is known for its high-quality mounted and unmounted pearls. It's at the southern end of Apu Bay.

Maison de la Vanille VANILLA FARM
(☎65 67 27; admission free; ⏰by reservation) On the right of the road into Haamene is this small family-run operation where you can see vanilla preparation and drying processes and also purchase vanilla pods. For more about vanilla cultivation, see p122.

FROM HAAMENE TO PATIO

A little further on the road climbs again, making a long sweeping ascent and descent westwards to beautiful **Hurepiti Bay** and the village of **Tiva**. As you round the end of the bay, keep an eye out for the stunning silhouette of Bora Bora.

The island's main quay is located at **Tapuamu**, but Patio, further north, is the administrative centre of the island, with offices, a post office, a bank and shops.

Love Here PEARL FARM
(☎65 62 62; www.loveherepearlfarm.com; admission free; ⏰7am-4pm) Make a beeline for this family-run pearl farm right on the seashore, approximately halfway between Tapuamu and Patio. Visitors learn about the technique of grafting to create cultured pearls, as well as the varieties and their characteristics. It has a gift shop that sells mounted and unmounted pearls as well as jewellery, and prices are great.

FROM PATIO TO VAITOARE

Continuing around the coast, the road passes copra plantations before reaching **Faaha** and the eponymous bay. From the bay the road climbs over a headland and drops down to Haamene Bay. Where the coast road meets Haamene Bay, you can turn east to get to Hôtel Hibiscus. From Hôtel Hibiscus the coast road goes around the northern side of the bay to the village of **Haamene**.

Vallée de la Vanille VANILLA FARM
(☎65 74 89; admission free; ⏰10am-6pm) This small operation is known for its quality vanilla pods at economical prices. Visitors will get the low-down on vanilla cultivation.

Foundation Hibiscus TURTLE REHABILITATION
(☎65 61 06; www.hibiscustahaa.com; admission free; ⏰9am-5pm) Run by Hôtel Hibiscus, this foundation is dedicated to saving turtles that have become entangled in local fishing nets. The hotel owners buy the trapped turtles and keep them in pens beside the hotel's pier. The turtles are fed every morning until they've grown large enough to be released.

WORTH A TRIP

JOE DASSIN BEACH

Part of coming to French Polynesia is finding that perfect strip of sand where you really feel like you've been stranded in paradise. On Taha'a, if you're willing to take a bit of a walk you can get to deserted Joe Dassin Beach, on the southwest side of the island, a 15-minute walk along the coast north of Pati. Ask a local in Pati to show you the trailhead, pack a lunch and get lost in paradise for the day. Oh, and don't forget your snorkel gear: there's fantastic snorkelling just offshore.

Activities

Walking

Taha'a's interior is dense and caters to bushwalkers. The only real hiking trail into the interior follows a little-used 7km track across the centre of the island from Patio to Haamene over **Col Vaitoetoe**. From Col Vaitoetoe, you'll get dazzling views of Haamene Bay.

Diving & Snorkelling

Taha'a has one dive centre, but dive centres on Ra'iatea (p113) regularly use the sites to the east of the island and will collect you from lodgings in the south of Taha'a. As on Ra'iatea, you have to go to the *motu* for swimming and snorkelling. Some guesthouses

VANILLA, VANILLA, VANILLA

Taha'a is accurately nicknamed 'the vanilla island', since three-quarters of French Polynesian vanilla (about 25 tons annually) is produced here. This is a far cry from the 150 to 200 tons produced a century ago, when vanilla cultivation flourished in the Society Islands.

Several vanilla farms are open to the public, and at these family-run operations you can buy vanilla pods at reasonable prices – about 2300 CFP per 100g. You can also find out about the technique of 'marrying' the vanilla, a delicate operation in which the flowers are fertilised by hand because the insects that do the job in other regions are not found in French Polynesia. Nine months later the pods are put out to dry, and they turn brown over four to five months. They are then sorted and packed before being sold locally or exported.

Jacqueline Mama, a Taha'a vanilla farmer, gives us tips on keeping vanilla pods: 'Once you buy your vanilla, keep it in an airtight place. Wrapping it tightly in plastic wrap usually does the job. If it starts to lose its sheen you can close it in a jar with a drop of rum to revive it.' (Be sure to check first if it's legal to import such products into your home country.)

will drop you on a *motu* for the day or you can join an organised pirogue tour. The healthiest coral gardens are off **Motu Tau Tau** and **Motu Atger** (Motu Toahotu). The channel off Motu Tau Tau is peppered with lots of coral formations in shallow waters.

Tahaa Diving DIVING, SNORKELLING
(☎65 78 37, 24 80 69; www.tahaa-diving.com) This low-key operation located in Tapuamu charges 6000 CFP for an introductory dive or a single dive and 11,000 CFP for a two-tank dive. Most dive sites involve a 20- to 45-minute boat trip across the lagoon. Snorkelling trips are also on offer. Cash only.

Tours

Tours allow you to get out to those sandy *motu* and provide easy access to local pearl farms and vanilla plantations. Many tour operators are based in Ra'iatea and offer pick-up services from Ra'iatea. Full-day tours range from 8500 CFP to 10,500 CFP. Book ahead as a minimum number of people (usually four) is required.

Tahaa Tour Excursions BOAT, 4WD TOUR
(☎65 62 18, 79 27 56) Fruit tasting, a *motu* visit with snorkelling, pearl- and vanilla-farm visits, and a copious home-cooked lunch are highlights of the highly recommended lagoon and land tour run by Edwin of Chez Edwin & Jacqueline. It also takes in Col Vaitoetoe. Based in Taha'a.

L'Excursion Bleue BOAT TOUR
(☎66 10 90; www.tahaa.net) Another good company. Offers full-day tours of Taha'a entirely by boat that include drinks and lunch on a *motu*, snorkelling off Motu Tau Tau and pearl- and vanilla-farm visits. Based in Ra'iatea.

Manava Tours BOAT TOUR
(☎66 28 26; www.manavapension.com) Offers full-day tours of Taha'a that include pearl-farm and vanilla-plantation visits. Lunch is served on a *motu*, and you'll also have a chance to snorkel in Taha'a's beautiful coral garden. Based in Ra'iatea.

Arii Moana Tours BOAT TOUR
(☎79 69 72) Offers full-day lagoon tours of Taha'a. Based in Ra'iatea.

Temehani BOAT TOUR
(☎66 12 88, 77 54 87; www.vacances-tahiti.com) This half-day or full-day cruise (7500/9500 CFP) on a monohull takes you to various scenic spots on the lagoon for swimming and snorkelling. The itinerary is flexible. Operates small groups only. Based in Ra'iatea.

Vanilla Tours BOTANIC TOUR
(☎65 62 46) Knowledgeable Alain Plantier runs excellent ethnobotanic-oriented tours that last about three hours. No tours on Saturday and Sunday. Based in Taha'a.

Vaituariki Taxi Motu BOAT TOUR
(☎70 56 94) Full-day lagoon tours. Based in Ra'iatea.

Vaipoe Tours BOAT, 4WD TOUR
(☎65 60 83) Half- and full-day lagoon tours and island tours aboard 4WDs. Based in Taha'a.

Dave's Tours 4WD TOUR
(☎65 62 42) Organises island tours aboard 4WDs. Based in Taha'a.

Sleeping

THE ISLAND

TOP CHOICE **Titaina** PENSION $$
(☎65 69 58, 29 17 13; www.pension-titaina.com; Poutoru; bungalows d 11,700-14,500 CFP;) At the end of the asphalted road north of Poutoru, this delightfully secluded retreat has three bungalows spread out on grassy grounds surrounded by blooming tropical gardens. They're far from fancy but are prettily decorated and kept scrupulously clean. Your courteous hosts speak English and go above and beyond to ensure you enjoy your stay. Lionel is a dive instructor and can arrange introductory dives, while his wife can cook up some seriously tasty dishes at dinner (3500 CFP). Breakfast (1400 CFP), served on your terrace, is a treat, too. There are (free) bikes and kayaks to keep you busy, and great snorkelling in a sheltered bay a short hop from the pension, if the mood strikes. Oh, and Joe Dassin Beach is a leisurely 30- to 45-minute stroll away along the seashore. No pick-up at Ra'iatea's airport, but the quay at Poutoru (for the *Maupiti Express 2*) is just 200m down the road. Cash only.

Chez Edwin & Jacqueline BUNGALOW $
(☎65 62 18; www.tahaatourexcursion.com; Haamene; house from 10,000 CFP;) Good for independent types or families, this modernish two-bedroom cement house has a big living room, TV, hot-water bathrooms and a full kitchen. Friendly Edwin and Jacqueline will drive you to get groceries and you can check out the family vanilla plantation. Take an island tour with Edwin, explore the island on free bikes or just hang out by the pool. The only drawback is that it's not on the water, which explains why it's brilliant value. Cash only.

Fare Pea Iti PENSION $$$
(☎60 81 11, 76 98 55; www.farepeaiti.pf; Patio; bungalows d garden/beach 18,000-36,000 CFP;) Fare Pea Iti has three well-designed and capacious bungalows with spiffing lagoon frontage; expect lots of bamboo, stonework and draped white fabrics. Hint: aim for the smaller, cheaper unit, which is slightly set back from the waterfront. That said, they're a tad overpriced for what you get, especially given swimming is not *that* tempting, with very shallow waters and a profusion of algae at certain times of the year. Fare Pea Iti's total capacity is eight guests at a time, making it wonderfully intimate. The homemade meals are delectable, but you will pay for them (half board is 9500 CFP per person)! Other features include a small pool and complimentary kayaks, bikes and DVDs. Transfers to Raiatea's airport cost 10,400 CFP per person return.

Chez Pascal GUESTHOUSE $
(☎65 60 42; Tapuamu; r & bungalows incl breakfast per person 4000 CFP) This backpacker crash pad is a popular spot for unfussy travellers. Nobody's going to be writing about the basic little bungalows and cramped rooms with shared cold-water bathrooms, but the rootsy Polynesian style and family atmosphere give this place a ramshackle charm. It's inland – forget about swimming – but you can make arrangements to be dropped off on Motu Tau Tau (1500 CFP). No meals, but there's a communal kitchen. Transfers to/from the quay at Poutoru (for the *Maupiti Express 2*) cost 2500 CFP per person.

Tiare Breeze VILLA $$$
(☎65 62 26; www.tiarebreeze.com; Haamene Bay; villa incl breakfast from 43,000 CFP;) There's only one ultraprivate hillside bungalow here, so if it's privacy you're after, this place may fit the bill. Plenty of deck space lets you lounge around and enjoy the outstanding view and great indoor-outdoor sound system, or you can trek down the hill to chill out in the posh overwater hang-out area on a pontoon. Everything is made with taste from local materials and you really feel you're in the lap of luxury. For meals you can cook in your own kitchen or the owner will drive you to nearby restaurants. Kayaks and bikes are free.

Hibiscus HOTEL $$
(☎65 61 06; www.hibiscustahaa.com; Haamene Bay; bungalows d from 10,600 CFP;) The haphazardly run Hibiscus gets mixed reviews, but its promo deals (stay three nights, pay for two) make it a bargain. Seven simply built bungalows of varying sizes and shapes are clustered in an Edenlike garden on a hillside overlooking Haamene Bay. They all have bathroom, terrace and fan, and there are eight free boat moorings with dock access.

There's an on-site restaurant and bar across the road, on the waterfront. Transfers from Raiatea cost 6000 CFP per person return.

Chez Louise CAMPGROUND $
(☎71 23 06; Tiva; campsites per person 1100 CFP) Louise, from the eponymous restaurant, allows travellers to pitch their tents in the garden beside the restaurant, right by the seashore, with Bora Bora as a backdrop. There's no proper ablution block, but a rudimentary outdoor shower. Toilets are inside the restaurant. Cash only.

THE MOTU

Some *motu* digs are set in private paradises that rival (and some would say exceed) the settings of Bora Bora's better resorts.

TOP CHOICE **Vahine Island Private Island Resort** RESORT $$$
(☎65 67 38; www.vahine-island.com; Motu Tuuvahine; bungalows d from 60,000 CFP;) In a picturesque location with white-sand beaches and translucent water, this intimate, traveller-recommended resort caters to couples who are seeking exclusivity. It has nine French Polynesian–style bungalows – three of which are perched over a shallow lagoon speckled with healthy coral formations. They are not as luxuriously appointed as the newer, high-luxe models on Bora Bora, but they are lovingly decorated with bright Tahitian bedspreads, coral and shell adornments, and comfy hammocks on spacious wooden terraces. Kayaks and snorkelling equipment are available for free; lagoon tours and fishing trips are organised. Airport transfers cost 8000 CFP per person return. For yachters, the resort can be reached on VHF Channel 70. Look out for internet deals.

La Pirogue RESORT $$$
(☎60 81 45; www.hotel-la-pirogue.com; Motu Rootava; bungalows d from 30,000 CFP;) If you want one of the country's best locations and enjoy natural environments (open, rustic, thatched-roof bungalows) more than hermetically sealed rooms, head straight to this small, secluded *motu* resort famous for its gorgeous sunsets over Bora Bora out on the horizon. It's intimate and friendly, and appeals to couples looking for a bit of luxury without an exorbitant price tag – although it also caters to families. No air-con here – but who needs it with the sea breezes puffing in? The restaurant has a varied menu and very good reputation. Airport transfers are 8400 CFP per person return. Special rates are available for honeymooners.

Pension Atger PENSION $$
(☎28 26 81; atgertheodore@mail.pf; Motu Atger; bungalows full board per person 9000 CFP;) The *motu* experience for less than 10,000 CFP per day? Yes, it's possible at this well-priced retreat on secluded Motu Atger (Motu Toahotu). The four bungalows are nothing flash but they're comfortably furnished, have private facilities and open onto the lagoon. The atmosphere is delightfully chilled out, swimming and snorkelling are excellent, and kayaks are complimentary. It's not perfect, though; some boat tours stop here at lunchtime (which feels less intimate) and the sharks and rays that are kept captive in a fenced-in underwater area out the front may not be to everybody's taste. Cash only.

Le Taha'a Private Island & Spa RESORT $$$
(☎60 84 00; www.letahaa.com; Motu Tau Tau; bungalows d from 85,000 CFP;) French Polynesia's only Relais & Chateaux resort is one of the most exclusive resorts in the country. In an exceptional setting on Motu Tau Tau, if you don't have an overwater bungalow facing either Taha'a or Bora Bora, you'll at least have your own pool. Every option is designed with luxurious creativity and offers space and a supreme level of privacy. Stairs cut into a tree in the main building lead up to a gourmet restaurant and cocktail bar, offering indoor and outdoor seating amid fabulous views. Le Taha'a is definitely a destination resort (it's very isolated), but the place offers enough activities to keep most guests entertained for days.

Eating & Drinking

There are shops in each village and a few *roulottes* open around the island at night, but the dining options are very limited. The *motu* resorts all have their own bars, but otherwise your drinking options are limited to the following restaurants.

Tahaa Maitai RESTAURANT $$
(☎65 70 85; Haamene; mains 1300-3500 CFP; ⌚lunch Tue-Fri & Sun, dinner Tue-Sat) Travellers recommend this restaurant right on Haamene Bay not only for its fabulous views but also for its delicious cuisine. The menu features lots of fresh seafood, local fruits and vegetables and delicious French desserts. There's also a long cocktail list, making this a popular local watering hole.

La Pirogue HOTEL RESTAURANT **$$**
(☎60 81 45; mains 1700-2400 CFP; ⊙lunch daily by reservation) With 180-degree views of the main island and a wide deck, alfresco dining doesn't get any better. Meals range from Italian specialities to *poisson cru* (raw fish) and tasty burgers. Transfers from the main island cost 1000 CFP per person return; the resort's boat dock is near Hipu. Excellent value.

La Plage RESORT RESTAURANT **$$**
(☎60 84 00; Motu Tau Tau; mains 1500-3000 CFP; ⊙lunch by reservation) Inside Le Taha'a Private Island & Spa, 'The Beach' is open to non-guests if it's not full (call ahead). Enjoy the five-star setting while savouring a frondy salad or grilled fish. Take the 11.30am shuttle at Tapuamu.

Chez Louise RESTAURANT **$$**
(☎71 23 06; Tiva; mains 1400-1900 CFP, set menu 4900 CFP; ⊙lunch & dinner) This is one of the best stops for lunch on a tour of Taha'a. Right beside the lagoon, the open-air terrace offers mesmerising views of Bora Bora to the west – a photographer's dream at sunset. Louise cooks simple but palatable Polynesian specialities and is famous for her 'marina menu', which includes lobster, shrimp and raw fish served in bamboo plates. Cash only.

L'Hibiscus HOTEL RESTAURANT **$$$**
(☎65 61 06; Haamene Bay; mains 2100-2600 CFP; ⊙lunch & dinner) This hotel restaurant has an ace location right on the water, but the menu is fairly limited and prices are quite steep. It's a great place for a sundowner, though.

Maina Nui SNACK **$**
(☎65 65 68; Patio; mains 1200-1300 CFP; ⊙lunch Mon-Fri) Good Chinese fare is served at this popular locale on the main road in the centre of Patio.

Snack Poutoru SNACK **$**
(☎21 81 54; Poutoru; mains 1200 CFP; ⊙lunch daily) Head here for a simple meal at lunchtime – grilled chicken, beefsteak or raw fish. It's on the coastal road, about 100m from the Poutoru wharf.

Shopping

Vanilla and pearl farms (see Sights) sell their products to visitors.

Tavita TATTOOS
(☎70 37 32, 65 72 09; Patio) Thinking about getting tattooed by one of the most charismatic tattoo artists in French Polynesia? Contact Tavita, who is also famous for his entirely tattooed face. He creates traditional-style black-ink tattoos and comes to your lodging upon request.

Information

There's internet and wi-fi access at the post offices in Patio and Haamene (with the Manaspot network).

The post offices in Patio and Haamene have an ATM. The Banque Socredo in Patio also has an ATM.

Getting There & Away

There is no airport on Taha'a. From the southern tip of Taha'a, the airport on Ra'iatea is only 15 minutes across the lagoon and some hotels will pick up guests from the airport or from the ferry quay at Uturoa on Ra'iatea.

See p120 for information on the *navette* service between Ra'iatea and Taha'a.

The **Maupiti Express 2** (☎67 66 99; www.maupitiexpress.com) ferry operates on Wednesday, Friday and Sunday between Bora Bora, Taha'a (Poutoru) and Ra'iatea.

Interisland ships stop at Tapuamu on Taha'a en route from Ra'iatea to Bora Bora, but not on every voyage.

Getting Around

There is no public transport on Taha'a. If you are contemplating hitching, remember that traffic is very light. Hiring a car or bike are the only ways to see the island independently. The coast road is mostly sealed and in good condition. If you do decide to tackle it by bicycle, keep in mind that there are some steep stretches on the south of the island that can be heavy going.

There are petrol stations in Patio and Tapuamu, which are open Monday to Saturday. You can save money on Taha'a's ridiculously expensive car costs by hiring a scooter on Ra'iatea and bringing it across on the *navette*.

Monique Locations (☎65 62 48) Near the church in Haamene, hires out cars for 11,000/14,000 CFP for eight/24 hours.

Tahaa Location Voitures (☎65 66 75, 72 07 71; www.hotel-tahaa.com) Has cars for 9500/10,000 CFP for four/24 hours. It's north of Faaha Bay.

Bora Bora

POP 5757

Includes »

Best Places to Stay

- Sunset Hill Lodge (p134)
- Intercontinental Bora Bora Resort & Thalasso Spa (p136)
- Sofitel Bora Bora Private Island (p136)
- Rohotu Fare Lodge (p134)

Best Places to Eat

- Maikai Bora Bora Marina & Yacht Club (p138)
- Bora Kaina Hut (p139)
- Fare Manuia (p140)
- Villa Mahana (p139)

Why Go?

This is it, the one. As you arrive by plane the view says it all. The promise of a wonderland is instantly made good: a ring of sand-edged *motu* (islets) encircle a glinting turquoise lagoon around soaring rainforest-covered basaltic peaks. With such a dreamlike setting, Bora Bora is, unsurprisingly, a honeymooners' choice. But there's much more to do than clinking glasses with the loved one in a luxurious hotel. Diving, snorkelling, lagoon tours, hiking and parasailing are readily available. What you shouldn't expect, though, is sweeping expanses of sand. With only one 'real' beach, Bora Bora is much more a lagoon destination. What makes the island so famous worldwide is those iconic over-the-water bungalows with piers reaching out like tentacles into the lagoon. This paradise is much more accessible than you think. As well as five-star resorts, a handful of quaint pensions and affordable midrange hotels beckon.

When to Go

Try to make your trip coincide with the Heiva i Bora Bora (p134) in July or the Hawaiki Nui canoe race (p230) in November – two highly engaging events. June to October, the island's driest months, are the most popular, but keep in mind that the lagoon doesn't *always* look like a turquoise-backed mirror, especially from June to August, when the *maraamu* (southeast trade wind) blows. The rainiest months are from December to April; this is when the lagoon is often flat.

History

James Cook sighted Bora Bora in 1769 on his first voyage to French Polynesia, and a London Missionary Society (LMS) base was established on the island in 1820. Bora Bora supported Pomare in his push for supreme power over Tahiti, but resisted becoming a French protectorate (established over Tahiti in 1842) until the island was annexed in 1888.

During WWII a US supply base was established here, prompted by the bombing of Pearl Harbor in 1941. From early 1942 to mid-1946 Operation Bobcat transformed the island and, at its peak, up to 6000 men were stationed on Bora Bora. Today the runway on Motu Mute is the clearest (and most useful) reminder of those frenetic days. Eight massive 7in naval cannons were installed around the island during the war; all but one are still in place.

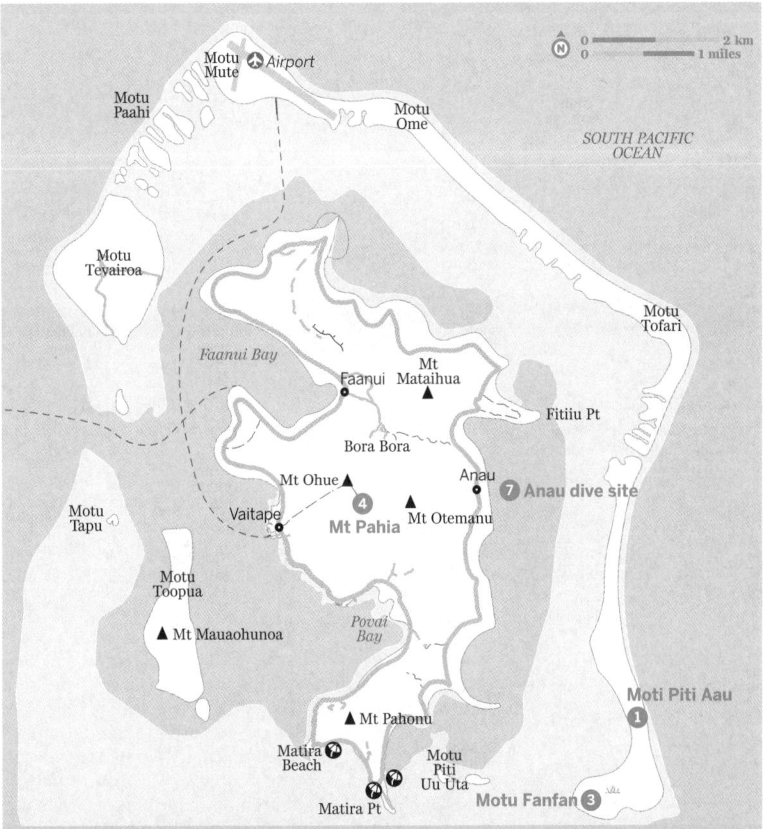

Bora Bora Highlights

1. Discovering all the perks of a world-class resort on secluded **Motu Piti Aau** (p136)
2. Ogling the stunning cerulean blue lagoon on a **boat tour** (p132) and enjoying a barbecue picnic on a *motu*
3. Working your tan on idyllic **Motu Fanfan** (p136)
4. Huffing to the top of **Mt Pahia** (p133) to admire the sensational views
5. Taking a **4WD tour** (p134) to spot rusty WWII relics and ancient ceremonial sites
6. Enjoying a romantic dinner with your partner in a gourmet **restaurant** (p138)
7. Diving with manta rays at **Anau dive site** (p131)

Bora Bora

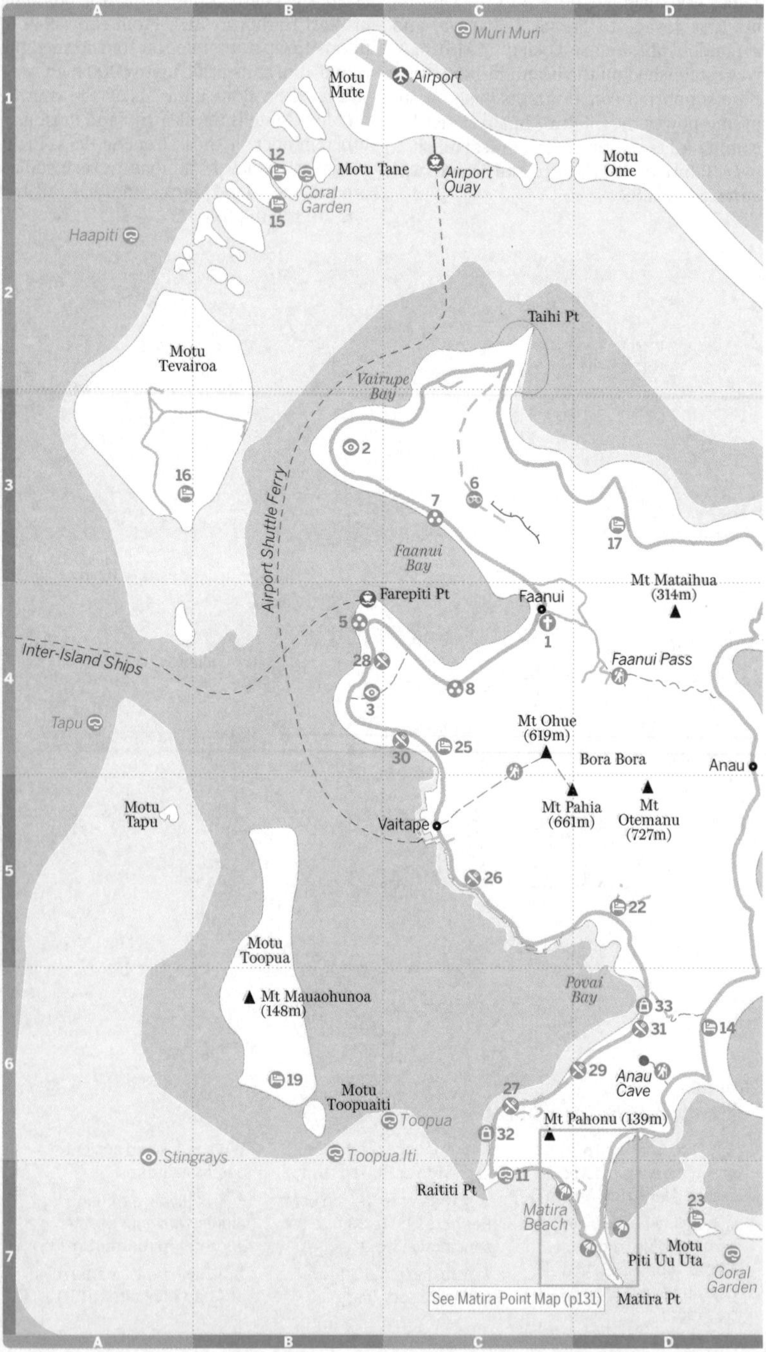

Muri Muri
Motu Mute
Airport
Motu Tane
Airport Quay
Motu Ome
Coral Garden
Haapiti
Motu Tevairoa
Taihi Pt
Vairupe Bay
Airport Shuttle Ferry
Faanui Bay
Farepiti Pt
Faanui
Mt Mataihua (314m)
Inter-Island Ships
Faanui Pass
Tapu
Mt Ohue (619m)
Bora Bora
Anau
Motu Tapu
Mt Pahia (661m)
Mt Otemanu (727m)
Vaitape
Motu Toopua
Mt Mauaohunoa (148m)
Povai Bay
Anau Cave
Motu Toopuaiti
Toopua
Mt Pahonu (139m)
Stingrays
Toopua Iti
Raititi Pt
Matira Beach
Motu Piti Uu Uta
Coral Garden
See Matira Point Map (p131)
Matira Pt

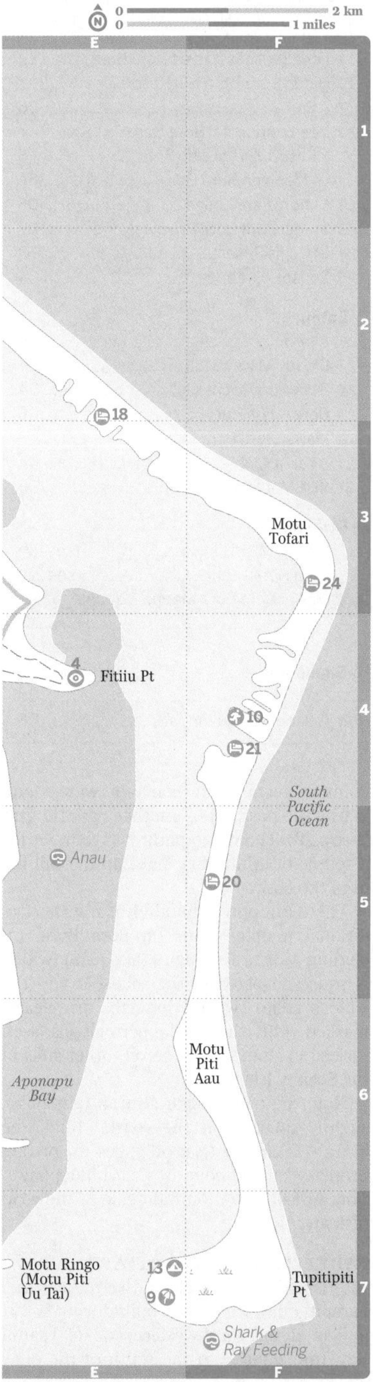

Sights

Sights are listed anticlockwise starting from Vaitape on the west coast.

VAITAPE

If arriving by air you'll be transported from the Motu Mute airport to Vaitape, the island's main settlement. It's not the most evocative town, but it's the only place on Bora Bora that doesn't feel as if it were built exclusively for tourists. Vaitape is a great place to do a bit of shopping, take care of banking and internet needs and just get a feel for the way locals really live. Busy during the day, by late afternoon it becomes altogether sleepy, with *pétanque* (boules) players taking centre stage.

Vaitape is at its liveliest on Sunday morning, when numerous **food stalls** selling such delicacies as *pahua taioro* (clams marinated in coconut seawater sauce) and *firifiri* (doughnuts) take position along the main road. For tourists, it's a great opportunity to catch local vibes.

A **monument** to Alain Gerbault, who in 1923 was the first yachtsman to achieve a nonstop solo crossing of the Atlantic, stands at Vaitape quay. Gerbault lived on Bora Bora in the 1930s.

MATIRA BEACH & MATIRA POINT

Beyond the overland road, the coast road passes several shops and the iconic Bloody Mary's, one of the island's most popular restaurants.

The former Hotel Bora Bora at Raititi Point marks the start of easily accessible Matira Beach, Bora Bora's only real beach. This stunning stretch of snow-white sand and pinch-me-I'm-dreaming turquoise sea is perfect for relaxing, swimming and evening up your sunburn. Though it's dotted with a few *snacks* (snack bars) and places to stay, its sheer size means that finding your own square of paradise is a snap. Matira Beach graces both sides of Matira Point, a narrow peninsula that extends south into the lagoon.

The final leg of the annual Hawaiki Nui canoe race (p230) finishes right on Matira Beach.

MATIRA POINT TO FITIIU POINT

From Matira Point, the coast road passes a collection of busy little shops, restaurants and hotels. The road rounds the point and passes the former Club Med, then drops back down to the coast just before the fishing village of **Anau**, a rather strung-out affair.

Bora Bora

Sights

1	Church	C4
2	Coastal Defence Gun	B3
3	Coastal Defence Guns	B4
4	Coastal Defence Guns	E4
5	Coastal Marae	B4
6	Lookout	C3
7	Marae Fare-Opu	C3
8	Marae Taianapa	C4
9	Motu Fanfan	E7

Activities, Courses & Tours

10	Bora Bora Lagoonarium	F4
11	Bora Diving Centre	C7
	Bora Diving Centre	(see 21)
	Martine Turtle Protection Centre	(see 21)
	Topdive	(see 16)
	Topdive	(see 20)
	Topdive	(see 30)

Sleeping

12	Blue Heaven Island	B1
13	Bora Bora Camping	E7
14	Bora Bora Ecolodge & Spa	D6
15	Bora Bora Ecolodge & Spa - Pension Motu	B2
16	Bora Bora Pearl Beach Resort & Spa	A3
17	Bora Vaïte Lodge	D3
18	Four Seasons Resort Bora Bora	E2
19	Hilton Bora Bora Nui Resort & Spa	B6
20	Intercontinental Bora Bora Resort & Thalasso Spa	F5
21	Le Méridien Bora Bora	F4
22	Rohotu Fare Lodge	D5
23	Sofitel Bora Bora Private Island	D7
24	St Régis Resort	F3
25	Sunset Hill Lodge	C4

Eating

26	Alfredo	C5
27	Bloody Mary's	C6
28	Bora Bora Yacht Club	B4
29	Bora Kaina Hut	D6
30	Maikai Bora Bora Marina & Yacht Club	C4
31	Villa Mahana	D6

Drinking

	Bloody Mary's	(see 27)
	Bora Bora Yacht Club	(see 28)
	Maikai Bora Bora Marina & Yacht Club	(see 30)

Shopping

32	Farm	C6
33	Galerie Alain et Linda	D6

A fingerlike peninsula extending out into the lagoon, Fitiiu Point features several interesting sites, but they all take a bit of effort to find. Up a small hill, a track peels off to the right and leads to well-preserved **WWII coastal guns** (Map p128). The **walking trail** along the ridge starts behind the first house, at the sharp bend in the road. If anybody is around, ask permission to take the trail. From the site there are fine views out over the lagoon to the *motu*.

NORTH COAST

The road beyond Fitiiu Point traverses the most lightly populated stretch of coast as it rounds several bays. The north coast of the island around Taihi Point is sparsely populated. Just after the point, a steep and often muddy track climbs up to an old WWII radar station atop a ridge and on to a **lookout** (Map p128) above the village of Faanui.

FAANUI BAY

Faanui Bay was the site of the US military base during WWII. At the end of Tereia Point, a rectangular concrete water tank marks the position of another **coastal gun** (Map p128). There's no path; just clamber for a couple of minutes straight up the hill behind the tank.

There are only a handful of *marae* (traditional temple) ruins on Bora Bora, including **Marae Fare-Opu** (Map p128), which is squeezed between the roadside and the water's edge. Two of the slabs are clearly marked with the turtle petroglyphs seen incised in stones at numerous other sites in the Society Islands.

Note the picturesque **church** (Map p128), slightly inland. On the coastal road, the **Marae Taianapa** (Map p128) lies on private property on the edge of a coconut plantation, just off the mountain side of the road (ask around).

FAREPITI POINT TO VAITAPE

Interisland ships dock at the rather drab Farepiti quay, which was built during WWII and is at the southwestern end of Faanui Bay. Immediately to the south of the quay lies a **coastal marae** (Map p128); it's on private property but you can see it from the quay.

Along the road from Farepiti Point to Pahua Point, one of the WWII defence guns can be seen silhouetted against the skyline. The road rounds the point, and two **coastal defence guns** (Map p128), placed here to guard the shipping route into the lagoon, overlook the point. The route is not well marked, so ask around if you get lost, or join a 4WD tour.

Activities

All operators listed below organise free pick-ups and drop-offs from hotels and pensions.

Diving & Snorkelling

Diving in the bath-warm waters of Bora Bora is amazing and features sloping reefs. Sharks, rays and other marine life abound, and can be seen in quite shallow waters in the lagoon, or outside the reef. Don't expect healthy coral gardens, though; the voracious crown-of-thorns starfish *(Acanthaster planci)* has taken its toll over the last few years, especially along the outside reef. Check out p33 for details about dive sites, which include **Anau** (Map p128), famed for its regular sightings of manta rays. Other killer sites are **Tapu** (Map p128), where you can approach lemon sharks in less than 20m, and, south of Teavanui Pass, Toopua and Toopua Iti. Bora Bora is also a great place to learn to dive.

There are three professional diving outfits on Bora Bora. They come with excellent reputations for equipment, safety and instruction. All employ qualified, English-speaking staff.

No visit to Bora Bora would be complete without a bout of snorkelling. The lagoon seems to be tailored to the expectations of avid snorkellers, with clear waters and a smattering of healthy coral gardens around. Schools of glittering fish and perhaps a stingray or a blacktip shark are just a few of the regulars. Many are so used to snorkellers that they'll go eyeball to face mask with you (well, not the sharks!).

Alas, the best snorkelling spots can't be reached from the shore – you will have to rent a boat or opt for a lagoon tour. At the site called Anau, you'll have the opportunity to observe majestic manta rays in the morning.

Matira Point

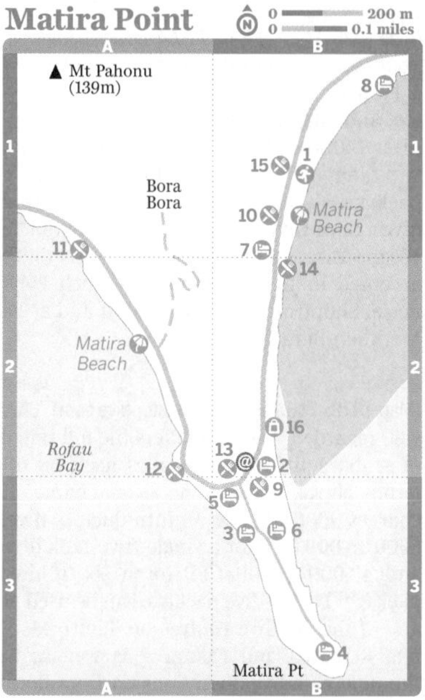

Matira Point

Activities, Courses & Tours

Bora Bora Parasail .... (see 1)
1 La Plage B1

Sleeping

2 Bungalows Temanuata B2
3 Chez Nono B3
4 Chez Robert & Tina B3
5 Hotel Matira B3
6 Intercontinental Bora Bora Le Moana Resort B3
7 Le Maitai Bora Bora B1
8 Sofitel Bora Bora Marara Beach Resort B1

Eating

9 Fare Manuia B3
10 La Bounty B1
11 Matira - Chez Julie A1
12 Moi Here A2
13 Roulotte Matira B2
14 Tama'a Maitai B2
15 Tiare Market B1

Drinking

Hurricane .... (see 8)

Shopping

16 Marama Tattoo B2

Bora Diving Centre DIVING
(Map p128; ☎67 71 84, 77 67 46; www.boradiving.com) A small outfit capably managed by a French couple; known for friendly service and small groups. Has introductory dives (9000 CFP), single dives (8000 CFP), two-tank dives (15,000 CFP), six-/10-dive packages (40,000/64,000 CFP) and Nitrox dives. Bora Diving Centre is a member of Te Moana Pass, an interisland dive pass that's accepted in 11 dive shops in French Polynesia. Shopfronts at Matira Point and at Le Méridien Bora Bora.

Topdive DIVING
(Map p128; ☎60 50 50; www.topdive.com) This well-regarded dive shop offers the full range of scuba activities and prides itself on offering Nitrox dives at no extra charge. It charges 9000 CFP for an introductory dive, 8500/15,000 CFP for a single-/two-tank dive and 43,000/70,000 CFP for a six-/10-dive package. The 10-dive package can be used at any of the Topdive centres on Tahiti, Moorea, Rangiroa and Fakarava as well as at the Blue Nui dive operations on Bora Bora, Manihi and Tikehau. The main base is on the northern edge of Vaitape, and there's an annex at Intercontinental Bora Bora Resort & Thalasso Spa and at Bora Bora Pearl Beach Resort & Spa.

Lagoon Excursions

Taking a cruise around Bora Bora's idyllic lagoon will be one of the highlights of your trip to French Polynesia. You'll get the chance to swim and snorkel in otherwise inaccessible places. Half- and full-day tours are available.

Competition is fierce among the various operators who provide trips on the lagoon and its surrounding *motu,* so don't hesitate to shop around. Ask what's included in a cruise, and which snorkelling and swimming spots are included. If you're staying at a fancy hotel, book a tour on your own as these places can tack on as much as 40% extra for the same excursion.

All full-day tours provide a barbecued fish lunch on a *motu*. Most boats have snorkelling gear but it's not a bad idea to bring your own. Bring waterproof sandals, an underwater camera, a hat and sunscreen.

Bora Bora Lagoonarium SNORKELLING, BOAT TOUR
(Map p128; ☎67 71 34; ⏲Sun-Fri) Half-/full-day tours are 7000/9000 CFP. Includes a visit to a 'lagoonarium' – a kind of mini underwater zoo where you can swim with (or observe) captive turtles, sharks and rays in a fenced-in underwater area – and a good lunch barbecue. No tours on Saturday.

Lagoon Service SNORKELLING, BOAT TOUR
(☎67 71 34; ⏲Sun-Fri) Luxurious boats with a maximum of eight people. Half-/full-day personalised tour is 12,500/24,000 CFP per person. It generally includes four swimming and snorkel stops, and a picnic on Motu Tane.

Pure Snorkeling SNORKELLING, BOAT TOUR
(☎76 43 43; www.puresnorkeling.com) Run by a dive instructor who arranges customised half-day tours (10,000 CFP per person, six people maximum) aboard a luxurious boat, with an emphasis on ecotourism (he doesn't dabble in shark or ray feeding and offers guided snorkelling trips on less crowded coral gardens). Includes a snorkel stop at Anau for the manta rays (mornings only).

Manu Tours SNORKELLING, BOAT TOUR
(☎79 11 62) Lagoon tour aboard a large outrigger canoe. Half-day tours are 6500 CFP, including fruit tasting on Motu Fanfan. Full-day tours cost 8500 CFP and include a picnic on Motu Fanfan.

Teiva Tours SNORKELLING, BOAT TOUR
(☎67 64 26; ⏲Sun-Fri) Enjoy a ray- and shark-feeding session, and a snorkel stop at a coral garden; all for 6000 CFP per person (half-day tours, mornings only).

SHARK & RAY FEEDING

Most lagoon tours bill themselves as 'safaris' because they include shark and ray feeding (they usually use tuna scraps), as well as snorkelling stops. Getting up close and personal with blacktip reef sharks and majestic stingrays is an extraordinary experience, but whether or not these artificial encounters are a good idea is open to debate. On the one hand, it undeniably disrupts natural behaviour patterns; sharks and rays that grow dependent on 'free lunches' may unlearn vital survival skills. On the other hand, it's undoubtedly spectacular (and safe), and it's a good way to educate tourists. You be the judge.

Teremoana Nono Tours SNORKELLING, BOAT TOUR
(☎67 71 38; www.cheznonobora.com) Based at Chez Nono. A long-time operator famous for its superb barbecue lunch. A full-day tour costs 9200 CFP and includes a shark- and a ray-feeding demonstration as well as several snorkel stops.

Moana Adventure Tours BOAT TOUR
(☎67 41 41, 78 27 37; www.moanatours.com; per person 4100 CFP) This outfit runs glass-bottom trips three times a week. During the 1¼-hour outing, the boat chugs around the lagoon and you're bound to see tons of rainbow-coloured fish species. Great for children and senior travellers. Prices include transfers from your hotel.

Undersea Walks

Aqua Safari UNDERSEA WALKS
(☎28 87 77; www.aquasafaribora.com; trips 8500 CFP) This company provides the unique experience of walking underwater, wearing a diver's helmet and weight belt. Pumps on the boat above feed air to you during the 30-minute 'walk on the wet side', in less than 4m. Walks are available to everyone over the age of eight. It's very reassuring that a dive instructor accompanies you on your walk. Perfect for families.

Parasailing

Picture yourself comfortably seated, gracefully drifting at 50m or 130m above the multihued lagoon at Matira, feeling the caress of the trade winds on your face... Parasailing in Bora Bora is an unforgettable experience, and you don't even get wet!

Bora Bora Parasail PARASAILING
(Map p131; ☎70 56 62, 78 27 10; parasail@mail.pf; ⏲Mon-Wed, Fri & Sat, closed Jan & Feb) Based at Matira Beach, this outfit offers 15-minute trips starting from 25,000 CFP for two (18,000 CFP for one). If you want to get high (literally), you can take the 25-minute trip with a 300m-long tow rope (23,000/32,000 CFP for one/two). Kids over four are welcome.

Kitesurfing

The steady winds that buff Matira Point mixed with the reef-sheltered lagoon are the perfect combination for kitesurfing. The warm, lovely Bora Bora waters are already on the radar of some local pros – but don't be put off, it's also a great place to learn. Chat to Alban at **Kitesurf School** (☎29 14 15; www.kitesurf-school-polynesie.com) to get hooked up with the how-to.

> DON'T MISS
>
> **SWIMMING WITH TURTLES**
>
> Looking for an unusual experience? Le Méridien Bora Bora (p137) plays host to the **Marine Turtle Protection Centre** (Map p128; www.boraboraturtles.com), which is a rehabilitation centre. Visitors can swim with the turtles in a protected lagoon and watch babies being cared for under the guidance of a conservationist. Good news: it's open to outside guests. It costs 5000 CFP (of which 3000 CFP can be deducted from a meal at the hotel restaurant). Contact the hotel reception to arrange transfers.

Hiking

Not all the action is in the water on Bora Bora, and we suggest that you take the time to explore the island's spectacularly mountainous interior. Choked in thick forest and dominated by bulky basaltic mountains, the island's centre is virtually deserted and can only be reached by walking paths. A guide is essential as the paths are notoriously difficult to find and to follow.

Arrange any hike with **Polynesia Island Tours** (☎29 66 60) or **Bora Bora Mountain Trek** (☎73 61 23), which have professional walking guides who speak passable English. Count on 6500 CFP for a half-day walk and anything between 12,000 and 14,500 CFP for the Mt Pahia ascent or the Anau Cave walk.

Mt Ohue & Mt Pahia HIKING
If you're really fit, you can try the arduous climb up to Mt Ohue (619m) and Mt Pahia (661m), two of Bora Bora's iconic summits. It's a five- to six-hour hard-going return hike from Vaitape, with some difficult uphill scrambles and a few treacherous sections, but the panoramic views will be etched in your memory forever. Don't attempt to do this hike on your own because there have been instances of walkers getting lost and injured along the way.

Kings' Valley & the Ancestors' Path HIKING
A half-day walk offered by Polynesia Island Tours, with a focus on flora, local legends and archaeology. It also includes the (easy) climb to Faanui Pass (views!). Moderate.

Anau Cave HIKING

From Anau, you'll climb to a spectacular cave into a cliff at a height of about 400m. No shade along the way. About five hours return. Moderate.

Anau Ridges HIKING

An easy, half-day walk along the ridges above Anau.

Tours

A couple of operators organise island tours aboard open 4WDs. They run half-day trips that visit American WWII sites along with locally important (and hard-to-find) archaeological areas and a few stops at lookouts. Guides are informative, providing interesting titbits on the island's flora and fauna. At about 7600 CFP per person, these tours are good value if you don't want to hire a car. Contact **Tupuna Mountain Safari** (☎67 75 06) or **Vavau Adventures** (☎72 01 21). Free pick-ups.

Festivals & Events

Heiva i Bora Bora CULTURE

This festival takes place every year in July in Vaitape, on a big stage set up near the quay. It features a program of parades, dance, singing and sports contests, as well as beauty pageants and floral floats. It's said to be the best Heiva after the one held in Pape'ete.

Hawaiki Nui CANOE RACE

The arrival of the Hawaiki Nui canoe race (p230) early November on Matira Beach is an indescribably cheerful event, with dozens of colourful pirogues (outrigger canoes) congregating on the beach.

Sleeping

Glossy brochures and promotional literature focus on Bora Bora's ultraswish resorts, which are as luxurious and as expensive as the hype leads you to believe. That said, a smattering of affordable pensions have sprung up over the last two decades (and are still largely ignored by most first-time visitors).

Although places to stay can be found all around the island, as well as on the *motu*, the majority are concentrated along the southern coast.

VAITAPE & WEST COAST

TOP CHOICE **Sunset Hill Lodge** BUNGALOWS $

(Map p128; ☎79 26 48; www.sunset-hill-borabora.biz; Vaitape; bungalows d 7000-12,000 CFP;) Who said Bora Bora was out of your financial reach? This is a real find if you're working to a tight budget. Sure, from the outside the property lacks the wow factor; but once you step inside you feel as if you've been teleported to a rejuvenating oasis. It features three immaculately furnished bungalows, one of which – 'Pilotis' ('on stilts') – has air-con, a full kitchen and lovely views of Vaitape bay. The whole place is centred on pleasantly landscaped grounds. The owner offers the most unbiased information in town and will take the time to explain all the options to travellers. Also on offer: bikes and kayaks for hire. On the northern outskirts of Vaitape. Cash only.

Rohotu Fare Lodge BUNGALOWS $$

(Map p128; ☎70 77 99; www.rohotufarelodge.com; Povai Bay; bungalows 19,000 CFP;) This 'lodge' features three local-style fully equipped bungalows cocooned in exotic gardens on the mountainside overlooking Povai Bay. You'll go giddy over the ever-so-slightly over-the-top interior, with a number of risqué statues in the bathrooms and kooky carvings. The two lagoon-view bungalows are the best, with stunning views over the bay. Perks include free transfers to Vaitape quay, free laundry service and free bikes. No beach nearby, but Matira Point is an easy bike ride away, or you can arrange transfer with Nir, your Israeli host, who speaks excellent English. If you don't fancy cooking, there are several restaurants nearby. Note: though it's only a hop and a skip from the coastal road, the access road is very steep.

MATIRA POINT & AROUND

Much of the island's accommodation is clustered around Matira Point, at the southern toe of Bora Bora. This area also features the island's best beach.

Hotel Matira BUNGALOWS $$$

(Map p131; ☎67 70 51, 60 58 40; www.hotel-matira.com; bungalows d from 22,000 CFP;) This is a good place to hang your hat if you don't want or need the amenities of a big resort, yet everything you might need or want – the beach, dining options, shopping – is virtually at the front door. That said, there are a few (minor) drawbacks; the property is screened from the coastal road by an incongruous concrete wall, there's no air-con, no wi-fi access and only the dearer bungalows (Nos 1 and 11) are right on the beach. The bungalows themselves are dotted around manicured lawns; they're not posh but comfortable and commodious, with large bedrooms, dark-wood furniture and the essential sun deck. And the beachfront location is terrific.

Le Maitai Bora Bora RESORT **$$$**
(Map p131; ☎60 30 00; www.hotelmaitai.com; r/bungalows d incl breakfast from 20,000/35,000 CFP;) While not as exclusive or as glam as its competitors, this sprawling resort is brilliant value, especially if you can score promotional rates. The overwater bungalows feature Polynesian designs but lack privacy (the coastal road passes just behind). Rooms across the road from the beach, in the hills amid lush jungle foliage, are impersonal but spotless and some upper-floor rooms have stunning lagoon views. It's a member of Earthcheck (www.earthcheck.org).

Bungalows Temanuata BUNGALOW **$$$**
(Map p131; ☎67 75 61; www.temanuata.com; bungalows d from 20,000 CFP;) On an island where affordable-but-beautiful hotels are a rarity, this venture ideally positioned on Matira Point is a no-brainer. The 15 bungalows are well arranged but are tightly packed together on a grassy property overlooking a narrow stretch of beach. Only two units have full lagoon views. Check out the website for off-season discounts.

Sofitel Bora Bora Marara Beach Resort RESORT **$$$**
(Map p131; ☎60 55 00; www.sofitel-frenchpolynesia.com; bungalows d from 30,000 CFP;) This matriarch of the Bora Bora luxury hotel dynasty (it was originally built by filmmaker Dino De Laurentis in 1977 to house Mia Farrow and the crew while shooting *Hurricane*) offers a wide range of facilities, including an infinity pool, a small spa and two restaurants. The bungalows come in a large range of categories, including beach units, garden units, overwater bungalows and the odd 'half overwater, half on the beach' bungalow. Bad news: the whole complex is sandwiched between the coastal road and the lagoon, which doesn't exactly make it ideal for peace or privacy. Good news: guests have full access (at no extra charge) to the dining and recreational facilities of the Sofitel Private Island, a sister property on a *motu* just five minutes away via the hotel's free shuttle – now that's a deal.

Intercontinental Bora Bora Le Moana Resort RESORT **$$$**
(Map p131; ☎60 49 00; www.borabora.interconti.com; bungalows d from 35,000 CFP;) The Moana Beach spreads along the eastern side of Matira Point (good for watching the sun rise, but not ideal for sunset), a thin stretch of beach is right out the front and there's sensational snorkelling offshore. The most sought-after units are bungalows 11 to 18, with magnificent lagoon views from the bedroom. The resort shows signs of wear and tear, the restaurant could use an upgrade and service is a bit lackadaisical, but it's competitively priced and within walking distance of various shops and restaurants. Best of all, guests can use the facilities at Intercontinental Bora Bora Resort & Thalasso Spa, the top-notch sister property; a boat shuttles between the two resorts. The hotel is a member of Earthcheck.

Chez Nono BUNGALOWS **$$**
(Map p131; ☎67 71 38; nono.leverd@mail.pf; bungalows d 13,200 CFP) Of the two round-shaped bungalows, one is right on Matira Beach; the other is just behind. They're both no-frills, the bathrooms are separated from the bedrooms by a curtain and the property needs some TLC, but overall it's not bad value given the irresistible location. Bonuses: free kayaks.

Chez Robert & Tina PENSION **$**
(Map p131; ☎67 72 92; pensionrobertettina@mail.pf; d with/without bathroom 9500/8400 CFP) This place is a heartbreaker. Right on the point, it's surely one of the most divinely situated pensions in Bora Bora – especially if you score an upstairs room with a balcony, with sensational views of the azure lagoon. Sadly, we've heard reports of variable service, indifferent owners and lack of maintenance. Rooms are in three functional, fan-cooled homes, all with shared kitchen. A few rooms have private facilities (cold-water bathrooms). The shore isn't sandy but Matira Beach is just a coconut's throw away.

EAST COAST

Bora Bora Ecolodge & Spa PENSION **$$**
(☎21 54 07; www.sejour-en-polynesie.com; Anau; bungalows d 12,000-14,000 CFP) The name is misleading – there's nothing vaguely 'eco' or 'lodge' in this modest pension featuring six self-contained bungalows. Despite being by the shore, the location is not idyllic (the lagoon is muddy, there's no beach and it's

isolated) but, for the price, it's an acceptable plan B if other pensions are full. Transfers from the Vaitape quay are free. There's another 'ecolodge' on a *motu*.

NORTH COAST

Bora Vaïte Lodge GUESTHOUSE $
(Map p128; ☎67 55 69, 73 57 71; www.boravaite.com; Hitiaa; dm 3000 CFP, s/d with shared bathroom 6000/8400 CFP, studios s/d/q 8400/9500/14,800 CFP;) Be warned: this friendly pension is in splendid isolation at the northern tip of the island, far from the main tourist highlights at Matira Point. That said, the owners can drive you to Matira (and back) once a day for 500 CFP per person. There are three bare but clean rooms in the main house as well as two large, comfortable and fully equipped studios downstairs. Shoestringers can opt for a bed in a three-bed dorm in a separate building. Prices include breakfast. Dinners (2800 CFP, on request) are served on a breezy verandah with good lagoon views. There's a grocery store nearby. Free transfers to Vaitape quay. Cash only.

THE MOTU

TOP CHOICE **Intercontinental Bora Bora Resort & Thalasso Spa** RESORT $$$
(Map p128; ☎60 76 00; www.tahitiresorts.intercontinental.com; Motu Piti Aau; bungalows d from 80,000 CFP;) Phenomenal. Seen from above, the layout of the 80 overwater bungalows resembles two giant crab claws. Inside, it's no less impressive, with floor-to-ceiling windows and Starck-inspired decor; think polished wood and chrome rather than exuberant Polynesian touches. Two highlights: the **spa** (www.deepoceanspa.com), possibly the most attractive in French Polynesia, and the seawater air-conditioning system, which is the pride of the hotel, and justifiably so – it saves 90% of the electricity consumed by a conventional cooling system of similar capacity. Another unique feature is the over-the-water wedding chapel, complete with a glass-floor aisle. One weak point? Snorkelling is just average (the sea floor is sandy). Free shuttles to the Intercontinental Bora Bora Le Moana Resort. It's been a member of Earthcheck since 2006.

Sofitel Bora Bora Private Island RESORT $$$
(Map p128; ☎60 56 00; www.sofitel-frenchpolynesia.com; Motu Piti Uu Uta; bungalows d from 45,000 CFP;) You'll be hard-pressed to find a mellower spot to maroon yourself for a languid holiday. This Sofitel strikes a perfect balance between luxury, seclusion, privacy (there are only 31 units) and convenience – on hilly Motu Piti Uu Uta, it's just five glorious minutes by shuttle boat from the main island, so you're not too far from the

MAKING THE MOST OF THE MOTU

Aah, the tantalising *motu* on Bora Bora. Although they're not far from the mainland, it's not that easy to enjoy their paradisiacal setting unless you're a guest at one of the luxurious resorts. Keep in mind that all *motu* are private, so don't treat the land as yours to explore without permission. We've found a few options, though:

Manu Taxi Boat (☎79 11 62; 9am-4.30pm) can arrange transfers to **Motu Fanfan** (Map p128), at the southernmost tip of Motu Piti Aau, for 3000 CFP. There are sun-loungers, hammocks, an ablution block and a sensational coral garden just offshore. Snacks (2000 CFP) and drinks are available. Bring your snorkel gear.

Rohivai Tours (☎67 54 26, 32 60 46) can drop you off on private **Motu Ringo** (Motu Piti Uu Tai) for 2500 CFP. It departs at 12.30pm and returns at 3.30pm. The *motu* has sun-loungers and an ablution block.

Bora Bora Lagoonarium (p132) can drop you off on its private *motu* at the northern tip of Motu Piti Aau (2500 CFP). It's a lovely spot, with sun-loungers and a small beach restaurant (lunch is 2500 CFP), but you may not like the 'lagoonarium'. Snorkelling is top notch.

La Plage (Map p131; ☎67 68 75, 28 48 66; laplage.bora@hotmail.com), based on the beach near hotel Maitai Polynesia Bora Bora, can transfer you to a *motu* adjoining Motu Fanfan (3500 CFP per person, minimum two people). If you prefer setting your own pace and fancy tootling around the lagoon yourself, La Plage rents small four-seater motor boats that are easy to drive; no licence is required. A detailed map featuring the lagoon is provided, as well as life jackets. Plan on 14,000/20,000 CFP per half/full day for the boat, petrol and transfers. Bring a picnic and your snorkelling gear.

action. The only dilemma: a well-appointed overwater bungalow or an elegant unit positioned on a greenery-shrouded hillside, with heavenly views of the lagoon? Due to its position, it gets plenty of sunshine, even in late afternoon. Another draw is the proximity of one of Bora Bora's best coral gardens.

St Régis Resort RESORT $$$
(Map p128; ☎60 78 88; www.stregis.com/borabora; Motu Ome; bungalows d from 95,000 CFP; ❄@🛜≋) The Saint Régis is a bubble of exclusivity that will render you speechless and never wanting to leave the premises. This is a romantic resort, extremely quiet and popular with couples. The 90 overwater and beach 'villas' (for these are not mere rooms at 145 sq metres for a standard!) have a gorgeous feel, with lots of wood, quality furnishings and elegant textiles. You can also book in for a beauty treatment in the serene **Miri Miri spa**. The two restaurants are of a very high standard.

Four Seasons Resort Bora Bora RESORT $$$
(Map p128; ☎60 31 30; www.fourseasons.com/borabora; Motu Tehotu; bungalows d from 90,000 CFP; ❄@🛜≋👪) Opened in 2008, the Four Seasons raised the bar again in the struggle for ultimate luxury on Bora Bora. The stadium-sized overwater bungalows are some of the most impressive in French Polynesia – each with its own sizeable pool on an enclosed deck overlooking the sea, with access to the lagoon down a staircase. The bedrooms and bathrooms are massive and both masterpieces of understatement despite including luxuries such as works of art adorning the walls, teak furnishings, high-quality linen and king-size beds. The international clientele is made up mainly of celebs, honeymooners and couples who spend the day by the pool and being treated at the spa, but it's also welcoming to families (young children and teenagers have their own entertainment program).

Le Méridien Bora Bora RESORT $$$
(Map p128; ☎60 51 51; www.borabora.lemeridien.com; Motu Piti Aau; bungalows d from 55,000 CFP; ❄@🛜≋) Renovated in 2011, Le Méridien is one of the best cures for winter blues – and the views of Mt Otemanu and the lagoon from your private terrace won't let you forget it. The vast glass floors in the overwater bungalows are mesmerising, the boat-shaped bar is fabulous and the infinity-edge pool is adorable. Le Méridien is strongly involved in sea-turtle protection work (see p133). Though artificial, the beach has chalk-white sand and the water is so clear you can see fish darting about your feet. With 98 units, including 82 overwater bungalows, Le Méridien is certainly not a hideaway but it's in harmony with its surroundings.

Bora Bora Pearl Beach Resort & Spa RESORT $$$
(Map p128; ☎60 52 00; www.spmhotels.com; Motu Tevairoa; bungalows d from 60,000 CFP; ❄@🛜≋) Of all Bora Bora's top-end options, the Pearl has the strongest Polynesian feel. The 80 units are all built from bamboo, thatch and wood and blend perfectly into the landscaped property. The 50 overwater bungalows are lovely, but the 20 garden suites, which come complete with their own swimming pool, and the 10 beach suites, equipped with an outdoor Jacuzzi, will really win your heart over. Other highlights include the dazzling infinity pool and the tropical spa, where only Polynesian treatments are utilised. It's a member of Earthcheck. We have one grumble: it's exposed to the prevailing winds.

Hilton Bora Bora Nui Resort & Spa RESORT $$$
(Map p128; ☎60 33 00; www.boraboranui.com; Motu Toopua; bungalows d from 60,000 CFP; ❄@🛜≋) This splendid resort with a dizzying array of accommodation options extends along a ravishing stretch of porcelain sand, on hilly Motu Toopua. It boasts 120 glorious units, including overwater bungalows and lovely hillside villas, as well as top-notch amenities, including the obligatory glass-floor viewing panels in the overwater bungalows, an infinity pool and a gourmet restaurant. Nestled in a grove overlooking the resort, the spa will make you go 'aah'. One quibble, though: facing west towards the sea, it lacks the iconic view of Bora Bora.

Bora Bora Camping CAMPGROUND $
(Map p128; ☎31 55 33; boraboracamping@gmail.com; Motu Piti Aau; campsites per person 2000 CFP; 🛜) The only camping on the island is at the southern tip of Motu Piti Aau. You couldn't possibly get a more idyllic position for a relaxing sojourn – swaying palm trees, gin-clear waters, a fantastic coral garden a few finstrokes away and mesmerising views of the spectacularly mountainous mainland. Amenities are very limited – cold showers and basic self-catering facilities – but at this price and in such an enviable location

nobody's complaining. Note that transfers to Matira Point are 2000 CFP per person return.

Blue Heaven Island PENSION $$$

(Map p128; ☎72 42 11; www.blueheavenisland.com; Motu Paahi; bungalows d 24,000 CFP) Location is the drawcard for Blue Heaven Island. This American-run pension on Motu Paahi features five wood-and-palm bungalows that are dotted around a huge coconut grove. It's no-frills but clean, and run on solar power. The property opens onto a wonderfully turquoise *hoa* (shallow channel) speckled with healthy coral formations; it's the most amazing snorkelling spot on Bora Bora. Despite its idyllic location, we can't help feeling that this place is overpriced for what you get. There are no self-catering facilities, no air-con and no wi-fi access, and meals (full board is 6500 CFP per person) have been rated as 'average' by some guests. The owners don't provide a free shuttle to the mainland, which means you'll feel a bit captive. Bring insect repellent, as mosquitoes seem to enjoy the place. Cash only.

Bora Bora Ecolodge & Spa PENSION

(Map p128; ☎21 54 07; www.sejour-en-polynesie.com; bungalow q 24,000 CFP) As with its sister property on the main island, there's no spa and no 'ecolodge' here but this is a good option if you want to stay on a *motu* without breaking the bank. Bear in mind that the three units are simply built and without frills (no hot water). Location is ace, near a superb coral garden. Half board is available for 4000 CFP per person. Cash only.

Eating

There's a good choice of restaurants on Bora Bora, ranging from European gourmet dining to *roulottes* (food vans) and *snacks*. Most top-end hotels have an in-house restaurant that is also open to nonguests. Other than the *snacks*, nearly all of the independent restaurants, as well as some of the resort restaurants, offer free transport to and from your hotel (call ahead) and accept credit cards.

All the luxury hotels have dance performances with buffet dinners several times a week, costing around 7500 CFP to 9500 CFP.

Most restaurants firmly shut their doors at 9pm, so don't wait until late or you might go hungry.

VAITAPE

There are a few good places for breakfast, a snack or a cheap meal in Vaitape. A string of stalls along the main road sell fruit and cold drinks. The in-house restaurants at Sofitel Bora Bora Marara Beach Resort and Intercontinental Bora Bora Le Moana Resort offer very reasonably priced lunch menus and are open to outside guests.

TOP CHOICE Maikai Bora Bora Marina & Yacht Club RESTAURANT $$

(Map p128; ☎60 38 00; www.maikaimarina.com; mains 1600-2500 CFP; ⊙lunch & dinner, closed Mon & Tue low season) This highly rated eatery offers excellent Polynesian cuisine with a refined twist, savoured in a vast local-style yet elegant dining room overlooking the lagoon. The menu varies, but you can expect your socks to be pretty well blown off. Excellent value. Same location as Topdive, on the northern outskirts of Vaitape.

Aloe Cafe SNACK, BAKERY $$

(☎67 78 88; mains 1400-2000 CFP; ⊙6.30am-5pm Mon-Sat) A busy place right in the centre of Vaitape. Pastries are the reason to come, with a tempting choice of homemade treats such as coconut pies and chocolate croissants. It's also a good place for a light meal at lunchtime; the *mahi mahi* (dorado) burger is superb. Good breakfasts too (including one featuring pancakes, bacon and eggs). Cash only.

Le St James RESTAURANT $$

(☎67 64 62; mains 1700-3000 CFP; ⊙lunch & dinner Mon-Sat) Don't be deterred by the odd location – the place is hidden in the back of a small shopping centre in Vaitape – for, once inside, you'll find French specialities with a bow to local ingredients. Let the sea breeze whip through your hair while dining alfresco on the deck above the lagoon. The lunch menus (from 1900 CFP) are good value.

Bora Bora Yacht Club RESTAURANT $$

(Map p128; ☎67 60 47; mains 1200-3600 CFP; ⊙lunch & dinner) This venerable yacht club has seen better days, and Maikai Bora Bora Marina & Yacht Club has been giving it hard times in recent years. That said, the wooden deck overlooking the lagoon is one of the best places in town for alfresco dining. The menu runs the gamut from grilled fish to meat dishes and salads. North of Vaitape.

EATING OUT AT A MOTU RESORT

Free shuttles, which generally operate until 11pm or midnight, allow you to enjoy the restaurants at most luxury hotels on the *motu* around Bora Bora. Note that reservations are mandatory, and you won't be allowed over if the hotel is fully booked. The Four Seasons, which is dubbed 'the fortress' on Bora Bora, has the most restrictive policy and usually doesn't accept outside guests on its premises.

Recommending restaurants in these hotels is quite hard because it all depends on the culinary skills of the current chef. By popular opinion, the restaurants at Saint Régis Resort and Intercontinental Bora Bora Resort & Thalasso Spa offered the best gourmet fare at the time of research. Anyway, you can't really go wrong at these places – their atmosphere is so wonderfully mellow and their setting so romantic that you're guaranteed to have a memorable lunch or evening out.

Dinner is usually a formal affair (no shorts and no thongs) with à la carte offerings, while lunch is more casual, with light snacks, salads and simple dishes. At dinner, expect to pay anything between 2500 CFP and 4000 CFP for a fish dish. They also offer evening performances with dinner buffets several times a week.

Use of the pool is usually not allowed, except if you buy a 'beach pass'. Ask at the hotel reception.

Alfredo SNACK **$$**
(Map p128; ☎67 58 68; mains 1300-3000 CFP; ⊙lunch & dinner Tue-Sun) As casual eats go, Alfredo is a good choice. It's relatively simple stuff, well prepped and filling; salads and burgers are standouts. It's south of Vaitape, past the post office, on the mountain side of the road.

Roulottes FOOD VAN **$**
(mains 1000-1500 CFP; ⊙dinner) The cheapest option in town. In the evening several *roulottes* take up position along the main road and serve unambitious dishes at economical prices.

Super To'a Amok SUPERMARKET **$**
(⊙5.30am-6.30pm Mon-Sat) A well-stocked supermarket. North of Vaitape.

Nunue SUPERMARKET **$**
(⊙5am-6pm Mon-Sat, 5-10am Sun) North of Vaitape.

Chin Lee SUPERMARKET **$**
(⊙5am-6pm Mon-Sat, 5-11am Sun) North of Vaitape.

POVAI BAY

TOP CHOICE **Bora Kaina Hut** RESTAURANT **$$**
(Map p128; ☎67 54 06; mains 1500-3500 CFP; ⊙dinner Sat-Thu) The Bora Kaina Hut ticks all of the boxes for an idyllic island experience. Romantic interior with candlelit tables, wooden furniture and sand floor: check. Well-presented food befitting the setting: check. Attentive service and soothing soundtrack: check. Be sure to try the divine homemade *uru* (breadfruit) gnocchi or the *mahi mahi* with passionfruit sauce cooked on volcanic stones – Kaina Hut's signature dishes. The catch of the day is equally popular, but skip dessert.

Villa Mahana RESTAURANT **$$$**
(Map p128; ☎67 50 63; www.villamahana.com; set menu 11,000-15,000 CFP; ⊙dinner) Yes, the set menu has the potential to flag a red alert to Amex, but it's the top-end darling of Bora Bora. A true alchemist, the Corsican chef Damien Rinaldi has got the magic formula right, fusing Mediterranean with Polynesian to create stunning cuisine, perfectly matched with French wines. Exquisite execution extends to the small dessert selection: the *fondant au chocolat* (chocolate cake) provides a flavour explosion. It's housed in a stylish villa reminiscent of Provence, with lots of ochre and yellow tones. Perfect for a romantic tête-à-tête, but be sure to book well in advance – there are only seven tables. No sign.

Bloody Mary's RESTAURANT **$$$**
(Map p128; ☎67 72 86; mains 2500-3700 CFP; ⊙dinner Mon-Sat) Bloody Mary's isn't just a restaurant, it's an experience. You walk on sand floors, sit on coconut stools under a thatched roof and are surrounded by exotic plants. The food impresses, too; you choose your meal from an extensive display at the entrance, with a presentation in English. Fish-lovers will get a buzz here, with a tantalising array of lagoon fish and pelagic species, but dedicated carnivores are also well catered for, with meat cooked the American-barbecue

way. Very touristy, but it's a concept that has been a cult since 1979, so go with the flow.

MATIRA POINT & AROUND

The area around Matira Point offers the island's most varied eating options.

Fare Manuia RESTAURANT **$$**
(Map p131; ☎67 68 08; mains 1500-3900 CFP; ⏰breakfast, lunch & dinner) The hardest thing about eating at this local favourite is deciding between the excellent meat or fish dishes, crunchy salads, filling and delicious pasta and mouth-watering pizzas. Big appetite? Opt for the huge wood-fired prime rib or the rack of New Zealand lamb. Excellent value. If only it had lagoon views, life would be perfect.

Matira – Chez Julie SNACK **$**
(Map p131; ☎67 77 32; dishes 500-2000 CFP; ⏰10am-3pm Tue-Sun) This unfussy little eatery could hardly be better situated: it's right on the beach at Matira (think terrific lagoon views). The menu concentrates on simply prepared dishes as well as burgers, salads and omelettes. Eat alfresco or grab your victuals and find your picnic spot on the beach.

Tama'a Maitai HOTEL RESTAURANT **$**
(Map p131; ☎60 30 00; mains 1500-2800 CFP; ⏰11.30am-9pm) A more mellow setting you'd be hard pressed to find. Part of Le Maitai Bora Bora hotel, Tama'a Maitai overlooks the lagoon and catches lots of breeze. All the usual suspects are featured on the menu including salads, pizza, fish and meat dishes, as well as a few vegetarian options.

La Bounty RESTAURANT **$$**
(Map p131; ☎67 70 43; mains 1300-3500 CFP; ⏰lunch & dinner) This buzzy restaurant in an open-air thatched-roof building is a good place to soak up the tropical climes and indulge in fine dining without breaking the bank. The menu is eclectic, with an emphasis on French specialities – salads and pasta sit happily alongside flavoursome pizzas and even *fondue bourguignonne* (Burgundy fondue). Alas, no lagoon views to speak of.

Roulotte Matira SNACK **$$**
(Map p131; mains 1200-1800 CFP; ⏰breakfast, lunch & dinner) This popular hang-out serves honestly prepared dishes such as burgers, grilled fish and beef steaks in a sand-floor dining room. It's just across the road from Hotel Matira.

Moi Here SNACK **$**
(Map p131; ☎67 56 46; mains 300-1800 CFP; ⏰7am-8pm) It's the location that's the pull here, rather than the food. Greasy burgers and sandwiches, salads, beef sirloin and fish dishes won't knock your socks off but you're literally hanging over the beach, with dizzying views of the turquoise lagoon.

Tiare Market SUPERMARKET **$**
(Map p131; ⏰6.30am-7pm Mon-Sat, 6.30am-1pm & 3-6pm Sun) Self-caterers can stock up the kitchenette at this local supermarket. It's well stocked with all the necessities, from wine and fresh bread to sunscreen and toothpaste.

Drinking

Frankly, the bar scene is tame on Bora Bora. However, there are a few cool spots where you can cut loose over some sunset cocktails in pleasant surrounds. If it's just the setting you want to absorb, check out the bars in the big hotels. It will cost you from 1200 CFP for a cocktail, and some even have happy hours. The *motu* hotels offer shuttle services, usually until about midnight.

Maikai Bora Bora Marina & Yacht Club BAR
(Map p128; ☎60 38 00; ⏰closed Mon & Tue low season) This swanky bar is the coolest venue on the island. There's an elegant indoor space with high ceilings and overhead fans. It has occasional live music.

Bloody Mary's BAR
(Map p128; ☎67 72 86; ⏰Mon-Sat) No trip to Bora Bora is complete without a pilgrimage to this iconic venue, which has been there for more than three decades. It's in Povai Bay.

Hurricane HOTEL BAR
(Map p131; ☎60 55 00) The in-house bar at Sofitel Bora Bora Marara Beach Resort is friendly and sociable, with a pleasant outdoor deck.

Bora Bora Yacht Club BAR
(Map p128; ☎67 60 47) This bar-restaurant with a large deck over the water is a good spot for sunset drinks. North of Vaitape.

Le St James BAR
(☎67 64 62; ⏰Mon-Sat) In Vaitape, this place has a cosy corner over the water. Killer cocktails.

Entertainment

If there's one thing you absolutely have to check out while you're on Bora Bora it's a **traditional dance show** held in one of

BORA BORA FOR...

Children

» Approaching rays and inoffensive blacktip sharks and colourful fish on a lagoon tour (p132)

» Splashing about on Matira Beach (p129)

» Swimming with turtles in a protected area (p133)

» Learning to dive in the calm, shallow waters of the lagoon (p131)

» Walking along the seabed (p133)

» Parasailing over the turquoise lagoon (p133)

Couples

» Luxuriating in a beachfront massage *a deux* at Intercontinental Bora Bora Resort & Thalasso's Spa (p136)

» Exploring the lagoon on a private boat tour (p132)

» Booking an overwater bungalow at a plush resort on Motu Piti Aau (p136)

» Shopping for the shiniest pearl at Pearla Joaillerie (p141)

» Enjoying a candlelit dinner at one of Bora Bora's intimate restaurants. Good picks include Villa Mahana (p139), Bora Kaina Hut (p139) – ask for the private corner – and the St Régis Resort's overwater restaurant (p137)

» Sipping a cocktail at Maikai Bora Bora Marina & Yacht Club (p140) or at any hotel bar

the luxury hotels. You can usually get in for the price of a drink at the bar, or for between 8000 CFP and 10,000 CFP you can also feast on a buffet dinner. There are performances once or twice a week; ask at the reception desks about the schedule and entry policy.

Other than that, nightlife is as restrained as it is on the other islands of French Polynesia.

Shopping

Black-pearl jewellery is sold in many places around Bora Bora, at prices that are often higher than in Tahiti. Apart from pearls, shopping on Bora Bora tends to mean hopping between the few galleries and boutiques that are scattered around the island.

TOP CHOICE Marama Tattoo TATTOOS
(Map p131; ☎74 57 92, 76 35 34; Matira Point; ⊙by appointment) For traditionally designed tattoos head to this highly rated tattoo studio. Popular, sterile and reliable. Book well ahead as Marama is something of a legend in French Polynesia.

TOP CHOICE Galerie Pakalola ARTS & CRAFTS
(Map p128; ☎67 71 82; Vaitape; ⊙9am-6pm Mon-Sat) Loads of Polynesian works of art, including paintings and carvings by local artists and artisans, are sold at this pretty special gallery just next to the post office. It also has quality jewellery and *pareu* (sarongs).

Pearla Joaillerie JEWELLERY
(☎67 63 91; Vaitape; ⊙9am-6pm) Jewel designer Laurent Rebstock is big name in the pearl business and has a superb selection of loose pearls and jewellery pieces on show. Prices start at 8000 CFP.

Farm JEWELLERY
(Map p128; ☎60 37 77; Povai Bay; ⊙8.30am-6pm Mon-Sat) Bora Bora does not produce black pearls but you can visit the Farm and see how it's done thanks to regular demonstrations at the back of the boutique. Loose pearls and jewellery pieces are on sale.

Centre Artisanal HANDICRAFTS
(Vaitape; ⊙8am-4pm) By the Vaitape quay, Centre Artisanal has lots of stalls selling *pareu,* basketwork and other crafts produced by island women.

Galerie Alain et Linda ARTS & CRAFTS
(☎67 70 32; www.borabora-art.com; Povai Bay; ⊙8.30am-6pm Mon-Sat) About halfway between Vaitape and Matira Point, this gallery has a little bit of everything – including a mix of art, books, etchings and pottery.

Information

Unless otherwise noted, the following places are all in Vaitape, where most of Bora Bora's services are found, including a medical centre, several private doctors and a pharmacy.

Aloe Cafe (internet per hr 1000 CFP; 6am-6pm Mon-Sat;) Internet and wi-fi access. At the back of a small shopping centre.

Banque de Polynésie (8am-noon & 1.15-4.30pm Mon-Thu, 8am-noon & 1.15-3.30pm Fri) Currency exchange and ATM.

Banque de Tahiti (8am-noon & 1-4pm Mon-Fri) Currency exchange and ATM.

Banque Socredo (7.30-11.30am & 1.30-3.30pm Mon-Fri) Currency exchange and ATM.

Bora Bora tourist office (67 76 36; info-bora-bora@mail.pf; 9am-noon & 1-4pm Mon-Fri, 9am-noon Sat) On the quay at Vaitape. It has pamphlets and other info. Mildly helpful.

Bora Spirit Matira (internet per hr 500 CFP; 9am-7pm;) Near Matira Point. Internet and wi-fi access.

Post office (OPT; internet per hr 500 CFP; 7am-3pm Mon-Thu, 7.15am-2.15pm Fri;) Internet and wi-fi access (with the Manaspot network). Has an ATM.

Getting There & Away

Bora Bora is situated 270km northwest of Tahiti and can be reached by air or boat from there.

Air

Air Tahiti (67 53 53, 86 42 42; www.airtahiti.pf; Vaitape; 7.30-11.30am & 1.30-4.30pm Mon-Fri, 8-11am Sat) flies between Bora Bora and Tahiti (16,700 CFP, 50 minutes, up to 10 flights daily), Huahine (9500 CFP, 20 minutes, one to two flights daily), Maupiti (8500 CFP, one to two flights weekly), Mo'orea (19,500 CFP, one hour, one to three flights daily) and Ra'iatea (7800 CFP, 15 minutes, one to three flights daily). Air Tahiti also has direct flights from Bora Bora to the Tuamotus, with a very handy flight to Rangiroa (26,000 CFP, 1¼ hours, five to six flights weekly) and onward connections to other atolls, including Tikehau, Fakarava and Manihi.

Boat

The passenger boat **Aremiti 4** (50 57 57; www.aremiti.pf) runs once a week between Pape'ete and Bora Bora (9500 CFP), stopping at Ra'iatea and Huahine en route. It generally departs on Friday and returns on Sunday.

Two cargo ships, the *Hawaiki Nui* and the *Taporo*, make two trips a week between Pape'ete and Bora Bora (via Huahine, Ra'iatea and Taha'a), leaving Pape'ete on Tuesday and Thursday around 4pm; they leave Bora Bora on Wednesday and Friday. Note that it's pretty difficult for tourists to get passage aboard the *Taporo* as it's usually booked out by locals. Both dock at the Farepiti quay, 3km north of Vaitape. See p250 for more information.

The **Maupiti Express 2** (67 66 69; www.maupitiexpress.com; Vaitape) runs between Bora Bora and Maupiti on Thursday and Saturday (4000/5000 CFP one way/return, two hours). The boat also serves Ra'iatea and Taha'a on Wednesday, Friday and Sunday (4000/5000 CFP one way/return, 1½ hours), departing at 7am on Wednesday and Friday and at 3pm on Sunday. Tickets can be bought on board or at the office on the Vaitape quay.

> **DAY TRIP TO MAUPITI**
>
> The *Maupiti Express 2*, which runs twice weekly between Bora Bora and Maupiti, departs the Vaitape quay at 8.30am and arrives at Maupiti at 10.15am; the return trip leaves Maupiti at 4pm on the same day and arrives back at Bora Bora at 6pm, which makes it quite possible to visit Maupiti as a day trip from Bora Bora. This is a good option if you're pressed for time, but keep in mind that Maupiti is well worth a few days!

Getting Around

Bora Bora's 32km coast road hugs the shoreline almost all the way around the island.

To/From the Airport

The airport is on Motu Mute, at the northern edge of the lagoon; transfers are offered to and from the Vaitape quay on two large catamaran ferries (included in the cost of your ticket). There's a regular bus from the quay to the hotels at Matira Point (500 CFP).

When leaving by air, you need to be at the quay at least 1¼ hours before the flight. The top hotels transfer their visitors directly to and from the airport; all other passengers are picked up at the quay by the catamaran ferries (the cost of this is included in the ticket).

Bicycle & Car

There are two petrol stations in Vaitape.

Bora Bora Rent a Car – Avis (67 70 15, 67 56 44; www.avis-tahiti.com; 7.30am-5.30pm Mon-Sat) Has its main office in the centre of Vaitape, as well as a desk right by Tiare Market, near Matira Point. Cars cost from a whopping 13,500 CFP per 24 hours. Bikes cost 2000 CFP per 24 hours.

Bora Spirit Matira (Map p131; 9am-7pm) At Matira Point. Rents bikes for 1000 CFP per day.

Maupiti

Includes »

Best Places to Stay

» Maupiti Résidence (p147)

» Pension Poe Iti – Chez Gérald & Joséphine (p148)

» Kuriri Village (p148)

Best Outdoor Activities

» Diving (p146)

» Snorkelling (p146)

» Kayaking (p147)

Why Go?

Close your eyes. And just imagine. You land on a strip of coral by the sea, you are garlanded at the traditional welcome with *tiare* (a highly fragrant gardenia) by a smiling-eyed islander. There's a shimmering lagoon with every hue from lapis lazuli to turquoise, a perfect ring of islets girdled with sand bars, palm trees leaning over the shore and large coral gardens packed with rainbow-coloured species. Brochure material? No, just routine in Maupiti, Bora Bora's little sister. This impossibly scenic creation of basalt and coconut trees has all you need to throw your cares away.

Unlike its glamorous neighbour, Maupiti has managed to hold on to that slow-down-it's-the-South-Pacific feeling, and that's why it's gaining popularity. There's only one road and virtually no cars, just bikes; there are no showy resorts, just a smattering of family-run pensions.

If working your suntan ceases to do it for you, there are walks, lagoon excursions, diving, kayaking, fishing and snorkelling to keep you buzzing.

When to Go

As with most Society Islands the drier season (June to October) is the most popular time to visit Maupiti. In July the island is in full swing with the Heiva cultural festivities. Divers and snorkellers might like April to June and September to November best, when the water is calmest. The manta-ray season runs from April to mid-September.

History

Dutch explorer Roggeveen is credited with the European 'discovery' of Maupiti in 1722, nearly 50 years before Wallis, Bougainville and Cook made their important landfalls on Tahiti. European missionaries were quick to follow, eventually succeeding in installing Protestantism as the major religion.

Bora Bora began to assert influence over Maupiti in the early 19th century; the power struggles continued throughout the century. French influence also reached the island during this period; missionaries and local chiefs continued to wield the most power until after WWII, when the French took over.

Maupiti has changed little over the last century; fruit crops grown on the *motu* (islets) are still major sources of income for the islanders.

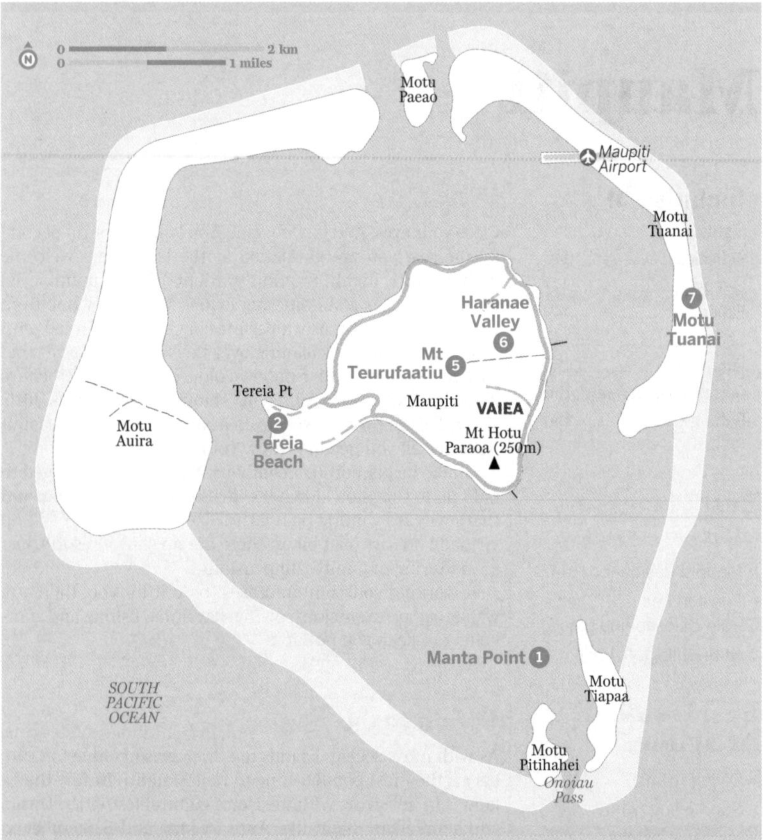

Maupiti Highlights

1. Exploring Maupiti's gin-clear lagoon while snorkelling with manta rays at **Manta Point** (p146)
2. Taking it real easy, basking lizardlike on heavenly **Tereia Beach** (p145)
3. Cavorting with grey sharks at one of Maupiti's excellent reef **dives** (p146)
4. Paddling a **kayak** (p147) across the azure lagoon
5. Scaling **Mt Teurufaatiu** (p148) and feasting your eyes on 360-degree views of the translucent lagoon
6. Reflecting on Maupiti's bizarre past while spotting well-preserved **petroglyphs** (p145)
7. Finding your own paradise in a delightful pension on **Motu Tuanai** (p148)

Sights

From the air, Maupiti resembles a miniature Bora Bora – a *motu*-fringed aqua lagoon with a rocky, mountainous interior. The high island mass is surrounded by a wide but shallow lagoon fringed with five *motu*, including Motu Tuanai, where the airport is located. There's only one pass, between the lagoon and the ocean, Onoiau, to the south.

THE MAIN ISLAND

The following sights are listed anticlockwise around the island.

Vaiea VILLAGE

The village spreads along the east coast and is dominated by a sharp ridge line running from north to south. Neat houses, brightened with hibiscus, are strung along the road and they often have *uru* (breadfruit) trees shading the family tombs fronting many of them.

Haranae Petroglyphs ARCHAEOLOGICAL SITE

Maupiti has some interesting and easily viewed petroglyphs etched into boulders in a rocky riverbed. The biggest and most impressive is a turtle image. To reach the petroglyphs, head north out of the village and round the point before passing the basketball court near the church. You're now in the Haranae Valley; on the mountainside is a signposted track heading inland. Follow it for 200m to a small pumping station, and then follow the rocky riverbed. After only 100m, on the left, you'll find the petroglyphs.

Tereia Point BEACH

A more scenic spot you'd be hard pressed to find. Here the lagoon is warm and crystal clear and the bone-white beach is nearly all sand (no smashed coral or broken rock). **Tereia Beach** is a stunning place to sun yourself, but not that great for swimming due to the shallow water. There are no facilities except a small beach restaurant. At sunset, the spot becomes downright romantic.

From Tereia Beach it's easy to wade across the lagoon to Motu Auira during low tide. Or you can walk along the coastline to the south and find a string of secluded coves past Tereia Varua point.

Marae Vaiahu ARCHAEOLOGICAL SITE

Maupiti's most important *marae* (traditional temple) features a large coastal site covered with coral slabs and a fish box. Made of four coral blocks set edgewise in the form of a rectangle, the box was used for ceremonial purposes to ensure successful fishing. Four fish kings are represented on the sides of the box. It's signposted, northwest of the main quay.

KNOW BEFORE YOU GO...

» Maupiti has no ATMs, and credit cards are only accepted at a couple of pensions, so you'll need to bring enough cash to cover your entire bill, plus a little extra for surprise add-ons.

» Beware of tricky currents when snorkelling or kayaking near Onoiau Pass (where a few of the pensions are).

» Maupiti has no resorts; digs are in simple family guesthouses.

THE MOTU

Maupiti's star attractions are its five idyllic *motu*, spits of sand and crushed coral dotted with swaying palms, floating in the jade lagoon that surrounds the main island. Many travellers choose to stay on these fabulous islets, but the mainland pensions will happily organise day trips for around 3000 CFP per person if you're staying on the island. Besides acting as quiet retreats, the *motu* also offer good beaches.

Motu Paeao, at the northern end of the lagoon, is ideal for swimming and snorkelling. There's an important melon-production plantation on **Motu Auira**, as well as a lovely coral sand beach. At low tide you can reach it from the mainland by wading across the lagoon – the water is warm and only waist high, but keep an eye out for rays.

Motu Tiapaa has beautiful, sandy, white beaches and good snorkelling on its ocean and lagoon sides. It's also the most developed *motu*, with several pensions, so it can seem crowded by Maupiti standards. If you have a kayak, however, you can paddle across to the completely isolated **Motu Pitihahei**, but be sure to steer way to the north of Onoiau Pass, which is very dangerous due to strong currents near the pass.

The airport and a few pensions are found on **Motu Tuanai**, another picture-friendly islet. However, the lagoon is shallow along this *motu*, which doesn't make it good for swimming except for young children.

Maupiti

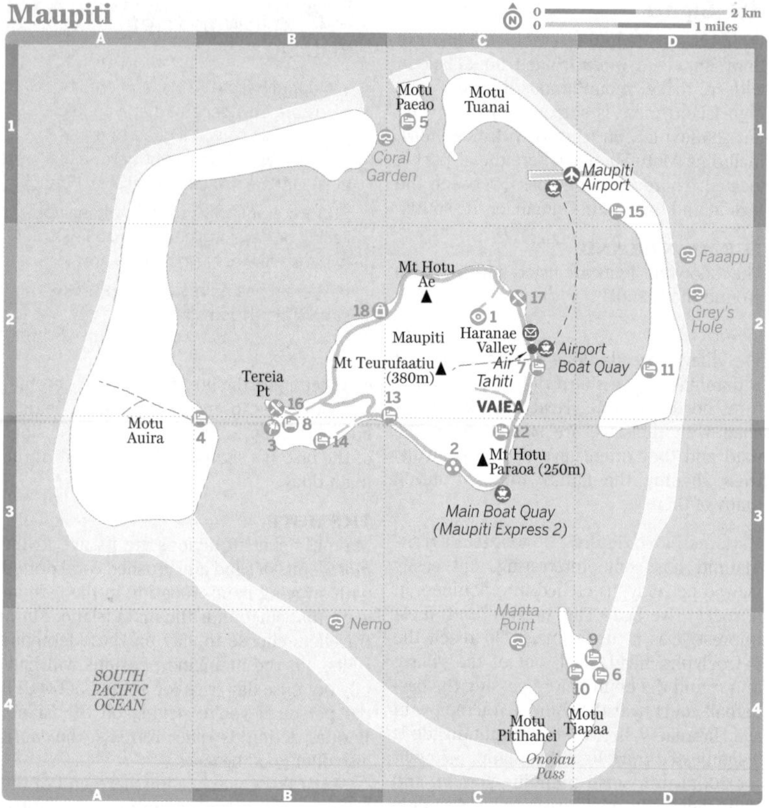

Activities

Diving

Maupiti is an excellent underwater playground (Manta Point is a particular attraction) and a good place to learn to dive, with a couple of very safe dive sites in the lagoon. There are also outstanding dive sites outside the lagoon, but they aren't always accessible due to the strong currents and swell in the pass. See p34 for more information on diving on Maupiti.

Manta Point DIVING

At this dive site to the south of the lagoon you can dive on a manta rays' cleaning station, where cleaner wrasses feed on parasites from the mantas' wings, in less than 8m of water. In theory they're here every morning between April and mid-September (but sightings can't be guaranteed).

Maupiti Nautique DIVING

(☎67 83 80; www.maupiti-nautique.com) This low-key diving venture is French-run and by all accounts reputable. It specialises in small groups (maximum four divers) and offers an intimate feel to its aquatic adventures. Single-dive trips or introductory dives cost 6500 CFP including gear, and two-tank trips are 12,000 CFP. An open-water course costs 41,000 CFP. Book well ahead. Cash only.

Snorkelling & Lagoon Excursions

Maupiti's magnificent lagoon is crystal clear, bath-warm and filled with all manner of tropical marine life, from schools of butterflyfish and parrotfish to manta rays and banks of flame-coloured coral. The best snorkelling sites are the reefs stretching north of Onoiau Pass (but beware of the currents) and Motu Paeao to the north. Most guesthouses have masks and snorkels

Maupiti

Sights

1 Haranae Petroglyphs C2
2 Marae Vaiahu C3
3 Tereia Beach B3

Sleeping

4 Auira - Chez Edna B3
5 Fare Paeao – Chez Jeanine C1
6 Kuriri Village D4
7 Mareta - Chez Manu C2
8 Maupiti Résidence B3
9 Maupiti Village D4
10 Papahani - Chez Vilna D4
11 Pension Poe Iti – Chez Gérald & Joséphine D2
12 Taputea C3
13 Tautiare Village C2
14 Teheimana B3
15 Terama D1

Eating

Ben Sa .... (see 12)
16 Chez Mimi B2
17 Tarona C2

Shopping

18 Vaitia Artisanat B2

you can borrow. The pensions also run lagoon tours; figure between 3000 CFP and 5500 CFP for a full-day trip in a pirogue (outrigger canoe) gliding through the blue and stopping periodically to snorkel and free dive. In season, the pensions also offer snorkelling trips to the manta rays' cleaning station (about 2000 CFP). One reputable operator is **Sammy Maupiti Tour** (☎76 99 28; half-/full-day trip 3000/5000 CFP), which promises a memorable day of snorkelling, fishing and shark feeding.

Kayaking

Sea kayaking is a popular activity of the DIY variety. Paddling around the quiet lagoon is very safe. Most accommodation places either rent or offer free sea kayaks for guests' use.

Whale- & Dolphin-watching

Apparently, humpback whales find Maupiti attractive too. Every year during the austral winter, from mid-July to October, they frolic off Maupiti's barrier reef. Whale-watching trips are available through the pensions. You may have the privilege of swimming right alongside these graceful giants, but don't stress them and always follow the guide's instructions. Dolphins can be spotted all year round along the reef. A three-hour excursion costs 7500 CFP.

Sport Fishing

Fishing outings can be organised with Tautiare Village and Teheimana pensions, which offer affordable boat charters: from 6000 CFP to 10,000 CFP (depending on distance travelled) for a half-day at sea, including gear.

Sleeping

THE MAIN ISLAND

Guesthouses are all either right on the lagoon or very close to it, but only Maupiti Résidence has a beach.

Maupiti Résidence BUNGALOW $$
(☎67 82 61; www.maupitiresidence.info; Tereia Beach; bungalow d 11,000-14,000 CFP, q 15,000-18,000 CFP; ❄📶) The location, right on Tereia Beach, is to die for. While hardly glitzy, the two bungalows contain enough room to accommodate a small troupe and exemplify functional simplicity with a living room, two bedrooms, a terrace that delivers full frontal lagoon views and a fully equipped kitchen. Perks include free bicycles and kayaks, hot water, daily cleaning service, air-con (add 500 CFP), TV and washing machine, making this one of the best-value stays you'll have. You can order breakfast and have your lunch or dinner delivered to your bungalow. The secret's out, so book early. Credit cards are accepted.

Teheimana PENSION $
(☎67 81 45, 71 29 97; tapututeheimana@live.fr; s/d half board with shared bathroom 7500/15,000 CFP; 📶) Tucked away in a beautifully landscaped garden, this pension with a definite family-run feel offers an affordable lagoonside tropical oasis. The house has three rooms that share bathrooms (hot-water showers) and a nice communal kitchen. It's very simple but clean and the atmosphere is relaxed and friendly. The outdoor setting features a profusion of plants and trees. What's missing is a swimmable beach; instead of sand at the front, it's sharp rock made of coral and limestone. Not exactly a great tanning spot, but don't despair – Tereia Beach is a short walk away. Airport transfers are free.

Taputea PENSION $
(☎67 82 78; s with/without bathroom 4000/3000 CFP, d 8000/6000 CFP; 📶) Right in the village, this modern house is a value-for-money pick. The three rooms are lacking in charm

but perfectly serviceable. The attached Ben Sa venture makes copious, hearty pizzas, or you can order dinner (about 2500 CFP). Prices include breakfast.

Mareta – Chez Manu PENSION $
(☎67 82 32; chezmanu@mail.pf; s/d with shared bathroom 3000/6000 CFP; @) In this family-run venture in the centre of the village you won't pay very much and you won't get very much – a sort of win-win. The three rooms are threadbare and share a cold-water bathroom. Guests may use the cooking facilities for an extra 300 CFP or order a meal (from 1500 CFP).

Tautiare Village PENSION $$
(☎60 15 90, 32 42 67; www.pension-tautiarevillage.sitew.com; s/d incl breakfast 8000/12,000 CFP, half board 10,000/16,000 CFP; wi-fi) An unfussy pension with unpretentious appeal. The four adjoining rooms are spotless and come equipped with big hot-water bathrooms. They are set on grassy garden areas and face the lagoon, but don't get too excited: swimming is not *that* tempting here due to shallow (and sometimes murky) waters, but Tereia beach is a 20-minute walk away. Fishing trips can be arranged.

THE MOTU

Pension Poe Iti – Chez Gérald & Joséphine PENSION $
(☎74 58 76; maupitiexpress@mail.pf; Motu Tuanai; bungalow s/d 5500/9500 CFP; air-con) This desirable pension ticks all the right boxes, with a spiffing lagoon frontage, a small strip of beach, lofty views and four well-proportioned bungalows (with hot water and air-con) scattered in a well-tended property – not to mention green credentials (power is supplied by two windmills). Sunbathing is top notch but swimming is not that enthralling, with very shallow waters; paddling to more idyllic swimming grounds expands your possibilities. When it comes to preparing Polynesian dishes for dinner (2600 CFP), Joséphine, your gracious host, knows her stuff. Airport transfers, kayaks and snorkels are free. Reserve well ahead.

Kuriri Village PENSION $$
(☎67 82 23, 74 54 54; www.maupiti-kuriri.com; Motu Tiapaa; bungalows half board per person 12,600 CFP; wi-fi) Watch dolphins frolicking in the waves from a little wooden deck (with Bora Bora looming on the horizon), take a dip in the lagoon, read a book from the well-stocked library – it's a tough life at Kuriri Village, isn't it? A series of simply designed yet tastefully arranged bungalows is scattered amid lovely gardens and coconut palms. It's intimate and laid-back, and appeals to couples looking for a bit of style without an exorbitant price tag. The property opens onto the lagoon and the ocean – two different settings, two different atmospheres. As befits a French-run outfit, you can expect to eat divinely. Free kayaks and fishing rods. Airport transfers are included and credit cards are accepted.

Papahani – Chez Vilna PENSION $$
(☎60 15 35; pensionpapahani@hotmail.fr; Motu Tiapaa; bungalows half board per person 9500-12,600 CFP; wi-fi) An atmosphere of dreamlike tranquillity characterises this well-run pension with a fab lagoon frontage. Your biggest quandary here: a bout of snorkelling (or kayaking) or a snooze on the white-sand beach under the swaying palms? The five bungalows blend perfectly into the tropical gardens. Try for one of the newer, slightly more expensive bungalows, as the two units at the rear are a bit long in the tooth. Airport transfers are free.

Auira – Chez Edna PENSION, CAMPING $
(☎67 80 26; Motu Auira; campsites per person 2100 CFP, garden bungalows 5000 CFP, beach bungalows half board per person 9000 CFP) Chez Edna has the reputation of being haphazardly run but the truly magical setting offers some compensation, with swaying palms, a porcelain-sand beach lapped by topaz waters and the

DON'T MISS

CLIMBING MT TEURUFAATIU

The ascent of Mt Teurafaatiu (380m) is vigorous, but the 360-degree panorama at the summit is worth the effort. Ribbons of blue water flecked with turquoise and sapphire, islets girdled with brilliant scimitars of white sand, lagoons mottled with coral formations, and Bora Bora in the background… hallucinogenic. The track starts virtually opposite Tarona *snack* (p149) and the climb is shaded for most of the way. The most difficult part is towards the end, with a climb up steep rock to reach the ridge. Allow three hours for the return trip and be sure to bring plenty of drinking water.

The track is not properly marked, so it's not a bad idea to go with a guide – contact your pension to organise one (about 3000 CFP).

TO MOTU OR NOT MOTU?

Your biggest decision: staying on a *motu* (islet) or on the main island? For the full Robinson Crusoe experience, places on the *motu* are hard to beat, as they offer plenty of remote and tropical tranquillity. Be prepared to feel a bit of a captive, though, except if you're ready to paddle to the village or pay anything from 500 CFP to 1500 CFP for a transfer by boat to the mainland. If island life is your top priority, stay on the main island. Better yet: combine the two options!

majestic silhouette of the main island in the background. While the garden bungalows are teeny and fairly ramshackle, the beach bungalows with private terrace cut the mustard. It's a good bargain for those who have a tent, with a sandy area and plenty of shade, but you'll have to deal with hordes of mosquitoes in the evening. One convenient point: it's the only place on the *motu* from where you can walk (well, wade across the lagoon) to the main island.

Terama PENSION $

(☎678196,710333;http://maupiti.terama.over-blog.com; Motu Tuanai; r & bungalows half board per person 7000 CFP) An acceptable option if you want to base yourself on a *motu* without paying the hefty price tag. Run by an affable French-Tahitian couple, it exudes low-key vibes and features three basic, boxy and neon-lit rooms in the family home, with two communal bathrooms (one with bucket). There's also a very simple bungalow right on a little stretch of sand; lying on your bed you can see the majestic silhouette of the main island. The water's not deep enough for swimming, although free kayaks offer adequate compensation. Airport transfers are free.

Maupiti Village PENSION $$

(☎67 80 08; Motu Tiapaa; dm/r/bungalows full board per person 6000/7000/12,000 CFP) This place is hit and miss. Some travellers like its casual atmosphere, some loathe it. On the plus side, the food is copious and flavoursome, and the location on the ocean side of Motu Tiapaa is good for snorkelling. Accommodation-wise, it's clean but spartan, with three particle-board rooms with a shared outside bathroom, a bare-bones 10-bed dorm and a few bungalows (ask for the one facing the beach), all with saggy mattresses. But if you can live with that, it's not a bad deal at these prices, especially given that kayaks are free and you won't be inside much anyway.

Fare Paeao – Chez Jeanine PENSION $$

(☎67 81 01; fare.pae.ao@mail.pf; Motu Paeao; s/d bungalows half board 15,200/20,000 CFP) This property edges onto fabulous coral gardens and jade waters. The six luminous and functional bungalows are sprinkled through gardens replete with fragrant shrubs of *tiare*. Guests can make use of the kayaks to explore the lagoon. Shame that it's a bit overpriced, especially considering what's available on the island.

Eating

Most visitors opt for the half- or full-board options with their accommodation. In the village, several small shops sell basic supplies and soft drinks.

Tarona SNACK $$

(☎67 82 46; mains 1200-1700 CFP; ⊙lunch & dinner Mon-Sat) Just north of the village, this place comes recommended for its hearty portions of traditional French Polynesian dishes such as raw fish, tuna sashimi, braised beef, and pork with taro.

Chez Mimi SNACK $

(Tereia Beach; mains 800-1200 CFP; ⊙9am-3pm) Feel the sand in your toes at this oasis of a place soothingly positioned right on Tereia Beach. It's an ideal spot for a filling lunch after (or before) working your tan. The menu concentrates on sandwiches and simply prepared fish dishes.

Ben Sa PIZZERIA $$

(☎33 18 68; pizzas 1200-1400 CFP; ⊙lunch & dinner) In this unpretentious joint you'll find about 20 varieties of crispy pizzas. The quality isn't exactly earth shattering, but neither is the bill. They can be delivered to your pension for an extra 250 CFP. Same location as Taputea pension.

Shopping

Vaitia Artisanat HANDICRAFTS

(☎67 83 23; ⊙daily) You can find some quality souvenirs made from oyster shells, urchins and seashells as well as pearls here; it's located in the north of the main island (it's signposted).

Information

There's no bank and no ATM, so bring a wad of cash. There's wi-fi near the *mairie* (town hall) and internet access at the pension **Mareta – Chez Manu** (per hr 250 CFP).

Getting There & Away

Maupiti is 320km west of Tahiti and 40km west of Bora Bora.

Air

Air Tahiti (☎60 15 05, airport 67 81 24, central reservation 86 42 42; www.airtahiti.pf; ⏲8-11am Mon, Wed & Thu, 8.45am-1pm Tue & Fri) flies from Maupiti to Tahiti (17,000 CFP, 1½ hours, five flights weekly), Ra'iatea (8500 CFP, 25 minutes, three flights weekly) and Bora Bora (8000 CFP, 20 minutes, one or two flights weekly).

Boat

Because of strong currents and a tricky sand bar in the Onoiau Pass, the lagoon can only be navigated by smaller ships, which are occasionally forced to wait for appropriate tidal conditions. The **Maupiti Express 2** (☎67 66 69, 78 27 22; www.maupitiexpress.com) ferry runs between Maupiti and Bora Bora on Thursday and Saturday (4000/5000 CFP one way/return). Leaving Vaitape (Bora Bora) at 8.30am, it arrives at Maupiti at 10.15am then departs for the return trip at 4pm, arriving back at Bora Bora around 6pm.

MAUPITI BY BIKE

Maupiti is small (and flat) enough to be explored by bike, which is by far the best – and most enjoyable – way to get around the island. A 10km coast road hugs the shoreline almost all the way around the island and rarely rises above sea level. Most pensions offer bike hire for about 1000 CFP per day. Operators also wait on the quay when the *Maupiti Express 2* arrives at Maupiti.

Getting Around

If you've booked accommodation you'll be met at the airport, although some places charge for the trip (around 2500 CFP return).

It's simple to arrange a boat out to the *motu* from the village and vice versa. It costs 500 CFP to 1500 CFP to go from the main island to the *motu*. All the pensions on the mainland or *motu* can arrange these transfers.

The Tuamotus

Includes »

Best Places to Stay

» Ninamu Resort (p164)

» Kia Ora Resort & Spa (p158)

» Ariiheevai – Chez Alphonsine (p166)

» Cocoperle Lodge (p173)

» Raimiti (p170)

» Tevahine Dream (p156)

Best Places to Eat

» Snack Te Anuanua (p171)

» Cocoperle Lodge (p173)

» Raira Lagon – Beach Raira (p160)

Why Go?

Life in the fast lane not your style? Head for the Tuamotus. It's the dream South Seas snapshot: the 77 atolls – narrow coral rings encircling turquoise lagoons – that make up this stunning archipelago are flung over an immense stretch of indigo-blue ocean.

Life in the atolls is equal parts harsh and paradisiacal: hardly anything grows so there's little fruit and vegetables, and the only drinking water is collected from the rain. Yet the silence, starry skies, coral beaches, blue lagoons, idyllic *motu* (coral islets) and languid pace of life captivate nearly everyone who makes it here. Most tourists visit Rangiroa, Tikehau, Fakarava and Manihi, which have the bulk of tourist infrastructure, but it's also possible to explore lesser-known beauties such as Ahe and Mataiva.

If you're into diving and snorkelling – the main reasons to come to the Tuamotus – you'll be ecstatic. The vast, pristine marine area offers unparalleled opportunities to encounter the menagerie of marine life. For nondivers, fantastic lagoon excursions beckon.

When to Go

The Tuamotus get more sunshine than any other archipelago in French Polynesia. The shoulder seasons (April to May and October to November) are the best times to visit. From December to March is the period when storms and rain are more likely. It's still very warm, but the humidity is higher. Between June and September the prevailing trade winds produce pleasantly mild weather but rough seas – not ideal for boat excursions. Diving is excellent year-round but the seas are calmer from October to May.

The Tuamotus Highlights

1 Diving the legendary **Tiputa Pass** (p154) and **Garuae Pass** (p167)

2 Watching a lustrous dark pearl being 'birthed' from an oyster at a pearl farm at **Manihi** (p171)

3 Walking along the pink- and white-sand beaches on **Tikehau** (p162)

4 Cycling to coconut plantations and past the emerald lagoon of **Mataiva** (p165)

5 Finding your own slice of heaven on the unspoilt sands of **Les Sables Roses** (p166) on Fakarava

6 Slowing things down on quietly charming **Ahe** (p173)

7 Leaving the world behind on remote **Makemo** (p167)

8 Seeing surreal, raised coral formations at **Île aux Récifs** (p154), south of Rangiroa

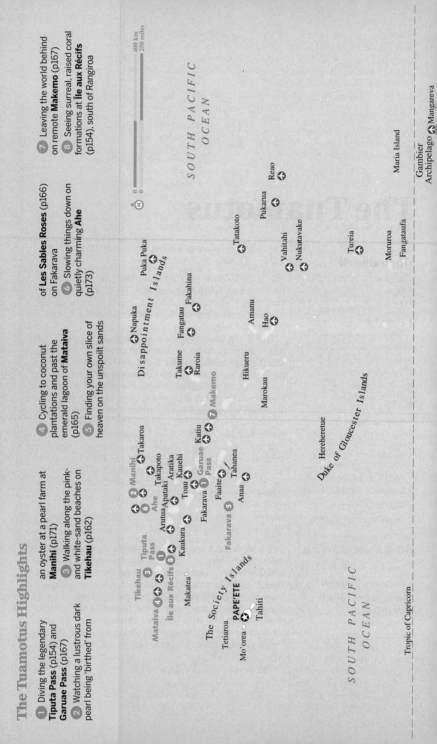

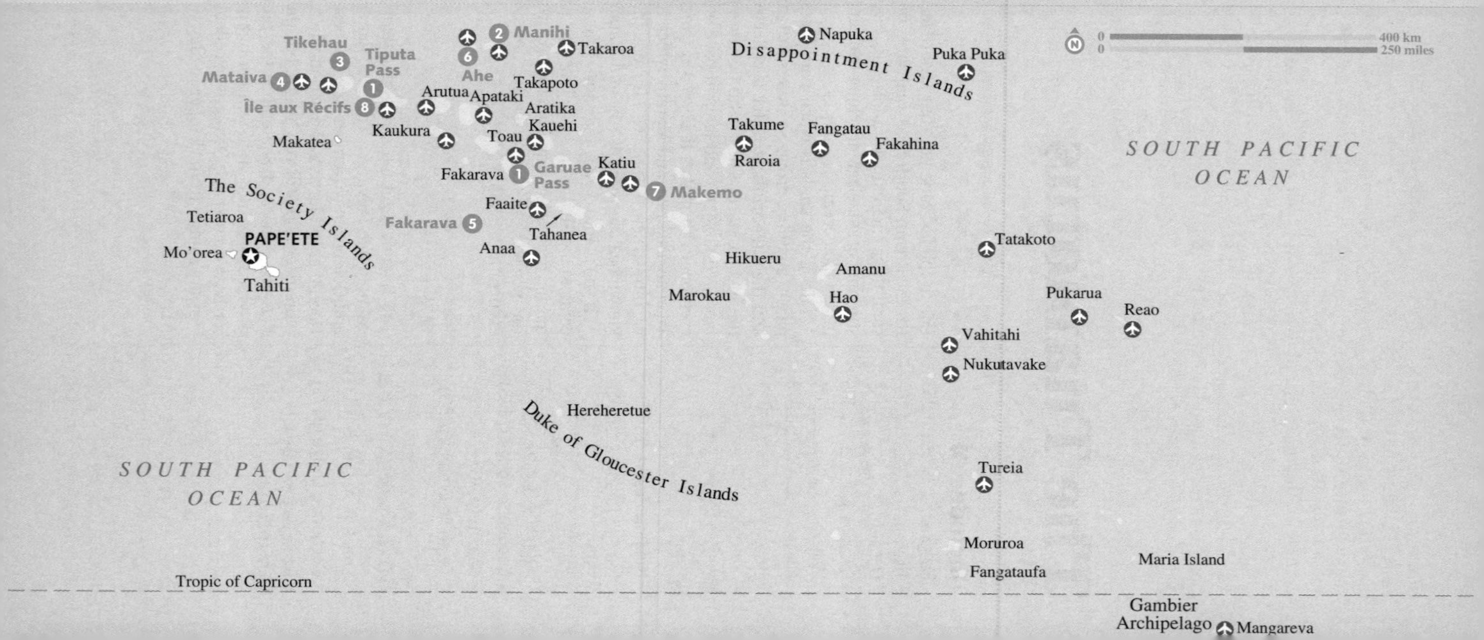

History

Early Tuamotu history is a mystery. One theory is that the Paumotu (people of the Tuamotus) fled from the Leeward and Marquesas Islands following conflicts during the 14th, 15th and 16th centuries. Another theory is that the eastern Tuamotus were populated at the same time as the major Polynesian diaspora moved on from the Marquesas to the Gambier Archipelago and Easter Island, around AD 1000.

European explorers were less than complimentary about the group – in 1616 Jacques Le Maire and Willem Schouten spoke of the 'Islands of Dogs', the 'Islands without End' and the 'Islands of Flies'. In 1722 Jacob Roggeveen called them the 'Pernicious Islands' and in 1768 French explorer Louis-Antoine de Bougainville dubbed them the 'Dangerous Archipelago'.

Thus the reputation of the group as an uninviting place was sealed and the Europeans turned their attention towards the more welcoming Society Islands.

Christian missionaries established copra production in the 1870s, and by 1900 copra represented 40% of the total exports of the colony. Pearl diving and mother-of-pearl production both enjoyed a golden age around 1850.

From 1911 until 1966, phosphate mining on Makatea was the principal export activity not only for the Tuamotus but for all of French Polynesia. The population of other islands began to decline dramatically in the 1960s as copra production fell away and plastic buttons killed off the mother-of-pearl button business.

In the 1970s, when airstrips were built on many of the islands, the population decline was slowed and the group's economic prospects began to brighten. The flights back to Tahiti carried not only suntanned tourists but loads of fresh reef fish for the busy markets of Pape'ete.

The 1970s brought another far less congenial employment prospect to the Tuamotus when France's Centre d'Expérimentation du Pacifique (CEP) took over the central atoll of Hao and began to test nuclear weapons on the western atolls of Moruroa and Fangataufa (see p224).

Pearl cultivation began in the 1980s and the atolls flourished with wealth and reverse migration from the late 1990s till around 2003 when pearl prices began to plummet. Today, on atolls such as Manihi and Tikehau, abandoned pearl farms dot the lagoon.

Getting There & Away

Most visitors fly into the Tuamotus, while others arrive by cargo ship or on their own boats.

AIR Flying is by far the easiest, fastest and most comfortable way to get to the Tuamotus, with **Air Tahiti** (www.airtahiti.pf) serving no fewer than 32 atolls. Most of the traffic is to and from Pape'ete, but there are also transversal connections between Bora Bora and the more tourist-oriented atolls, including Fakarava, Rangiroa and Tikehau, which eliminates the need to backtrack to Pape'ete. Within the archipelago, Rangiroa is the major flight hub.

BOAT Starting from Pape'ete, there is a network of cargo vessels that run between the atolls. They include the *Saint-Xavier Maris-Stella, Dory, Mareva Nui* and *Kura Ora*, and take a limited number of passengers along with their main freight transport. Their 'schedules' are prone to last-minute changes and comfort is very limited.

See p250 and individual Getting There & Away sections for details on how to reach the Tuamotus by cargo ship.

Getting Around

Public transport is virtually nonexistent in the Tuamotus. Outboard motorboats, bicycles and scooters are the most convenient ways to get around. Only Rangiroa and Fakarava have sealed roads; elsewhere, roads are often just crushed-coral tracks, perhaps a few kilometres long, linking the village to the airport or to the areas where copra is produced.

Airports are sometimes near the villages, or sometimes on remote *motu* on the other side of the lagoon. If you have booked accommodation, your hosts will come and meet you but transfers are not necessarily free.

RANGIROA

POP 3016

Rangiroa (rung-ee-roh-ah) is one of the biggest atolls in the world, with a lagoon so vast that it could fit the entire island of Tahiti inside of it. While visitors coming directly from Bora Bora or Tahiti will probably find Rangi (as it's known to its friends) to be a low-key, middle-of-nowhere sort of a place, this is the big city for folks coming from anywhere else in the archipelago. With paved roads, a few stores, resorts, plentiful internet and gourmet restaurants, there's really everything here you need – and in the Tuamotus, that's a really big deal!

But it's only the beginning: Rangiroa's richest resource lies below the surface. It's a diving mecca, with world-renowned dive sites blessed with prolific marine life just minutes from your hotel or pension.

For landlubbers the never-ending string of remote *motu* is the real draw and boat trips across the lagoon to the stunning Île aux Récifs and Lagon Bleu are not to be missed.

Sights

TOP CHOICE Île aux Récifs NATURAL SITE
(Island of Reefs; Map p155) South of the atoll, an hour by boat from Avatoru, Île aux Récifs is an area dotted with raised *feo* (coral outcrops), weathered shapes chiselled by erosion into petrified silhouettes on the exterior reef. They stretch for several hundred metres, with basins and channels that make superb natural swimming pools. There's a good *hoa* (shallow channel) for swimming and a picturesque coconut grove by the beach.

Lagon Bleu NATURAL SITE
(Blue Lagoon; Map p155) Lagon Bleu is a popular spot about an hour away from Avatoru by boat. This is what many people visualise when imagining a Polynesian paradise: a string of *motu* and coral reefs has formed a natural pool on the edge of the main reef, a lagoon within a lagoon. The lagoon isn't deep and offers safe snorkelling among the myriad little fish, but don't expect much from the coral.

Avatoru VILLAGE
(Map p156) Avatoru won't leap to the top of your list of preferred villages in French Polynesia but its location, right by Avatoru Pass and the lagoon, is stunning. It's a modern and bustling place by Tuamotu standards. The two churches – one Catholic and one Mormon – are about the only buildings of interest.

Tiputa VILLAGE
(Map p156) Around the middle of the day, you could pretty safely fire a gun along the main street in Tiputa and not hit anyone. It's a charming little village; getting a boat across the Tiputa Pass adds to the whole experience. After the village the track continues east through coconut plantations until it's halted by the next *hoa*.

FREE Gauguin's Pearl PEARL FARM
(Map p156; ☎93 11 30; www.gauguinspearl.com; ⊙guided tours 8.30am, 10.30am & 2pm Mon-Fri) Free tours are offered of the pearl farm directly next to the boutique (p161).

Plage Publique BEACH
(Map p156) This artificial beach near Kia Ora Resort & Spa is nothing special but has a few shady trees and a good vibe from a mix of locals and tourists.

Activities

Diving & Snorkelling

The number-one activity on Rangiroa is diving, and it's no wonder. The **Tiputa Pass** and the **Avatoru Pass** have reached cult status in the diving community and offer some of the best drift dives in the world. Sharks and manta rays are the big attractions, but you'll also encounter countless reef species as well as shoals of barracuda and trevally. Most sites are suitable for both experienced and novice divers, but novices would be advised to start with easier sites before tackling more intimidating drift dives in the Tiputa Pass.

For beginners, **Motu Nuhi Nuhi** (The Aquarium; Map p156) is an ideal spot to take a first dive: it's shallow and thick with neon-coloured fish. Other sites include the stunning **Les Failles** (Map p155) at the opposite side of the atoll, which is dived infrequently due its remoteness, and **L'Éolienne** (Map p156); see p34 for details. For thrill-seekers, Le Bleu is a great dive in the open ocean. A bait is used to attract sharks, from silvertips and nurse sharks to grey sharks and sometimes tiger sharks.

Snorkelling is another great way to visit the lagoon. You can just grab a snorkel and splash around near your hotel or guesthouse (many of which provide snorkelling gear for guests), but to really experience life under the sea it's necessary to sign up with

DON'T MISS

WATCHING DOLPHINS FOR FREE

Dolphin-watching has never been so straightforward. Near Les Relais de Josephine (Map p156), a small site overlooking Tiputa Pass has been cleared so that visitors can watch the daily performances of dolphins that dance in the waves created by the outgoing current.

Rangiroa

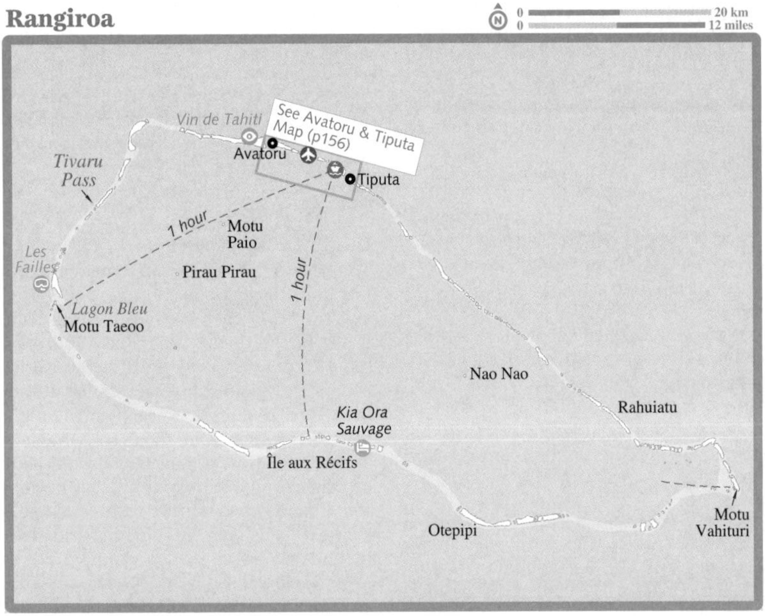

Rangiroa Plongée, the Six Passengers or a boat tour operator and go out to further marine wonderlands.

Rangiroa Plongée DIVING, SNORKELLING
(Map p156; ☎77 65 86, 27 57 82; www.rangiroaplongee.pf) This small dive outfit (two instructors) provides personalised service at affordable prices (6800 CFP for an introductory dive or single dive). The dedicated two-hour snorkelling trip through the Tiputa Pass (5000 CFP) comes highly recommended (no experience is required). It's at the eastern end of Avatoru.

Six Passengers DIVING, SNORKELLING
(Map p156; ☎96 02 60; www.the6passengers.com) The Six Passengers is a fully fledged, well-organised dive shop offering a full menu of underwater adventures, including introductory dives (7900 CFP), single dive trips (7000 CFP), snorkelling trips and certification courses. Five- and 10-dive packages go for 33,500/63,000 CFP, and Nitrox dives are also available (7500 CFP). There's a 10% discount for divers who have their own gear. It's located in a modern base on a small coral beach.

Topdive DIVING
(Map p156; ☎96 05 60; www.topdive.com) A professional and highly recommended dive shop that offers the full range of scuba activities and prides itself on offering Nitrox dives at no extra charge. Introductory dives go for 8000 CFP while single dives cost 8500 CFP. Six- and 10-dive packages are 43,000/70,000 CFP.

Y'aka Plongée DIVING
(Map p156; ☎20 68 98; www.yakaplongeerangiroa.com) Opened in 2011, this dive outfit is run by Marco and Cathy, two of Rangiroa's long-standing dive instructors. They have an excellent reputation for service and instruction, and offer introductory dives (7500 CFP), single-dive trips (7500 CFP) and courses. Prices drop by about 10% for more than four dives. Y'aka also runs day trips to Les Failles (23,000 CFP per person, including two dives and lunch onboard, minimum four people). It's next to Topdive.

Lagoon Excursions

Organised tours are really the only way of exploring the most scenic spots on the lagoon and, if you happen upon a nice group, make for a wonderful day. The most popular excursions – the Lagon Bleu and Île aux Récifs – are to the opposite side of the lagoon from Avatoru, which takes at least an hour to cross and can be uncomfortable if the sea is rough. Usually a minimum of four to six people is required.

Avatoru & Tiputa

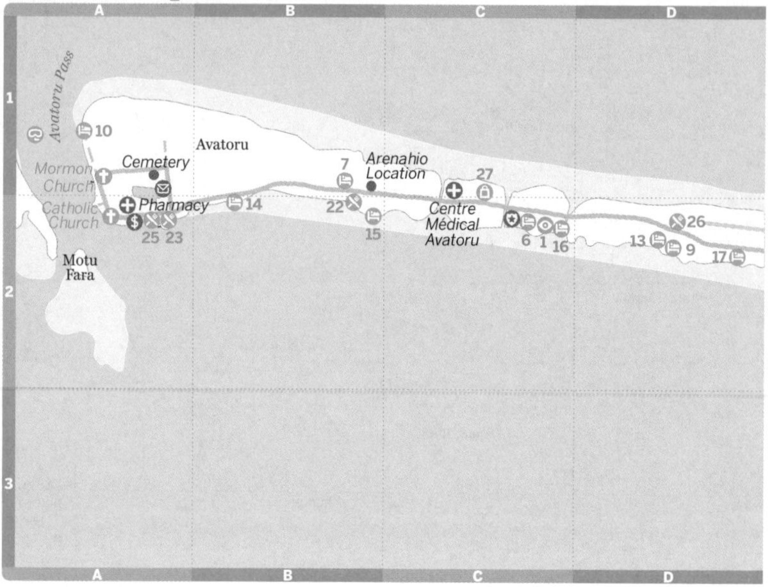

Snorkelling gear can be arranged, although you may have to pay extra for this. Full-day tours generally depart at 8.30am and return at 4pm. When the weather's bad or the winds are too high, excursions are cancelled.

Trips to the Lagon Bleu or Île aux Récifs cost around 7500 CFP including lunch. All bookings can be made through your hotel or pension, but you can also make direct arrangements with the boat tour companies. Transfers are provided.

Hiria Arnoux CRUISE, SNORKELLING
(☎21 85 91) A good-value half-day cruise (5300 CFP) on a monohull that takes you to various scenic spots on the lagoon for swimming, snorkelling and trying your hand at fishing. The itinerary is flexible. Operates small groups only. Private charters also available.

Spirit Excursion BOAT TOUR, SNORKELLING
(☎96 76 62, 71 29 90) Standard tours to Île aux Récifs and the Lagon Bleu.

Pa'ati Excursion – Léon BOAT TOUR, SNORKELLING
(☎96 02 57) Offers well-run tours to Île aux Récifs that include swimming, snorkelling and a short guided walk to the raised coral outcrops. Another draw is the excellent beach barbecue at lunchtime; leftovers are discarded into the sea, which attracts a gang of (harmless) blacktip sharks near the shore.

Tereva Excursions – Jean Pierre BOAT TOUR, SNORKELLING
(☎96 82 51, 70 71 38) Has the most popular tours to the Lagon Bleu. You can walk ankle-deep across a (mostly dead) coral seabed to visit a bird island. Feasting on barbecued fish, playing ukulele and feeding the sharks are on the itinerary. On the way back, a snorkel stop is usually made near Avatoru Pass.

Sleeping

Most places to stay and eat are dotted along the string of islets east of Avatoru village. Besides a few hotels, options on Rangiroa are mostly in family pensions. Except where noted, credit cards are accepted.

Tevahine Dream PENSION **$$**
(Map p156; ☎93 12 75; www.tevahinedream.com; bungalows d half board per person 12,500-16,500 CFP; 📶) Tevahine Dream gets rave reviews from honeymooners who want something more personal and intimate than a hotel. Five rustic chic bungalows are designed in a Zen-meets-Polynesia style, dripping with wood and draped white fabrics. Bathrooms are mini-oases with ferns and coral gravel,

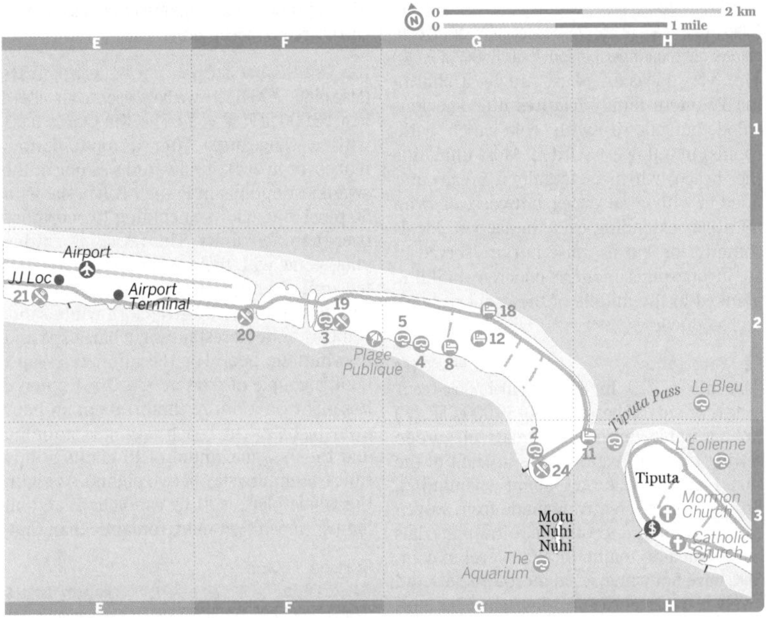

Avatoru & Tiputa

Sights

1 Gauguin's Pearl C2

Activities, Courses & Tours

2 Rangiroa Plongée G3
3 Six Passengers F2
4 Topdive G2
5 Y'aka Plongée G2

Sleeping

6 Chez Cécile C2
7 Chez Loyna B1
8 Kia Ora Resort & Spa G2
9 Le Maitai Rangiroa D2
10 Le Merou Bleu A1
11 Les Relais de Josephine H3
12 Pension Bounty G2
13 Raira Lagon D2
14 Rangiroa Lodge B2
15 Tevahine Dream B2
16 Tuanake C2
17 Turiroa Village – chez Olga D2
18 Vahaui Paradis G2

Eating

Chez Obelix .... (see 17)
19 Heirani F2
Kia Ora Resort & Spa – Te Rairoa. (see 8)
20 Lagoon Grill F2
21 Le Kai Kai E2
Le Maitai Rangiroa – Le Lagon Bleu .... (see 9)
22 Ma'a Mika B2
23 Magasin Daniel A2
24 Moetua - Ohotu G3
25 Puna A2
Raira Lagon – Beach Raira .... (see 13)
26 Vaimario D2

Shopping

Arno .... (see 5)
Gauguin's Pearl .... (see 1)
27 Ikimasho C1

and the garden units, built of pine planks, have their own tiny pool. Norbert, the owner, will treat you with excellent Polynesian and Chinese dishes served in an appealing dining room overlooking the lagoon. The only downside is the lack of shade on the property. Prices include bikes and kayaks. Minimum stay of two nights. Cash only.

Chez Cécile PENSION $

(Map p156; ☎93 12 65; pensioncecile@mail.pf; bungalows half board per person 7500-8500 CFP; 📶) This very pleasant place run by a charming Paumotu family features nine spacious wood bungalows (with cold-water bathrooms) in a flowery garden. Most units line the 'beach', which is actually a breakwater filled in with coral gravel, but you can swim off a pier extending over the lagoon. Meals come in for warm praise but are served in an incongruous modern concrete building plonked in the middle of the property, with no lagoon views.

Le Merou Bleu PENSION $$

(Map p156; ☎79 16 82; www.merou-bleu.com; bungalows s/d half board 16,000/30,000 CFP; 📶) An agreeable option in a magical garden setting right on Avatoru Pass in front of the surf break (but forget about swimming). Bungalows are creatively made from woven coconut thatch and other natural materials but manage to maintain a fair level of comfort, have hot water, good mosquito nets and lovely terraces perfect for lounging. It's a bit isolated, but this actually adds to the charm, as does the friendliness of Sonya, the French owner from Alsace. The half-board option is a good deal as she's an adept cook, too. Enjoy your dinner in a traditional-style *fare* (dining room) opening onto the pass. Credit cards are not accepted.

Kia Ora Resort & Spa LUXURY HOTEL $$$

(Map p156; ☎93 11 11; www.hotelkiaora.com; villas d from 55,000 CFP; ❄📶🏊) The Kia Ora is back with a vengeance. After a top-to-bottom makeover in 2011, it now ranks as one of the swankiest options in French Polynesia, with 50 plush bungalows, including 10 enormous over-the-water units. The ravishing garden villas come with their own pool and are dotted around a magnificent coconut plantation situated on a fine li'l stretch of white sand. It incorporates a restaurant, a bar, a spa and a swimming pool. For the ultimate escape, book a couple of days at **Kia Ora Sauvage** Map p155), on Motu Avearahi, about an hour away by boat. The beach setting is stunning and there's a maximum of 10 guests at any time (minimum stay of two nights). At night, the whole place is lit by candlelight and oil lamps – it can't get more romantic than that.

Turiroa Village – Chez Olga BUNGALOW, DORM $

(Map p156; ☎96 04 27, 70 59 21; pension.turiroa@mail.pf; dm 2500 CFP, bungalows tr 10,500 CFP) Popular with budget-minded divers, this venture is a freakishly good deal for the Tuamotus. The airy, six-bed dorm with an ace location on the lagoon easily wins the heart of backpackers, while the four bungalows are modern, well appointed and can sleep three people. OK, there's no beach, but a pontoon gives you access to a swimming area, and kayaks are free. No meals are provided except breakfast (500 CFP) but you can whip up something in the clean guest kitchen, or you could head to Chez Obelix, which is a thong's throw away. Our only gripe: this place doesn't have the Polynesian character of some of the other pensions.

Raira Lagon HOTEL $$

(Map p156; ☎93 12 30; www.raira-lagon.pf; bungalows incl breakfast/half board per person from 11,600/13,700 CFP; ❄📶) A cross between a family-run place and a hotel, Raira Lagon is a reassuring choice with no surprises (good or bad) up its sleeves. It features 10 bungalows that meet modern standards. They're spread throughout a garden fringed by one of the better swimming areas on the atoll, and the more expensive ones come with a lagoon view. The restaurant balcony faces the lagoon and serves large, buffet-style breakfasts in lieu of the usual bread and coffee. Bonuses: free kayaks and snorkelling gear.

WHERE ARE THE BEACHES?

Let's be frank: high hopes of sweeping expanses of silky sand might be dashed upon arrival on Rangiroa. Although the atoll boasts clear, aquamarine water and a brochure-esque appeal, it's not a beach holiday destination, and swimming and sunbathing opportunities are scarce. You come here for the lagoon and the diving, less so for the beach. While most accommodation options are right on the lagoon, nearly none have sandy beaches. That said, they usually do have plenty of coral and good snorkelling, just steps from your bungalow, which provides for some compensation. You can also work your tan on the public beach or sign up for an excursion to Lagon Bleu or Île aux Récifs, which are blessed with superb sandy areas.

If lazing on a beach is your priority, be sure to make a trip to Tikehau or Fakarava – both have lovely strips of coral sand edging the lagoon.

Chez Loyna PENSION $
(Map p156; ☎96 82 09, 29 90 30; www.pensionloyna.com; r/bungalows half board per person 6500/7500 CFP; 📶) Although it's not directly beside the lagoon, this venture popular with unfussy divers is a bargain, with three modest yet clean rooms with bathroom (hot water) and a handful of larger bungalows out the back. Food here is a definite plus, with generous meals using local ingredients. Tuna carpaccio? More please.

Tuanake PENSION $$
(Map p156; ☎96 03 52; www.tuanake.pf; bungalows s/d half board 10,500/16,800 CFP; 📶) Under new management that was doing a good job of revitalising this pleasant place when we visited, Tuanake is a haven of peace set in a coconut plantation on the coral gravel–lined lagoon. Some bungalows (with hot-water showers) show some signs of wear and tear (there are plans to renovate them) but the congenial atmosphere and excellent cuisine more than make up for this. Bikes are free.

Le Maitai Rangiroa HOTEL $$$
(Map p156; ☎93 13 50; www.hotelmaitai.com; bungalows d incl breakfast from 26,000 CFP; ❄📶) This midrange hotel has undergone quite a few sprucings, and they've all been for the better. The 38 bungalows are tightly packed on a small property, but otherwise it's well run and serviceable. The six units that are right on the lagoon are a better option and well worth the extra bucks. Bar a small sunbathing patch of crushed coral, Le Maitai doesn't have any beach (the shoreline is craggy) nor a swimming pool, but there's a pontoon with lagoon access. The on-site restaurant is a plus.

Vahaui Paradis BUNGALOW $
(Map p156; ☎96 02 40, 74 29 56; arorii@mail.pf; bungalows d incl breakfast 11,000-12,000 CFP; 📶) Hats off to the owners: they dared build this venture directly on the ocean side of the atoll – this is the only place in the Tuamotus with such a location. Pros: crashing waves, exposed reef, prevailing winds. Cons: crashing waves, exposed reef, prevailing winds. The large, fully equipped Fare Arenui has a floor of crushed coral and is just steps from the reef, thus proffering unobstructed ocean views, while the Fare Tinihau – a refurbished bungalow from hotel Kia Ora – is slightly set back from the shore. They're both large, comfy and cheery. The coral shelf is very high here and much of the reef is exposed at low tide; for a dip, head to the public beach which is just a few minutes' walk away.

Pension Bounty PENSION $$
(Map p156; ☎96 05 22; www.pension-bounty.com; s/d incl breakfast 12,500/17,000 CFP; 📶) Lodging here is in four adjoining rooms rather than bungalows, but these are well scrubbed and modern, and have mosquito screens and hot water. They're slightly claustrophobic and the decor is more motel than boutique but the whole place is kept shipshape and the French hosts are helpful. One downside to staying at Bounty, though, is the lack of lagoon vistas available at most of the other pensions, but a coral path leads to a small beach beside the Kia Ora Resort & Spa, a coconut's throw from the pension. Dinner is available (add 3500 CFP per person) but you also have your own equipped kitchen. English, Spanish and Italian are spoken.

Les Relais de Josephine PENSION $$
(Map p156; ☎96 02 00; http://relaisjosephine.free.fr; bungalows half board per person from 16,000 CFP; 📶) The setting of this very French interpretation of the Polynesian pension, in full view of the dancing dolphins on Tiputa Pass, is arguably the prettiest on the atoll. Lounging on the deck here is a truly decadent experience, as is dining on the elegant French-style food made from local ingredients. That said, there's no beach, no pool and no swimming access. The seven bungalows are decked out in minimalist colonial-style elegance but are not luxurious. The three garden units are a tad sombre; try and get a pass-facing bungalow if you can. Couples, take note: some front walls don't make it to the ceilings (good for natural ventilation, less so for privacy).

Rangiroa Lodge GUESTHOUSE, CAMPGROUND $
(Map p156; ☎20 09 22; www.rangiroalodge.com; campsite per person 1400 CFP, dm 2800 CFP, d with/without bathroom incl breakfast 7100/6100 CFP; 📶) This no-frills backpackers is housed in a ramshackle building at the entrance of Avatoru village. The six shoebox-sized rooms are spartan and stifling hot during the day, but that's not why folks – mostly cash-strapped divers – come here. They come for cheap beds and easy access to conveniences. If you're into that (and not fancy bungalows) this is an acceptable option. It also takes campers. The ablution block is in good nick and there's a communal kitchen. The best part of the 'lodge' is the spiffing lagoonside location, with good snorkelling just steps away.

Eating & Drinking

Most visitors opt for half board at their hotel or pension but there are also a few good independent eating options. Be sure to notify your pension that morning if you plan to eat elsewhere for dinner. Avatoru has a few supermarkets; they generally open Monday to Saturday, and close for lunch.

Raira Lagon – Beach Raira HOTEL RESTAURANT **$**

(Map p156; ☎93 12 30; mains 1600 CFP, set menu 3500 CFP; ⏲breakfast, lunch & dinner) Breakfast attracts mostly hotel guests, but the alfresco restaurant has been positioned as an independent restaurant to attract both guests and nonguests for lunch and dinner. Lunch is a good bet if you need to recharge the batteries post-diving, or are just looking for a good meal in a friendly spot blessed with cracking lagoon views. Chow down on a thick fish burger or a succulent tuna carpaccio with pesto sauce, but be sure to leave room for the devilish homemade *flan coco* (a custard-like dessert flavoured with coconut). Brilliant value.

Ma'a Mika SNACK **$**

(Map p156; ☎34 91 71; mains 500-1300 CFP, set menu 2000 CFP; ⏲9am-6pm Wed-Mon) Formerly a chef at Le Maitai Rangiroa, Mika decided to open this eatery along the main road in Avatoru. Snacking at its best, with a shortlist of palate pleasers: fish burger, catch of the day, savoury pies. The best part? Everything's under 1300 CFP, and the set menu, at 2000 CFP, is a steal. If only Ma'a Mika had a lagoonside setting!

Lagoon Grill RESTAURANT **$$**

(Map p156; ☎96 04 10; mains 1600-3500 CFP; ⏲lunch & dinner Wed-Mon) The well-respected Lagoon Grill is a terrific spot for a lagoonside meal, with alfresco tables under large shade trees. Carnivores, you'll find nirvana here: this place majors in flawlessly cooked grilled beef rib (word to wise: order your meat bloody or rare), *magret de canard* (duck breast) and *andouillettes* (chitterlings). It also offers a good selection of seafood dishes. Offers pick-up service at dinner. And oh, that view!

Moetua – Ohotu SNACK **$**

(Map p156; ☎78 30 38; mains 1000-1400 CFP; ⏲lunch Mon-Sat) Talk about location! The dining deck of this buzzing *snack* (snack bar) at the eastern tip of Avatoru is on the lagoon, literally. The menu concentrates on simply prepared fish and meat dishes served in generous portions. Sandwiches (from 400 CFP), burgers and salads are also available. It's a good place to catch local vibes and enjoy plenty of local colour.

Kia Ora Resort & Spa – Te Rairoa HOTEL RESTAURANT **$$**

(Map p156; ☎93 11 11; mains 1500-3300 CFP; ⏲breakfast, lunch & dinner) As fancy as Rangiroan cuisine gets. The overwater restaurant is lovely. Here the chef prepares gourmet international food, combining fresh seafood and meat with delicious sauces and flavours. Finish up with a poolside martini.

Le Maitai Rangiroa – Le Lagon Bleu RESTAURANT **$$**

(Map p156; ☎93 13 50; mains 1500-3000 CFP; ⏲breakfast, lunch & dinner) Familiar French fare with a local twist – salads, fish and meat dishes – won't inspire devotion, but the atmosphere is relaxed and the tropical decor appealing. Breakfast is a lavish buffet (2500 CFP).

Puna SNACK **$**

(Map p156; ☎73 76 10; mains 400-2000 CFP; ⏲lunch & dinner Tue-Sun) A local favourite that serves excellent, fresh food in massive portions. Light eaters can order single fish brochettes (400 CFP each) or big side orders of salad, fries and more. For dessert try hot delicious *gaufres* (Belgian-style waffles; from 400 CFP) with a choice of sweet toppings. At the marina.

CORAL WINE

A vineyard? On an atoll? Surreal but true. Vin de Tahiti has a 20-hectare vineyard planted on a palm-fringed *motu* about 10 minutes by boat from Avatoru village. This is the only atoll vineyard in the world, making the only wines produced from coral soil. It produces coral white wine, dry white and rosé. Since October 2010 the wine has been made using the principles of biodynamic agriculture. Vin de Tahiti should be awarded organic certification by the time you read this. Wanna sample a glass (or two)? Most restaurants on the atoll have it, and it's also on sale at the supermarkets.

For more on Vin de Tahiti's history go to www.vindetahiti.pf.

Le Kai Kai RESTAURANT $
(Map p156; ☎96 03 39; mains 1200-2600 CFP; ⏰lunch & dinner Fri-Wed) A French garden restaurant along the main road (no views). Beautifully grilled fresh tuna, *mahi mahi* (dorado) and meat specialities are embellished with flavours such as orange and ginger, and then dished up with a medley of vegetables. Transfers from your pension or hotel are free. Credit cards are not accepted.

Vaimario RESTAURANT $$
(Map p156; ☎96 05 96; mains 1400-3000 CFP; ⏰closed Wed & lunch Sat) The extensive menu takes in seafood, meat and pizza and combines French tradition with an eye to local flavours. The irresistible *crêpe au miel de Rangiroa* (pancake with local honey) will finish you off sweetly. The weak point is its unassuming position along the road, with no sea views. Free transfers are offered (at dinner only) and there's a decent wine list and spirits.

Heirani RESTAURANT $
(Map p156; ☎28 65 61; mains 1100-2000 CFP; ⏰lunch Tue-Sun, dinner Tue-Sat) Wholly unpretentious and bearing not an ounce of belaboured design, this popular locale next to the Six Passengers dive centre whips up cheap eats that make the perfect lunch on a budget. The chow mien, salads and grilled fish are excellent.

Chez Obelix RESTAURANT $$
(Map p156; ☎96 02 07; mains 1600-2000 CFP; ⏰lunch & dinner Wed-Mon) Although there's nothing out of the ordinary on the menu and the roadside setting isn't spectacular, travellers and locals rave about the well-prepared food here. Daily specials include steaks and grilled fish served with rice or vegetables. It's closed for several months of the year.

Magasin Daniel SUPERMARKET
(Map p156; ⏰closed 11.45am-2.30pm) The best of Avatoru's supermarkets is near the post office in Avatoru.

Shopping

Arno HANDICRAFTS
(Map p156; ☎96 02 41; ⏰10am-6pm) A good find. Arno is renowned for its high-quality earth paintings that represent traditional designs. It also sells shirts as well as shell necklaces and bracelets. It's just behind Y'aka Plongée.

Gauguin's Pearl JEWELLERY
(Map p156; ☎93 11 30; www.gauguinspearl.com; ⏰8am-5pm Mon-Fri, 9am-noon & 3-5pm Sat) Has an excellent selection of set and loose pearls directly from the pearl farm (p154), which is on the premises. Employs professional, English-speaking staff. You can be picked up for free from your place of lodging.

Ikimasho JEWELLERY
(Map p156; ☎96 03 91; http://ikimasho-black-pearls.com; ⏰9am-5pm Mon-Sat) Has an interesting selection of creative local jewellery, including earrings, necklaces, pendants and rings, some of which are made of pearl and bone. In Avatoru village.

Information

Note that there are only two ATMs on Rangiroa – one in Avatoru and one in Tiputa.

Banque de Tahiti (☎96 85 52; Avatoru; ⏰8-11am Mon, Tue, Fri & Sat, 1-4pm Mon & Fri) Currency exchange.

Banque Socredo (☎96 85 63; Avatoru; ⏰7.30-11.30am & 1.30-4pm Mon, Wed & Fri, 1.30-4pm Tue & Thu) Currency exchange. Has a 24-hour ATM.

Centre Médical d'Avatoru (☎96 03 75; ⏰7.30am-3.30pm Mon-Fri) Medical centre. There are also two private doctors in Avatoru.

Chez Obelix (per hr 1000 CFP; ⏰lunch & dinner Wed-Mon) Internet access.

Gendarmerie (police station; ☎96 73 61)

Le Kai Kai (per hr 700 CFP; ⏰Fri-Wed, no set hours) Internet access.

Pharmacy (Avatoru; ⏰7am-12.30pm & 2.30-6.30pm Mon-Sat, 10.30am-12.30pm Sun)

Post office Avatoru (OPT; ⏰7am-3pm Mon-Thu, 7am-2pm Fri; wi-fi) Internet and wi-fi access (with the Manaspot network); Tiputa (OPT; ⏰7am-12.30pm Mon-Thu, to 11.30am Fri) Has a 24-hour ATM.

Six Passengers (per hr 500 CFP; ⏰8am-noon & 2-5pm; wi-fi) This dive shop offers internet and wi-fi access (with the Iaoranet network).

Getting There & Away

AIR The airport is smack in between Avatoru (to the west) and Tiputa (to the east). **Air Tahiti** (☎93 14 00, 86 42 42; www.airtahiti.pf) offers two to three flights daily between Pape'ete and Rangiroa (one hour, 19,000 CFP). Rangiroa is also connected by air to Bora Bora and other atolls in the Tuamotus. One-way fares on offer include Bora Bora–Rangiroa 26,000 CFP, Rangiroa–Tikehau 7500 CFP, Rangiroa–Fakarava 7500 CFP and Rangiroa–Mataiva 7500 CFP (see p248 for more details).

BOAT The *Dory, Mareva Nui* and *Saint-Xavier Maris-Stella* are the only cargo ships serving Rangiroa that take passengers, besides the *Aranui*, which stops on Rangiroa on its way back from the Marquesas.

For details, see p250.

Getting Around

A sealed road runs the 10km from Avatoru village at the western end of the string of islets to the Tiputa Pass, at the eastern extremity. There's no public transport on Rangiroa, but there's a rather casual approach to hitchhiking (which is never entirely safe, although you'd be unlikely to run into problems on Rangiroa): if you're walking along in the hot sun, someone will often stop and offer you a ride.

To/From the Airport

If you have booked accommodation, your hosts will be at the airport to welcome you. If your pension is near the hotel, transfers will probably be free; places further away tend to charge (ask when you book).

Bike, Car & Scooter Hire

The easiest way to get around is to hire a bicycle or a scooter, but keep in mind that the road is not lit at night. Car hire is also available.

Arenahio Location (☎96 82 45) Hires out cars/scooters/bicycles for 8500/5500/1300 CFP for a full day. Credit cards are accepted.

JJ Loc (☎27 57 82) Offers bikes/scooters for 1400/5500 CFP for a full day.

Rangi Rent a Car (☎96 03 28) Car hire from 6500 CFP per day.

Boat

Manu Taxi Boat (☎78 13 25) offers a shuttle service between Ohotu wharf and Tiputa village for 500 CFP return; taking a bicycle over costs 500 CFP extra.

TIKEHAU

POP 407

Tikehau is a joy. Its unparalleled beauty, endless coral beaches and low-key yet reasonably developed tourist infrastructure make it a real charmer. Time has eroded the ring of coral into sweeping, twisting *motu* of white and pink sands that engulf little bays, craggy nooks and the vivid turquoise lagoon. Idyllic picnic spots abound and the atoll's secluded shores are some of the best in the Tuamotus for lounging, loafing and lollygagging. And unlike on Rangiroa, you don't have to travel far to find that perfect strip of strand. Below the turquoise waters, a vast living world beckons divers of all levels.

Sights

Tuherahera VILLAGE

Most islanders live in Tuherahera, in the southwest of the atoll. Find peace in this pretty village, bursting with *uru* (breadfruit), coconut trees, bougainvillea and hibiscus. There is an uncommon variety of faiths including Catholic, Sanito, Seventh Day Adventist and Protestant, all of which have their own church. It's easy to cycle your way around – follow the dirt track that skirts the picturesque ocean side of the *motu* until the airstrip and pedal back to the village taking the lagoonside road.

Fancy a dip? Head to one of Tuherahera's coral **beaches**. The best one lies east of the village, near the airstrip, and is lined by several pensions. The sand is wide and the waters are calm and translucent. Another beauty lies at the western tip of the village; this strip is lapped by a glassy turquoise *hoa* and has pinkish sands.

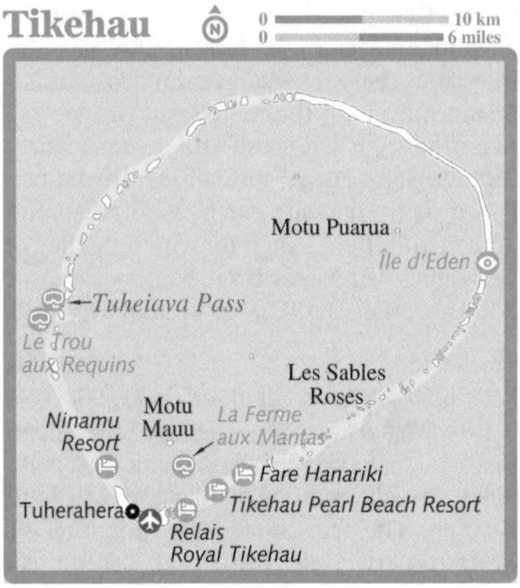

Les Sables Roses BEACHES

(Pink Sands) Southeast of the atoll the shores are fringed with truly amazing 'Pink Sands Beaches' that really do glow a light shade of pink, a result of finely pulverised coral.

Motu Puarua NATURAL SITE

(Île aux Oiseaux, Bird Island) Lying almost in the middle of the lagoon, the rocky Motu Puarua hosts several species of ground-nesting birds including brown noddies and *uaau* (red-footed boobies) that can easily be approached.

Île d'Eden FARM

(Eden Island) It's hard to describe Île d'Eden. It's not a traditional tourist site per se, but a working farm operated by a handful of families belonging to the Church of the New Testament. They have created a vibrant, organic garden in the infertile sands of their superb *motu*. Most visitors to Île d'Eden arrive on an organised tour, usually in combination with Motu Puarua and Les Sables Roses.

Activities

Diving & Snorkelling

On the diving scene, Tikehau seems to play second fiddle to the better-marketed Rangiroa or Fakarava. But, after having checked out several dive sites here, we say: injustice! The extraordinary Tuheiava Pass, to the west of the atoll, about 30 minutes by boat from Tuherahera village, is an unspoilt underwater idyll teeming with all sorts of fish and marine life; see p36 for details about sites. Inside the lagoon, La Ferme aux Mantas is another killer site.

Topdive DIVING, SNORKELLING
(☎96 22 40, 96 23 00; www.topdive.com) This respected dive centre is based at Tikehau Pearl Beach Resort, but transfers from most pensions can be arranged. A small yet well-organised dive outfit, it has introductory dives (9000 CFP), single dives (7800 CFP), two-tank dives (15,000 CFP) and six-/10-dive packages (37,500/70,000 CFP). At most dive sites, snorkelling is also possible.

Lagoon Excursions

The easiest way to get a broad look at the delights around the lagoon is to take a one-day tour. All pensions and hotels can organise excursions, sometimes through an outside operator, and trips cost from 7500 CFP per person. They usually take in La Ferme aux Mantas, Motu Puarua and Île d'Eden, and include a barbecue picnic on one of many paradisiacal *motu* dotted along the Sables Roses.

DON'T MISS

LA FERME AUX MANTAS

Every morning or so, several manta rays (up to eight individuals) congregate around a lagoon site aptly named 'La Ferme' – there was a pearl farm here before – in order to be cleaned by wrasses that feed on parasites from the mantas' wings. Snorkellers and divers can easily approach these majestic creatures in less than 8m of waters. One downside: as the sea floor is sandy, the water clarity is not exceptional – underwater photographers may be disappointed. Most lagoon tours stop here on their way to Motu Puarua. Blue Nui offers dives to this site on a regular basis. Note that it's not a zoo and sightings can't be guaranteed.

Sleeping

Unless otherwise noted, prices quoted include transfers to the airport. All places bar one accept credit cards.

TUHERAHERA VILLAGE & AROUND

Options here are near the village and airport and are lined up along the lagoon side of the *motu*.

Hotu PENSION $
(☎96 22 89; www.pensionhotu.com; bungalows half board per person 9500 CFP; Wi-Fi) Deservedly popular and occupying a divine stretch of sand, Hotu is a great place to enjoy the coral beach in low-key surroundings. It features five fan-cooled bungalows with private facilities (hot showers that are heated with solar energy); they're teeny but have a little more artistic flair than the others in this price bracket, via hand-painted *pareu* (like sarongs) on the walls and cool coral and wood decoration. Kayaks and bikes are available for hire (500 CFP for the duration of your stay). Fishing trips can be organised.

Tikehau Village PENSION $$
(☎96 22 86, 76 67 85; www.tikehauvillage.com; bungalows s/d half board 13,000/20,000 CFP; Wi-Fi) You can't argue with the location. It's right on the beach, so your biggest worry is tracking sand into your bungalow. Beautiful views are augmented by well-appointed bungalows that come decorated with local wood, coconut-palm fronds and coral stonework – plus the bathrooms have hot water. The shady terraces look out over white-sand and turquoise-lagoon bliss. There are kayaks and bikes for guests' use. Some English is spoken.

Chez Justine PENSION, CAMPGROUND $
(☎96 22 87, 72 02 44; campsite for 2 persons incl breakfast 4000 CFP, bungalows half board per person 8000 CFP; @Wi-Fi) This family-run pension is a reliable abode. Ask for one of the three big beachfront bungalows here, which cost the same as the four basic, humbly furnished rooms tucked away behind. They all feel a little past their prime on the inside, but they are clean and the location, on a wide sandy beach lapped by topaz waters, is divine. Note

that bathrooms have cold-water showers. Campers can pitch tents on a sandy, shady plot just 10m from the lagoon – bliss! Kayaks and bikes are complimentary.

PRIVATE MOTU

TOP CHOICE **Ninamu Resort** RESORT **$$$**
(☎73 78 10; www.motuninamu.com; bungalows full board per person 30,000 CFP; 📶) Anchored on a private white- and pink-sand *motu* a 10-minute boat ride from the village, this Australian-run venture is the kind of haven stressed-out city slickers dream about. The massive bungalows are built from gnarled hunks of wood, coral stonework and coconut thatch, and the restaurant is another Crusoe-with-style masterpiece. The feel is much more of a private club than a resort here, with most things, from snorkelling equipment to use of the kayaks, being free. Prices also include daily excursions. There are only six units, which ensures intimacy. The ethos here is laid-back, ecological – everything is powered by wind and sun – and activity-oriented. Ninamu appeals to honeymooners, families and outdoorsy types in equal measures – a winning formula.

Tikehau Pearl Beach Resort RESORT **$$$**
(☎96 23 00; www.spmhotels.com; bungalows d from 59,000 CFP; ❄📶🏊) A hot favourite with Italian honeymooners, this intimate resort (there are only 38 units) boasts a stunning position between endless swathes of white- and pink-sand beaches and bright blue waters. Walk for hours along empty beaches, spend the day in the water or take off on one of many offered water activities. There are free shuttle boats to the village four times a day. The over-the-water suites offer the extra bonus of privacy and are so big and exquisitely designed that you might never want to leave your private dock. All options except the over-the-water standard bungalows have air-con. There's a dive centre on-site.

Relais Royal Tikehau PENSION **$$**
(☎96 23 37; www.royaltikehau.pf; s/d half board 16,000/26,000 CFP, bungalows s/d half board from 21,000/32,000 CFP; @📶) What a magical setting! This upscale pension sits on a secluded *motu* about a 20-minute walk across some shallow waterways to the village, meaning that you get a sense of exclusivity without feeling captive. The property is lapped by a glassy turquoise *hoa* on one side and fronted by a swath of pinkish sand on the other side. Bungalows are big and comfy, but perhaps a little overpriced for the simplicity of the furnishings and lack of air-conditioning. Rooms are much less exciting, and have neither the views nor the cooling breezes that the bungalows have. The whole place is run on solar and wind power. Free kayaks. Airport transfers are 1500 CFP per person return. Minimum stay of two nights.

Fare Hanariki BUNGALOWS **$$**
(☎21 69 33; farehanariki@mail.pf; bungalows full board per person 11,000 CFP; 📶) If you're looking to get away from it all, make a beeline for this lovely haven on an isolated *motu* a 10-minute boat ride from the village. It consists of four charmingly simple bungalows scattered amid a sprawling coconut grove. The whole *motu* is girdled with superb white-sand and pink-sand coral beaches. This is not a place for those looking to be pampered – air-con and hot showers are unknown – but for those who appreciate tropical charm and a laid-back atmosphere, look no further. Cash only.

Eating

Tikehau Village PENSION RESTAURANT **$$**
(☎96 22 86; set menu 2500-3500 CFP; ⏰lunch & dinner by reservation) The restaurant at the Tikehau Village is one of the prettiest spots around, overlooking the water with cool breezes and a social vibe – nonguests are welcome. The set menu is a bit pricey but it makes for a pleasant change from the standard fare served at most pensions. Lunch is cheaper than the evening version.

Snack Gilbert SNACK **$$**
(☎74 86 25; mains 1200-1300 CFP; ⏰lunch Mon-Sat by reservation) Lovely setting, right by a beach overlooking a turquoise *hoa* at the western end of the village. What to expect? Simple meals incorporating organic ingredients. Call ahead, as the eponymous Gilbert can be a little grumpy when people simply drop by unannounced.

Tikehau Pearl Beach Resort RESORT RESTAURANT **$$**
(☎96 23 00; mains 1300-3200 CFP; ⏰lunch daily) Call for the shuttle times to lunch at this swanky resort. Light meals are available, and you can enjoy the fabulous setting without breaking the bank.

Chez Cindy SNACK **$$**
(☎96 22 67; mains 1200-1400 CFP; ⏰lunch & dinner Sun-Fri) This modest eatery in the village serves massive portions of good *poisson cru* (raw fish), *steak frites* (steak and chips), chow mein and more.

Poeiti SNACK **$**
(mains 300-1000 CFP; ⏰Mon-Fri 7am-4pm) A tiny *snack* near Tikehau Village, where you can order a sandwich, steak and chips or fried chicken.

Information

There is no bank or ATM on Tikehau. There's wi-fi access (with the Hotspot network) near pensions Hotu and Chez Justine.

Getting There & Away

Tikehau lies 300km northeast of Tahiti and 14km north of Rangiroa.

AIR The airport is about 1km east of the village entrance. **Air Tahiti** (☎96 22 66, 86 42 42; www.airtahiti.pf) has daily flights between Pape'ete and Tikehau (18,500 CFP). There are also several weekly flights between Bora Bora and Tikehau (26,000 CFP), via Rangiroa. The Tikehau–Rangiroa flight costs 7500 CFP.

BOAT The *Mareva Nui* and *Saint-Xavier Maris-Stella* (p161) offer transport to Tikehau.

Getting Around

A 10km track goes around Tuherahera, and passes by the airport. Bicycles can be hired (1200 CFP per day) at your pension, or if you stay at Chez Justine they're free.

MATAIVA

POP 235

Like stepping into a time machine, this tiny, picturesque atoll is the sort of hideaway that you search for your whole life to discover. Despite the limited tourist infrastructure, it provides a delightful escape holiday and is becoming one of the more popular spots in the archipelago. There are superb coral beaches, numerous snorkelling spots, well-priced pensions, lots of fish and one of the few noteworthy archaeological sites in the Tuamotus.

The structure of the Mataiva lagoon gives it an unusual appearance: the coral heads create walls 50m to 300m wide that form about 70 basins with a maximum depth of 10m. Seen from the plane it looks like a mosaic of greens. Unforgettable.

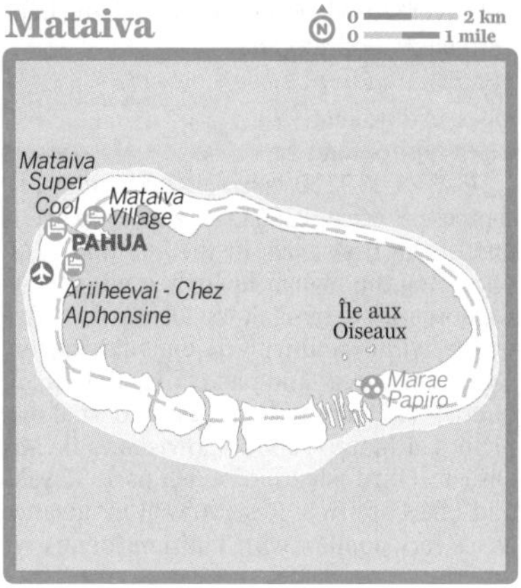

Sights & Activities

The village of **Pahua** is divided by a pass a few metres wide and no deeper than 1.5m, suitable only for very small boats. A bridge spans the pass and links the two parts of the village.

Don't miss the chance to help fishermen catch fish in one of the **fish parks** around the lagoon and the pass. Sorted, scaled and gutted, the fish are sold in the village.

In the south, along the edge of the lagoon, you'll find a series of appealing coral **beaches**. They're narrow but utterly secluded. The best **snorkelling** is in the channels near Marae Papiro, to the southeast of the lagoon.

Marae Papiro ARCHAEOLOGICAL SITE
Marae Papiro is a well-kept *marae* (traditional temple) on the edge of a *hoa*, about 14km from the village. In the centre of this *marae* you can see the stone seat from which, according to legend, the giant Tu guarded the pass against invasion.

Île aux Oiseaux NATURAL SITE
(Bird Island) To the east of the lagoon, a crescent-shaped coral spit covered in small shrubs is a favourite nesting place for *oio* (brown noddies), *tara* (great creasted terns) and red-footed boobies.

Tours

The pensions organise trips to the various sites by motor boat and by car, costing about 3000 CFP for the day, including a picnic.

Sleeping & Eating

The three pensions are in the village. Prices include airport transfers. Credit cards are not accepted. There are several small shops with basic food supplies.

TOP CHOICE **Ariiheevai – Chez Alphonsine** PENSION $
(☎76 73 23, 96 32 50; bungalows full board incl excursions per person 8500 CFP; ❄) This place is one of the best deals in the Tuamotus. Alphonsine, the owner, lovingly tends the six well-organised bungalows all on the edge of the white-sand-fringed emerald lagoon. The food is great and plenty of activities are offered, including flower-garland making, picnics at Marae Papiro and visits to Île aux Oiseaux (Bird Island) or a fish park. Kayaks and bikes are free. Reserve well in advance as it's very popular with Tahiti residents.

Mataiva Village PENSION, CAMPGROUND $
(☎96 32 95; campsite per person 1500 CFP, bungalows full board incl excursions per person 8500 CFP; ❄) Following Ariiheevai, Mataiva Village has embraced the same concept of an all-inclusive formula at bargain rates. That said, the location is a bit less appealing than at Ariihevai; the eight comfortable bungalows grace the pass but there's not really a beach. Kayaks and bikes are free if you stay in a bungalow; campers pay 500 CFP per day.

Mataiva Super Cool PENSION $
(☎96 32 53, 76 06 25; bungalows s/d half board incl excursions 7000/13,000 CFP) Overlooking the pass, this place has three well-organised bungalows with cold-water bathrooms and terraces. Kayaks and bikes are free. Add an extra 1500 CFP for lunch. Prices include a daily excursion.

Information

Bring stash of cash for there is no bank on the atoll. Pahua has a post office.

Getting There & Away

Mataiva is 350km northeast of Tahiti and 100km west of Rangiroa.

AIR There are two Pape'ete–Mataiva flights (18,500 CFP one way) a week, and one flight to/from Rangiroa (7500 CFP one way) with **Air Tahiti** (☎96 32 48, 86 42 42; www.airtahiti.pf).

BOAT Mataiva is on the routes of the *Mareva Nui* and *Saint-Xavier Maris-Stella* (p161).

Getting Around

A track goes almost all the way around the island through the middle of the coconut plantation for about 28km. Cycling is an excellent way of getting to Marae Papiro. You can hire a bicycle from pensions for about 1000 CFP per day.

FAKARAVA

POP 800

Welcome to paradise. One of the largest and most beautiful atolls in French Polynesia, Fakarava is the stuff of South Seas fantasy. Heavenly white and pink sand, ruffled coconut trees and an unbelievable palette of lagoon blues are the norm here. The atmosphere is supremely relaxed and the infrastructure is quite good, with an assortment of well-run pensions and a few swish options.

Garuae Pass, in the north of the atoll, is the widest pass in all of French Polynesia. There's also a second pass, Tumakohua in the far south, that the locals reckon is the most beautiful in the Tuamotus and it's hard not to agree. The atoll's particularly diverse ecosystem has made it a Unesco-protected area.

Fakarava is a great place to unwind, but for those looking for more than a suntan, it offers a number of high-energy distractions. The fantastic diving and snorkelling is legendary among divers, who come for a truly exhilarating experience in the two passes.

Whatever your inclination, one thing is sure: after several days here, you'll find it difficult to pack and leave.

Sights

TOP CHOICE **Les Sables Roses** NATURAL SITE
A double crescent of dreamy beaches split by a narrow spit of white-and-pink coral sands, Les Sables Roses seems to come right out of central casting for tropical ideals. The turquoise water laps both sides of the sandy strip and there's only one boat: yours. It's perfect for relaxing, swimming and evening up your sunburn. It's near the southernmost tip of the atoll, not far from Tetamanu, and is reached only on lagoon-excursion boats.

Lagon Bleu (Motu Tehatea) NATURAL SITE
Simply divine. Near the northwestern corner of Fakarava, Lagon Bleu features an indescribably lovely stretch of white-sand coral beach, turquoise-blue water, palm trees leaning over the shore – and not a soul in sight. Twitchers are sure to get a buzz too – there are a number of desirable new ticks for their list, including two endemic species: the atoll fruit dove and the Tuamotu reed warbler. Seabirds, notably noddies and frigate birds, can also easily be spotted here.

You'll need to take a boat tour to get to Lagon Bleu. One proviso: it's usually *nono* (gnat)-infested.

WORTH A TRIP

MAKEMO

Spectacular undersea landscapes, pristine *motu* and an off-the-beaten-track charm make Makemo an ideal destination for anyone looking for an authentic Paumotu experience or seeking an escape from the modern world. **Pouheva** village is an administrative and school centre for the central Tuamotus. The church and the lighthouse near the pass are the only sights of significance.

Makemo is the place to go for unspoilt scuba diving. The waters are pristine and prized for the effort required to get there. **Scuba Makemo** (98 03 19, 78 49 13; makemodive@mail.pf) is run by Ludovic, a French instructor who's been conducting dives in the Tuamotus for more than 15 years. Prices are among the cheapest in French Polynesia; count on 6000 CFP for an introductory dive, 5400 CFP for a single dive, 13,000 for a two-tank dive at a remote site and 25,500/48,000 CFP for a five/10-dive package. See p37 for details about dive sites. He also runs **Relais Scuba Makemo** (98 03 19, 78 49 13; makemodive@mail.pf; bungalow half board per person 7000 CFP), which comprises three lagoon-facing bungalows on the outskirts of the village. You'll eat with the family; meals are local-style and tasty. Makemo has another pension, **Teanuanua Beach Pearls** (77 12 09, 98 02 18; bungalow s/d full board 8400/11,600 CFP), which is 24km from the village, completely isolated. Both pensions can organise lagoon tours and picnics on one of many idyllic *motu*.

Tempted? Contact **Air Tahiti** (86 42 42; www.airtahiti.pf), which has three weekly flights to Makemo (46,000 CFP return) or, if you're adventurous, embark on the *Kura Ora* cargo ship (see p250 for boat transport details).

Rotoava VILLAGE

Most islanders live in Rotoava village at the northeastern end of the atoll, 4km east of the airport. Aside from Rangiroa's Avatoru, this is the most developed and busiest town in the Tuamotus but it's still pretty quiet by most people's standards. With only a few streets, a couple of churches and grocery stores, a bakery and a school, it's easy to explore. Behind Relais Marama, on the ocean side, the **Phare de Taputavaka** is worth a gander. This pyramid-shaped lighthouse built of stones is one of the oldest in French Polynesia, said to be more than 80 years old.

Ancien Phare de Topaka LIGHTHOUSE

This photogenic 15m-tall grey turret (dating from 1957) looks as if it's on loan from a medieval castle. The lighthouse is no longer in operation. To get here, follow the road to the airport and look for PK2.5 *(point kilométrique)*, from where a dirt track leads to the lighthouse.

Marae Tahiri Vairau ARCHAEOLOGICAL SITE, BEACH

This partly restored *marae* built of coral slabs sits beside a lovely strip of coral sand, about 300m past Plage du PK9. The beach offers shimmering waters and is great for sunbathing, picnicking, swimming and snorkelling.

PK10.5 NATURAL SITE

The PK10.5 marks the end of the dirt road, just on the edge of the phenomenal **Garuae Pass**. By incoming or outgoing current, the pass gets really rough, with waves than can easily exceed 2m in the middle of the pass.

Tetamanu VILLAGE

A handful of inhabitants also live in Tetamanu village, a tiny settlement on the edge of **Tumakohua Pass**, which is as backwater as backwater gets. It has a cute coral **chapel** built in the 19th century and an old **graveyard** with coral tombstones.

Activities

Diving & Snorkelling

Rangiroa, watch your back! The underwater wonders of **Garuae Pass** (also known as 'Northern Pass') and **Tumakohua Pass** (also known as 'Southern Pass') are now firmly on the map in diving circles (for details, see p36). Divers can't gush enough superlatives about the fabulous array of fish life, especially grey sharks, blacktip sharks, manta rays, tuna and barracuda, that can be found in both passes. Good news for novice divers: most sites are accessible with an Open Water certificate. Another draw is the coral, which is much healthier than on Rangiroa. The catch? The two passes are 60km away

DON'T MISS

PLAGE DU PK9

A bit of a local's secret, **Plage du PK9** is – you guessed it – 9km northwest of Rotoava (go past the airport and follow the dirt track towards the northern pass; at the PK9 marker, take the path to the left). Tan junkies will rejoice: it's a thin, laid-back, postcard-perfect stretch of white coral sand backed by palms and lapped by calm, sparkling turquoise waters. It's equally good for sunning and swimming and there's excellent snorkelling not far offshore. Bring a picnic and plenty of water.

from one another, which makes logistics a bit tricky if you want to dive the two passes in a limited period of time. If you're based in or near Rotoava, day trips to the Southern Pass are organised on a regular basis by the local dive shops but they're weather-dependent and require a minimum of divers. Check what is planned closer to the time of your visit. Recommended operators are listed below.

Fakarava Diving Center DIVING
(☎93 40 75, 73 38 22; www.fakarava-diving-center.com) In Rotoava, this husband-and-wife team specialises in small groups (maximum five people). Prices are very reasonable: 7000 CFP for an introductory dive, 6500 CFP for a single dive and 18,000 CFP for a day trip to Tumakohua Pass (including two dives and lunch). Book early as there's only one boat.

Tetamanu Diving by Eleuthera DIVING
(☎77 65 68, 77 10 06; www.dive-tahiti.com) At Tetamanu Village, this outfit offers the full slate of diving adventures, including introductory dives (6100 CFP), single dives (6100 CFP), courses and packages. It specialises in diving the Tumakohua Pass, which is only two minutes away by boat. Free pick-ups can be arranged from Motu Aito Paradise and Raimiti.

Topdive DIVING
(☎98 42 50, 29 22 32; www.topdive.com) This reputable outfit in Rotoava also has an annex on a *motu* near Motu Aito Paradise. It offers introductory dives (from 8500 CFP), one-/two-tank dives (8500/15,500 CFP) and dive passes (43,000/70,000 CFP for six/10 dives). Day trips to Tumakohua Pass cost 23,000 CFP including lunch.

Lagoon excursions

As in Rangiroa, here organised tours are the only way of exploring the idyllic, remote spots on the lagoon, including Lagon Bleu, Tetamanu (if you're based in the north) and Les Sables Roses. Usually a minimum of four to six people is required.

Half-/full-day trips to Lagon Bleu cost around 7000/8500 CFP. A full day excursion taking in Les Sables Roses, Tetamanu and a snorkelling stop in the southern pass usually costs 12,000 CFP, including a barbecued lunch at Les Sables Roses. All bookings can be made through your hotel or pension. Transfers are provided.

Note that it's at least a 90-minute boat ride to get to the southern sites from Rotoava. For Lagon Bleu, it takes about 30 minutes by boat from Rotoava.

Sleeping

ROTOAVA & AROUND

A couple of places are in the village; the others are to the south. Unless otherwise noted they accept credit cards and offer free airport transfers.

Havaiki Pearl Guesthouse PENSION $$
(☎93 40 15, 74 16 16; www.havaiki.com; bungalows s/d half board from 13,000/20,000 CFP; wi-fi) On the southern end of the village, this is the liveliest pension on Fakarava and the ambience is like a small hotel. The beachfront bungalows are very simple wooden structures that feel a tad hanky-sized but they're all well decorated with local fabrics, have good mosquito nets and offer a lovely lagoon frontage. If you're seeking space, opt for the two-bedroom garden units, which are built on stilts (nice views). All are equipped with private bathrooms (with 'tepid' water, as the owner puts it). Good English is spoken and airport transfers cost 2000 CFP return. Bikes and kayaks are free. There's a three-night minimum stay. Cash only.

Relais Marama BUNGALOWS, CAMPGROUND $
(☎98 42 51, 76 12 29; www.relais-marama.com; campsite incl breakfast per person 2600 CFP, bungalow with shared bathroom per person incl breakfast 6000 CFP; @ wi-fi) On the ocean side of the *motu* at Rotoava (no beach), behind the *mairie* (town hall), this backpackerlike option has all the hallmarks of a great deal; eight basic but immaculate bungalows in a verdant compound, two well-scrubbed ablution blocks (with cold water), a tranquil

location and a tab that won't burn a hole in your pocket. The bungalows are well spaced out and catch lots of breeze. All prices include breakfast and for other meals you can use the tip-top communal kitchen, go to nearby eateries or have a meal delivered to the Relais. Campers share the same facilities as the bungalows. There's a fee of 1000 CFP for internet and wi-fi access (valid for the length of your stay). Bikes are free.

Tokerau Village PENSION **$$**

(☎98 41 09, 70 82 19; www.tokerau-village.com; bungalows s/d half board 12,600/23,400 CFP; wi-fi) This is one of the most comfortable pensions on Fakarava. Flora the owner spends her days fine-tuning the garden and making sure there's not a speck of dust in any of the four well-proportioned, modern wood bungalows. Each unit has a big terrace, mosquito net and TV, but for the price you'd expect a fan. The food is creative, delicious and usually involves vegetables as well as fresh fish. If only the dining room was positioned near the lagoon, life would be perfect. Some English is spoken and the whole place runs on solar energy. Kayaks are free. Airport transfers are 2000 CFP return. It's 7km south of Rotoava.

Paparara PENSION **$$**

(☎98 42 66; www.fakarava-divelodge.com; bungalows half board s 9500-12,600 CFP, d 17,000-21,000 CFP) You have two options here: one of two small and basic *fare* that are right on the water and share a cold-water bathroom (ask for the 'Robinson' unit, which is as cosy as a bird's nest), or four better equipped beachside bungalows with private bathrooms. A big hit with divers, and the food here is good, plentiful and eaten family-style. It's 7km south of Rotoava.

Vaiama Village PENSION **$$**

(☎98 41 13, 70 81 99; www.fakaravavaiama.com; bungalows d half board 19,500 CFP; wi-fi) One basic two-storey house sleeps five people while three smaller and prettier coconut-thatch bungalows sleep two. All have attached bathrooms with coral-gravel floors and big ferns for a tropical-oasis effect. The beach is only so-so but there's a pontoon and good snorkelling out the front. There's a family atmosphere and airport transfers cost 1500 CFP return.

White Sand Beach Resort RESORT **$$$**

(☎93 41 50; www.whitesandfakarava.com; bungalows half board per person 16,000-23,000 CFP; air-con, internet, wi-fi) If you're looking for the classic Tuamotu setting, complete with shady palms, lagoon views and a splendid white stretch of sand just steps from your door, then this resort-style operation won't disappoint. With 30 spacious wooden bungalows, a restaurant and various activities on offer, this is the biggest and most up-market option on Fakarava. The beach is good and there's a picturesque, sunset-friendly pontoon with fabulous snorkelling options, but the hotel is understaffed, beds lack mosquito nets, the garden needs some TLC and some bungalows are in need of a lick of paint (or varnish). Note that only the Premium bungalows have air-con. Despite its shortcomings, it's not a bad deal considering the price and location. It's 7km south of Rotoava.

Kiria PENSION **$$**

(☎98 41 83, 73 41 12; www.pensionkiriafakarava.com; s/d bungalow half board 11,000/19,000 CFP) Each of the four bungalows here is made from coconut thatch and a variety of local materials – each is different from the others and pleasingly simple. The attached

BLACK PEARL, THE DECLINING JEWEL OF THE TUAMOTUS

Black Tahitian pearls were once the black gold of the Tuamotus. Though farming officially began in the 1960s, the industry didn't have the technology to make it viable till the 1980s. For the next decade and a half the world market price for these 'rare' pearls was so high that many farmers became ridiculously rich ridiculously fast. By the year 2000 so many farmers had begun mass-producing that the market became saturated and prices began to drop. With very little centralisation or government organisation, the future of pearling now looks bleak. (For more on the industry, see p215.)

The Tahitian pearls that are 'farmed' are cultured; a cultured pearl is created by an operation called a graft. This culturing process takes approximately four years from the time the first oyster spawn are collected to the harvest of those oysters' first pearls.

For more information on pearl grafting go to www.pearl-guide.com/tahitian-pearl-farming.shtml; for buying tips, see p63.

bathrooms are filled with ferns and the grounds are covered in coral gravel, which keeps the place especially tidy (and no sand in your bed); there's a fine ribbon of sand beyond the coral, however. The smiles of the owners stand out even by Paumotu standards. Airport transfers are 2000 CFP return. Kayaks are free. Cash only. It's about 8.5km south of Rotoava.

Veke Veke Village PENSION $$
(☎70 45 19; www.pension-fakarava.com; bungalows s/d half board 13,000/19,000 CFP; 📶) What an exquisite spot! Imagine a small, sandy bay fringed with coconut palms and lapped by turquoise waters. Choose between two family-sized semi-over-the-water bungalows or four smaller bungalows right on the beach. All options are on the old side but are generally well maintained. A real hit is the dining area with coral-gravel floor; it has beautiful sunset views over the lagoon. If you're serious about fishing, book here as the owner can arrange fishing outings. Airport transfers are 1000 CFP return. It's 4km south of Rotoava.

Fare Kohei BUNGALOWS $$
(☎28 89 26, 79 88 14; http://farekohei.jimdo.com; bungalow d 12,000 CFP) Opening in 2012, this venture sports a self-contained bungalow right in Rotoava village. It's nothing fancy but well managed and well priced, and it's conveniently close to shops, restaurants and dive centres.

TETAMANU & AROUND

At the other end of Fakarava, near Tumakohua Pass and a two-hour boat ride from the airport, is the village of Tetamanu (population: six).

TOP CHOICE **Raimiti** PENSION $$$
(☎71 07 63; www.raimiti.com; s/d bungalow full board for 2 nights from 54,000/99,000 CFP) Travellers in search of romance enthuse about this Crusoe-chic and very isolated spot with only nine units – five rustic but tastefully done-out lagoonside cabins constructed from local materials as well as four larger oceanside darkwood bungalows. Meals are excellent and are served either in a lagoonside, shell-fringed hut or under the stars. There's no electricity, but you'll come to love your oil lamps lighting the scene at night. Unfortunately Raimiti sits beside a rocky stretch of lagoon shoreline but there's good swimming and snorkelling out the front. Prices include excursions and transfers (be warned that it's an open boat, which can be uncomfortable in bad weather). Gay-friendly.

Motu Aito Paradise PENSION $$
(☎74 26 13; www.fakarava.org; bungalows full board per person 14,800 CFP) This pension is a feat of artistic ingenuity. The *motu* is really nothing special (and there's not even a proper beach), but the owners have built such beautiful coconut-thatch structures and planted enough flowers that they've transformed the land into something appealing. There's excellent snorkelling just offshore. The weak point is the food: some hungry divers have reported it lacks variety and quantity. Prices are for a three-night minimum stay and include daily excursions and airport transfers (be prepared to get wet if it's raining). Topdive (p168) has a dive base on a neighbouring *motu*. Cash only.

Tetamanu Village PENSION $$
(☎77 10 06; www.tetamanuvillage.pf; bungalows full board per person per 3/4/5 days 50,000/62,000/70,000 CFP) This place is a real heartbreaker. It sits on a paradisiacal *motu* overlooking the stunning Tumakohua Pass, with exceptionally healthy coral reefs just metres away, and comprises five local-style bungalows overlooking the lagoon and a delightful overwater dining room. An annex called **Tetamanu Sauvage** on a nearby *motu* connected to the 'Village' by a makeshift wooden bridge harbours another cluster of beachfront units. Alas, we've heard reports of irregular service, which can be worrisome in such a remote setting. Divers should ask for package room-and-scuba deals with the on-site dive centre.

Eating & Drinking

Otikao – Chez Anita SNACK $
(☎70 82 09; mains 1100-1300 CFP; ⏰lunch Mon-Sat by reservation) A very pleasant spot for lunch if you're cycling along the island – it's 1km south of White Sand Beach Resort and 8km south of Rotoava. Run by friendly Anita, this humble affair boasts an ace location right on the edge of the turquoise lagoon and whips up simple yet tasty meals. Bring your snorkelling gear: spectacular coral gardens beckon just offshore.

Havaiki Pearl Guesthouse PENSION RESTAURANT $$
(☎93 40 15; Rotoava; lunch 500-1500 CFP, dinner menu 3500 CFP; ⏰lunch daily, dinner by reservation) It's not right on the beach and

DON'T MISS

SNACK TE ANUANUA

You wouldn't necessarily expect to find a chic eatery in the modest village of Rotoava. But then there is **Snack Te Anuanua** (☎93 40 65; Rotoava; mains 1600-3500 CFP; ⏲lunch daily, dinner Wed-Sun), beating all the odds. A surprisingly hip open-air restaurant with swoon-worthy lagoon views, this culinary outpost specialises in *tartares* (raw meat or fish), grilled meat and fish dishes served in a variety of sauces, healthy salads and lip-smacking desserts. It's also the perfect venue for a sundowner. French owner Cecile speaks good English and can arrange free pick-up from all the pensions at the north of the island. Cash only.

the setting is frustratingly bland (think an oversized, tiled dining room with no lagoon view) but there's an appetising menu at dinner. Light meals and burgers are offered at lunch. The bar has a good selection of tipples available by the glass. Offers pick-up service.

White Sand Beach Resort – Kura Ora HOTEL RESTAURANT $$
(☎93 41 50; mains 1600-3500 CFP; ⏲breakfast, lunch & dinner) The gentle breezes waft in and the views across the lagoon are fantastic. The menu has some new twists on old island favourites and many dishes use organic ingredients. Unfortunately the food is hit-and-miss and the service sometimes amateurish. It's a cool spot where you can cut loose over some sunset cocktails, and there's live music at night on certain weekends.

Faka Faapu SELF-CATERING $
(☎32 56 78; Rotoava; ⏲7am-3pm Mon, Tue, Thu & Fri, 8am-noon Sun) For fruit and vegies, stop at this roadside stall, which has a selection of imported fruit and some other produce from around French Polynesia. It's across the street from Topdive.

Roulotte SNACK $
(Rotoava; mains 1000-1300 CFP; ⏲lunch Mon-Sat, dinner Tue-Sat) This modest eatery across the street from Topdive serves local plain fare such as chow mien and grilled tuna.

Getting There & Away

The atoll is 488km east-northeast of Tahiti.

AIR **Air Tahiti** (☎93 40 25, 86 42 42; www.airtahiti.pf) flies from Pape'ete to Fakarava every day (20,000 CFP one way), twice weekly from Fakarava to Rangiroa (7500 CFP), four times weekly from Rangiroa to Fakarava (7500 CFP) and once or twice weekly to/from Manihi (12,200 CFP).

BOAT The *Saint-Xavier Maris-Stella* and *Mareva Nui* (p161) stop at Fakarava and take passengers.

Getting Around

The airport is 4km west of Rotoava. A scheduled visit by former French president Jacques Chirac (he never actually showed up) brought funding to pave a 20km road from the airport to the southeast side of the atoll. From the airport, a dirt track goes as far as the edge of Garuae Pass, about 5.5km away to the west.

Faka Location (☎78 03 37) hires out bikes (2000 CFP per day) and scooters (8000 CFP per day).

Tetamanu is accessible by boat only.

MANIHI

POP 800

Considered the birthplace of the Tahitian pearl industry, Manihi is a classically gorgeous atoll with one deep pass in the southwest and great fishing. Since pearl prices began to plummet around 2000 (see p169), approximately 50 farms have gone out of business, but there's still a smattering of pearl farms dotted around the lagoon.

The atoll is 28km long and 8km wide. The best beaches and picnic spots are at the south of the lagoon where white sand, ruffled palms and sapphire waters make for the perfect escape. Swimming and sunbathing will be big on the daily checklist for most visitors, but energetic types can fill their holiday with diving, kayaking and snorkelling.

Sights

The not-very-pretty village of **Turipaoa** takes about five minutes to wander round, but is a good place to get a sense of atoll life. Manihi is now eclipsed by its quiet neighbour, Ahe, in terms of numbers of pearls produced, but it's still a great place to visit a **pearl farm** – ask at your accommodation.

Manihi

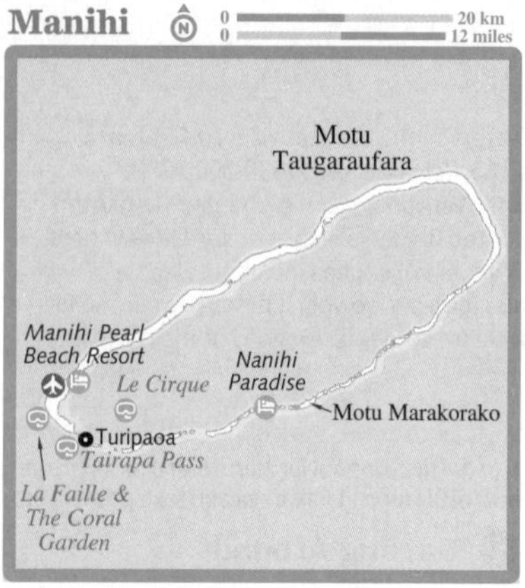

Activities

Diving & Snorkelling

The novice diver will find Manihi's waters fascinating and filled with life, but those who have travelled to other atolls might find that it compares unfavourably. That said, the sites near **Tairapa Pass** are excellent, as is **Le Cirque**, inside the lagoon, where manta rays can regularly be spotted. See p36 for details. The coral reefs and coral outcrops that are dotted around the lagoon are perfect for snorkelling.

Topdive DIVING
(☎96 42 17; www.topdive.com) Based at Manihi Pearl Beach Resort, this is the only dive outfit on the atoll. It has introductory dives (9000 CFP), single dives (7800 CFP), two-tank dives (15,000 CFP) and six-/10-dive packages (37,500/70,000 CFP).

Lagoon Excursions

All the places to stay can organise lagoon excursions, which include snorkelling stops and picnic lunch on a deserted *motu.*

Sleeping & Eating

Manihi Pearl Beach Resort RESORT $$$
(☎96 42 73; www.spmhotels.com; bungalows d from 48,000 CFP; ❄📶🏊) Embedded in a thick tropical garden near the airport, this well-run resort is the quintessential island sanctuary. It's one of the older establishments in the Tuamotus, and the atmosphere is more laid-back than sophisticated. Accommodation ranges from a smattering of individual bungalows on the beach to overwater units. All bungalows are positioned to get the best view first thing in the morning. The overwater units aren't the largest but they are charmingly designed; only the more expensive ones have air-con. The catch? They're exposed to the prevailing winds, which can produce uncomfortable waves and noise. The faux beach is no great shakes but a slew of daily activities on offer, ranging from village visits to lagoon excursions to pearl-farm visits, will keep you occupied. It has a restaurant, a bar, a spa and a dive shop.

Nanihi Paradise PENSION $$
(☎93 30 40; www.nanihi-paradise.com; bungalow full board per person 13,500 CFP; 📶) On a tiny *motu,* this quirkily laid-out place has three clean, flower-bedecked two-bedroom bungalows with fully equipped kitchen and outdoor bathrooms (cold-water showers). Various excursions and lagoon tours can be arranged, but if you're intent on diving, be aware that the local dive centre doesn't provide pick up from the pension because of the lengthy boat ride (about 30 minutes). The overall vibe is superbly relaxed. Round-trip airport transfers are 2500 CFP per person (and can be rough in bad weather).

Manihi Pearl Village PENSION $$
(☎96 43 38; pension.ppv@mail.pf; bungalows half board per person 10,500 CFP) This pension in the village lacks the wow factor (no beach, no seclusion) but it fits the bill if you're not intent on staying on a *motu.* The three bungalows are neat, spacious and functional, and overlook a little private marina which is swimmable. Kayaks and bikes are complimentary. If you want to dive, the Manihi Blue Nui dive centre will pick you up on the way to the dive sites. A good plan B. Airport transfers are included.

Information

There is no bank on the atoll, so bring a wad of cash. The post office in Turipaoa village has internet and wi-fi access (with the Manaspot network).

Getting There & Away

AIR **Air Tahiti** (☎96 43 34, 86 42 42; www.airtahiti.pf) has almost daily flights between Pape'ete and Manihi (22,100 CFP one way), direct or via Rangiroa, Tikehau or Fakarava (11,000 CFP one way). There's also a twice-weekly flight to Fakarava (12,200 CFP one way).

BOAT The *Mareva Nui* and *Saint-Xavier Maris-Stella* (p161) service Manihi and accept passengers.

Getting Around

The only track on Manihi links Motu Taugarau-fara to the airport, covering a total distance of only about 9km. The Manihi Pearl Beach Resort has bicycles but you can't get too far and the road is barren and shadeless.

AHE

POP 377

This 20km-long by 10km-wide ring of coral is a charmer. The many hues of its pure aqua-blue water, the foaming breakers around the reef and the thin strips of coral-sand beach of its many deserted *motu* make for an enchanting scene. It is less developed than many other surrounding atolls because of its geography. The only pass is at the northwest of the atoll; the village of Tenukupara is in the far southwest and the airport is at the northern extremity. The atoll's beauty draws in a large number of yachties between May and August and the two pensions here are among the best in the archipelago.

The aim of the game on Ahe is to relax – but if you're keen to get the blood flowing a bit there are a few options available. It's also great place to buy pearls direct from the pearl farm.

Sights & Activities

A great way to get a feel of the island is to get to **Motu Manu** (Bird Island), which has the only remaining patch of primary forest in the Tuamotus. Activities on offer at the pensions range from cruising around the *motu* and **snorkelling** spots to **kayaking** and **fishing**. **Pearl farm** visits are also popular. Cocoperle Lodge organises renowned **deep-sea fishing** charters and **spearfishing** trips.

Archimède Expéditions DIVING
(☎70 13 04; www.archimede-expeditions.com) Based in Tahiti, this outfit organises diving weekend trips to Ahe, usually once a month. Divers stay at Chez Raita.

Sleeping & Eating

The following places are run by solar power.

Cocoperle Lodge PENSION **$$**
(☎96 44 08; www.cocoperlelodge.com; bungalows half/full board per person from 11,000/13,000 CFP) An eco-boutique hotel that's a step up in organisation from your standard family pension, Franco Polynesian-run Cocoperle Lodge is set in a coconut plantation facing the lagoon. It has six well-decorated bungalows made with local materials; private bathrooms (with hot water; three of the bathrooms, though private, are separated from bedrooms); fans; and mosquito screens. Excellent meals are served in a *fare* by the lagoon and the bar is open all day. There's a whole menu of other free and costed activities on offer, and free kayaks. The lodge packs its rubbish to Pape'ete for proper disposal and is a member of the Reef Check program (www.reefcheck.org). Credit cards are accepted, and English and some Italian are spoken.

Chez Raita PENSION **$$**
(☎96 44 53; www.pension-raita.com; bungalows half/full board per person 9500/12,500 CFP) If you're hoping to partake in the Tuamotuan pension experience look no further – Raita and her husband offer local hospitality at its finest. Digs are in three bungalows that lip out onto the blue-on-blue vista of lagoon and sky, on the east side of the atoll. They're beautifully appointed and have lots of local charm, though the best thing they offer is the lullaby of the wavelets. Various excursions can be organised, including picnic excursions to Tenukupara village and other *motu* (minimum four people) as well as line fishing in the lagoon and snorkelling. Free kayaks. Credit cards are accepted.

Getting There & Away

AIR Air Tahiti (☎86 42 42; www.airtahiti.pf) flies from Pape'ete to Ahe three to four days weekly (22,200 CFP one way).

BOAT The *Saint-Xavier Maris-Stella* and *Mareva Nui* (p161) service Ahe.

The Marquesas

POP 8600

Includes »

Best Places to Stay

» Temetiu Village (p195)

» Keikahanui Nuku Hiva Pearl Lodge (p180)

» Hotel Hanakéé Hiva Oa Pearl Lodge (p196)

Best Archaeological Sites

» Iipona (p198)

» Kamuihei, Tahakia & Teiipoka (p183)

» Tohua Koueva (p178)

Why Go?

Grand, brooding, powerful and charismatic: that pretty much sums up the Marquesas. Here, nature's fingers have sculpted intricate jewels that jut up dramatically from the cobalt-blue ocean. Waterfalls taller than skyscrapers trickle down vertical canyons, the ocean thrashes towering sea cliffs, sharp basalt pinnacles project from emerald forests, and scalloped bays are blanketed with desert arcs of white or black sand.

Some of the most inspirational hikes and rides in French Polynesia are found here, allowing walkers and horse riders the opportunity to explore the islands' rugged interiors. Here the past is almost palpable, thanks to a wealth of archaeological remains dating from pre-European times.

Another highlight is the culture. In everything from cuisine and dances to language and crafts, the Marquesas do feel different from the rest of French Polynesia. But don't expect turquoise lagoons, swanky resorts and an electric nightlife – the Marquesas are an ecotourist's dream, not a beach-holiday destination.

When to Go

Closer to the Equator than the rest of French Polynesia, the Marquesas' climate is a bit different. Temperatures and humidity tend to be slightly higher than in Tahiti. There is no bad time to visit: in theory, June to September sees heavier rain while November to March is drier (exactly opposite to the rest of French Polynesia) and experiences calmer seas (better for boat excursions and diving). An absolute minimum of 10 days is required if you plan to visit the two main islands (Nuku Hiva and Hiva Oa) plus one secondary island.

History

Among the first islands to be settled by the Polynesians during the great South Pacific migrations, the Marquesas served as a dispersal point for the whole Polynesian triangle from Hawaii to Easter Island and New Zealand. Estimates of the islands' colonisation vary from prehistory to between AD 900 and 1100.

The Marquesas' isolation was broken in 1595 when Spanish navigator Alvaro de Mendaña y Neira sighted Fatu Hiva by pure chance. Mendaña's fleet then sailed along past Motane and Hiva Oa, and anchored for around 10 days in Vaitahu Bay on Tahuata. Mendaña christened these four islands Las Marquesas de Mendoza in honour of his sponsor, the viceroy of Peru, García Hurtado de Mendoza.

In 1774 James Cook lingered for four days on Tahuata during his second voyage. Ingraham, the American commander of the *Hope*, 'discovered' the northern group of the Marquesas in 1791, arriving slightly ahead of Frenchman Étienne Marchand, whose merchant vessel took on fresh supplies at Tahuata and then landed on 'Ua Pou. In 1797 William Crook, a young Protestant pastor with the London Missionary Society (LMS), landed on Tahuata, but his attempts at evangelism were unsuccessful.

French interest in the region grew as a means of countering English expansion in the Pacific. After a reconnaissance voyage in 1838, Rear Admiral Abel Dupetit-Thouars took possession of Tahuata in 1842 in the name of French King Louis-Philippe.

Under the French yoke, the Marquesas almost fell into oblivion – the French administration preferred to develop Pape'ete on Tahiti, which they thought had a more strategic value. Only the Catholic missionaries, who had been active since their arrival on Tahuata in 1838, persevered, and Catholicism became, and still is, firmly entrenched in the Marquesas.

Upon contact with Western influences, the foundations of Marquesan society collapsed. Whaling crews brought alcohol, firearms and syphilis. In a stunning decline, the population plummeted from around 18,000 in 1842 to 2096 in 1926.

In the 20th century the Marquesas were made famous by Hiva Oa residents Paul Gauguin and Belgian singer Jacques Brel. Slow but sure development of infrastructure has helped lessen the archipelago's isolation,

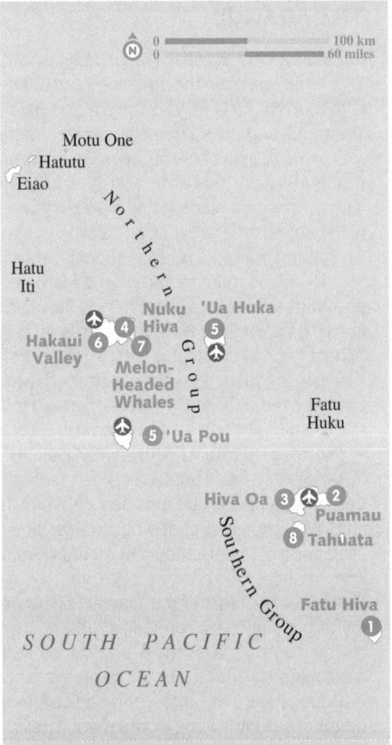

The Marquesas Highlights

1. Forgetting what day it is on hard-to-reach **Fatu Hiva** (p201)
2. Wandering flabbergasted amid *tiki* (sacred statues) at **Puamau** (p198)
3. Clip-clopping across the fecund interior of **Hiva Oa** (p194)
4. Gazing down impenetrable valleys while hiking across the **Nuku Hiva** heartland (p180)
5. Experiencing timeless traditional village life on **'Ua Huka** (p185) or **'Ua Pou** (p189), lodging in homestays and meeting master carvers
6. Exploring on foot the spectacular **Hakaui Valley** (p182) on Nuku Hiva
7. Spotting (and maybe snorkelling with) **melon-headed whales** (p178) off Nuku Hiva's east coast
8. Enjoying a picnic in a secluded bay on **Tahuata** (p199)

THE ARANUI

If there's an iconic trip in French Polynesia, it must be on the *Aranui*. For nearly 25 years, this 117m ship has been the umbilical cord between Tahiti and the Marquesas and a hot favourite with tourists. Its 14-day voyage, departing from Pape'ete, takes it to one or two atolls in the Tuamotus and the six inhabited islands of the Marquesas. There are 17 trips per year.

The *Aranui* has been supplying the remote islands of the Marquesas since 1984 and that is still its primary mission. Its front half looks just like any other cargo ship of its size, with cranes and holds for all types of goods. The back, however, is like a cruise ship, with cabins, several decks and a small swimming pool. There's nothing glitzy about it – everything is simple and functional. Unless you're on a yacht, there's simply no other way to visit so many islands in the Marquesas (along with two Tuamotu atolls thrown in as a bonus) in such a short period. It's also a sustainable approach, because you get to know the island life. Note that this is an organised journey; if you don't like to be tied to a schedule or forced to live with a group, it may not be for you.

There are four classes of accommodation, from large cabins with balcony, double bed and bathroom (€3500 to €4900 per person) to dorm-style beds with shared bathroom facilities (€2100 per person). All the accommodation has air con. Prices include all meals and taxes. It is also possible to join the *Aranui* on Nuku Hiva for eight days in the Marquesas.

While the ship is unloading and loading freight – a major event on the islands – passengers take excursions ashore, which typically include picnics, scuba diving, snorkelling, 4WD trips to archaeological sites and remote villages, horse riding, and stops at craft centres, where they can meet craftspeople and make purchases. No nights are spent ashore; all shore visits last just a day or half-day and include multilingual guides. European and North American art history experts, archaeologists and ethnologists are invited on the cruise, providing cultural insights.

You may try to use the *Aranui* as a means of transport from one island in the Marquesas to another, but it's at the captain's discretion; don't rely too much on this option.

Bookings are essential, and peak periods (July, August and December) are booked up months in advance. Contact your travel agency, or the shipowner, **Compagnie Polynésienne de Transport Maritime** (CPTM; ☎Pape'ete 42 62 42, 43 48 89; www.aranui.com), directly.

while archaeological surveys are uncovering a culture that was lost only a comparatively short while ago.

Getting There & Away

AIR The Marquesas are connected to Pape'ete. There aren't any direct services to other archipelagos – you'll have to go through via Pape'ete. All flights are handled by **Air Tahiti** (☎86 42 42; www.airtahiti.pf).

Nuku Hiva and Hiva Oa are well connected with Tahiti, with daily direct flights from Pape'ete. Pape'ete–Nuku Hiva costs 33,000 CFP one way while Pape'ete–Hiva Oa is 33,200 CFP. Flights from Pape'ete to 'Ua Huka (36,000 CFP one way, daily) and 'Ua Pou (36,000 CFP one way, daily) are via Nuku Hiva.

There are also several flights a week between Hiva Oa and 'Ua Pou (9800 CFP one way), and between Hiva Oa and 'Ua Huka (9800 CFP one way). There's a daily flight between Nuku Hiva and Hiva Oa (12,500 CFP one way).

BOAT The *Taporo IX* and **Aranui** (☎42 62 40; www.aranui.com) service the Marquesas, departing from Pape'ete and travelling via the Tuamotus (Fakarava and/or Rangiroa). The *Aranui* does about 17 trips a year. Note that the *Taporo IX* doesn't take passengers.

Getting Around

Given the lack of public transport, it's still a bit of an adventure to get around the Marquesas, but that can be part of the fun.

BETWEEN ISLANDS The easiest and quickest way to island-hop within the archipelago is by regular Air Tahiti flights. *Bonitiers* ('skipjack boats') can be individually chartered and you can hop on the cargo ship *Aranui* if your timing is right (ask about arrival dates). Tahuata and Fatu Hiva are only accessible by boat and it takes some ingenuity to organise this. See the individual islands' Getting There & Away sections for more information.

ON THE ISLANDS Guides and taxis are the main modes of transport for getting around the islands' web of 4WD tracks (and, increasingly, surfaced roads). It is possible to hire your own vehicle on Nuku Hiva and Hiva Oa. On Tahuata, Fatu Hiva and 'Ua Pou, you'll have to charter a 4WD with driver.

NUKU HIVA

POP 2632

The wow factor kicks in fast when you land on the airstrip at Terre Déserte (Desert Land) at Nuku Hiva's northwestern tip and head for Taiohae, the 'capital' of the Marquesas. The 4WD transfer along innumerable twists and turns offers drama, seemingly around every other bend, with stunning landscapes and explosive vistas. This huge, sparsely populated island (the second largest in French Polynesia after Tahiti) boasts a fantastic terrain, with razor-edged basaltic cliffs pounded by crashing waves, deep bays blessed with Robinson Crusoe–like beaches, dramatic waterfalls and timeless valleys that feel like the end of the world.

Horse riding is top notch and there's exceptional hiking, too. Diving is also available and if you want to watch a pod of melon-headed whales, Nuku Hiva is your answer. And culture? The island has a gob-smacking portfolio of archaeological sites, with more *tiki* (sacred statues) and *tohua* (open-air gathering places) than you can count, and there are some beautiful handicrafts available.

With daily flights from Pape'ete and good connections to other islands in the archipelago, there's no excuse not to spend at least three (preferably four) days here to do the island justice.

> **TIME ZONE**
>
> Be sure to adjust your watch when you arrive in the Marquesas, as they are half an hour ahead of Tahiti time. When it's noon in Tahiti, it's 12.30pm in the Marquesas.

Getting There & Away

The **Air Tahiti** (☎91 02 25, 92 01 45, 86 42 42; www.airtahiti.pf; ⏲8am-noon & 1.30-4.30pm Mon-Thu, 8am-noon & 1.30-3.30pm Fri) office is in the centre of Taiohae.

The *Aranui* cargo ship makes a stop at Taiohae.

Getting Around

Slowly but surely the roads of Nuku Hiva are being paved. At the time of writing a sealed road ran from Taiohae to within a few kilometres of the airport and to the Teavaitapuhiva Pass.

TO/FROM THE AIRPORT It takes at least 1¼ hours to reach the airport from Taiohae along a winding road, longer if it has rained and the ground is muddy. Licensed 4WD taxis generally wait for each flight. It is nevertheless wise to

Nuku Hiva

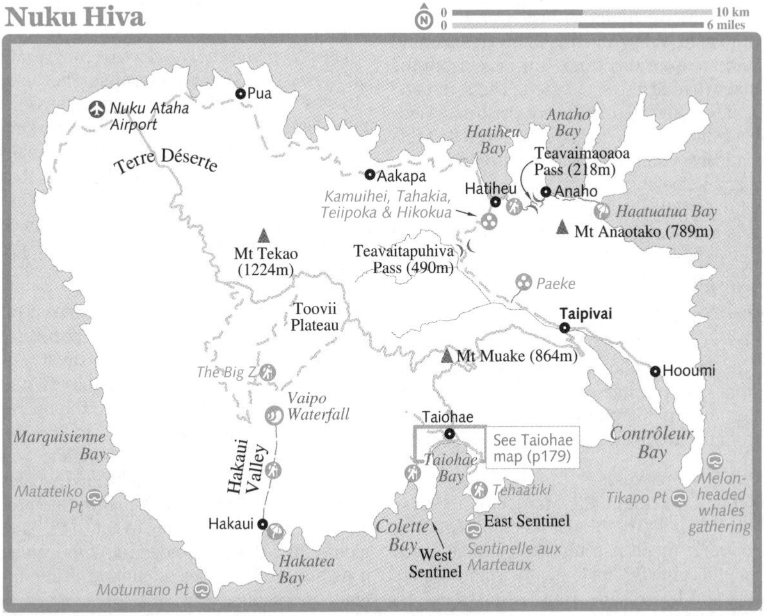

book through your hotel or pension. Transfers to Taiohae cost 4000 CFP per person.

CAR 4WDs without driver can be hired from 11,500 to 13,500 CFP per day. Rates include insurance and unlimited kilometres but not petrol. Contact the hotel **Moana Nui** (☎92 03 30; pensionmoananui@mail.pf) in Taiohae.

Taiohae

POP 1700

The first glimpse of Taiohae after the journey from the airport at Terre Déserte will take your breath away. Nestled at the base of soaring mountains, the town deploys itself along a perfectly crescent-shaped bay. On a clear day, the jagged peaks of 'Ua Pou loom on the horizon. While it's the Marquesas' 'capital', Taiohae oozes the kind of sunny languor you'd associate with the tropics, and it's easy to wind down a few gears here. Spend your Sunday morning in church, take a stroll along the seafront, meet a few woodcarvers and toss back a cool Hinano at sundown. Taiohae also offers useful services, including a tourist office, ATMs, internet access, a few shops and a handful of accommodation options. This is the obvious place to base yourself in Nuku Hiva.

Sights

TOP CHOICE Tohua Koueva ARCHAEOLOGICAL SITE
This massive *tohua* is just over 1.3km up the Pakiu Valley on the Taipivai road, and 700m along a dirt track. Turn east from the main road at the sign 'Site déchets verts de Koueva' then go past the poorly situated garbage dump by the river. It's believed that this extensive communal site, with its paved esplanade, belonged to the war chief Pakoko, who was killed by the French in 1845. Today it is a peaceful spot full of massive banyan trees and flowers. All the stone carvings are contemporary.

Notre-Dame Cathedral of the Marquesas Islands MONUMENT
This striking building is built from wood and stones on a former sacred site venerated by the ancient Marquesans. The stones come from the archipelago's six inhabited islands.

Pae Pae Piki Vehine ARCHAEOLOGICAL SITE
Rebuilt for the 1989 Marquesas Festival, this *pae pae* (traditional meeting platform) contains modern sculptures and a dozen magnificent *tiki* made by the island's sculptors and by artisans from Easter Island. Its central, breezy location makes it a popular hang-out for local kids.

FREE Musée Enana MUSEUM
(☎92 03 82; ⌚8-11.30am & 2-4.40pm Mon-Fri, 8-11.30am Sat) This little museum has a few documents and artefacts focusing on traditional Marquesan culture. It also doubles as a small craft shop. It's on the same property as the Hee Tai Inn.

Monument to the Dead MONUMENT
On the seafront, opposite the Kamake shop, you can't miss this obelisk fronted by a cannon constructed in honour of Étienne Marchand.

Activities

Horse Riding

Horse riding is a good way to soak up the drop-dead-gorgeous scenery.

Sabine Teikiteetini HORSE RIDING
(☎92 01 56, 25 35 13; half-day rides incl transfers 8000 CFP) Sabine is a qualified guide who can arrange lovely rides on Toovii Plateau. You don't need any riding experience, as Sabine caters to all levels of proficiency. Rides last about three hours.

Whale-Watching

At sea, Nuku Hiva's main claim to fame is a bewildering whale gathering 'event'. Dozens (and at times, hundreds) of melon-headed whales *(Peponocephala electra)* congregate off the east coast in the morning. They usually stay at the surface, vertically or horizontally, sometimes playing, sometimes basking motionless. Though their habits remain largely unknown, some experts think that the east coast is their resting area during the day. The site itself is impressive, since it's anywhere between 100m and 1km off the coast, in a deep-blue sea.

Marquises Plaisance WHALE-WATCHING
(☎92 08 75, 73 23 48; e.bastard@mail.pf; half-day cruise for 2 people 15,000 CFP) This small outfit runs whale-watching excursions. While an encounter is not guaranteed, the operator claims a success rate of 50% to 70% depending on the season. If you're game, you can snorkel with the melon-headed whales (but don't attempt to touch them). One proviso: the one-hour journey to get to the site, along Nuku Hiva's pounded sea cliffs, can be a nightmare if the sea is choppy. Prices include snorkelling gear.

Taiohae

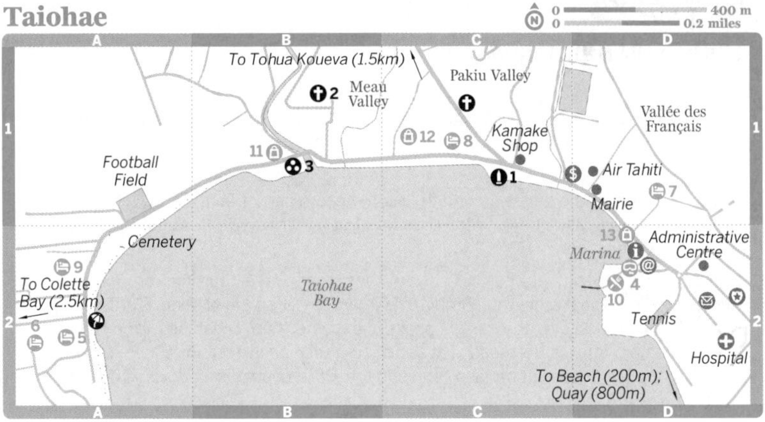

Taiohae

Sights

1 Monument to the Dead C1
Musée Enana .... (see 5)
2 Notre-Dame Cathedral of the Marquesas Islands B1
3 Pae Pae Piki Vehine B1

Activities, Courses & Tours

4 Centre Plongée Marquises D2

Sleeping

5 Hee Tai Inn A2
6 Keikahanui Nuku Hiva Pearl Lodge A2
7 Mave Mai D1
8 Moana Nui C1
9 Paahatea Nui A2

Eating

10 Café Vaeaki D2
Keikahanui Nuku Hiva Pearl Lodge .... (see 6)
Moana Nui .... (see 8)
Snack Tuhiva .... (see 13)

Shopping

Boutique du Centre Plongée Marquises .... (see 4)
11 Damas Taupotini B1
12 Edgar Tamarii C1
13 Fare Artisanal D2

Diving

There are a dozen magnificent diving sites, which are very different from those of the Society group or the Tuamotus. The Marquesas don't boast coral reefs, peaceful lagoons or crystalline waters. The water is thick with plankton and visibility is consequently reduced (generally 10m to 20m). These specific conditions guarantee regular sightings of very unusual creatures, such as scalloped hammerheads and melon-headed whales, which are not encountered elsewhere in French Polynesia. All kinds of rays – mantas, eagles and stingrays – also swim close to the shore.

Since Nuku Hiva is devoid of any protective barrier reefs, divers should be prepared to cope with sometimes difficult conditions, particularly the swell, to get to the sites. Most sites require a half-hour or so boat trip. For details of dive sites in the area, see p37.

Centre Plongée Marquises DIVING
(☎92 00 88; marquisesdives@mail.pf) This small operation runs on a charter basis only. An outing costs 35,000/45,000 CFP for up to three/four divers. Prices include equipment and two successive dives. Dives are not guided, so you need to be experienced, but there's a comprehensive briefing before each dive. Book ahead.

Quad Biking

Revving up the motor and hitting the trail on a quad bike (ATV) is a great way to explore the area around Taiohae.

DON'T MISS

HIKING ON NUKU HIVA

To date, hiking is *the* very best Nuku Hiva has to offer, and it's dizzying (literally), with a couple of exceptional walks that take in some awe-inspiring viewpoints, without another traveller in sight. A guide is essential because trails are not marked and it's easy to get lost.

Tehaatiki Explore the ridges around the southeastern part of Taiohae Bay. There are magnificent views of the bay and the coastline, but few shady areas. About five to six hours, moderate.

Peaks & cliffs near Aakapa & Hatiheu A very scenic hike. Starting from Toovii Plateau, the path snakes its way through a primary forest on the plateau. Right on the plateau rim, the view over the Aakapa peaks and the northern coastline will be etched in your memory forever. It's mostly flat and shady. Keep an eye out for endemic birds, including the Marquesan imperial pigeon and the white-capped fruit dove. About six hours, moderate.

Big Z An altogether different atmosphere. The western part of the island is barren. Starting from Toovii Plateau at an altitude of about 1000m, you follow a volcanic ridge to the west. Highlights include a lookout over a 'hidden valley', featuring snaggle-toothed peaks tangled together. Expect to see wild goats, white-capped fruit doves and white-tailed tropic birds. No shade, but lots of breeze. About six hours, moderate.

The hike to the **Vaipo Waterfall** (p182) is another stunner. DIYers have two good options for solo walking: **Colette Bay** (p182) and from **Hatiheu to Anaho** (p184).

For guides, contact the following:

Marquises Rando (☎92 07 13, 29 53 31; www.marquisesrando.com) Run by a professional guide, Marquises Rando charges 6600 CFP for Tehaatiki, 8500 CFP for Peaks and Cliffs near Aaakapa and Hatiheu, and 10,000 CFP for Big Z. Prices include transfers, water, biscuits and fruits.

Richard Deane – Terama (☎74 86 78, 28 08 36) This guide specialises in walks near Taiohae and Taipivae (from 3500 CFP per half-day).

Marquises Quad Aventure – ATV Tours ADVENTURE TOUR
(☎32 18 37; by reservation) This quad-biking operator runs a variety of guided tours that visit Colette Bay, Taipivai and Hatiheu. Guided trips for two-person quads cost 12,000/15,000 CFP per half/full day.

Tours

Jocelyne Henua Enana Tours GUIDED TOUR
(☎92 08 32, 74 42 23; www.marquisesvoyages.com.pf) Jocelyne knows just about everything there is to know about Nuku Hiva. She is one of the only guides available on Sundays, speaks English and takes credit cards. Her 4WD day tours offer a good overview of the island (16,000 CFP for two).

Sleeping

Credit cards are accepted unless otherwise noted.

Keikahanui Nuku Hiva Pearl Lodge HOTEL $$$
(☎92 07 10; www.pearlodge.com; bungalows d 26,000-31,000 CFP;) Nuku Hiva's only upmarket option, the Keikahanui occupies a wonderfully peaceful domain at the western tip of the bay. Digs are in 20 Polynesian-style bungalows hidden along a steep hill smothered in juicy tropical foliage. They are commodious and decked out with *tapa* (cloth made from beaten bark and decorated with traditional designs) and woodcarved panels. Plus, each bungalow has a private balcony with a simply

eye-popping view over the bay. Need more? There's a sweet swimming pool (the size of a teacup, though), a bar and a restaurant.

Moana Nui HOTEL $
(☎92 03 30; pensionmoananui@mail.pf; s incl breakfast/half board 6500/9000 CFP, d incl breakfast/half board 9900/16,000 CFP; ❄📶) All eight rooms are clean, well organised (air-con, a small balcony, private facilities, hot shower, daily cleaning) and utilitarian. Rooms 1 and 2 have good views of the bay. There are plans to renovate the place during the lifetime of this book; let's hope prices will be kept reasonable. What won't change, though, is the handy location, right in the middle of the bay. The on-site restaurant is an added bonus. The owner is helpful if you need to hire a car or book activities.

Hee Tai Inn HOTEL $$
(☎92 03 82; www.marquesas-hinn.com; s/d 9000/10,500 CFP; ❄📶) Can't speak a single word of French? Here you'll be glad to be welcomed in flawless English by Rose Corser, an American lady who fell for Nuku Hiva a long time ago and who is a mine of information on all things Marquesan. It's a pity then that the accommodation is in a rather characterless building. The eight motel-like rooms are spacious and meticulously clean. It's at the western tip of the bay, beneath the Keikahanui Nuku Hiva Pearl Lodge.

Paahatea Nui PENSION $
(☎92 00 97; paahateanui@mail.pf; bungalows s/d incl breakfast 6000/10,000 CFP) The good people at Paahatea Nui – husband Justin and wife Julienne – are not setting out to win any 'best in its class' awards with their establishment, but the virtue is that it's kept in tip-top shape. The six bungalows are not well spaced out but the garden, overflowing with blossoming tropical flowers, ensures you're sealed off from your neighbours. No meals are available except breakfast, but you can use the kitchen. One downside: it's a bit far from the 'action'. Cash only.

Mave Mai PENSION $$
(☎92 08 10; pension-mavemai@mail.pf; s/d incl breakfast 9000/11,000 CFP, half board 11,000/15,000 CFP; ❄📶) Peacefully reposed over sloping grounds above the marina, this pension features eight rooms in a two-storey motel-style building. They're not terribly Polynesian, but they're light and well appointed, with private facilities (hot water) and air-con, as well as a kitchenette in two of the rooms. The real draw is the small terrace (or balcony upstairs) overlooking the bay. The place can feel a bit deserted during the day because the owner doesn't live on the premises.

Eating & Drinking

You'll find several well-stocked supermarkets on the seafront, as well as a bakery, a small market and a few *roulottes* (mobile food vans) – your best bargain for cheap eats.

Moana Nui HOTEL RESTAURANT $$
(☎92 03 30; mains 1000-2900 CFP; ⏲lunch & dinner Mon-Sat) Basking in a convivial buzz, the restaurant at this hotel has an eclectic menu, from salads and burgers to fish and meat dishes. Or opt for a pizza cooked in a wood-fired oven (evenings only).

Keikahanui Nuku Hiva Pearl Lodge HOTEL RESTAURANT $$
(☎92 07 10; mains 1300-3500 CFP; ⏲lunch & dinner) The chef at this upscale hotel fuses quality local ingredients with Gallic know-how. The Marquesan goat with coconut milk will certainly win your heart. Bag a table on the terrace and savour the views of the bay and the twinkling stars. Light meals are available at lunchtime. The bar is great for a sunset cocktail.

Café Vaeaki CAFE $
(mains 800-1100 CFP; ⏲closed dinner Sun) At this little place right on the quay you can fuel up with simple dishes such as raw fish, sandwiches and fruits. Cash only.

Snack Tuhiva SNACK $
(mains 1000-1200 CFP; ⏲breakfast & lunch Mon-Sat) This low-key venue inside the market is a good spot to catch local vibes. Devour a comforting breakfast or munch on well-prepared fish dishes at lunchtime. Cash only.

Shopping

Fare Artisanal HANDICRAFTS
Next to the tourist office, the *fare artisanal* (craft centre) is a good place to stock up on *monoi* (fragrant oil), necklaces, bracelets and carvings.

COLETTE BAY

Want to see the base camp for *Survivor Marquesas* (2002)? Head to Colette Bay, about 3.5km from Taiohae. Take the track going up to the Keikahanui Nuku Hiva Pearl Lodge, at the western side of the bay. Instead of branching left to the hotel, keep right and continue for about 2km. The track zigzags along the western side of the cove up to a pass, where you'll see a cattle fence, to the left. Open the gate and follow the dirt road that descends to the pebble beach at Colette Bay. It's ideal for a gentle stroll (or a picnic), but bring plenty of insect repellent.

Damas Taupotini HANDICRAFTS
Master carver Damas Taupotini has a workshop across the road from Pae Pae Piki Vehine. He carves pieces from bone, wood and stone.

Edgar Tamarii HANDICRAFTS
(☎92 01 67) Another renowned carver is Edgar Tamarii, whose workshop is located near Moana Nui hotel. He specialises in woodcarvings.

Boutique du Centre Plongée Marquises SOUVENIRS
(⏲8-11am & 2.30-5pm) Here you'll find a few curios, *pareu* (sarongs) and shell necklaces.

Information

Banque Socredo (☎92 03 63; ⏲7.30-11.30am & 1.30-4pm Mon-Fri) Currency exchange, as well as two ATMs.

Hospital (☎91 20 00) Has a dentist, too.

Keikahanui Nuku Hiva Pearl Lodge (☎92 07 10; ⏲7am-9pm; wi-fi) Internet and wi-fi access.

Moetai Marine – Yacht Services (☎92 07 50; ⏲8am-12.30pm Mon-Fri; wi-fi) On the quay. Has internet and wi-fi access (900 CFP per hour), laundry service (1000 CFP) and can help yachties with formalities.

Post office (⏲7-11.30am & noon-3.30pm Mon-Thu, 7-11.30am & noon-2.30pm Fri; wi-fi) Internet access and wi-fi (with the Manaspot card). Has an ATM.

Tourist office (☎92 08 25; ⏲7.30am-12.30pm Mon-Fri) Has a few brochures and can help with simple queries.

Hakaui Valley

Of all the marvels that Nuku Hiva offers, few equal the awe-inspiring majesty of the Hakaui Valley, which slices through the basaltic landmass, west of the island. On either side of the canyon, vertical walls rise to nearly 800m and **Vaipo Waterfall**, the highest in French Polynesia at 350m, plummets into a natural swimming pool at the end of the valley. In the drier months the volume of the falls lessens and can be reduced to a mere trickle.

The Hakaui Valley is also of strong historical interest. The valley was once the fiefdom of King Te Moana and Queen Vaekehu, and the ancient royal road follows the river past numerous ancient sites, namely *pae pae* and *tohua,* hidden behind a tangle of vegetation.

Next to the Hakaui Valley, in Hakatea Bay, you'll find the magnificent **Hakatea Beach**. Waters are generally calm and good for swimming, but you'll have to deal with *nono* (gnats; see p185). Bring lots of repellent.

Marquises Plaisance (☎92 08 75, 73 23 48; e.bastard@mail.pf) can arrange guided trips to the waterfall. It costs 13,500 CFP for two people for the full-day excursion, but no picnic is provided. From Taiohae, it takes about 40 minutes by speedboat to reach Hakatea Bay, where the boat anchors. From the bay, allow about 2½ hours to reach the waterfall on foot. The path is flat and follows the river (be prepared to get wet) and includes stretches of the ancient paved royal road. Note that it's not advised to walk the last 300m or so because the narrow canyon is subject to falling rocks. Back in Hakatea Bay, you can recharge the batteries on Hakatea Beach before returning to Taiohae.

Toovii Plateau

'Where am I?' is probably what you'll be wondering on reaching Toovii Plateau, which spreads out at an average altitude of 800m at the heart of the island. With its conifer forests and vast pastures where cattle graze, it seems straight out of a Brothers Grimm fairy tale. The mountain setting and cooler climate can be a very welcome change from the muggy coastal areas. At times, ghostly mists add a touch of the bizarre. Toovii used to supply the whole archipelago with meat, dairy produce and timber, but serves now as a playground for various activities including horse riding and hiking.

Taipivai

Quiz: who was on board the American whaler *Acushnet,* which put in at Taiohae in July 1842, jumped ship, spent three weeks at Taipivai and wrote his unusual experiences in *Typee* (1846)? Answer: Herman Melville (you know, who also wrote *Moby Dick* and *Billy Budd*).

Forget about stories of fierce warriors and cannibals – now Taipivai is a charming village that carpets the floor of a river valley. At the eastern end of the village the river rushes into the majestic **Contrôleur Bay**.

It takes about half an hour by 4WD on a paved road in good condition to reach Taipivai from Taiohae.

The main reason to stop in Taipivai is to visit the **Paeke** archaeological site, which lies on a hillside at the exit of the village on the way to Hatiheu (the path that leads to the site is not signed, so ask around). It features two well-preserved *me'ae* (traditional sacred sites) flanked by a set of brick-coloured *tiki*. The *me'ae* further up the hill has a pit into which human remains were thrown. From the main road, it's a 20-minute walk uphill on a path.

Hatiheu

Hatiheu is a graceful little village dominated by a crescent of black sand, soaring peaks and immaculate, colourful gardens; it's no wonder that Robert Louis Stevenson succumbed to its charms when he passed through in 1888. On one of the peaks to the west, at a height of 300m, is a white statue of the Virgin Mary, erected in 1872.

From Taipivai, follow the main road 7.5km as it climbs to the impressive **Teavaitapuhiva Pass** (490m), from which there are magnificent views over Hatiheu Bay.

Sights

TOP CHOICE **Kamuihei, Tahakia & Teiipoka** ARCHAEOLOGICAL SITE

About 300m towards Taipivai from the Hikokua site, these three connecting sites make up the largest excavated archaeological area of Nuku Hiva. A team led by the archaeologist Pierre Ottino began restoration in 1998.

The importance and sheer number of these structures testify to the dense population this valley once sheltered. With its large moss-covered basalt rocks and huge banyans, the largest of which has been estimated to be over 600 years old, Kamuihei exudes *mana* (spiritual power).

At the foot of the largest banyan is a deep pit, presumably dug for the remains of sacrifices or for taboo objects. Other pits are scattered about the site; these are mostly *ua ma,*

LOCAL KNOWLEDGE

PIERRE OTTINO, ARCHAEOLOGIST

French archaeologist Pierre Ottino has supervised numerous restorations in the Marquesas over the last two decades and was involved in all Marquesas Arts Festivals.

Why are the Marquesas so special? Most archaeological sites are still untouched, and there's exceptional diversity. We have statues, gathering places, ceremonial centres and houses, all set within powerful landscapes. And there's not a soul in sight.

What are the not-to-be-missed archaeological sites? The Kamuihei-Tahakia-Teiipoka complex on Nuku Hiva is a must-see as it's the most comprehensive site in the Marquesas. On Hiva Oa, I recommend Taaoa and, if you want to admire massive *tiki,* Iipona in Puamau.

What's the best way to learn about local culture? Visit the archaeological museum in Hatiheu and take a tour with a knowledgeable guide.

Good multiday trip in the archipelago? You would want to spend three to four days exploring Nuku Hiva before heading to Hiva Oa – allow another three to four days to make the most of the island.

WORTH A TRIP

ANAHO & HAATUATUA

One of the best-kept secrets in the Marquesas is the sublime **Anaho Bay**, on Nuku Hiva's northeast coast, where it's hard to feel connected with the outside world. The fact that it's only accessible by speedboat (15 minutes from Hatiheu; 7000 CFP) or a little less than 1½ hours by foot (also from Hatiheu) adds to the sense of seclusion. A few families make their living harvesting copra among the swaying coconut plantations; there is a tiny chapel and not much else. It's a popular anchorage for visiting yachts and, with the only coral reef on Nuku Hiva, the bay is lagoonlike and inviting. Small wonder that back in 1888 Robert Louis Stevenson was inspired to write many pages eulogising its unsettling beauty.

Take the paved road at the end of Hatiheu up towards the valley. About 300m uphill there's a small clearing and a well-marked trail to the left. From the **Teavaimaoaoa Pass** (218m), reached after about 45 minutes, Anaho Bay appears like a mirage. Both the ascent from Hatiheu and descent to Anaho are quite steep, but the track is in good condition and is well marked. Bring mosquito repellent and plenty of water.

If Anaho's not enough for you, head to **Haatuatua Bay**, a 30-minute stroll to the east, on an easy-to-follow trail. A crescent-shaped bay fringed with a yellow scimitar of sand, framed by lofty volcanic ridges, it is bound to satiate any contemplative mind. Just you, the caress of the sea breeze, the sand in your toes...and a few wicked *nono* to mar the experience!

which stocked the all-important breadfruit. A little higher, on Teiipoka, are two large rocks about 2.5m high by 3m wide and decorated with petroglyphs that represent turtles, fish and the eyes of a *tiki,* along with human figures. It's estimated that the valley contains more than 500 other petroglyphs like these.

On the other side of the track is the restored *tohua* Tahakia, one of the biggest in the Marquesas, as well as some *pae pae.*

Hikokua ARCHAEOLOGICAL SITE

One of the most powerful archaeological sites in the Marquesas, Hikokua was discovered by the archaeologist Robert Suggs in 1957 and has been restored and maintained by Hatiheu locals since 1987. It dates from around AD 1250 and was in use until the 1800s.

The vast, central, rectangular esplanade *(tohua)* was used for dance performances at community festivals. It's flanked by tiers of small flat basalt blocks that were once used as steps for the spectators.

On the terrace stand two modern **stone carvings** by a local artist, and a flat rock that was used for various purposes, including solo dances and rituals associated with puberty.

Near the centre of the esplanade are nine Christian **tombs**. They probably date from the time of the first missionaries' arrival, after the abandonment of the site.

The platform at the bottom, on the northern side of the esplanade towards the ocean, was the *tuu* (ceremonial activity centre), upon which sacrifices and displaying of the victims' bodies took place. The chief's residence stood at the northeast corner of the esplanade.

Hikokua is just off the dirt road, at the entrance to the village.

FREE **Museum** MUSEUM

(on request) This modest yet well-organised archaeological musem does a good job of explaining the archipelago's history and culture. It features artefacts, exhibits and replica. The detailed signs in English are very informative. Ask for the key at Chez Yvonne, next door.

Tours

Given the scarcity of explanatory signs, it makes sense to hire a knowledgeable guide to visit Hatiheu's archaeological sites. Contact **Jocelyne Henua Enana Tours** (92 08 32, 74 42 23; www.marquisesvoyages.com.pf) in Taiohae or Chez Yvonne in the village.

NASTY NONOS

Even the hardiest of adventurers can be brought to their knees (and the edges of their fingernails) by the nearly invisible but undeniably hostile *nono*. Cover yourself in lightweight trousers and long-sleeved shirts and whip out the jungle juice. This little gnat's bites can leave welts that itch like no other. Fortunately, they are found almost uniquely on beaches and in some valleys and are not disease carriers.

Eating

Chez Yvonne – Restaurant Hinakonui RESTAURANT $$
(☎92 02 97; mains 1700-3000 CFP; ⊙lunch & dinner Mon-Sat, by reservation) This authentic Marquesan restaurant is a relaxing spot, with an open-air thatched terrace opening onto the seafront. Signature dishes include lobster flambéed with whisky (from February to October) and goat with coconut milk. Bookings are recommended, otherwise you might find the kitchen closed if there aren't enough customers. Avoid the five boxy bungalows (single/double half board 8000/12,000 CFP), which show too many signs of wear and tear, including saggy mattresses and sombre bathrooms.

'UA HUKA

POP 582

This low-key, less-visited island remains something of a 'secret' and you'll probably have it all to yourself. There are only three villages, and after a day or two the community seems to absorb you like a giant, friendly sponge. Here's your chance to buy carvings from master carvers, zigzag up the flanks of an extinct volcano to reach mysterious archaeological sites tucked away in the jungle, take a boat excursion to intriguing offshore islets and delve right into Marquesan life.

Sights

Vaipaee VILLAGE
The island's main town is at the end of a very deep, narrow inlet, about 1km long and rightly named Invisible Bay. Next to the mayor's office, a little **museum** (admission free) features pestles, *tiki,* finely carved sculptures, *pahu* (drums), jewellery and period photos as well as a *ha'e* (traditional house). Donations are appreciated. Hours are erratic; ask at the mayor's office.

FREE **Arboretum** BOTANICAL GARDEN
(⊙Mon-Sat) A wide variety of plants, including 200 species of citrus fruits, are cultivated in these botanical gardens halfway between Vaipaee and Hane. The species best adapted to the climate are used for reforestation where the vegetation has been destroyed by wild goats and horses.

Manihina BEACH
Near the airport, Manihina Beach is a wonderfully scenic pebbly beach framed by basaltic cliffs. Sadly there are lots of *nono.* It's accessible by a dirt road.

Hane VILLAGE
Experts believe that the first Polynesian settlement on the Marquesas was here, tucked away in a bay protected on the east by the impressive **Motu Hane**. The white house on the seafront contains the craftcentre as well as a modest **marine museum** (admission free), which shows the evolution of traditional pirogues (outrigger canoes) as well as hooks used for shark fishing. Ask around for someone to help you get the key.

Meiaute ARCHAEOLOGICAL SITE
High up in the valley of Hane, the site of Meiaute includes three 1m-high, red-tuff **tiki** that watch over a group of stone structures, *pae pae* and *me'ae,* which are partly overgrown. Two of these *tiki* have projecting

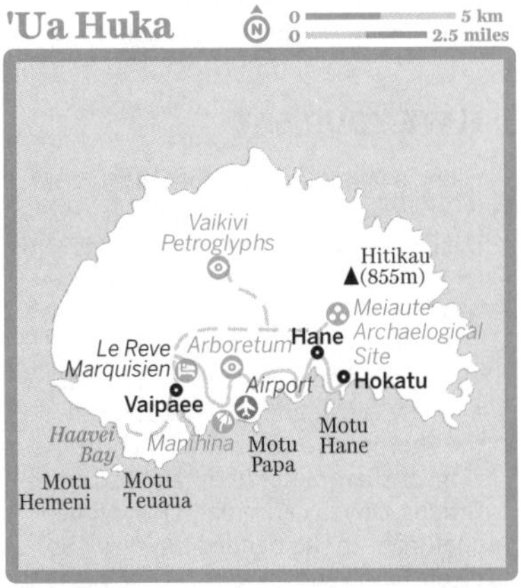

ears, one has legs and a phallus, while the other two have only a head and trunk. The clearing forms a natural lookout with magnificent views of Hane Bay on one side and the caldera on the other. It's a 25-minute walk from the village of Hane. You don't really need a guide to get there; follow the main road inland, until you reach a concrete stairway on your right, 30m after a sharp bend. Climb the steep hill to the *pae pae*. A little higher up, in a clearing, you will find the *tiki*. If you're not sure, villagers will point you in the right direction.

Hokatu VILLAGE
Everybody loves Hokatu – it's so mellow. And very scenic: about 3km east of Hane, it lies in a sheltered bay edged with a pebble beach pounded by frothy azure seas and offers direct views of imposing sugar-loafed Motu Hane. On the waterfront there's a small **museum** (admission free) that displays well-presented photographs of the petroglyphs around the island.

Motu Teuaua & Motu Hemeni ISLANDS
Thousands of *kaveka* (sooty terns) nest year-round on the islets of Hemeni and Teuaua, near the southwestern point of 'Ua Huka, and they lay thousands of eggs daily.

Access to Hemeni is prohibited in order to protect the species. Teuaua, the neighbouring islet (also known as Île aux Oiseaux or Bird Island), is accessible by speedboat when the sea is calm. You can accompany the islanders when they gather the eggs (which are considered a delicacy). It's not for the fainthearted, because you'll need to jump on to a rocky ledge and clamber up the rock using a permanently fixed rope. As you approach the nests, the *kaveka* become extremely angry and their cries deafening. The bravest birds start swooping at you.

If, despite all this, the experience still attracts you, wear a hat.

Vaikivi petroglyphs ARCHAEOLOGICAL SITE
This little-visited archaeological site on the Vaikivi Plateau is well worth the detour, if only for the walk or horse ride to get there. The petroglyphs represent an outrigger canoe, a human face, an octopus and various geometric designs.

Activities

Walking

Any chunk of the coastal route between Haavei Bay to the west and Hokatu to the east offers jaw-dropping views. For other walks, a guide is essential because the trails are unmarked. Ask at your pension for a guide; the usual cost is about 5000 CFP, picnic included.

Vaikivi petroglyphs WALKING
From Hane, it's a three-hour walk inland to the Vaikivi petroglyphs. A steep path wiggles up to the edge of the caldera, from which you'll get cardiac-arresting views of Hane Bay (plan on one hour from Hane). You can save this section by getting there by 4WD from Vaipaee. Then it's another two hours or so, well inland, amid a variety of landscapes – from thick vegetation to tree ferns and a dramatic finish of hacking through pandanus.

Small Crater WALKING
A lovely, easy walk around the rim of an ancient volcano, located east of Vaipaee. Lunar landscapes and fantastic views. About 1½ hours.

Big Crater WALKING
Around the rim of the big crater west of Vaipaee. About four hours.

Hokatu to Hane WALKING
There's an inland track that connects the two villages. It goes over a small pass. If the trail has been cleared, a guide may not be necessary.

Horse Riding

A fantastic ride is from Vaipaee to Hane, passing the arboretum, airport and windswept plateaus before reaching the coastal road, which plunges down towards Hane.

ARCHAEOLOGY IN THE MARQUESAS – LEARN YOUR BASICS

You don't need to have a PhD to appreciate the archaeological remains that are typical of the Marquesas, but a few explanations will greatly enhance your trip.

Tohua

The *tohua* refers to a paved rectangular platform with several tiers of basalt block rows on either side. The *tohua* were used as meeting places and also hosted festivals and dance performances. Flat boulders form a sort of stage on which solo dances took place, and which was also used by young chiefs to show off their tattoos.

Me'ae

The *me'ae* is the Marquesan equivalent of the Tahitian *marae*. *Me'ae* are religious sites built from basalt blocks placed side by side and piled up. Generally found in the valleys and away from secular places, the *me'ae* was the sacred precinct par excellence and was a place of worship, burial and human sacrifice. It was strictly *tapu* (forbidden); access was restricted to a few priests or chiefs endowed with *mana* (spiritual power). *Me'ae* were also used for cannibalistic rituals. They were generally built near a banyan, a sacred tree.

Pae Pae

Pae pae are platforms of stone blocks, on which *ha'e* (human habitations) were built from native plants and wood. The *pae pae* was divided into two sections. The front level was reserved for daily activities, while the back section, which was covered and slightly raised, served as a sleeping area. The roof was made of leaves from the *uru* (breadfruit) tree and coconut palm. Only the stone foundations have survived; the vegetation and wooden structures have been destroyed.

Foundations of *pae pae* are ubiquitous in the Marquesas. Some modern houses are even built on them!

Tiki

One of the Marquesas' most pervasive images, the enigmatic *tiki* are carved humanlike statues, the height of which varies from a few dozen centimetres to almost 3m (they're definitely shorter than the monumental *moai* on Easter Island). Since they were generally erected on or near a holy place, experts believe *tiki* had a religious and symbolic function, possibly representing deified clan ancestors. They also marked the boundaries of places that were *tapu*. The highly stylised mouth and eyes are the most striking features; the mouth is represented by a long and narrow rectangle, while the eyes are large concentric circles. Sculpted in the form of statues, *tiki* were also carved in bas-relief, on weapons, paddles and dugout canoes. According to many locals, some *tiki* are still possessed of *mana* and have a potential for evil that can manifest itself if they are moved or handled.

Petroglyphs

Petroglyphs are designs carved on stones. They feature sharks, turtles, whales, outrigger canoes, facial features and geometric patterns... Ancient works of art? Possibly, according to local experts.

If you want to explore the interior and reach a secluded archaeological site, then nothing beats the ride from Hane to the Vaikivi petroglyphs.

Horse-riding trips can be organised through your pension. A ride typically costs 6000 CFP for a half day or 10,000 CFP for a full day, including a guide.

Tours

Pension owners have 4WDs and can take you to visit the island's villages (about 5000 CFP per day).

BIRD-WATCHING IN THE MARQUESAS

Serious birdwatchers rate the Marquesas as a top birding hot spot in Polynesia, with rare endemic species, some of which are classified as endangered. Keep your eyes peeled for the following feathered creatures:

Fatu Hiva monarch *(Pomarea whitneyi)* Fatu Hiva.

Iphis monarch *(Pomarea iphis)* 'Ua Huka.

Marquesan ground dove *(Gallicolumba rubescens)* Hatutu and Fatu Huku.

Marquesan imperial pigeon *(Ducula galeata)* Nuku Hiva and 'Ua Huka.

Marquesan kingfisher *(Todiramphus godeffroyi)* Tahuata.

Marquesan (Motane) monarch *(Pomarea mendanae motanensis)* Motane.

Marquesan reed warbler *(Acrocephalus mendanae)* Throughout the archipelago.

Marquesan swiftlet *(Collocalia ocista)* Throughout the archipelago.

Ultramarine lorikeets *(Vini ultramarina)* 'Ua Huka.

White-capped fruit dove *(Ptilinopus dupetithouarsii)* Throughout the archipelago.

For more information, go to www.manu.pf and www.birdlife.org.

Sleeping

Chez Maurice et Delphine PENSION **$**

(☎92 60 55; Hokatu; bungalows half board per person 6500 CFP) This pension has five ramshackle and very simply furnished bungalows on a little knoll on Hokatu village outskirts, with sweeping views of Hokatu Bay and Motu Hane. Delightful hosts: Maurice is a master carver (his living room resembles a craft museum) and he'll be happy to teach guests some of his techniques, while his wife Delphine (who can get by in English) is adept at preparing flower garlands. Try to book the bungalow Mata Otemanu, which boasts a perfect position – lying on your bed you can see the bay and the ocean. Airport transfers are 2000 CFP return.

Le Reve Marquisien PENSION **$$**

(☎79 10 52; revemarquisien@mail.pf; Vaipaee; bungalows s/d half board 16,400/21,000 CFP) Scene: a secluded clearing surrounded by a lush coconut grove. Soundtrack: birds twitching in the jungle. Close up: totally relaxed, you're sipping a fruit juice on your private terrace. The four bungalows are of good standard, with wooden floors, firm beds, hot water and TV. Le Reve Marquisien is a perfect escape hatch, but it feels a bit too isolated, about 2km from Vaipaee. Airport transfers are free.

Chez Alexis Scallamera PENSION **$**

(☎92 60 19, 79 09 48; scallamera.florentine@mail.pf; Vaipaee; r with shared bathroom per person 2000-4000 CFP; ❄📶) Two home-style rooms with shared (hot-water) bathroom right in the thick of the owners' sprawling home. Rooms lack intimacy, but sport tip-top mattresses. Meals are available on request.

Information

Infrastructure is very limited on 'Ua Huka. Bring a wad of cash – there's no bank and no ATM, and credit cards are not accepted.

Post office (⏲7-11am Mon-Fri; 📶) In Hane, has internet and wi-fi access (with the Manaspot card).

Getting There & Away

Air Tahiti (☎91 60 16, 92 60 44, 86 42 42; www.airtahiti.pf) has offices at the airport and in Vaipaee.

The *Aranui* cargo ship (p176) stops at Vaipaee. Speedboats can be hired to travel to 'Ua Pou and Nuku Hiva (from 55,000 CFP).

Getting Around

A surprisingly good 13km road links Vaipaee to Hokatu via Hane.

'Ua Huka's airport is on an arid plateau midway between Vaipaee and Hane. Some pensions charge 2000 CFP return for airport transfers.

'UA POU

POP 2110

'Ua Pou's geology is fascinating. A collection of 12 pointy pinnacles seem to soar like missiles from the basaltic shield. Almost constantly shrouded in swirling mist and flecked by bright sunlight, they form one of the Marquesas' most enduring images. Completing this natural tableau of otherworldly proportions are a few oasislike valleys bursting with tropical plants, as well as a handful of tempting beaches.

'Ua Pou's jewel-like natural setting will frame everything you do here, from hiking and horse riding across the island to visiting secluded hamlets. For culture buffs, the island musters up a handful of powerful archaeological sites.

Getting There & Away

There is an office for **Air Tahiti** (☎91 52 25, 86 42 42; www.airtahiti.pf; ⏲7.30am-noon & 1.30-3.30pm Mon-Fri) in Hakahau. The *Aranui* cargo ship (p176) stops at Hakahau and Hakahetau.

Getting Around

One dirt 4WD track runs most of the way around the island, with the only inaccessible bit being the section between Hakamaii and Hakatao.

The airport is at Aneou, about 10km west of Hakahau. Your hosts will come to collect you if you have booked accommodation; it usually costs 4000 CFP per person return.

Ask at your pension about hiring a 4WD with driver; expect to pay 15,000 CFP to 20,000 CFP per day.

Hakahau

'Ua Pou's largest settlement, Hakahau is blessed with a photogenic location. A huge bite chomped out of the fretted coastline of 'Ua Pou's northern coast, Hakahau Bay resembles a giant mouth about to swallow up its prey, with the iconic basalt peaks in the background. Hakahau is a relaxed coastal town blessed with a sweeping black-sand beach – fairly suitable for a dip – and wicked waves that keep local surfers happy. With a couple of pensions and useful services, it's a convenient base.

Sights

Hakahau Bay NATURAL SITE

For a beautiful view of Hakahau Bay head east from Restaurant-Pension Pukuéé along a track until you reach a small pass. At the pass, take the right fork and climb steeply for about 10 minutes until you reach a small flight of steps leading to a white cross, which you can see from the quay.

Anahoa Beach BEACH

From Hakahau, it's a 30-minute walk east to deserted Anahoa Beach. From the Hakahau quay, follow the sign for Restaurant-Pension Pukuéé and continue along the paved road beyond the restaurant.

Catholic church CHURCH

Right in the centre of town is this enticing church made of wood and stone. Inside you'll find some fantastic woodcarvings of religious figures with a distinctly Marquesan touch.

Activities

The activity of choice on 'Ua Pou is **walking**. Without a guide you can walk along the 4WD tracks that connect the villages (but there's no shade). For deeper exploration, it's advisable to hire a walking guide since it's easy to get lost. Ask at Restaurant-Pension Pukuéé. A full-day guided walk is about 12,000 CFP for two. Recommended hikes:

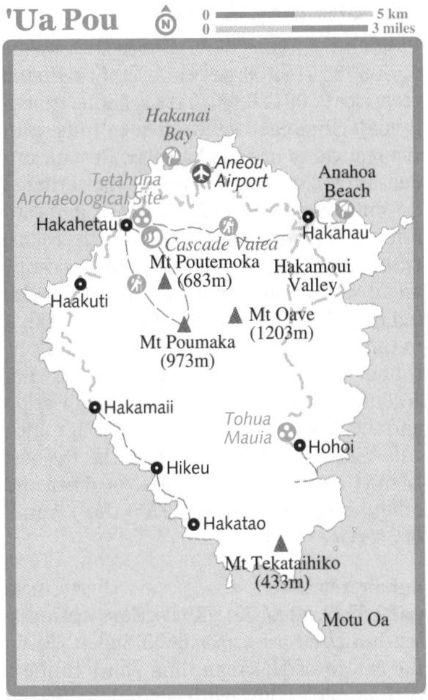

DON'T MISS

PLAGE AUX REQUINS (SHARK BEACH)

Shortly beyond the airport at Aneou, **Hakanai Bay** appears like a mirage from around a sharp bend: a long curve of wave-lashed beach, and the only footprints to be seen other than your own are those of crabs and insects (except at weekends, when locals enjoy picnics here). It has been named Plage aux Requins (Shark Beach) because of the sharks that are occasionally seen in the cove (it's safe for a dip nonetheless).

Hakahau–Hakahetau WALKING
The cross-island path from Hakahau to Hakahetau takes three to four hours. It ends at Hakahetau where you can take a dip at the waterfall. Easy to moderate.

Poumaka Loop WALKING
The more challenging Poumaka loop takes about four hours and goes around Mt Poumaka. It affords hauntingly beautiful panoramas of the iconic basaltic 'pillars' that jab the skyline.

Sleeping & Eating

Pukuéé PENSION, RESTAURANT $$
(☎92 50 83, 72 90 08; pukuee@mail.pf; r half board per person 9000 CFP;) It's reliable, friendly and fabulously sited on a hillside with swoony views of Hakahau Bay. Restaurant-Pension Pukuéé garners points for daring to do something a bit different, as the layout attests: the four smallish, no-frills rooms with shared bathrooms (hot water) occupy an all-wood house that resembles a chalet (couples, take note: the walls don't make it to the ceilings), and there's a little pool surrounded by eye-soothing greenery. Owner Jérôme is great with excursion organisation and well versed in ecotourism. Jérôme's wife, Elisa, will treat you with the freshest island ingredients (vegetables, local fish and other seafood) at dinner (2700 CFP). Laundry service is available.

Pension Vehine PENSION $$
(☎92 53 21, 70 84 32; r & bungalows incl breakfast/half board per person 6600/8800 CFP) In the centre of Hakahau, this pension offers two simple rooms with shared bathroom (hot-water showers) in a house and two beautifully finished bungalows in the garden (alas, no views). Meals are served at Snack Vehine, the family's restaurant.

Chez Dora PENSION $$
(☎92 53 69; r incl breakfast/half board per person 5000/7000 CFP, bungalows incl breakfast/half board per person 6000/7000 CFP) At the far end of the village, this is a mixed bag. The three rooms with shared bathroom in the owners' house have nothing to excite the senses (and might be noisy if the whole family is around). More charming are the two standalone bungalows in the garden.

Snack Vehine SNACK $
(☎92 50 63; mains 1100-1600 CFP; lunch & dinner Mon-Sat) Located a mango's throw from Pension Vehine, this casual eatery is your spot for chow mein, grilled or raw fish, and steaks.

Information

There's a small medical centre with a doctor and dentist in the south of the village.

Banque Socredo (7.30am-noon & 1-3pm Mon-Fri) Currency exchange and an ATM.

Post office (OPT; 7-11.30am & 12.15-3pm Mon-Thu, 7-11.30am & 12.15-2pm Fri;) On the seafront. Internet and wi-fi access (with the Manaspot network). Has an ATM.

Hakahetau

This tranquil village springs up like an oasis after driving along the west coast on a dusty track. There aren't many things to see, but the addictive peaceful atmosphere could hold you captive longer than expected.

Sights

Cascade Vaiea WATERFALL
At the entrance of the village a sign marks the mountainside track to a waterfall. It has a deep round bathing pool that looks like something out of a tonic-drink advert.

Tetahuna ARCHAEOLOGICAL SITE
At the far end of the village, make a beeline for this grandiose *tohua*, which hosted numerous dance and cultural performances during the Marquesas Arts Festival in 2007.

Flat Stone LOOKOUT
At the northern entrance of the village there's a large flat stone that you can walk out onto to see a view of the village and bay. It's now used to dry copra, but in ancient

times it had the more grisly job of drying human remains before they were transported in a pirogue up the mountain for 'burial'.

Sleeping & Eating

Pension Leydj PENSION **$**
(☎92 53 19; r half board per person 5500 CFP) In a plum setting on a hill at the edge of Hakahetau, this mellow pension offers clean, well-swept yet impersonal rooms at a nice price. Bathrooms (cold water) are shared. Owner Tony is a renowned master carver and the living room is like a small art gallery – you won't find a better place to buy high-quality souvenirs. His spouse Célestine can cook some seriously good Marquesan meals. Various excursions can be organised.

Ti' Piero SNACK **$$**
(☎92 55 82; mains 900-1900 CFP; ⊙lunch & dinner Wed-Sun) This family-run eatery does a wonderful job of preparing well-executed Marquesan specialities, such as the *chèvre de sept heures* (goat cooked for seven hours) and breadfruit rolls. A good place to recharge the batteries after the Hakahau–Hakahetau walk. It's best to reserve.

Hakamaii

At the end of the 4WD track from Hakahetau, on the west coast, this one-street village stretches along the Kahioa River. The facade of the town's stone church, facing the ocean, has unusual yellow, blue and red wooden panels that are meant to imitate stained-glass windows.

A path running up the hill next to the church leads up to a ridge for some fantastic views.

Hohoi

Tranquillity reigns supreme in this little charmer, located about 12km southeast of Hakahau, and nobody's complaining. Apart from its lovely setting and peaceful ambience, Hohoi is a definite must-see for culture vultures.

Situated above the village, the magnificent **Tohua Mauia** comprises a huge L-shaped stone platform as well as numerous *pae pae* dotted around the main complex. Even if your interest in ruins is only slight, the enchanting setting and the almost mystical hush are reason enough to come here.

Further down in the village, look for the pagoda-shaped **Catholic church**. Continue down to the beach; if you are lucky, you might come across *pierres fleuries* (flowering stones) – pieces of phonolite that have crystallised to form amber-coloured flower shapes.

DON'T MISS

THE MARQUESAS ARTS FESTIVAL

Powerful, grandiose, visceral – words do little justice to the Marquesas' premier festival, which lasts about one week and is held once every four years, usually in December, either on 'Ua Pou, Nuku Hiva or Hiva Oa. It's so colourful that it's definitely worth timing your trip around it. The last edition was held in December 2011 on Nuku Hiva, so you'll have to wait until December 2015 for the next one, on Hiva Oa. If you don't have the patience, 'mini festivals' are held on the smaller islands (on 'Ua Huka in 2013) in between two 'big' festivals.

The Marquesas Arts Festival revolves around a series of music, dance and cultural contests, with dance performances being the highlights. Groups from all the Marquesan islands demonstrate their skills at traditional dances, including the spine-tingling Haka Manu (Bird's Dance) and Haka Pua (Dance of the Pig). Groups from other Polynesian archipelagos are invited and they join the contests, too. Most dancing contests take place on restored archaeological sites, which strengthens the visual appeal of the performances. Events also include traditional Marquesan meal preparations as well as arts and crafts displays.

The Marquesas Arts Festival is your top chance to immerse yourself in traditional Marquesan culture. All islanders take it very seriously. Book your Air Tahiti flight a few months in advance.

HIVA OA

POP 1991

Scenery- and atmosphere-wise, Hiva Oa is worthy of an Oscar. This serpentine island is a picturesque mix of lush jungle, sea-smashed coastal cliffs and towering volcanic peaks. Many of the bays that fret the coastline make wonderful photo ops with their combinations of indigo water, white- or black-sand or pebble-stubbled foreshores and nodding palms – not to mention a smattering of typical Marquesan hamlets where time has stood still. After a few days here, you'll understand why the artist Paul Gauguin and the Belgian singer Jacques Brel chose to call it home.

But wait! There's more to Hiva Oa than grandiose landscapes and laid-back vibes. Pre-European history is achingly prominent here, with a collection of enigmatic archaeological sites scattered in the jungle, including the most intriguing *tiki* in French Polynesia, which will give you plenty to ponder.

Hiva Oa is also the optimal launching pad for exploring Tahuata and Fatu Hiva.

Getting There & Away

The *Aranui* cargo ship (p176) stops at Atuona and Puamau and, less frequently, at Hanapaaoa and Hanaiapa. To get to Tahuata, you can charter a private boat and share the costs with any other passengers (you're looking at about 20,000 CFP from Atuona to Vaitahu). To get to Fatu Hiva, see p202.

Air Tahiti (☎92 70 90, 86 42 42; www.airtahiti.pf)

Getting Around

TO/FROM THE AIRPORT The airport is 13km from Atuona. If you have booked your accommodation, your host will come and collect you for about 3600 CFP return. You can also hitch a ride to town.

CAR **Atuona Rent-a-Car** (☎92 76 07, 72 17 17) and **Hiva Oa Location** (☎92 70 43, 24 65 05) have 4WDs for hire (without driver) for about 13,000 CFP per day, with unlimited kilometres.

Hiva Oa & Tahuata

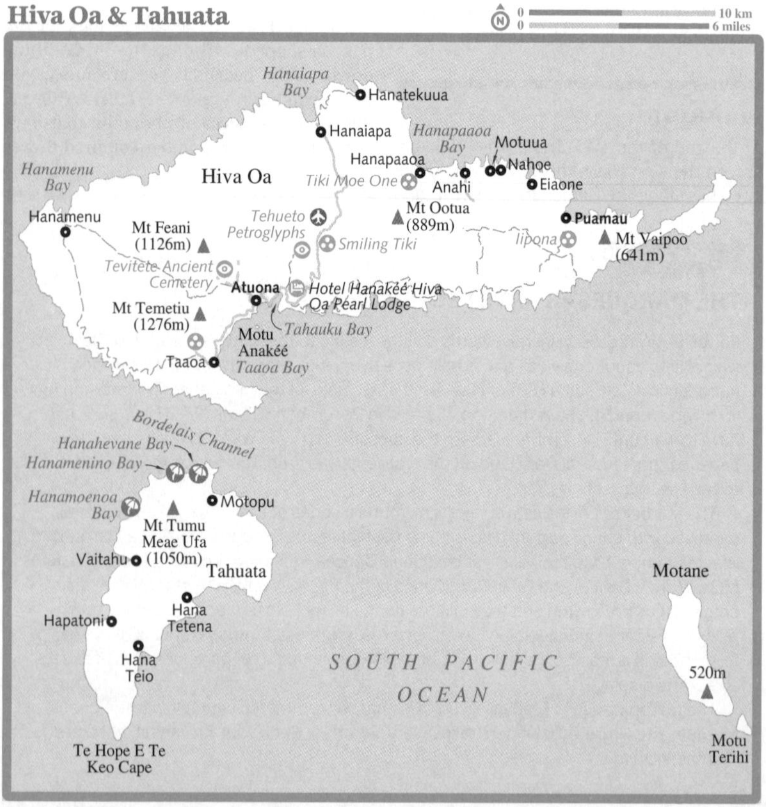

Atuona & Around

POP 1300

Atuona is the southern group's administrative capital and one of the Marquesas' most attractive settlements. Nestled at the mouth of a lovely bay, it's framed by forested mountains that rise steeply up behind it to converge on a crenellated central ridge. It's the only town with any sort of bustle (by Marquesan standards) on Hiva Oa, and has a small selection of restaurants and guesthouses. Neat, modern houses cling like limpets to a rocky peninsula that separates the town centre from the majestic Tahauku Bay to the east, a favourite anchoring place among yachties.

Atuona is particularly famous for having once been home to Paul Gauguin and Belgian singer Jacques Brel (1929–78), whose memories are kept alive by a regular trickle of visitors.

Sights

Espace Culturel Paul Gauguin MUSEUM

(adult/child 600/300 CFP; ⌚8-11am & 2-5pm Mon-Thu, 7.30am-2.30pm Fri, 8-11am Sat) For Gauguin fans, a visit to this refurbished museum is a must. Don't get too excited, though; you won't find any originals, just digital copies of his work. The detailed signs in English are very informative. Once you've done a full round of the paintings, timeline and literature, head outside and have a look at the Maison du Jouir (House of Pleasure), a replica of Gauguin's own house.

Centre Jacques Brel MUSEUM

(adult/child 600/300 CFP; ⌚8-11am & 2-5pm Mon-Thu, 7.30am-2.30pm Fri, 8-11am Sat) Behind the Espace Culturel Paul Gauguin you'll find a big aircraft hangar. In the centre is Brel's plane, *Jojo;* posters tracing the musician's life adorn the walls and his music plays dreamily over the sound system. For more on Brel's life, see p195.

Calvaire Cemetery CEMETERY

Another must-see for Gauguin and Brel devotees is the Calvaire Cemetery, perched on a hill overlooking Atuona. You will find this frangipani-filled graveyard an appropriately colourful place for Paul Gauguin's tomb. While most of the tombs are marked with white crosses, Gauguin's is a simple round stone with his name painted in white. Right behind, a replica of the statue *Oviri* (meaning 'wild') stands guard. Jacques Brel's grave is a bit below, near the access steps, on the left. The gravestone, lovingly planted with flowers, is adorned with a medallion depicting the singer with his female companion, Madly.

To get there, head north on the road just east of the *gendarmerie* (police station). Continue for about 600m until you reach a fork in the road and follow the sign to the cemetery 100m further on. It takes about 20 minutes on foot.

Tehueto petroglyphs ARCHAEOLOGICAL SITE

Anyone with an interest in ancient Marquesan civilisation shouldn't leave Atuona without a visit to the Tehueto petroglyphs. Hidden high up in the Tahauku Valley, they are a good walk from Tahauku Bay (approximately 2.5km inland), but it's usually quite overgrown and the path is confusing; we suggest hiring a guide (ask at your pension). You'll find a massive rock with prolific carvings on two sides, including stylised human figures. Then follow the trail that leads up a small hill to an overgrown *tohua* sporting a *tiki* carved in bas-relief in the side of the stone platform (you can't miss it).

Tevitete Ancient Cemetery HISTORIC SITE

This isolated, poignant site about 2km up in a valley (ask for directions) features a series of tombs made of volcanic stones; note the small *tiki* that are carved in bas-relief on a few tombs. At the back of the cemetery, a big trunk is carved in the shape of a *tiki*. From the cemetery, you'll also get ample views of the valley and Atuona.

Catholic church CHURCH

The Catholic church, right in the centre, is worth a peek for its elegant architecture that combines wood and stone.

Tohua Pepeu ARCHAEOLOGICAL SITE

Restored for the 1991 Marquesas Arts Festival, the Tohua Pepeu faces Banque Socredo in the centre of town. It's used today as a festivities centre, where dances and cultural activities are performed.

Atuona Beach NATURAL SITE

Framed by basaltic cliffs, this wide curve of black sand is very scenic – it inspired painter Paul Gauguin, which is saying a lot – but it's not appropriate for swimming because of strong currents.

Atuona

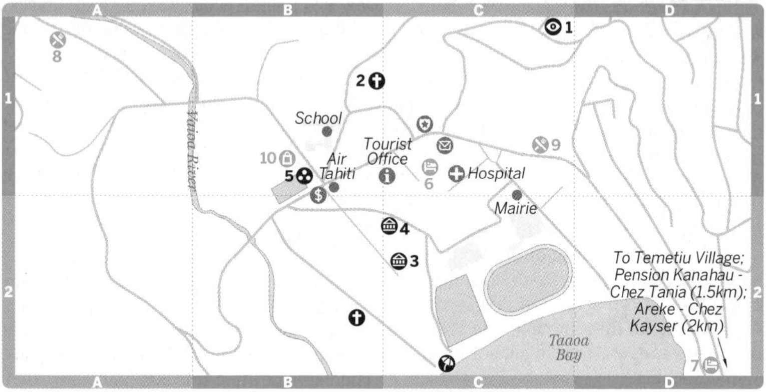

Activities

Hiking

There are some truly excellent hiking possibilities on Hiva Oa, including the strenuous cross-island trek from Atuona to Hanamenu (about 11 hours). Sadly, there's no waymarked trail and no guide was available on the island at the time of writing. Ask at your pension or contact Paco, from Hamau Ranch – Chez Paco, who may organise something for you if he's given enough advance notice.

Horse Riding

Seeing the island from the saddle is a typical Hiva Oa experience and a low-impact way to imbibe the majestic scenery. A network of trails leading to some of the most beautiful sites can be explored on horseback.

Hamau Ranch – Chez Paco HORSE RIDES
(☎92 70 57, 28 68 21; hamauranch@mail.pf; rides 7000-14,000 CFP) Paco organises three-hour jaunts on the plateau near the airport. No previous experience is necessary. The ultimate is a full-day ride to Hanatekuua Bay (p198), to the north of the island, along undulating ridges and the coastline. Riders must be at least six years old. Transfers can be arranged.

Diving

Hiva Oa is certainly not possessed of dazzling tropical reefs (there's no barrier reef and no turquoise lagoon in the Marquesas, remember), but there are many excellent diving sites along the crumpled coastline of Hiva Oa and Tahuata.

Atuona

Sights

1	Calvaire Cemetery	C1
2	Catholic Church	B1
3	Centre Jacques Brel	C2
4	Espace Culturel Paul Gauguin	C2
5	Tohua Pepeu	B1

Sleeping

6	Bungalows Communaux d'Atuona	C1
7	Pension & Relais Moehau	D2

Eating

8	Hoa Nui	A1
9	Snack Make Make	C1

Shopping

10	Marquises Creation	B1

SubAtuona DIVING, BOAT TOUR
(☎92 70 88, 27 05 24; eric.lelyonnais@wanadoo.fr; Atuona) This small diving outfit (one instructor) offers personalised tours and a wealth of experience in Marquesan waters. Including all gear, the cost of a single/two-tank dive is 7000/13,000 CFP (minimum two divers). SubAtuona also offers day trips to Tahuata that combine one dive and a tour of Tahuata's main villages. The price is 15,000 CFP and includes a picnic on a secluded beach. Payment is by cash only. Note that the owner had plans to sell his operation at the time of writing.

Boat Excursions

Taking a boat excursion to nearby Tahuata will be one of the main highlights of your visit to Hiva Oa and it's well worth the expense (especially given the lack of reliable boat services to Tahuata). Daylong trips usually include stops at Hapatoni and Vaitahu and a picnic lunch at Hanamenino Bay or Hanahevane Bay. Your pension will make arrangements with a local operator. Plan on 11,500 CFP per person.

Tours

Daylong excursions by 4WD cost about 12,000 CFP for two people. Plan on two days if you want to take in Taaoa, Hanaiapa, Hanapaaoa and Puamau. For information, contact pension owners. Guides have a very limited knowledge of English and act more as drivers than proper guides, so don't expect high-profile historical comments.

Sleeping

Accommodation options on Hiva Oa are fairly limited. All places are in (or near) Atuona, bar one in Puamau. Unless otherwise noted, credit cards are accepted.

TOP CHOICE **Temetiu Village** PENSION $

(91 70 60; www.temetiuvillage.com; Tahauku Bay; bungalows standard s/d 7100/9000 CFP, large d 10,200 CFP;) Seeking a stress-melting cocoon in Hiva Oa with efficient hosts and a big dollop of atmosphere, without an exorbitant price tag? This well-run pension has all the key ingredients, with four shiny-clean bungalows perched scenically on a lush hillside, each enjoying wraparound views of Tahauku Bay. There are also two older (and slightly cheaper) bungalows, but they show signs of wear and tear. The small pool is a joke, though. The food here is a definite plus.

PAUL GAUGUIN & JACQUES BREL

The Marquesas are closely associated with painter Paul Gauguin (1848–1903) and singer-songwriter Jacques Brel (1929–78). Both were won over by the archipelago's powerful landscapes and serenity, and both chose to live out their lives on Hiva Oa. They rest in the Calvaire Cemetery (p193), which has become something of a pilgrimage site for numerous devotees.

The evocative paintings of Paul Gauguin are largely responsible for Polynesia's enduring reputation as a paradise lost. Constantly in search of an escape, he first voyaged to Brittany, Martinique and Provence, but this was still not enough to appease his tormented mind. In Mataiea on Tahiti, where the Musée Gauguin now stands, he concentrated on capturing images of daily life and, in 1892 and 1893, experienced an intensely productive period. Exuberant settings and flamboyant colours, with yellows, reds and blues predominating, increasingly pervaded the artist's painting.

Impoverished, Gauguin sailed back to France in 1893 but, short of any recognition, he set off for the South Seas once again in 1895. His most powerful compositions date from this second and final stay in Polynesia, which was marked by illness and distress. After a failed suicide attempt, Gauguin took refuge on Hiva Oa in the Marquesas, where he defended the inhabitants against the colonial administration and the all-powerful Catholic Church. Although weakened, he did not stop writing, drawing, sculpting and painting, and it was during this period that he produced one of his most beautiful nudes, *Barbaric Tales* (1902). Gauguin died in May 1903.

Belgian-born artist (and a legend in France and in Belgium) Jacques Brel was as iconoclastic as Gauguin and he derided the flaws of society in his powerful songs, including the poignant 'Dans le Port d'Amsterdam' and 'Les Marquises'. In an attempt to escape media pressure, he set out to sail around the world on the *Askoy*, his private ketch, accompanied by his female companion, Madly, who was from Guadeloupe. In November 1975 they arrived at Atuona. In 1976 Brel and Madly set up a small home on the hillside above the village and became involved in village life. Brel equipped himself with *Jojo*, a Beechcraft airplane, with which he would perform medical evacuations to Pape'ete from time to time. Jacques Brel died of cancer in October 1978 at the age of 48. His tomb is near that of Gauguin.

DON'T MISS

THE SMILING TIKI

Hiva Oa's most bizarre statue, the Smiling Tiki (no joke), can be found near the road to the airport, about 10km from Atuona. About 1m in height, it stands alone in a clearing. Its two clearly outlined eyes resemble big glasses, and its curved lips suggest a smile – it looks like a puppet that you just want to hug! To find it (no sign), ask your hosts to draw you a map or ask for the little sketch map that's on sale at the tourism office (it's surprisingly reliable).

Hotel Hanakéé Hiva Oa Pearl Lodge HOTEL **$$$**
(92 75 87; www.pearlodge.com; bungalows d 26,000-31,000 CFP;) Recipe for romance: a secluded property on a mound overlooking Tahauku Bay, with Mt Temetiu as a backdrop; 14 well-designed bungalows deployed in a blooming tropical garden; a small pool with sunloungers; and a good restaurant. Some units have views of the bay while others face the valley and the mountainous interior. One minus: it feels a bit isolated.

Bungalows Communaux d'Atuona BUNGALOW **$**
(commune@commune-hivaoa.pf; Atuona; bungalows s/d 3000/4000 CFP) An obvious choice for thrifty travellers. In theory, the seven bungalows with bathroom (cold water) and kitchenette, next to the *mairie* (town hall), are reserved for officials, but they may be let to tourists depending on availability. Pluses: affordable, well located, serviceable. Minuses: crude and sticky hot (no fans are provided). Credit cards are not accepted. For booking, call the **mairie** (92 73 32; 7.30-11.30am & 1.30-4pm Mon-Thu, to 3pm Fri).

Pension Kanahau – Chez Tania PENSION **$**
(91 71 31, 70 16 26; http://pensionkanahau.com; Tahauku Bay; s/d incl breakfast 10,000/12,500 CFP;) Tania, your chirpy host, does a superb job in keeping her place shipshape. Locationwise, this pension plays in the same league as nearby Temetiu Village, with a flower-filled garden and stupendous views of Tahauku Bay and the mountain amphitheatre. The four bungalows are well furnished, spacious and sparkling clean (hot water is available); two units are equipped with cooking facilities. Tania may prepare meals, or she does drive guests to town for lunch or dinner and takes them back to the pension, for free. No credit cards are accepted, but you can pay in dollars or euros. There's a 15% drop in price if you stay more than three nights.

Pension Moehau PENSION **$**
(92 72 69; www.relaismoehau.pf; Atuona; s/d incl breakfast 8100/12,200 CFP;) While the front rooms are light-filled and face a bay-view terrace, those at the back face the dark hill behind. The moral of the story: ask for an oceanside room (especially rooms 2 and 3). All rooms are scrupulously clean, amply sized and well appointed (hot water, fan and plump bedding) but they lack charm. There's a good restaurant downstairs.

Areke – Chez Kayser PENSION **$$**
(92 76 19, 23 48 17; www.pension-hivaoa.com; Tahauku Bay; r half board per person 10,500 CFP;) This aerie affords glorious views of Tahauku Bay and has a nice little pool in the garden. The modern house is charmless, but this place enjoys a good reputation for its delicious home cooking and convivial atmosphere. All three rooms are simple and fresh, but there's not much in the way of decoration. Don't even consider walking to town – the access road is incredibly steep, but the owner provides free transfers by car. Prices drop by 10% if you stay more than three nights. Cash only.

Eating

Most restaurants provide free transport for their dinner guests (call ahead). You will find several well-stocked grocery stores in Atuona.

Hotel Hanakéé Hiva Oa Pearl Lodge HOTEL RESTAURANT **$$**
(92 75 87; mains 1500-3900 CFP; lunch & dinner) Probably the number-one spot for fine dining in Hiva Oa, and certainly the most suitable place for a *moment à deux*. The sweeping views from the terrace are impressive enough, but the excellent French-influenced cuisine is better still, and makes imaginative use of the island's rich produce. The Sunday brunch (3300 CFP) is a steal.

Relais Moehau RESTAURANT **$**
(92 72 69; mains 1400-2500 CFP; lunch & dinner) It might feel weird to sit down for a pizza on a South Pacific island, but the fish pizza is too flavoursome to ignore (at dinner

only). Other headliners include *chaud froid de thon* (cooked tuna served cold), grilled wahoo, and raw shrimps with coconut sauce. The tiled terrace overlooking Atuona bay is agreeable. Note the opening hours at lunchtime: 11.30am to 1pm. Credit cards are accepted (minimum 5000 CFP).

Temetiu Village PENSION RESTAURANT **$$**
(☎91 70 60; set menu 3000 CFP; ⏰lunch & dinner, by reservation) What's the draw here? The panoramic views from the open-air dining room? The convivial atmosphere or the delectable (and copious) Marquesan specialities, such as seafood or goat? Come and see for yourself. Credit cards are accepted.

Areke – Chez Kayser PENSION RESTAURANT **$$**
(☎92 76 19, 23 48 17; www.pension-hivaoa.com; set menu 2500 CFP; ⏰by reservation) The Kaysers are *bons viveurs* and Madame knows her stuff when it comes to cooking lipsmacking Marquesan specialities such as goat with coconut sauce or chicken with papaya sauce. Wash it all down with a glass (or two) of French wine. Cash only.

Snack Make Make SNACK **$**
(☎92 74 26; mains 1300-2300 CFP; ⏰lunch Mon-Fri) Opposite the post office, this longstanding joint serves inexpensive fish and meat dishes. It may also be open for dinner certain days (call ahead). Cash only.

Hoa Nui RESTAURANT **$$**
(☎92 73 63; set menu 2500 CFP; ⏰lunch & dinner, by reservation) Hidden amid junglelike foliage, this modest eatery specialises in Marquesan cuisine (think pork, fish, seafood or goat), though the desserts are disappointing. Cash only.

Shopping

There's no craft centre in Atuona but you'll find a few outlets selling curios and local handicrafts. Relais Moehau has a good selection of woodcarvings. The gift shop inside Hotel Hanakéé Hiva Oa Pearl Lodge has woodcarvings and objects made of bone from Fatu Hiva and Tahuata.

Makivi Curious HANDICRAFTS
(☎79 40 57) Sells woodcarvings and stonecarvings as well as tapa and jewels made of bone, all made in the Marquesas. Call ahead and the owners will pick you up.

Marquises Creation CLOTHING, JEWELLERY
(☎92 70 77) A small shop behind the Tohua Pepeu, Marquises Creation specialises in clothing and jewellery.

Tuarae Peterano HANDICRAFTS
(☎92 70 64) Tuarae is famous for his woodcarvings and bamboo items poker work. His son specialises in bone carving. Call ahead for an appointment.

MARQUESAN HANDICRAFTS

If there is one place in French Polynesia where it's really possible to spend some cash, it's the Marquesas. *Tiki* (sacred sculptures), pestles, *umete* (bowls), adzes, spears, clubs, fish hooks and other items are carved from rosewood, *tou* (dark, hard-grained wood), bone or volcanic stone. These treasures are pieces of art, items you will keep for a lifetime. Less expensive buys include seed necklaces and *umu hei*, an assortment of fragrant plant material such as ylang-ylang, vanilla, pieces of pineapple covered in sandalwood powder, and various other fruits and plants, held together with a plant fibre. Fatu Hiva prides itself on being the only island in French Polynesia to have perpetuated the manufacture of *tapa* (cloth made from beaten bark and decorated with traditional designs). Before visiting the Marquesas, be sure to check the customs regulations in your home country regarding things like wood carvings or *tapa*.

In most villages there is a small *fare artisanal* (craft centre) where you can shop around. They may open only when requested or when the *Aranui* is in port. It's also well worth approaching craftspeople directly. Some work is done to order only, so if you stay several days on an island it's worth making a visit as soon as you arrive.

Bring enough cash because you cannot pay by credit card. Prices may be relatively high, but they're still lower than in Pape'ete and are well worth it for the time and artistic effort put into the works. Expect to pay at least 2000 CFP for a small *tapa* piece (up to 15,000 CFP for a piece 1m long), 3000 CFP for a small 15cm *tiki* (and up to 100,000 CFP for a large one) and 5000 CFP for a bowl or plate of about 50cm. Bargaining is not a Pacific tradition so don't expect to be able to beat the prices down very much.

Information

Banque Socredo (☎92 73 54; ⏰7.30-11.30am & 1.30-4pm Mon-Fri) Currency exchange. Has a 24-hour ATM.

Cyberservices (☎92 79 85, 23 22 47; VHF 11) Laundry service, wi-fi and can help yachties with formalities (just call to be picked up).

Hospital Small but well equipped; it's behind the mayor's office.

Post office (⏰7am-noon & 12.30-3pm Mon-Thu, 7am-noon & 12.30-2pm Fri; 📶) Internet and wi-fi access (with the Manaspot card, available at the counter). Has an ATM, too.

Tourist office (☎92 78 93; ⏰8.30-11.30am & 2-4pm Mon-Fri) Right in the centre. Hands out useful brochures and sells sketch maps of most tourist sites. Opening hours are erratic.

Taaoa

This is a sweet, picturesque hamlet. About 7km southwest of Atuona, accessed by a scenic paved road, Taaoa really feels like the end of the line. It boasts a marvellous setting, with jagged green mountains as the backdrop, and an extensive archaeological site.

About 1.5km from Taaoa, high up in an uninhabited valley, **Tohua Upeke** doesn't have the impressive *tiki*, as at Iipona near Puamau, but its sheer size makes it just as interesting. Surrounded by thick overhanging trees (including huge banyan trees), it's not hard to imagine the power such sacred sites once had for the pre-Christian islanders. On arrival at the site, you will find yourself facing a vast *tohua* built on several levels. Try to find the well-preserved *tiki* more than 1m in height sitting on a platform under big banyan trees. From a distance it looks like a plain block of basalt, but as you get closer you can clearly pick out the contours of the eyes and mouth – thrilling!

Puamau

Chances are great that you'll come to this east-coast settlement to visit the Iipona archaeological site lying on the outskirts of the village. Puamau itself is a delightful, timeless village that occupies a coastal plain bordered by a vast amphitheatre of mountains. On the way from Atuona you'll pass through the picturesque hamlets of **Motuua** and **Nahoe** and the incredibly scenic **Eiaone Bay**.

WORTH A TRIP

HANATEKUUA BAY

One of Hiva Oa's best-kept secrets is this impossibly scenic bay fringed with a pristine stretch of white-sand beach and backed by a lovely coconut grove. This slice of paradise is accessible by foot only (or by boat). From Hanaiapa, it's a fairly easy 90-minute walk, although the path is not marked. Ask locals to show you the trailhead. After an ascent of about 20 minutes, you'll reach the **Hanahaoe Pass** (159m), from where there are superb views in all directions. From here the path veers due south along a ridge (don't take the path that descends into a small valley to the east). Some 45 minutes of relatively easy walking after leaving the pass, the bay of Hanatekuua comes into view – a fantastic sight. From here it's less than 30 minutes, downhill all the way, to the beach. Enjoy!

Sights

TOP CHOICE **Iipona** ARCHAEOLOGICAL SITE

Iipona is one of the best-preserved archaeological sites in French Polynesia. You'll be moved by its eeriness and impressed by the five monumental *tiki* – it pulsates with *mana*.

As you advance towards the first platform, you'll first notice the reclining **Tiki Maki Taua Pepe**, representing a woman lying on her stomach, her head stretched out and arms pointing to the sky. Experts believe she represents a woman giving birth. The petroglyphs on the pedestal represent dogs but their meaning is unknown.

Tiki Takaii, at 2.67m, is the largest *tiki* in French Polynesia; it's named after a warrior chief renowned for his strength. **Tiki Te Tovae E Noho** is to the left of Takaii, on a lower platform. Less finely worked than the others, its upper torso is hard to make out and the head has disappeared. Note that its hands each have six fingers. Further back stands **Tiki Fau Poe**. Measuring about 1.8m, it is sitting with its legs stretched out, a position typical of women when they work in the fields. Experts believe it to be Takaii's wife. **Tiki Manuiotaa** is in complete contrast to the others: less massive, its proportions are harmonious and balanced. The hands are clearly recognisable, as is its female sex. It was decapitated, but its head has been replaced by archaeologists.

Known to ethnologists and archaeologists in the 1800s, the Iipona (Oipona) site was extensively restored in 1991 by French archaeologists Pierre and Marie-Noëlle Garanger-Ottino.

To reach the site from Puamau, follow the track directly back from the seafront, next to the football ground, and continue for about 1.5km. You will need to pay 300 CFP to the person who maintains and guards the site.

Tohua Pehe Kua ARCHAEOLOGICAL SITE
On the property of Pehekua – Chez Marie-Antoinette, shortly before the Iipona site, is a small graveyard with the tomb of the valley's last chief and his partner, who died early in the 20th century. One of the four tombs at the site is flanked by two *tiki*. You'll also find an imposing *pae pae*.

Eating

Pehekua – Chez Marie-Antoinette RESTAURANT $
(☎92 72 27; set menu 2300 CFP; ⊙by reservation)
Most visitors on a day trip from Atuona usually have lunch here (by reservation only). The dining room looks tired but the real hit is the tasty Marquesan food (fresh fish, goat, pork). The *tohua* Pehe Kua is in its grounds. You can also purchase vanilla pods. The rooms feel too neglected to be recommended. Cash only.

Hanapaaoa

It's a winding but scenic 1½-hour journey by 4WD to wild and beautiful Hanapaaoa from Atuona. The track passes the airport and then splits shortly after; the first turn-off goes to Hanaiapa and the second one leads to Hanapaaoa and Puamau. About 14km after the first turn-off, a 4WD track branches hairpinlike on the left. Soon the track snakes along the coast, offering ethereal vistas around every other bend – indigo-blue ocean, plunging cliffs and stunning bays – before reaching the hamlet of Hanapaaoa.

In Hanapaaoa, ask a local to take you to the **Tiki Moe One**, hidden on a hillside. One of the quirkiest statues in the Marquesas, it features a carved crown around the head and is said to be endowed with a strong *mana*. It's modestly sized at under 1m in height. According to legend, the inhabitants used to take it down to the beach every year where they bathed it and coated it with *monoi* (fragrant oil) before putting it back in place.

Hanaiapa

Picturesquely cradled by striking mountains carpeted with shrubs and coconut trees, Hanaiapa is a gem. Stretching for more than 1km along a single street, this neat and flower-filled village feels like the end of the line. The majestic Hanaiapa Bay is fringed with a pebble beach. An imposing rock sits in the middle of the bay.

Hanaiapa is a cul-de-sac, but you can walk to Hanatekuua Bay. At the entrance of the village (coming from Atuona), about 200m off the main road, to the right, you'll find some well-preserved **petroglyphs**. A big boulder sports elaborate geometric patterns. It's not easy to find (no signs); ask passers-by if you're stuck.

If you're looking for souvenirs, it's not a bad idea to stop at the premises of **Jean & Nadine Oberlin** (☎92 76 34), a couple from Alsace who fell in love with Hanaiapa long ago. They make lovely *tapa* (with a contemporary twist) as well as engraved calabashes. Look for the 'Artisanat' sign at the entrance of the village.

TAHUATA

POP 671

Just as lush but not as steep, Tahuata is Hiva Oa's shy little sister. Separated from Hiva Oa by the 4km-wide Bordelais Channel, it is the smallest inhabited island in the archipelago.

Most travellers visit Tahuata on a day tour from Hiva Oa, which is a shame as it deserves a couple of days to do it justice. So stretch that schedule and meet the bone carvers and tattoo artists at work, splash about on a deserted beach and explore the archaeological sites.

Sights

TOP CHOICE **Hanahevane Bay** BEACH
This glorious bay is caressed by jade-green waters and is studded with a broad strand

GETTING A TATTOO

Fancy looking like a fierce Marquesan *toa* (warrior) or a queen, thanks to indelible geometric patterns on your chest/shoulder/butt/neck/ankles/arms (take your pick)? Marquesan tattooists rank among the best in the South Pacific. Ironically, most Marquesan tattooists are not in the Marquesas, but work either on more touristy islands in French Polynesia (especially Tahiti, Mo'orea and Bora Bora) or abroad. On Nuku Hiva, ask for **Brice Haiti**; on Hiva Oa, **René Aukara**, **Tamatai Lecordier**, **Louis Bonno** and **Axel Kimitete** have a good rep. The most charismatic tattooist is certainly **Felix Fii**, on Tahuata. No two tattooists do the same designs. They all work to high-quality standards and use sterile needles. See p232 for more information.

of golden sand. It's a good picnic spot (despite a number of pesky *nono*) and has shallow, calm waters and a few coral formations, making it suitable for snorkelling. It's accessible by boat only.

Vaitahu VILLAGE

This tiny village, built against the steep slopes of the central ridge, retains a few vestiges of its stormy past. On the seafront stands a modest **memorial** topped by a rusty anchor, recalling the first meeting between Admiral Dupetit-Thouars and Chief Iotete in 1838.

Near the post office is a tiny **museum** (admission free) with some archaeological items including fish hooks and stone pestles. There are no set opening hours – just ask at the *mairie* next door.

The monumental stone **Catholic church** is opposite the seafront. Opened with great pomp and ceremony in 1988, it recalls the importance of Tahuata in the evangelisation of the archipelago. The church has beautiful stained-glass windows and some interesting woodcarvings.

Vaitahu is a good place to have a wander. Copra-drying sheds are dotted here and there, and brightly coloured traditional outrigger canoes (known locally as *vaka*) line the shore.

Hapatoni VILLAGE

Hapatoni curves around a wide bay and is accessible by boat in less than 15 minutes from Vaitahu, or by a track.

The **royal road** is the village's main attraction. Built on a dyke on the orders of Queen Vaekehu II in the 19th century, this paved road, lined with 100-year-old tamanu trees, extends along the shore. At the promontory a path leads up to a **lookout**, with a magnificent view of the bay.

In the middle of the village there's a lovely **me'ae** (ancient religious site). Next to it, you'll find a church built from stones and a cemetery.

Hanamoenoa Bay BEACH

This quiet, sheltered bay is popular with yachties. It's fringed by a ribbon of white sand, lapped by multihued waters and backed by lush hills.

Hanamenino Bay BEACH

Another secluded bay lined with a golden-sand beach, Hanamenino is also used for picnics. Access is by boat only.

Activities

The track that joins Vaitahu and Motopu in the northeast, a distance of about 17km, is suitable for **walking**.

Sleeping

Every village has one or two small shops. Tahuata has only one place to stay.

Amatea PENSION **$$**

(☎92 92 84, 76 24 90; Vaitahu; d 6000 CFP, d half board per person 7500 CFP) This property is secure and well maintained, with helpful hosts and a good location near the seafront in Vaitahu. The four rooms share two bathrooms (cold water). The owners can help arrange any activity and also transport to and from Tahuata.

Shopping

In Vaitahu try to meet **Félix Fii** and **Teiki Barsinas** (also known as 'Topi'), two renowned wood and bone carvers. Félix is also an excellent tattooist. Both villages have an artisanal shop.

Information

Tourist infrastructures are as scarce as hens' teeth on Tahuata. Bring cash, as there is no bank. The post office is in Vaitahu.

Getting There & Away

Tahuata is accessible only by boat (there's no landing strip) from Hiva Oa. There's no regular service, but locals frequently travel by boat between the two islands – ask around and hook onto a shared boat ride. Pension Amatea can also help arrange passage with private boats but it's much more expensive. You can also try to board the *Aranui* cargo ship (p176) at Hiva Oa.

By far the most convenient option is to take an excursion from Hiva Oa, which includes visits to Hapatoni, Vaitahu and a picnic on a beach at Hanamenino or Hanahevane.

Getting Around

A 17km track, accessible to 4WD vehicles, crosses the island's interior to link Vaitahu with Motopu and Vaitahu with Hapatoni. A 4WD costs 10,000 CFP for a day's hire with driver.

Hapatoni is less than 15 minutes from Vaitahu by speedboat. It costs about 6000 CFP to hire a boat between Vaitahu and Hapatoni, and 7000 to 10,000 CFP between Vaitahu and Hanahevane Bay.

FATU HIVA

POP 562

As far away from the rest of the world as it's possible to get in these modern times (despite mobile phones and satellite TVs), Fatu Hiva is a marvellous 'stop the world and get off' place. When arriving by boat (there's no landing strip), expect a visual shock: wrinkled cliffs tumble into the ocean and splendid bays, including the iconic Bay of Virgins, indent the coastline.

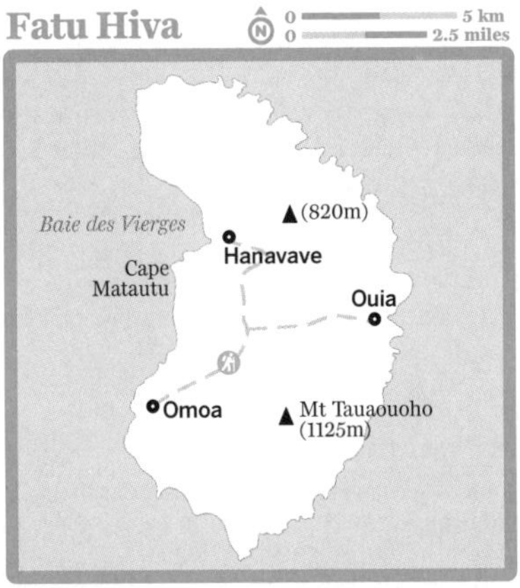

There are only two villages, one good pension and one dirt track, so there are plenty of opportunities to move into slow gear. For some cultural sustenance, a couple of giant petroglyphs – the biggest in French Polynesia – hidden in the forest beckon.

It's a bit challenging to get to Fatu Hiva, but for travellers who relish the idea of being marooned for a few days, this hard-to-reach island way off most people's radar (bar yachties) is hard to beat.

Sights

Omoa VILLAGE

Time moves at a crawl in Omoa. The most striking monument is the **Catholic church**, with its red roof, white facade and slender spire. It makes a colourful scene on Sunday morning, when it's bursting at the seams with a devout congregation neatly dressed and belting out rousing *himene* (hymns).

Omoa is famous for its two **giant petroglyphs**, which are in two different locations. The first site is easily accessed after a 10-minute walk from the main road (ask around) and features a huge fish (probably a dorado) as well as a few small anthropomorphic designs inscribed on big basaltic boulders. The second site is a 20-minute walk from Chez Lionel Cantois. It has a clearly outlined whale incised on a big slab – an eerie sight. To get there, you'll need a guide (Lionel will be happy to show you the site).

Hanavave VILLAGE

Hanavave boasts a splendid setting, at the mouth of a steep-sided valley, best enjoyed from the sea (lucky yachties!). When the setting sun bounces purple halos off the towering basaltic cones of **Baie des Vierges**, with a cluster of yachts at anchor, it's a hallucinatory wonderland. Truth is, these cones resemble giant phalluses protruding out of the ocean. This risqué natural tableau was originally (and aptly) named Baie des Verges in French (Bay of Penises). Outraged, the missionaries promptly added a redeeming 'i' to make the name Baie des Vierges (Bay of Virgins).

There's a small, sober **church** with an elaborate wooden altar in the village, as well as a **waterfall** at the end of the valley (ask for directions).

North of Hanavave, the stunning **Vaipo Cave** is carved into black cliffs. It's accessible only by boat.

Activities

Most activities on Fatu Hiva are of the DIY variety, including **walking** and **horse riding**. Why not follow the 17km-long track that links Omoa to Hanavave via the interior? The four-hour walk is not too difficult and you can't get lost. The first part of the walk goes up the Omoa Valley along a cliff-top path with sweeping views over the village below. The trail then crosses through the island's interior. It's a steep descent to Hanavave and there's not much shade along the way, but the views of the village and the dramatic coastline are well worth the effort. You can also horse-ride it – ask at your pension.

Sleeping

Chez Lionel Cantois PENSION **$**
(☎92 81 84, 70 03 71; chezlionel@mail.pf; Omoa; s/d incl breakfast 4500/6500 CFP, bungalow s/d incl breakfast 6500/9500 CFP; @) Basking in familial warmth, this pension at the far end of Omoa has an air of *Little House on the Prairie*. Lionel, who is from Normandy and who is a mine of local information (his English is passable), can take you virtually anywhere on the island, while his Marquesan wife Bernadette is an adept cook (dinner from 1500 CFP). The bungalow with bathroom (hot water) in the manicured garden is as cosy as a bird's nest but, if funds are short, the two rooms in the owners' house cut the mustard (the walls don't make it to the ceilings, though). Not a bad place to get stuck on Fatu Hiva (fear not, Lionel will help you arrange transport back to Hiva Oa). Transfers to the quay costs 1000 CFP return.

Shopping

Fatu Hiva is renowned for its *tapa* and *umu hei* (see the boxed text, p197), carved coconuts and woodcarvings.

Information

Bring a stash of cash – there's no bank on the island and credit cards are not accepted. There is a post office in Omoa.

Getting There & Away

Fatu Hiva is the most difficult island to get to in the Marquesas, but sorting out transport is manageable if you're flexible. In Hiva Oa, find out if boat charters to Fatu Hiva are being organised during your stay and you may be able to share the costs. There's no regular service; it all depends on the needs of locals (for instance, going back to Fatu Hiva after medical consultation in Atuona). Another option is to hop on the *Aranui* (p176) cargo ship when it stops at Atuona (Hiva Oa), Omoa or Hanavave. If you've got the dough, you can charter a private *bonitier* (about 50,000 CFP for the whole boat). Also contact Lionel at Chez Lionel Cantois, who's well clued up on the subject. The crossing between Hiva Oa and Fatu Hiva takes anything between three and five hours, depending on conditions and can be very uncomfortable if the sea is choppy.

Getting Around

The only dirt road is 17km long and links Hanavave with Omoa, but it's quicker (and cheaper) to hire a speedboat to travel between the two villages (about 7000 CFP per boat).

Enquire at your pension about hiring a 4WD; expect to pay 15,000 CFP a day with driver.

The Australs & the Gambier Archipelago

Includes »

Best Places to Stay

- Manôtel (p206)
- Rurutu Lodge (p206)
- Raivavae Tama (p209)
- Maro'i (p211)

Best Outdoor Experiences

- Walking (p206)
- Lagoon touring (p209)
- Exploring caves (p205)
- Whale-watching (p206)
- Horse riding (p206)

Why Go?

Isolated and straddling the Tropic of Capricorn, the magnificent and pristine Austral Islands are arguably French Polynesia's most underrated destination. The climate here is temperate, but everything else befitting of a tropical paradise is here: flower-filled jungles, sharp peaks, outrageously blue water and genuinely friendly people. The islands are wonderfully varied, from the limestone caverns of Rurutu and the Bora Bora–like lagoon of Raivavae to the fertile slopes and windy bays of Tubuai – heaven on earth for ecotourists.

If, after visiting the Australs, you still feel the urge for more off-the-beaten-track adventures, consider travelling to the Gambier, where visitors are an absolute rarity. All the makings of an island holiday paradise can be found in this jaw-droppingly beautiful archipelago, but it's so far away (about 1700km southeast from Tahiti) and expensive to get to that it remains one of the best-kept secrets in French Polynesia.

When to Go

During the dry season (May to October), the climate is milder than in other parts of the country. With average daily temperatures around 20°C, July and August are not the best time to visit if you're hoping to laze around on a beach, but are an ideal time for hiking. The islands are hottest in January and February. The Australs have two important religious festivals: the Tere, which is held in early January, and the Me, which is celebrated in May. The whale-watching season runs from July to October.

THE AUSTRALS

The islands here have had less of a history with Europeans and less influx from the outside world, so have kept their culture and delicious local-style cuisine alive. Pandanus weaving is still a mainstay and these crafted items are greatly sought after by islanders in other archipelagos. The climate means that peaches and carrots grow alongside banana trees and vast taro plantations.

History

The Australs were the last of the Polynesian islands to be settled; the first arrivals were believed to have come from Tahiti between AD 1000 and AD 1300. The islands came to European attention during the second half of the 18th century.

Apart from a colourful chapter in the *Bounty* saga, when the mutineers unsuccessfully tried to establish themselves on Tubuai, contact with Europeans and the Western world was limited until the late 19th and 20th centuries. This long period, during which English missionaries (or more frequently their native representatives) held sway, has ensured that Protestantism remains strong to this day.

Getting There & Away

Rurutu, Tubuai, Raivavae and Rimatara are about 600km south of Tahiti.

AIR **Air Tahiti** (www.airtahiti.pf) flies to Rurutu and Tubuai four days a week and to Raivavae and Rimatara three days a week. One-way fares include Tahiti–Rurutu (22,500 CFP), Tahiti–Tubuai (25,000 CFP), Tahiti–Raivavae or Tahiti–Rimatara (27,000 CFP).

Within the archipelago, interisland flights cost between 10,000 CFP and 18,000 CFP. You can also add an 'Australs Extension', which includes Raivavae, Rurutu and Tubuai to some Air Tahiti air passes (see p249).

BOAT The cargo ship *Tuhaa Pae IV* arrives three times monthly in the Australs; see p251 for details.

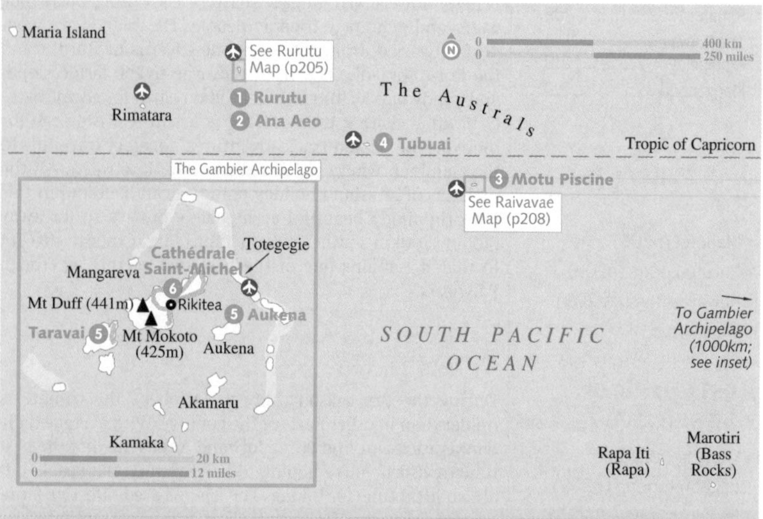

The Australs & The Gambier Highlights

1. Swimming with awe-inspiring humpback whales at **Rurutu** (p206)
2. Exploring the surreal limestone cave of **Ana Aeo** (p205) on Rurutu
3. *Motu*-hopping in the radiant Raivavae lagoon and picnicking on idyllic **Motu Piscine** (p209)
4. Imagining the glorious past of **Tubuai** (p207) while visiting its unique *marae* (traditional temple)
5. Taking a lagoon and island tour to **Taravai** and **Aukena** (p210) in the Gambier archipelago
6. Marvelling at the imposing **Cathédrale Saint-Michel** (p211) of Rikitea

KNOW BEFORE YOU GO...

» Many businesses don't accept credit cards.

» There are very few restaurants, so you'll probably need to take at least half board at your pension.

» If you visit between May and November, expect some cold nights – and even days – so pack warm clothes.

» The Gambier Islands (but not the Australs) are one hour ahead of Tahiti.

» There are no banks or ATMs in the Gambier Islands, so bring lots of cash.

Rurutu

POP 2098

The island's geology makes it unique; Rurutu is one of the South Pacific's largest raised atolls *(makatea)*. Vertical limestone cliffs pockmarked with caves line the coast, while the volcanic interior is a fertile, mind-bogglingly abundant jungle. While there's very little fringing reef, there are plenty of white-sand beaches where you can flake out.

What brings many people to Rurutu is the whales. When the whales aren't around, there are plenty of other activities and lots of unique natural attractions to keep you busy.

Sights

Rurutu has a circumference of about 32km, but the road cuts inland through the mountains, making the island feel much bigger. Apart from the Moerai to Marae Tararoa section, which is practically flat, the route is very hilly.

Of the three main coastal villages, **Moerai** is the largest. A sealed road runs about a third of the way around the island, linking the airport with Moerai and the village of **Auti**. Another sealed road climbs over the centre of the island to link Moerai with **Avera**, the third village.

Ana Aeo CAVE

This cave, with its massive, oozy-looking stalactites and stalagmites, is the most stunning on the island. It's 500m north of the Teautamatea pension; there's a signposted track going to the right that leads to the cave.

Ana Tane Uapoto CAVE

Turning right out of the main village of Moerai, you'll find a large roadside cavern with stalactites and stalagmites, called Tane Uapoto. Traditionally this cave was used to salt (for preservation) and divide whale meat among the islanders. Just beyond the cave there's a **whale-watching platform**. About 3km from here is another cavern that's accessible from the road called **Ana Tiana Taupee**.

Toataratara Point BEACHES, ARCHAEOLOGICAL SITE

At the southern end of the island, you'll find the small **Marae Poreopi** (a small traditional temple consisting of a platform made of stones) and a series of beautiful little **beaches** that run east of the point.

Marae Tararoa ARCHAEOLOGICAL SITE

Behind Teautamatea pension on the west side of the island are the well-preserved remains of Marae Tararoa, the *marae* (traditional temple) of the last Rurutu royal family.

Activities

All pensions offer worthwhile full-day **island tours** for around 5000 CFP, usually with guides who are very knowledgeable about the history of the island.

Rurutu

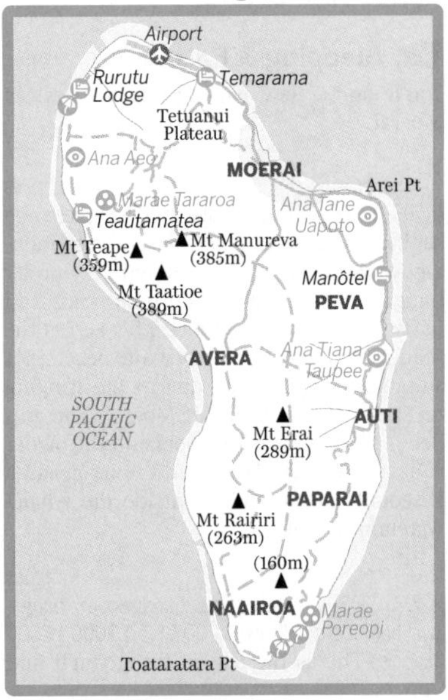

DON'T MISS

WHALE-WATCHING

There are few activities in the world as fantastic as the opportunity to swim with humpback whales. Rurutu, which has been nicknamed 'Island of Whales', actually has fewer of these mammals visiting its coastlines each year than Mo'orea or Tahiti, but what makes this an ideal place to see them is the absence of a lagoon, which causes the whales to come closer to shore. The incredible visibility makes the experience all the more impressive.

The whales come to Rurutu from around late July to mid-October to reproduce before heading back to the icy waters of the Antarctic. There are no promises that you will see any (it's not uncommon to experience a few weeks in a row with no sightings), but the best chance of seeing the whales is in August and September. Whale-watching trips are open to all – operators will even pull unconfident swimmers along on a boogie board if it's not too rough. **Raie Manta Club** (☎74 07 03; half-day tours 11,000 CFP) has been offering very professional whale-watching tours for over 10 years. You can also contact **Rurutu Baleines Excursion** (☎94 05 61, 70 37 29; half-day tours 8000 CFP).

For **horse riding**, contact Viriamu at Teautamatea pension. Superb trips, suitable for all levels, pass some stunning viewpoints in the island's interior (5000 CFP for a half day).

The interior is perfect for **walking**. A network of tracks criss-crosses the Tetuanui Plateau (200m), leading to the peaks of Taatioe (389m), Manureva (385m) and Teape (359m). **Reti Mii** (☎25 97 08) is a professional guide who leads half-day hiking tours and cave tours to some otherwise hard-to-access caves for 3000 CFP.

Sleeping & Eating

You'll find a few *snacks* (snack bars) in Moerai.

TOP CHOICE **Manôtel** PENSION $$
(☎93 02 25; www.lemanotel.com; bungalows s/d half board 11,100/15,600 CFP; wi-fi) The exceptionally well-run Manôtel has seven very pretty bungalows with fans, good bathrooms and particularly inviting terraces; it's across the road from a long stretch of white beach (not suitable for swimming due to the fringing reef) about 3km south of Moerai. The garden is blooming with colours and the owner runs some of the best island tours around. Discounts are available outside the whale-watching season.

Rurutu Lodge HOTEL $$
(☎93 03 30; www.hotelrurutulodge.com; bungalows half board s 7000-14,200 CFP, d 9000-19,500 CFP; wi-fi) This is the closest thing you'll find to a hotel in the Australs. You won't get much of a connection with the locals here but it's pleasantly designed, has flower-filled gardens and a lovely stretch of white-sand beach that's great for sunbathing (but not great for swimming because of coral rock). Note that the sea-facing units cost twice as much as the garden bungalows. There's a good on-site bar and restaurant.

Teautamatea PENSION $
(☎93 02 93, 70 34 65; pension.teautamatea@mail.pf; s/d half board 8500/13,000 CFP; wi-fi) Run by a British-Rurutu couple, the cosy rooms here are tastefully decorated in a Polynesian-meets-European-countryside chic. It's in a stunning setting in front of Marae Tararoa and just across the road from one of Rurutu's best beaches. Excellent English is spoken. Free bikes.

Temarama PENSION $
(☎93 02 80; pensiontemarama@mail.pf; s/d half board 7500/12,500 CFP; wi-fi, pool) Near the airport, this option has eight rooms with bathrooms in a big modern house. Although the setting is nothing special and the building is not particularly Polynesian, it's spotlessly clean, the welcome is warm and the food has a good reputation.

Information

Banque Socredo (7.30-11.30am & 1.30-4pm Mon-Fri) In Moerai. Has an ATM outside.

Post office (7am-noon & 1-3.30pm Mon-Thu, to 2.30pm Fri; wi-fi) Has an outdoor ATM and wi-fi access; near Banque Socredo.

Getting There & Around

Air Tahiti (☎94 02 50, 86 42 42; www.airtahiti.pf) has about four flights a week from Tahiti to Tubuai. Cargo ships dock at Moerai.

If you've booked accommodation you'll be picked up at the airport (sometimes for a fee of 500 to 1000 CFP round trip). Bicycles can be hired from most pensions for 1000 to 1600 CFP a day.

Tubuai

POP 2049

With its spreading, fertile plains, low hills and temperate climate, Tubuai is the fruit bowl and veggie patch of French Polynesia. This very scenic island is blessed with sandy beaches, a string of idyllic *motu* (islets), a fantastic lagoon and a few archaeological sites. Two mountain ranges slope down to the flat plains by the sea and a low-lying central region bisects the two. A cross-island road connects Mataura and Mahu, the island's main villages.

Sights

You'll need a guide to access the following sites. Contact Wilson Doom from Wipa Lodge.

Marae Raitoru, Haunarei & Hariitaata ARCHAEOLOGICAL SITE

Over 200 *marae* have been found in Tubuai and the few that have been cleared are among the most fascinating in the country. Raitoru and Haunarei Marae are two connected *marae* that were for birthing and umbilical cord-cutting ceremonies respectively. Nearby is Marae Hariitaata, which once served as a meeting place for chiefs.

Vaitauarii ARCHAEOLOGICAL SITE

At Vaitauarii are the remains of a site dedicated to tattooing Tubuai royalty. Until 2007 it was believed that the ancient Tubuai people were not tattooed, but now this site and shell tattoo combs found on the island have confirmed otherwise.

Fort George HISTORIC SITE

The *Bounty* is remembered by a sign on the northeastern corner of the island marking the site of Fort George, where the mutineers attempted to set up camp for two months in 1789.

Activities

Lagoon excursions offered by the pensions cost about 7000 CFP per person, with a picnic provided. For history buffs, very interesting **marae tours** (3000 CFP) are run by effervescent Wilson Doom from Wipa Lodge. They take three hours and visit the best-preserved *marae*.

There are several good **walking** opportunities, the best being to the summit of Mt Taitaa (422m). The route is signposted along the cross-island road and the return journey takes about three hours.

The steady winds that buff Tubuai mixed with the reef-sheltered lagoon are the perfect combination for **kitesurfing**. Contact Wilson Doom at Wipa Lodge, who's also well clued up on the subject. Bring your own gear as it can't be hired here.

Sleeping & Eating

There is one supermarket in Mataura, plus a scattering of smaller stores and snack bars around the island. You'll also find a couple of restaurants.

Wipa Lodge PENSION, CAMPGROUND $

(☎93 22 40, 73 10 02; maletdoom@mail.pf; campsites per person 2500 CFP, s/d 4500/7500 CFP; wi-fi) This well-run, centrally located pension on the cross-island road has five rooms with bathroom. They're tiny but well scrubbed and the garden setting is very pleasant. Campers can pitch their tent on a grassy, shady plot. All activities can be organised, including *marae* tours run by Wilson, the owner. His wife Gisèle does a good job of cooking delicious French-inspired meals (half board is 4300 CFP per person). Airport transfers are 1000 CFP and there are bikes for hire. Cash only.

Toena PENSION $

(☎95 04 12, 73 81 84; www.toena.pf; bungalows s/d half board 7500/13,000 CFP; wi-fi) Perched on a small plateau in the hills that dominate the eastern part of the island, this pension feels a bit isolated, but it's the perfect place to decompress. The two bungalows are very neat and tidy and have stupendous lagoon views. Cash only.

Chez Yolande PENSION $

(☎95 05 52; Mataura; s/d 6000/7000 CFP; wi-fi) This place has six immaculate rooms with bathroom in a modern and functional house. The upstairs rooms are the most private. There's a beach across the road. It's a good option, but don't expect dollops of atmosphere. Cash only.

Information

Mataura, about 4km east of the airport, is the main village and has a post office with public internet and an outside ATM, a **Banque Socredo** (8am-noon & 1.30-4pm Mon-Fri) with an ATM outside, and a basic hospital.

Getting There & Around

Air Tahiti (93 22 75, 86 42 42; www.airtahiti.pf) has an office at the airport. Cargo ships dock at Mataura.

Airport transfers are free if you have booked accommodation. Wipa Lodge and Toena have cars (about 6000 CFP per day) for clients' use.

Raivavae

POP 1049

Visitors to Raivavae (ra-ee-va-va-eh) rave that this is what Bora Bora must have been like 50 or even 75 years ago. It's a paradise not only because of the sweeping blue lagoon, idyllic white-sand *motu* or the green mountainous interior dominated by square-topped Mt Hiro (437m), but also because the warm Polynesian welcome and traditional way of life you'll find here is one of the most authentic and heart-warming in all of French Polynesia. Amazingly, the island receives only a small trickle of tourists.

Sights & Activities

Although the lagoon is the main highlight, Raivavae also has a few archaeological sites that are worth a peek. **Marae Pou Muavau**, across the road from the airport, is falling down after having been restored a few years back, but better care has been given to **Marae Mauna-Oto** on a private property on the east coast. This is also known as the 'princess *marae*' because of the tomb near the entrance, in which a little girl is buried – some say she was a princess. Another well-maintained *marae,* **Marae Pou Pou Tiare**, can be found about 1km from the Vaiuru entrance of the cross-island road (ask for directions as it's not easy to find).

The only remaining **tiki** on the island stands in a private garden just to the west of the village of Mahanatoa.

All pensions offer **lagoon tours** and excursions to *motu* (3000 CFP to 5000 CFP) and **hikes** up steep Mt Hiro (3500 CFP), plus a tour of the island by car.

Raivavae

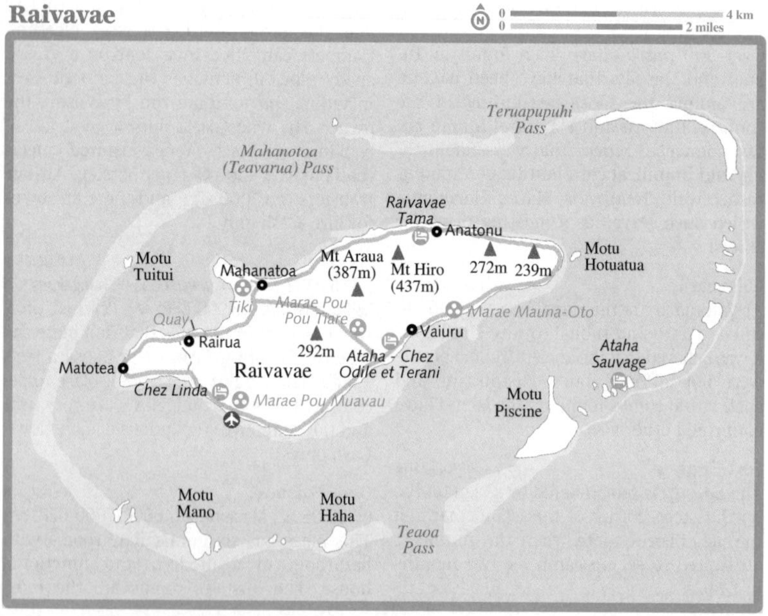

DON'T MISS

MOTU PISCINE

Raivavae's stunning lagoon, brimming with marine life and ringed by *aito*-covered *motu*, is one of the treasures of the South Pacific. Motu Piscine ('Motu Swimming Pool'; Motu Vaiamanu) is the best-known *motu*, fringed with white beaches and divided from its neighbour by a glassy turquoise channel that's teeming with tropical fish. Fa-bu-lous. All pensions can arrange a lagoon tour, including picnic, on Motu Piscine.

Sleeping & Eating

Raivavae Tama PENSION $
(☎95 42 52; www.raivavaetama.com; Anatonu; d half board per person 6500 CFP, bungalows s/d half board 8500/13,000 CFP) Three rustic, coconut-thatched bungalows with bathrooms sit on a skinny stretch of white sand, with fabulous lagoon views; there are also two basic rooms with shared bathroom in the family's home (which is across the road), two comfortable bungalows in the garden at the back and a secluded cabin out on a white-sand *motu* (meals are delivered). The local-style food and welcome here are extraordinary and excellent English is spoken. Kayaks and bikes are available for hire. Credit cards are accepted.

Ataha – Chez Odile et Terani PENSION $
(☎95 43 69, 28 92 35; pension.ataha@live.fr; s/d half board 8500/13,000 CFP, Ataha Sauvage per person 1500 CFP) Ataha has several options: a two-bedroom house (for families), three hanky-sized adjoining rooms, one more spacious room in the owner's house (with its own private entrance) and **Ataha Sauvage**, a rustic hut on stilts situated alone on a *motu* of white sand. Odile and Terani, the warm and happy owners, serve excellent *ma'a Tahiti* (traditional Tahitian food) at the pension or bring it out by boat to the *motu*. Cash only.

Chez Linda PENSION $$
(☎95 44 25, 78 80 24; www.pensionlindaraivavae.pf; Rairua; s/d half board 7400/10,600 CFP, bungalows s/d half board 10,600/16,200 CFP; wi-fi) This is a well-kept place with three Polynesian-style bungalows with private bathrooms and three tiny, modest rooms in the owner's house with shared bathroom. Linda, the young owner, cooks delicious traditional food. Cash only.

Information

Rairua has a **post office** with public internet (and wi-fi access) and an outside ATM.

Getting There & Around

Raivavae is 200km southeast of Tubuai. **Air Tahiti** (☎86 42 42; www.airtahiti.pf) operates flights to/from Pape'ete three days a week, sometimes via Tubuai. The ship *Tuhaa Pae IV* comes by about twice a month.

Pensions provide free airport transfers and bike hire. Cycling the flat 20km of coast road is easy.

Rimatara

POP 791

Rimatara looks like a mini Rurutu and is circled by a fringing reef and beautiful white-sand beaches. It's the most densely populated of the Austral Islands with three small villages, **Anapoto**, **Amaru** and **Mutua Ura**. Pandanus work and shell necklaces, plus the plantations, support the islanders, who have preserved their own distinct dialect. Air Tahiti began servicing the island in 2006, but it has yet to get under the tourist radar. The exception is birders, who visit in search of the rare and exquisitely coloured Rimatara lorikeet – locally known as the *ura*.

Ue Ue (☎94 44 03, 74 66 13; www.pensionueue.pf; Amaru; bungalows s/d half board 10,500/16,800 CFP) has no view, but the four modern bungalows, all with hot-water bathrooms, terraces and fans, are in a lovely garden with a pair of caged Rimatara lorikeets to liven it up a bit. Expect delicious *ma'a Tahiti* made from local ingredients. Cash only.

Getting There & Around

Rimatara is located about 150km west of Rurutu. **Air Tahiti** (☎86 42 42; www.airtahiti.pf) flies to/from Pape'ete three times a week, stopping en route at Rurutu.

BASKETRY IN THE AUSTRALS

The Australs are renowned for their mats, hats and baskets woven from pandanus. There are a few artisanal shops on Rurutu, including the one at the airport. On Tubuai, Raivavae and Rimatara, locals will point you to families who produce such items.

THE GAMBIER ARCHIPELAGO

POP 1400

The geology here is unique: one reef, complete with sandy *motu*, encircles a small archipelago of lush high islands dotting an exquisitely blue lagoon that's as clear as air. Adding to the allure are some of the eeriest and most interesting post-European structures in the country, a legacy of the Gambier's history as the cradle of Polynesian Catholicism. Today the archipelago is known for producing some of the finest and most colourful pearls in Polynesia.

History

The Gambiers were populated in three waves from the 10th to the 13th centuries, and they may have been a stopping point on the Polynesian migration routes to New Zealand or Easter Island.

The Sacred Heart Congregation, the first Catholic mission in French Polynesia, was established here in 1834 and Father Honoré Laval and his assistant François Caret became virtual rulers of the archipelago. Laval ran the islands like his own personal fiefdom until persistent complaints about his behaviour led to his exile on Tahiti in 1871.

Moruroa lies just 400km northwest of Mangareva and between 1966 and 1974, when above-ground nuclear tests were conducted (see p224), the population of the island was herded into fallout shelters (now demolished) if winds threatened to blow towards the Gambier.

Getting There & Around

AIR **Air Tahiti** (☎97 82 65, 86 42 42; www.airtahiti.pf) flies once to twice weekly to the Gambier Archipelago (72,000 CFP return, about 3½ hours). The airport is on Motu Totegegie, on the northeastern side of the lagoon. A communal ferry from Mangareva meets every flight. The journey takes 45 minutes and costs 500 CFP.

BOAT From Tahiti the cargo ship *Nuku Hau* is the only one serving the Gambier that takes passengers and it sails once a month; see p251 for details.

Mangareva

The bulk of the population lives on Mangareva, in and around the miniscule, fruit-tree-fringed village of **Rikitea**.

Sights & Activities

All the pensions can help organise daylong lagoon and island tours for 6000 CFP to 8500 CFP per person.

WORTH A TRIP

TARAVAI, AUKENA & AKAMARU

Got a fantasy of a deserted island with idyllic beaches? You've just pictured Taravai, Aukena and Akamaru. They not only fit the picture-postcard ideal, but they also have some fascinating historic buildings. For tours, ask at your pension.

Taravai

Taravai had a population of 2000 when the missionaries arrived, but today only about five people live here. The 1868 **Église Saint-Gabriel** (Church of St Gabriel), with its gorgeous shell decoration, is well maintained and has a decaying, picturesque arch that welcomes you from the shore. Five distinct colours of sand can be found on the island's beaches.

Aukena

Aukena also has reminders of the missionary period, including the 1839 **Église Saint-Raphaël** (Church of St Raphael) and the hexagonal **lookout tower**, still used as a landmark. The white-sand beach leading to the tower is one of the prettiest in all of French Polynesia.

Akamaru

Akamaru was the first island to be visited by Laval, and his majestic, 1841 **Église Nôtre-Dame-de-la-Paix** (Our Lady of Peace Church) still stands on the sparsely inhabited island. Groups from Mangareva occasionally come over to hold services.

Cathédrale Saint-Michel CATHEDRAL

Fully restored in 2011, the imposing Cathedral of St Michael was built between 1839 and 1848 and was Laval's most ambitious project. It makes a colourful scene on Sunday morning, when it is bursting at the seams with a devout congregation singing moving *himene* (hymns).

Couvent Rouru RUIN

The eerily beautiful remains of Rouru Convent, which once housed 60 nuns, stands south of the cemetery and is quickly becoming engulfed by weeds. It's said that Laval hid the entire female population of the island in the convent whenever whaling ships paid a visit.

Mt Duff HIKING

A hiking trail to Mt Duff is signposted about 2km north of Rikitea and it's about a 1½-hour climb to the peak (441m) from this point.

Sleeping & Eating

Maro'i PENSION $

(☎97 84 62; www.pensionmaroi.com; bungalows 1-3 people 9600 CFP;) This well-regarded option has four immaculate bungalows laid out on a grassy, fruit-tree-studded lawn lined with a small beach. It's on the opposite side of the island from Rikitea. Meals (breakfast/dinner 1600/2700 CFP) are available. Credit cards are accepted.

Chez Bianca & Benoît PENSION $$

(☎97 83 76; www.chezbiancaetbenoit.pf; Rikitea; s/d half board 11,100/17,000 CFP, bungalows s/d half board 13,200/19,000 CFP; closed Jul) Big bungalows sleep three to four people and have bamboo woven walls and decks with views over Rikitea and the lagoon. There are also four rooms in the owners' house. This is a central location with dynamic owners and good food. Cash only.

Understand Tahiti & French Polynesia

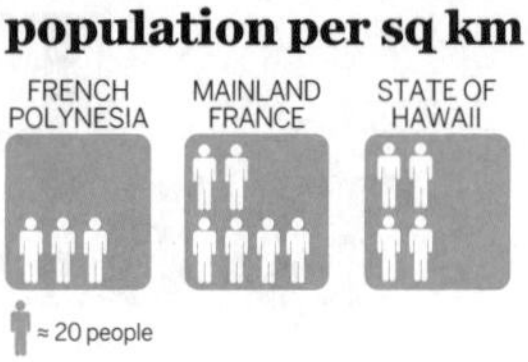

Tahiti & French Polynesia Today

Cultural Renaissance

Culturally, French Polynesia is rediscovering itself. In the last 20 years, the Tahitian language has been reclaimed as a subject now required in schools and as a university-level discipline. Tahitian dance is flourishing, tattoos have become the norm and *ma'a Tahiti* (traditional Tahitian food) has been transformed into haute cuisine. Even a few pre-European Tahitian events are being resuscitated, such as the Matari'i i Ni'a in November, marking the beginning of the 'season of abundance' – Westerners more pessimistically call this the 'wet season'.

Government Gymnastics

While technically a part of France, French Polynesia is, for the most part, self-governing. Since 2004 the government has been in turmoil as the main political parties battle it out and try to woo members of the assembly to flip-flop the balance of power. While democratic elections decide how many assembly seats go to each party, once there the members can switch allegiances. When it's a fragile majority, which is usually the case, one or two changes can overturn the entire government. From 2004 to 2009 this happened eight times, but since 2010 things have stabilised a bit; Oscar Temaru has been in power since April 2011.

- Population: 270,000
- Land-mass area: 3500 sq km
- Total area: 2.5 million sq km
- Number of islands: 118
- Tourists in 2011: 150,000

Motions of Independence

Now that Temaru has seemingly secured his presidential seat, he has begun to work on his lifelong goal: independence from France. He has gained little international backing aside from some Pacific island nations, though, and his support at home is oft-criticised. With the country's top

Documentaries

The Ultimate Wave Tahiti (2010) The Teahupoo monster.
The Last Reef (2012) Gorgeous underwater footage.
Blood & Ink (2012) Exploration of tattoos.
Les Possédés de Faaite (2009) Real-life witch hunts.

Fruity Faux Pas

It's illegal and highly discouraged to bring local fruit and vegetables from Tahiti to islands in other archipelagos, since you might also be bringing unwanted insect pests that could disrupt the balance of these fragile ecosystems.

Greeting People

- Greet women with a kiss on each cheek, or a handshake if professional.
- Men greet men with a handshake.
- Men can greet with cheek kisses if good friends or relatives.

belief systems
(% of population)

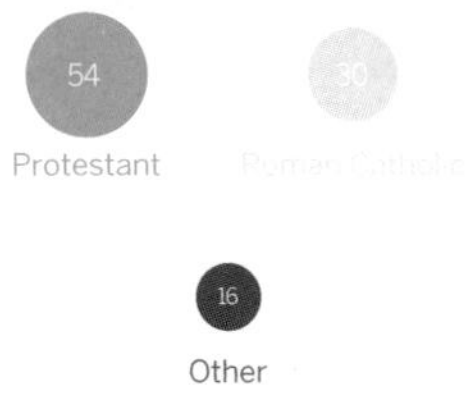

if French Polynesia were 100 people

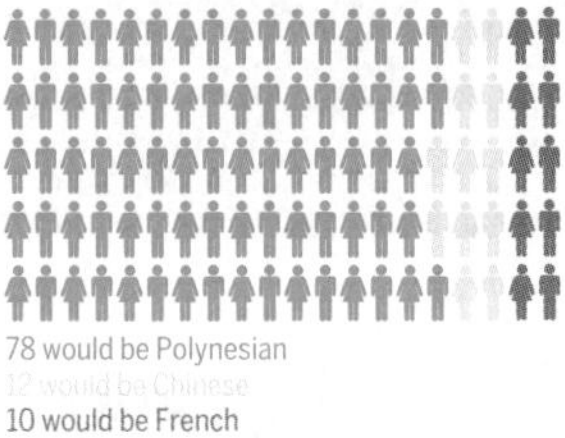

products – tourism and Tahitian pearls – in shambles, and a firm reliance on France for everything from imports to education, popular opinion is that the country is not ready to separate itself from France's teat.

Plentiful, Unprofitable Pearls

The 1990s were the gold-rush years for Tahitian pearls. But the country's infrastructure wasn't able to deal with the business that was generated. A lack of government regulation meant there were no production limits or quality guidelines. Buyers became wary; worse, an imposed export tax made pearls more expensive. Add a global recession and the availability of cheap Chinese-produced pearls, and the market collapsed. Today, with the price of a Tahitian pearl at one-quarter of what it was in 2000, only a few larger farms and a scattering of family-run farms are still in business.

Tourism in Free Fall

What happens in a global recession when a destination's publicity campaign is based on being elite and expensive? It suffers. Badly. There simply aren't enough well-off honeymooners to keep French Polynesia's overwater bungalows full. While elsewhere in the Pacific tourism is back on the rise, Tahiti's 2011 stats fell to equal those of 1996 (around 150,000). The costly airfare may also be to blame. It's sad, because the destination has so much more to offer than its packaged image suggests. It's possible to visit French Polynesia on a budget, but the country seems afraid to let folks know this.

» *Tiare* flowers harvested per day: 300,000

» Highest point: Mt Orohena (2241m), Tahiti

» Distance from Paris: 15,700km

» Tonnes of copra produced each year: 9054

Dos & Don'ts

» Do eat Tahitian food with your fingers.

» Do take your shoes off before entering a home.

» Don't tip unless there's a sign or the service was exceptional.

» Don't forget to smile – you're in French Polynesia!

Top Books

Mutiny on the Bounty (Charles Nordhoff and James Norman Hall)
Breadfruit (Celestine Hitiura Vaite)
To Live in Paradise (Renée Roosevelt Denis)
Piracy in the Pacific (Henri Jacquier)

Myths & Facts

Myth: French Polynesia is all five-star resorts.
Fact: family-run pensions and hotels are everywhere.
Myth: if you wear a flower behind your right ear you're single.
Fact: no one follows this tradition anymore.

History

The isolated islands of Polynesia were among the last places on earth to be settled by humans and, a thousand or so years later, were also some of the last places to be colonised by Europeans. Without written language, little is known of the islands' history before the first Europeans arrived. As soon as the islands were 'discovered' by Western explorers in the late 1700s, word of an idyllic way of life, a beautiful people and a tolerance of culture turned the region into a dream destination that, in many ways, retains the same allure today. Unfortunately, through the 1800s visiting sailors and traders brought disease, alcohol and guns, and within 100 years of first contact the population of most islands had plummeted by 60% or more, as islanders died of diseases they had no immunity against, drank themselves to death or, some say, died of sadness watching their culture die.

British Protestant missionaries first landed in 1772, significantly converting the region by 1815. Meanwhile the French were converting the Marquesas and Gambier Archipelagos to Catholicism. When they tried to do the same on Tahiti, sparks flew with the British, eventually leading to French ships taking aim at Tahiti and winning the islands for France.

Cotton plantations, mother-of-pearl harvesting and phosphate mining led the economy through the first half of the 20th century but none had staying power. The French saw a perfect hole to fill in the economy and between 1963 and 1996 the nuclear test sites in the remote western Tuamotus provided over 100,000 jobs. The tourism industry began with the opening of Faa'a International Airport in the early 1960s and peaked in the 1980s and 1990s.

From 1984, French Polynesia gained increasing autonomy from France. After the long-ruling pro-French leader Gaston Flosse was voted out in 2004 the government became (and still is) unstable, with power constantly being exchanged between Independentist party leader Oscar Temaru and the more French-aligned Gaston Tong Sang. In 2011 Temaru, backed by his majority assembly, made bold motions to gain complete independence from France.

Best History Museums

- Musée de Tahiti et des Îles, Tahiti
- Espace Culturel Paul Gauguin, Hiva Oa, the Marquesas
- House of James Norman Hall, Tahiti
- Museé Gauguin, Tahiti

TIMELINE

1500 BC

Polynesia's westernmost islands of Samoa and Tonga are populated via Melanesia. This Great Polynesian Migration is believed to have originally begun in Taiwan or Southeast Asia.

200 BC–AD 400

Eastern islands, including French Polynesia, Hawaii and Easter Island, are populated. It is also theorised that during this time there was trade between these islands and South America.

1520

Ferdinand Magellan (Spanish), the first European to sail across the Pacific Ocean, sights Puka Puka in the northeast Tuamotus but manages to miss the rest of French Polynesia.

MYSTERIOUS SWEET POTATOES & PRE-COLUMBIAN CHICKENS

Current genetic and linguistic evidence has proved Thor Heyderdahl's Kon Tiki theory – that the first Polynesians came from South America – to be incorrect. That doesn't mean that South America is completely out of the picture, however. All of the plant species introduced by the first Polynesians were of Southeast Asian origin save one, the sweet potato, which hails from Peru and Columbia. Studies show that this wily tuber arrived first to the Marquesas islands sometime around AD 300. The Peruvian word for sweet potato is *kumar*. The Polynesian word is umara or *kumara*. You do the math.

Then there's the chicken. Chickens are originally from Asia and until recently it was believed that Europeans were the first to introduce poultry to South America. But in late 2006 chicken bones found in southcentral Chile were carbon dated to be from over 100 years before the first European explorers arrived on the continent. DNA testing has proved that these pre-Columbian chickens are nearly identical to those found on Easter Island.

Getting There Is Half the Fun

The Great Polynesian Migration is one of the world's most outlandish yet mysterious historical events. Early Polynesians (hailing, it's believed, from either Taiwan or Southeast Asia) some 3000 to 4000 years ago tossed chickens, dogs, pigs, vegies and the kids into canoes and sailed into the wild blue yonder. And they found islands, lots of them. Using celestial navigation as well as now-forgotten methods of reading cloud reflections, wave formations and bird-flight patterns, Polynesians could find islands in the vast Pacific far better than we could find a last-minute seat on Air Tahiti during Christmas holidays.

Nothing remains of the boats used to make these voyages, so we have to make do with descriptions given by 18th-century Europeans. Forerunners of the catamaran, the canoes had two parallel hulls fused together by cross beams or platforms; they could be driven by sail, paddle or both. They could carry up to 70 people – the plants, seeds and animals needed to colonise the new land were carried on the connecting platform.

The first settlers in French Polynesia landed in the Marquesas, having journeyed via Samoa, sometime around 200 BC. From here they went on to discover the Society Islands around AD 300.

Paradise: Behind the Scenes

The Polynesian islands, and thus French Polynesia, were blessed with a situation unique in history: habitable, fertile islands where the pioneers could create their own society and religion in a place nearly devoid of danger. What this society was like before European contact is up to speculation but

1567

Alvaro de Mandaña (Spanish) comes across the northeast Polynesian islands and names them Las Marquesas de Mendoza after the viceroy of Peru. His visit is bloody and without cultural connection.

1615–16

Dutch captain Jacob Le Maire sails through the Tuamotus. It isn't until 1722 that the Society Islands are sighted by another Dutchman, Jacob Roggeveen, who 'discovers' Maupiti.

1767

Samuel Wallis arrives in Tahiti, kills many Tahitians and names the island 'King George's Land'. He sets up the first trade with the islanders and claims the island for England.

1768

Louis-Antoine de Bougainville visits Tahiti, ogles the women and begins the myth of 'New Cythera'. Not knowing that Wallis had already been there, Bougainville claims Tahiti for France.

for most of their island history Polynesians would have lacked very little. Music, dance and the arts were revered and a big part of island life.

Yet it wasn't free from problems. Overpopulation caused shortages of farming areas, particularly for taro, and wars frequently broke out between clans. The outcome of these wars was cruel: the defeated were often massacred and their *marae* (traditional temples) destroyed. The victors would then take possession of the defeated clan's lands.

Society also wasn't as sweet as European explorers perceived it. Underneath the smiles was an extremely hierarchical, structured and aristocratic system that was nearly feudal in nature and heavily ritualised. High chiefs known as *ari'i* ran the show and their positions were inherited; *tahua* were the priests; middle-class landowners were called *raatira;* the *arioi* were a group of itinerant artist-troubadours whose role it was to entertain everyone; and last were the *manahune,* which consisted of the bulk of the population including fishermen, farmers and servants. Human sacrifices were occasionally needed in religious rituals and these would invariably come from the *manahune*. Infanticide was also practised in circumstances where a girl of lower stature got pregnant by an *ari'i*. The *arioi* were not allowed to have children at all so would practise infanticide if primitive birth-control or abortion methods didn't work.

Top Archaeological Sites

- » Marae Taputapuatea, Ra'iatea
- » Opunohu Valley, Mo'orea
- » Maeva, Huahine
- » Iipona, Hiva Oa
- » Hikokua, Kamuihei & Tahakia, Nuku Hiva
- » *Marae* around the Relais de la Maroto, Tahiti

Despite this dark side, the unanimous reports from the first European explorers told of an exceptionally happy population who were uninhibited in showing their emotions; they were as quick to cry as they were to laugh.

Paradise & Its Droll, Wanton Tricks

Imagine months at sea in cramped, squalid quarters, with many of the crew suffering from scurvy, and happening upon a mountainous isle exploding with fruit, water and women. It was in these circumstances that, around 1500 years after the islands were settled, the first European explorers ventured into the region.

First came Captain Samuel Wallis on his ship the *Dolphin,* which he anchored at Matavai Bay in Tahiti's lagoon in late June 1767. A quarter of the crew was down with scurvy and Wallis himself was incapacitated during most of his visit. Initially the arrival was greeted with fascination as hundreds of canoes surrounded the ship, including canoes carrying young women 'who played a great many droll wanton tricks'. But the locals' fascination turned to fear and they attacked the *Dolphin*. Wallis retaliated by firing grapeshot at the Tahitians and then sending a party ashore to destroy homes and canoes. Following this a trade relationship somehow developed: the crew was desperate for fresh supplies and the Tahitians, who had not yet discovered metals, were delighted to receive knives, hatchets and nails in exchange.

1769

Captain James Cook makes his first voyages to Tahiti to observe and record the transit of Venus, but his equipment proves unworthy for the job.

» Captain James Cook

1772

Don Domingo de Boenechea dispatches missionaries at Tautira – the missionaries, fearing the Tahitians, lock themselves inside and scarcely come out till their Peru-bound boat picks them up in 1775.

1772–75

On Cook's second expedition to Tahiti he picks up Omai, a Huahine islander and brings him to London. Omai, the first Polynesian to visit Europe, becomes a popular socialite.

WHAT'S A MARAE?

Scattered throughout the islands, the most visible remains of ancient Tahitian culture are in its *marae,* open-air places of worship. Today Polynesians have fully embraced Christianity and many of these temples have been destroyed in the name of agriculture, dismantled to construct churches, used as house foundations or simply left to become engulfed by vines and weeds.

Births, deaths and family events were celebrated at simple family *marae;* larger *marae* were temples of chiefs where village meetings, sacrifices and wider religious ceremonies were practised. The largest and most important temples were the royal *marae,* such as Ra'iatea's Taputapuatea, which had influence over the whole of Polynesia, attracting chiefs from afar who would pledge allegiance to the kings.

Back in Europe, Wallis's official report of Tahiti focused on the geographical beauty of the region; this was soon overshadowed by gleeful rumours of uninhibited and beautiful women greeting the sailors with 'lascivious gestures'.

With his ships *La Boudeuse* and *L'Etoile,* Louis-Antoine de Bougainville arrived on Tahiti in April 1768. At this time Wallis was still homeward-bound, so Bougainville was completely unaware that he was not the first European to set eyes on the island. His visit only lasted nine days, but unlike Wallis, Bougainville had no unfriendly clashes with the Tahitians.

Bougainville explained that the Tahitians 'pressed us to choose a woman and come on shore with her; and their gestures, which were not ambiguous, denoted in what manner we should form an acquaintance with her'. Bougainville's reports of Venus-like women with 'the celestial form of that goddess', and of the people's uninhibited attitude towards sexual matters, swept through Paris like wildfire. Captain James Cook, who arrived a year after Bougainville, was less florid, but his reports confirmed the view that Tahitian women would 'dance a very indecent dance' while 'singing most indecent songs'.

In reality, Polynesian women were probably not hanging around waiting to seduce a shipload of strange white men. Sex was a natural part of everyday life, so it wouldn't have been surprising that Polynesian women wanted to check whether these funny-looking guys had all the right bits and pieces. Serge Tcherkézoff in his book *Tahiti 1768: Jeunes Filles en Pleur* (Young Girls in Tears) theorises that the girls sent to the ships were not seducing sailors for their own curiosity, but had been given orders by Tahitian priests to become pregnant by the strangers in order to capture their essence. Alexander H Bolyanatz in his book *Pacific Romanticism: Tahiti and the European Imagination* takes another

1776–80
Cook brings Omai back to Huahine, leaves many gifts that ultimately estrange Omai from his people, then later 'discovers' the Hawaiian Islands where the captain is killed and possibly eaten.

1789
Fletcher Christian sets Captain Bligh adrift in a small boat then returns to Tahiti on the *Bounty*. Some mutineers remain on Tahiti while the rest sail away to Pitcairn Island.

1790
The British navy arrives in Tahiti to pick up the mutineers who stayed on the island – the mutineers who ended up on Pitcairn don't get caught.

1797
The London Missionary Society arrives with 25 missionaries at Pointe Vénus in Tahiti – the Tahitians are welcoming but hard to convert, so only a few of the missionaries stay.

TUPAIA & OMAI: POLYNESIAN DIPLOMATS

Europeans explorers were enchanted and fascinated by Tahiti and its people and they were both thrilled and honoured when the opportunity arose to take adventurous islanders on as shipmates.

On James Cook's first voyage, Tupaia, a high priest of noble lineage, joined the *HMS Endeavor* near Tahiti (with his servant Taiata) and sailed onward with the ship's exploration of the Pacific. A highly educated man and brilliant navigator, Tupaia also proved to be a skilled diplomat and linguist. The Tahitian language was similar enough to other Polynesian languages that Tupaia was able to announce the European's intentions on their arrival to new island groups. His noble stature also impressed his Polynesian cousins – in New Zealand he was welcomed as a near god and in Maori oral history Tupaia is remembered and mentioned far more than Cook. Unfortunately Tupaia never made it to Europe – he died along with a huge number of Cook's usually healthy crew, of dysentery in Batavai (modern day Jakarta) on the long trip back to Britain.

During Cook's second Pacific voyage, the mission's flagship *HMS Adventure* took aboard Omai (although it's now thought his name was just Mai), an islander from Ra'iatea. Omai sailed back with the ship to England where he lived for two years before returning to Polynesia on Cook's third voyage. During his stay in London, Omai became popular with the aristocracy, not only for his exotic background but for his charm and good looks. His most famous encounter is a meeting with King George III whom Omai greeted with 'How do King Tosh!'

It's said that when Omai returned to live in Huahine that his many European possessions instilled jealousy in his fellow Polynesians and that the adventurer was never able to fully re-integrate back into island life. When Captain Bligh visited Tahiti on the *HMS Bounty* (before the mutiny) in 1789, he was told that Omai died about two and a half years after Cook's departure.

angle and says that the women's overtly sexual behaviour was defensive since the Tahitians had learned early on to fear European weaponry; by seducing the sailors the islanders would have more power over their often violent visitors.

Whatever the case, this uninhibited approach to sex was soon exploited by sex-starved sailors, whalers and traders, who began buying sex with nails (coveted by the locals for making fish hooks), clothes and alcohol, creating a demand for prostitution, spreading European diseases and palpably contributing to the rapid decline of the Polynesian culture.

1819

The Code of Pomare is established, forming a Christian alliance between the Leeward Islands; governing is based entirely on the scriptures establishing an unofficial missionary rule.

1842

Herman Melville deserts his whaling ship on Nuku Hiva and spends three weeks in remote Taipivai Valley – his book about the escapade, *Typee*, is published in 1846.

1842

The French take power and disperse Catholic missionaries. Queen Pomare IV pleads for British intervention to no avail. She flees to Ra'iatea then returns to Tahiti in 1847 as a figurehead.

1864

The first 329 Chinese immigrants arrive to work at American-run cotton fields on Tahiti. Workers continue to arrive from China through the 20th century and will eventually become successful merchants.

The Expeditions of Captain Cook

History depicts Captain James Cook as one of the greatest explorers of all time. Indeed, Cook's navigational and surveying skills, his ability to control unruly crews and keep them healthy and, above all, his cultural understanding, did set him apart. He is described as having been a dispassionate and tolerant man; it's often claimed he did not want to harm or offend the islanders, and that he made concerted efforts to befriend them.

In three great expeditions between 1769 and 1779, Cook filled out the map of the Pacific so comprehensively that future expeditions were reduced to joining the dots. Cook had been sent to the Pacific with two ambitious tasks. One, which was for the Royal Society, was to observe the transit of Venus as it passed across the face of the sun. By timing the transit from three very distant places it was hoped that the distance from the earth to the sun could be calculated. Tahiti was selected as one of the three measuring points (the other two were in Norway and Canada). Cook's second objective was to hunt for the mythical great continent of the south.

The instruments of the time proved to be insufficiently accurate to achieve Cook's first objective, but Cook's expeditions did yield impressive scientific work. As a result Cook's voyages communicated the wonders not only of Tahiti but also of New Zealand and Australia to an appreciative European audience.

But Cook's composure was far from impenetrable, and during his last voyage in particular his footsteps were not as light as he had claimed he wanted them to be. Stories of the voyage show that the once-tolerant man became less so – in particular he was angered deeply by any sort of theft and in one instance even ordered an islander's ear be cut off for stealing the ship's property.

The reasons for Cook's death and possible consumption (his remains were 'cooked', although no one is sure if he was eaten) in Hawaii have been debated. His journal, in which he had dutifully written for almost every instance of his journeys, remains uncharacteristically blank in the period before his death. Some speculate a cultural misunderstanding may have occurred, while others say Cook had become increasingly tyrannical and insensitive. Whatever the case, even though he was murdered, the captain's bones were distributed among Hawaiians in a manner usually reserved for the highest chiefs.

Western Vestiges

- » Paul Gauguin's tomb, Hiva Oa, the Marquesas
- » Cathédrale Saint-Michel, the Gambier Archipelago
- » WWII coastal defence guns, Bora Bora

Guns, Disease, Whisky & God

Once the Europeans came on the scene, traditional Polynesian society took a beating. It was a three-pronged affair: a jab to the ribs with high-

1877

Queen Pomare IV is succeeded by King Pomare V, who isn't interested in the job and effectively abdicates to the French four years later; then he drinks himself to death.

» Queen Pomare IV

1884

Half of the port of Pape'ete is destroyed by fire, instigating a law banning traditional architecture within the city. A cyclone in 1906 further damages the town.

1888

Robert Louis Stevenson arrives in Pape'ete aboard his ship *Casco* with his wife Fanny. The couple anchored for a few months in Tautira on Tahiti Iti.

tech European weaponry, a blow to the head by an influx of diseases and hard liquor and, finally, a kick in the groin by some Old World Christianity.

First enter the guns. At the time of first contact, islands consisted of chiefdoms that warred with each other over resources. This was quick to change once the Tahitians realised the power of European weaponry. Most explorers resisted when clans pressed them to take sides in local conflicts, but the *Bounty* mutineers, along with whalers and traders, were happy to offer themselves as mercenaries to the highest bidder. The highest bidders were the Pomares, one of a number of important families, but by no means the most important at that time.

A fire tragically destroyed half of the town of Pape'ete in 1884. After the disaster it became illegal to use local building materials within city limits.

The mutineers and their weapons helped create the political environment where one group could feasibly control all of Tahiti. Pomare I, the nephew of Obarea, the 'fat, bouncing, good looking dame' who Wallis had assumed was the island's chief back in 1767, already controlled most of Tahiti when he died in 1803. His son, Pomare II, took over from there and today the Pomares still consider themselves the royal family of French Polynesia.

But guns weren't the only problem. Whalers and traders began frequenting Tahiti from England and the USA in the 1790s, escaping their harsh shipboard life, buying supplies, introducing alcohol and spreading diseases. Traders also started to appear from the convict colonies in Australia; they exchanged weapons for food supplies, encouraged prostitution and established stills to produce alcohol.

Listless and plagued by diseases against which it had no natural immunity, the Polynesian population plummeted. The population of Tahiti in the late 1760s was estimated around 40,000; in 1800 another estimate put the population at less than 20,000; by the 1820s it was down to around 6000. In the Marquesas the situation was even worse: it has been estimated the population dropped from 80,000 to 2000 in one century.

In 1918 an influenza epidemic wiped out approximately 20% of Tahiti's population. There were so many dead the bodies were burned in great pyres.

In March 1797, 25 members of the London Missionary Society (LMS) landed at Pointe Vénus. While the new religion wasn't quick to catch on, the missionaries were able to closely associate themselves with King Pomare II, and Christianity was established as the dominant religion in 1815 and carried through the reign of Queen Pomare IV who ruled for 50 years.

The missionaries were an unyielding bunch and, although they had the best intentions, smothered many important, ancient customs with a rigid interpretation of Protestantism. A century later, the English writer Robert Keable, who had been a vicar with the Church of England, commented about pioneering missionary William Ellis that 'it was a thousand pities that the Tahitians did not convert Mr Ellis'.

Although the missionaries get a bad rap for destroying so much of the beauty of the Polynesian culture, in certain ways they very much helped the Polynesians by creating a spiritual framework in which to

1891

Post-Impressionist painter Paul Gauguin sails from France to Tahiti. He moves to the Marquesas in 1897 and dies there in 1903 of syphilis at age 54.

1911

Phosphate mining begins on Makatea in the Tuamotu Archipelago and becomes a major component of the economy; mining continues till the supplies are exhausted in 1966.

1918

An influenza pandemic thought to have originated in the USA kills approximately 20% of Tahiti's population. The disease spreads around the Pacific and is still considered one of the deadliest in history.

1932

Mutiny on the Bounty by Nordhoff and Hall is published, stoking the mythic fires of a Tahitian paradise and providing the base for three movies over the next 50 years.

MUTINY ON THE BOUNTY

There have been some colourful chapters in the history of European exploration in the Pacific, but none captures the imagination like the mutiny on the *Bounty*. It all started when Captain Bligh, an expert navigator who had learnt his trade under James Cook and had already visited Tahiti, was sent off to convey breadfruit from Tahiti to the Caribbean after someone had the bright idea that breadfruit would be a good food source for Caribbean slaves.

Bligh's expedition started late in 1787. After an arduous 10-month voyage, he arrived at a time when breadfruit-tree saplings could not be transplanted. The crew remained on Tahiti for six long, languorous months. Eventually, with the breadfruit trees loaded on board, the *Bounty* set sail, westbound, for the Caribbean.

Three weeks later, on 28 April 1789, when passing by Tonga, the crew, led by first mate Fletcher Christian, mutinied and took over the ship. The storybook version has Bligh depicted as a tyrant who deserved mutiny, but it's speculated that the reasons for the crew's takeover could have been due to Christian's mental instability or that a good portion of the crew had fallen in love with Tahitian women.

Bligh was pushed onto the *Bounty's* launch with 18 faithful crew members and set adrift. Proving his unmatched skill as a champion navigator, Bligh sailed his overloaded little boat across the Pacific and amazingly made landfall in Timor after a 41-day, 5823km voyage that was promptly written into the record books. By early 1790 Bligh was back in England; an inquiry quickly cleared him of negligence and a ship was dispatched to carry British naval vengeance to Tahiti.

Meanwhile, Christian and his mutineers returned to Tahiti before sailing off to find a more remote hideaway. Ultimately 16 mutineers decided to stay on Tahiti while a smaller group left with Christian and the *Bounty* to inhabit Pitcairn Island. Today, thanks to Fletcher Christian's mutiny, the odd Tahitian-British colony still on Pitcairn Island is one of the last vestiges of the British Empire.

Vengeance arrived for the mutineers on Tahiti in 1791 in the shape of Captain Edward Edwards, who made Bligh look like a thoroughly nice guy. He quickly rounded up mutineers and informed the men's new Tahitian wives that the men were going back to Britain to get their just desserts.

Bligh himself was back on Tahiti in 1792, this time in command of HMS *Providence* and with 19 marines to ensure there was no repeat performance. Bligh duly picked up his breadfruit saplings and transported them in record time to the Caribbean. As it turned out, the slaves never developed a taste for the fruit.

deal with all the new challenges (such as alcohol and prostitution) that were being introduced by less savoury Europeans. Today, Christianity is the country's best advocate and tool in the fight against alcoholism, domestic violence and incest, as well as providing exceptionally strong support for community.

1942

Five thousand American soldiers descend on Bora Bora to build the territory's first airstrip. The American military use the island as their supply base through WWII.

1947

Thor Heyerdahl makes his voyage to the Tuamotus from Peru aboard a balsa raft to prove Polynesians came from South America. His journey is a success but his theory is later disproved by genetics.

1957–58

The territory is officially named French Polynesia and votes to remain part of France amid riots in Pape'ete. Pouvana'a a Oopa, leader of the separatist movement, is exiled to France.

1961

Faa'a International Airport is constructed on landfill covering a coral reef. French Polynesia is opened up to the world and the tourism industry takes off.

BOENECHEA & THE FIRST MISSIONARIES

In 1772 Don Domingo de Boenechea, a Spaniard, sailed the *Aguilla* from Peru and anchored in the lagoon off Tautira on Tahiti Iti. Boenechea installed two missionaries and established Tautira as the first long-term European settlement on the island.

In 1775 the *Aguilla* again returned from Peru. The two Spanish missionaries, who had been spectacularly unsuccessful at converting 'the heathen', and who from all reports were terrified of the islanders, were more than happy to scuttle back to Peru. Boenechea died on Tahiti during this visit, and thus ended the Spanish role on Tahiti. He is buried by the Catholic church that today bears his name in Tautira on Tahiti Iti.

Enter the French

The French takeover of what is now French Polynesia was essentially a war of the missionaries. British clergy were an unofficial colonial power via the Pomare clan in the Society Islands, the Australs and the Tuamotus, but the French Catholic missionaries were in firm control in the Gambier Archipelago from 1834 and the Marquesas from 1838. In 1836 two French missionaries from the Gambier Archipelago were quietly dropped off near Tautira at the eastern extremity of Tahiti Iti; they were promptly arrested and deported by the British.

The deportation of the two French missionaries was considered a national insult to the French. Demands, claims, counterclaims, payments and apologies shuttled back and forth until 1842, when Rear Admiral Dupetit-Thouars arrived in *La Reine Blanche,* pointed his guns at Pape'ete and took power. Queen Pomare IV was forced to yield to the French.

TV wasn't in French Polynesian homes until the early 1980s, when RFO (Radio France Overseas) began the first local broadcasts.

The queen, still hoping for British intervention, fled to Ra'iatea in 1844 and a guerrilla rebellion against the French broke out on Tahiti and other islands. The presence of French forts around Tahiti confirms that it was a fierce struggle, but eventually the rebels were subdued, and by 1846 France had control over Tahiti and Mo'orea. In 1847 Queen Pomare was persuaded to return to Tahiti, but she was now merely a figurehead.

Queen Pomare died in 1877 and was succeeded by her son, Pomare V. He had little interest in the position and effectively abdicated power in 1881; he drank himself to death in 1891.

The Nuclear Era

French Polynesia continued to be a valuable strategic port for the French, especially when the islands' economies of vanilla, cotton, copra and mother of pearl were flourishing during WWI, and during WWII, when American forces used Bora Bora as a military base. But postwar, as the

1963

French Centre d'Expérimentation du Pacifique for nuclear testing opens on Moruroa and Fangataufa. The first atmospheric tests begin in 1966; in 1981, underground shafts are dug for underground testing.

1963–64

Jean Domard, associated with an Australian company, seeds the first pearl oysters. The first farm opens on Manihi in 1968, but it isn't until the 1980s that pearl farming takes off.

1984

French Polynesia gains internal autonomy from France, which is later expanded in 1990 and again in 1996. In 2004 it gains the unique French status of 'Overseas Collectivity'.

1985

French secret agents blow up the New Zealand–based Greenpeace ship *Rainbow Warrior* as it prepares for a protest voyage to the nuclear test site on Moruroa.

territory's exports declined, a more practical usage of it was devised. In 1963 Moruroa and Fangataufa, atolls in the Tuamotus, were announced to become France's nuclear test sites. Atmospheric nuclear explosions began in 1966. The Centre d'Expérimentation du Pacifique (CEP; Pacific Experimentation Centre) soon became a major component of the French Polynesian economy.

Over the next 30 years, 193 tests were performed on the two atolls and more than 130,000 people worked for the CEP. In 1981, 17 years after the USA, Britain and the USSR agreed to halt atmospheric testing, the French drilled bomb shafts under the central lagoons of the atolls and finally moved the tests underground. In 1995 French president Jacques Chirac announced a new series of underground tests, and a storm of protest erupted worldwide. Rioting broke out in Pape'ete but fell on deaf ears in France. The final rounds of tests were concluded in early 1996, and it was announced there would be no further testing in the Pacific.

For many years the French government denied that the tests posed any ecological threat to the region. Finally, in 1999 a French study reported that there had been radioactive leakage into underground water, and later that same year the existence of cracks in the coral cones of Moruroa and Fangataufa were also acknowledged. A 2006 study conducted by the French Polynesian Territorial Assembly concluded that Tureia in the eastern Tuamotus and the Gambier Archipelago would have been exposed to nuclear fallout during atmospheric testing; because there were never any dosimeter measurements taken on these islands, what the levels of radiation would have been has not been proved.

In November 2008 the French defence minister announced a bill setting the standards for nuclear-test workers' compensation, which passed in 2010. Still, two associations, the Association of Nuclear Test Veterans (AVEN), which is made up of former French military personnel, and Moruroa e Tatou, which has over 4000 French Polynesian members, have been lobbying the French government for any compensation for well over a decade, with little – or no – gains. On top of this, the environmental impacts of the tests have been disregarded by the legislation.

In January 2012, France approved a motion that would restore Moruroa and Fangataufa (previously under control of the French defence ministry) to French Polynesia's public domain. The bill would, among other things, let French Polynesia monitor radiation levels rather than rely on French reports, which it has come to mistrust. Pundits say this bill has little chance of passing.

Income tax was only introduced to French Polynesia in 1994, although it is still very low compared to France or even the US.

1995–96
Rioting against nuclear testing breaks out in Pape'ete and at Faa'a International Airport. The testing continues despite worldwide criticism until the series is complete in 1996.

2004
Oscar Temaru's pro-independence party is elected to power, temporarily ending Gaston Flosse's 20-year reign. For the next two years the government changes several times, mostly between Flosse and Temaru.

2006
Gaston Tong Song is elected president and becomes a part of a constant flip-flopping of power, now mostly between himself and Temaru over the next five years.

2011
During one of his longer terms of presidency, Temaru, supported by his Assembly, champions decolonisation of French Polynesia from France.

Environment

It's impossible to talk about the French Polynesian landscape without sounding clichéd. From the lush slopes of the high islands to the white-sand, palm-ruffled atolls with lagoons bluer than well, anything, this is the place that stereotypical ideals of paradise come from.

The Land

French Polynesia's 118 islands are scattered over an expanse of the Pacific Ocean stretching more than 2000km – an area about the size of Western Europe. Still, the islands and atolls make up a total land mass of barely 3500 sq km (less than one-third the size of the US state of Connecticut). Five archipelagos, the Society, Tuamotu, Marquesas, Austral and Gambier, divide the country into distinct geological and cultural areas.

High islands – think Tahiti, Mo'orea and Bora Bora – are essentially mountains rising out of the ocean that are often encircled by a barrier reef. A protected, shallow lagoon, with that flashy blue colour of postcards and brochure fame, is formed by the reef.

An atoll is a ring of old barrier reef that surrounds a now-sunken high island. Over time the reef was built up and mini-islands called *motu* were formed. These *motu,* which encircle the lagoon, reach a maximum height of 6m and are usually covered in low bushes and coconut palms. *Motu* are separated by shallow *hoa* (channels) that link the inner lagoon to the ocean. A *hoa* that's deep enough for boats to pass through is called a 'pass'.

Wildlife

The bulk of the Pacific's fauna originated in Asia/Melanesia and spread east; the further east you travel, the less varied it becomes. Don't come looking for wildlife safaris here, unless they're underwater.

Land Animals

Basically, any fauna that couldn't swim, float or fly to French Polynesia has been introduced. The first Polynesians, knowing they would be settling new lands, brought pigs, chickens and dogs in their canoes. They also brought geckos and the small Polynesian rat, probably as stowaways.

PROTECTION OF FLORA & FAUNA

Marine reserves in French Polynesia are few: Scilly and Bellinghausen (remote islands in the Leeward group of Society Islands) and eight small areas within Mo'orea's lagoon are the only ones protected by the country itself. Fakarava and its surrounding atolls (Aratika, Toau, Kauehi, Niau, Raraka and Taiaro) are a Unesco biosphere reserve. The only terrestrial reserves are the Marquesan Nature Reserves, which include the remote uninhabited islands of Motu One, Hatutu, Eiao and Motane. Several species are protected and there are limits placed on the fishing of some fish and crustaceans. Unfortunately, fish continue to be caught indiscriminately and shells are still collected. Although turtles are highly protected, they continue to be poached for their meat and their shells.

WATER HAZARDS

» Cone shells have a deadly poisonous stinger that protrudes from the hole at the cone's bottom.

» Pencil urchins live in crevices by day and dot the reefs at night – watch your feet, as stepping on the spikes can cause extreme pain. Urinating on the wounds can soothe them.

» Stonefish are French Polynesia's biggest, most prolific shallow-water hazard, yet are so well camouflaged they're nearly impossible to see; if you get stung, apply heat immediately and head for the hospital. Wearing plastic, waterproof sandals provides the best protection.

You'll surely see plenty of bugs – mosquitoes are omnipresent and *nono* (see the boxed text, p185), a nearly invisible biting fly, are fierce. The only real land shark is the centipede, which can grow up to 20cm long and has venom-injecting fangs that can cause swelling and pain for several hours. It's best to shake out towels, clothes and shoes just in case.

The endemic bird life of French Polynesia is as fragile as it is fabulous. Of the 29 land species, 12 are introduced and have driven many local species to near extinction. The 27 species of sea birds, including terns, noddies, frigates and boobies, make French Polynesia one of the richest tropical areas for marine species.

For information about French Polynesia's bird life check out www.manu.pf, the official site of SOP Manu, the Tahitian organisation for the protection of bird species.

Sea Animals

Any dismay about the lack of animal diversity on land is quickly made up for by the quantity of underwater species – it's all here.

At the top of the food chain, sharks are found in healthy numbers throughout the islands. Blacktip and whitetip reef sharks are the most common and pose little danger. More aggressive and sometimes unnervingly curious, the grey reef shark is common in the Tuamotus. Large sleeper or nurse sharks, distinguished by their broad head and oversized dorsal fins and tail, look daunting but generally keep to themselves on the bottom of channels and sandy banks.

Other large creatures you are likely to encounter are graceful manta rays; smaller, spotted leopard rays; stingrays; and moray eels. Five of the seven species of sea turtle (all endangered) make their home in French Polynesia, but you're most likely to see the green and hawksbill turtles, which often come to feed in the lagoons.

Between July and October, humpback whales can be seen primarily off the shores of Tahiti, Mo'orea and Rurutu. There are actually at least 24 species of whale that pass through French Polynesia, but startlingly few species other than the humpbacks are ever observed. Dolphins can be seen year-round, especially spinner dolphins. Electra dolphins are a major attraction around Nuku Hiva, where they gather in groups of several hundred, a phenomenon seen nowhere else in the world.

Hundreds of species of fish of all colours, shapes and sizes flutter about the reefs. Lobsters, slipper lobsters and crabs are found on the outer slopes of reefs or the bottom of caves and cliffs. Black-lipped pearl oysters and *pahua* (giant clams) are found on reefs inside the lagoons. Porcelain and cat-eye kauri are valued by collectors, but as shells are so scarce in French Polynesia it is not advised to take any living shells.

The comedians of the islands are hermit crabs. They are very fashion-conscious and will quickly swap their old shells for prettier ones; they act tough and threaten to pinch you, and will try to eat your sandwich off your picnic blanket if you're not careful. In the Tuamotus the enormous

Common Deep-Sea Fish

» tuna

» *mahi mahi* (dorado)

» bonito

» wahoo

» swordfish

NUCLEAR LEFTOVERS

The environmental repercussions of French nuclear testing are still hotly debated. It was confirmed in 1999 that Moruroa and Fangataufa were fissured by tests and that radioactivity has been allowed to escape from cracks in the atolls' coral cones. Evidence has been found of low-level activity in certain areas of the Gambiers, but long-ranging conclusive evidence has yet to come forth. See p224 for details on the political implications of this catastrophe. Travellers can rest assured that any radiation threat (which was only ever present in remote areas of the Tuamotu and Gambier Archipelagos) has long since passed.

and impressively colourful *kaveu* (coconut crab) feeds at night and is prized for its coconut-flavoured flesh. *Tupa* (land crabs) are found on all of the islands and have a penchant for getting squashed by cars.

Plants

Before human habitation, the variety of vegetation was limited to the seeds and spores that could travel by means of wind, sea or bird droppings. Polynesians brought *uru* (breadfruit), coconut, taro and bananas, and early missionaries introduced sugar cane, cotton, pineapples, citrus fruits, coffee, vegetables and other staples. Over the years botanists and enthusiasts have brought in various tropical plant species, which have thrived in the favourable climate. Today, visitors will encounter all of the sumptuousness of a tropical paradise: papayas, star fruit, mangos, avocados, guavas, pomelos and rambutan grow among birds of paradise, hibiscus and allamanda.

The *tiare,* a small, white, fragrant gardenia, is the symbol of French Polynesia. The significance of this flower runs deep. It is the first thing visitors are offered on arrival at Faa'a airport, it is used in many traditional medicines, it's used as a perfume and it is the classic flower to string as a *hei* (flower crown or necklace) or wear behind your ear.

The *uru* tree was the lifeline of ancient islanders, who used the bark for *tapa* (paperlike cloth), the trunk for canoes, the roots and leaves for medicine, and of course the fruit was the dietary staple. Taro, a root vegetable, is the secondary staple; the leaves of yellow taro resemble spinach when cooked, and this is called *fafa*.

COCONUT

The Tahitian language has at least seven words for the coconut; each describes a different stage of the nut's maturity.

The atolls are a stark contrast to the lush high islands. Made up primarily of sand and coral rock, the land lacks the minerals to support much vegetation. Coconut palms and an endemic shrub, the small-leafed, red-barked *miki miki,* dominate the landscape. Adding grace and much-needed shade to the atolls is the grand *kahaia* tree with its large, glossy leaves and fragrant white flowers.

Environmental Issues

Atolls and high islands are ecologically fragile, but French Polynesia has been slow to implement environmental protection. Despite a limited number of 'green' establishments that are springing up, and the rigorous requirements of public buildings and hotels to blend in with the landscape, pollution is steadily chipping away at the picture of paradise.

Although there are many low-lying atolls in French Polynesia, the effects of climate change, including rising sea levels, have so far been minimal. Higher water temperatures are one of the biggest threats to the health of the country's coral reefs and, during El Niño years in particular, huge amounts of coral die, which affects the entire ecosystem.

Islander Life

If French Polynesia had a national slogan it might be *haere maru* (take it slow), words that often fall from the lips of Tahitians to their busy French and Chinese cohabitants. It's hard not to take it slow out here. With one road encircling most islands, you'll often get caught driving behind an old pick-up truck at 50km/h with no chance of passing; national holidays seem to close up the shops and banks once every week or so; and getting served in a restaurant can take an eternity. This can be frustrating to anyone in a hurry, but somehow it all works out: you make it to wherever you were going even if it does take twice as long, the bank can wait till tomorrow and your food arrives once you are really, really hungry. The Tahitian people know this and always seem amused by anyone who tries to break the rhythm of calm.

Go to www.ica.pf (Institut de la Comminication Audiovisuelle, in French) for podcasts and videos of everything cultural in French Polynesia. Download or buy old films, and watch music videos, Tahitian news, clips of Tahitian dance and much, much more.

Family & Multiculturalism

The traditional Tahitian family is an open-armed force that is the country's backbone. Although modern girls are increasingly less likely to stay home and have baby after baby, an accidental pregnancy is considered more of a blessing than a hindrance, and babies are passed along to another eager, infant-loving family member. *Faamu* (adopted children) are not thought of as different to blood brothers and sisters, although the birth mother, and occasionally the father, sometimes remains a peripheral part of the child's life. Once a child is in a family, he or she is in no way obligated to stay; children move about to aunties, uncles and grandparents as they wish.

This family web is vitally important to an individual. When people first meet, the conversation usually starts with questions about family and most people are able to find a common relative between themselves within minutes. This accomplished, they are 'cousins' and fast friends.

But it's not all roses in what appears to be such a warm, fuzzy family framework. Domestic violence and incest are prevalent. This is closely connected with high rates of alcoholism. The government has launched

GENDER BENDER

You'll find that some women serving food in restaurants or working in hotels or boutiques aren't actually women at all. *Mahu*, males who are raised as girls and continue to live their lives as women, were present when Europeans first arrived on the islands. Although the missionaries attempted to halt this 'unnatural crime', nowadays *mahu* are an accepted part of the community. In today's lingo, another category of *mahu*, called *raerae*, refers to more flamboyant transvestites. These people face more discrimination than their *mahu* counterparts, who act more like very effeminate men.

It remains unclear whether this practice has a sexual or social origin, but it is generally assumed to be the latter, as *mahu* don't necessarily have sex with men. *Raerae*, however, do prefer men.

numerous programs addressing these issues but little progress has been made.

The majority of the population claims to be Polynesian (although most have some other ethnicity in the mix), 12% of the population is Chinese and the rest is European. Racial tension is rare but does exist. A few insults exist for each race, although they are usually only uttered on drunken binges or in schoolyards. Outward displays of racism are usually from Polynesians to French, while the more insidious kind goes from the French to the Polynesians. The Chinese generally try to stay out of it.

Sport

The national sport is, without dispute, *va'a* (pirogue, or outrigger-canoe) racing. You can admire the pirogue teams training on any lagoon, and if you're around in late October or early November, you can catch the Hawaiki Nui canoe race.

During the Heiva and a few scattered cultural festivals, Polynesians pull some interesting traditional sports out of their hats, including *amoraa ofae* (rock lifting), *patia fa* (javelin throwing), fruit-bearing races and coconut-husking competitions.

Surfing was an ancient Tahitian sport. The Billabong Pro international surf competition, held every August at the nearly mythically scary wave at Teahupoo on Tahiti Iti, brings worldwide coverage to Tahitian surfing.

Polynesians are great believers in *tupapau* (ghosts) and most people will have a good story to tell about the supernatural if you ask them.

Religion

Historically, Polynesians were polytheistic, worshipping *atua* (gods) who were surrounded by a pantheon of secondary gods. The main gods were Ta'aroa (god of creation), Tu (man god), Tane (god of craftsmen), 'Oro (god of war) and Hiro (god of thieves and sailors).

The arrival of Protestant missionaries at the end of the 18th century, followed soon after by the Catholics, marked the suppression of traditional religious beliefs. The missionaries changed the religious and cultural landscape forever, and today French Polynesia has a surprising number and variety of churches relative to its population. This includes a few takes on Mormonism, but around half of the population is Protestant and 30% are Catholic.

A few pre-Christian rituals and superstitions still exist alongside Christianity. Christian Polynesians continue to respect and fear ancient *tapu* (taboo) sites, and nothing would persuade a Polynesian to move a *tiki* (sacred statue) or *marae* (traditional temple) stone. On occasion, a *tahua* (faith healer or priest) is still consulted, and *raau tahiti* (traditional herbal medicine) is making a comeback.

Types of Dance

- **Otea** Fast hip action
- **Aparima** Free-flowing, graceful
- **Hivinau** Inspired by anchor hoisting
- **Paoa** Seated legend recitation
- **Fire dance** Juggling flaming torches

Arts

The zealous work of the missionaries managed to rid the existing Polynesian art and culture of many of its symbols and practices. Among other things, temples and carvings were destroyed and tattooing and dancing were banned. Fortunately, some traditions survived this period, and in recent years there has been a revival of Polynesian culture.

HAWAIKI NUI CANOE RACE

The sporting spectacular that has French Polynesians glued to their TV sets and talking passionately about favourites and challengers is a canoe race. The three-day, four-island Hawaiki Nui *va'a* (pirogue, or outrigger-canoe) race pits around 60 of the islands' best pirogue teams against each other and against anyone brave enough from overseas.

The 116km race, held in late October or early November, starts on Huahine, heads across the open sea to Ra'iatea, then to Taha'a and then finally on to Bora Bora.

Check out www.hawaikinuivaa.pf (in French) for more details.

THE HEIVA

Each year for a month, from late June to late July, islanders from all of the archipelagos join together for a full program of festivities in Pape'ete, on Tahiti, and on some of the other islands. The emphasis is on traditional-dance contests (both professional and amateur) and singing competitions, but there is a huge range of other activities on offer. Craft-making demonstrations include *niau* (woven coconut-palm leaves) and *tapa* (paper-like cloth) and a stone-carving competition. There's a procession of floral floats, a vote for Miss Heiva and Mr Heiva, a funfair, fireworks displays, fire walking and tattoo displays. Meanwhile, there's an outrigger-canoe race and traditional-sports competitions.

The Heiva is organised by Tahiti Nui 2000 (☎50 31 00). Reservations for the evening dance contests can be made from May onwards at the kiosk at Pl Toata in Pape'ete. You can also enquire at the tourist office. The evening will set you back between 1000 CFP and 3500 CFP. Dance performances take place at Pape'ete's Toata Amphitheatre.

Dance

Tahitian dance is not just a tourist attraction, it's a vibrant expression of Maohi (Polynesian) culture. The dances that visitors see are not created for tourists – they are authentic performances that take months of rehearsals and are based on rigorously standardised choreography depicting specific legends. In this land of oral traditions, dance is not merely an aesthetic medium but also a means of preserving the memory of the past.

Many luxury hotels offer quality dance shows about twice a week. On Tahiti and Mo'orea they are performed by semiprofessional groups and range from small groups dancing to piped-in music (in the worst cases) to theatrical extravaganzas with live orchestras (the show at the Intercontinental Resort Tahiti is arguably the best). These shows include a buffet and are open to all.

Warning! At a local dance performance, prepare to shake your hips: tourists are often asked up to the stage to dance once the show is over.

Music

Traditional Polynesian music, usually performed as an accompaniment to dance, is heard reverberating across the islands. Ukuleles and percussion instruments dominate, and the music is structured by a fast-paced and complex drum beat. Sunday *himene* (hymns) at churches feature wonderful harmonies.

Drums are the Maohi instruments par excellence and the most common is the *toere,* a cylindrical, hollowed-out piece of wood with a narrow slit down its length. String instruments are of European origin, though the ukulele, a miniguitar with four strings, comes by way of Hawaii.

Modern Polynesian music by local artists is the blaring soundtrack to everyday life, whether it's in a bus, at a cafe or on the radio – some groups also perform in hotels and bars. This music ranges from rock to folksy ballads usually accompanied by a guitar or ukulele.

Recommended Listening

- **Bobby** Dreamy
- **Te Ava Piti** Ukulele riffs
- **Angelo Neuffer** Poetic
- **Ester Tefana** Ukulele mood
- **Tapuarii Laughlin** Modern classics
- **Fenua** Traditional-techno fusion
- **Trio Kikiriri** Synth/ukulele

Sculpture, Woodcarving & Tapa

Traditionally, the best sculptures and woodcarvings have come out of the Marquesas, where fine *tiki,* bowls, mortars and pestles, spears and clubs are carved from rosewood, *tou* wood or stone. You can find these pieces in the market of Pape'ete, as well as gift shops around the islands, but the best deals are had in the Marquesas themselves.

Some woodwork sold in French Polynesia is actually made elsewhere (usually Indonesia), so if you see several of the same item, chances are it wasn't made in the country. Ask around to ensure you are getting the real thing.

Traditionally made throughout the Pacific, *tapa* (paperlike cloth) is a nonwoven fabric made from the bark of *uru* (breadfruit), banyan or

MONOI

What can't *monoi* do? This local concoction, made from coconut oil and *tiare* (fragrant gardenia, and the national flower), is deliciously perfumed with sandalwood, vanilla, coconut or jasmine. It's used liberally as hair oil, ointment, sunscreen and even mosquito repellent. It costs from 400 CFP to 600 CFP a bottle, is great on the skin after a day of sizzling in the sun and makes a great gift (although it does solidify in cooler climates).

aute (paper mulberry) trees. It was the semidisposable clothing fabric of pre-European Polynesia. Finished pieces are dyed with the sap of various plants or decorated with traditional artwork. Today, designs are sometimes just drawn on with ink.

Plaiting & Basketwork

Baskets and hats, and the panels used for roofing and the walls of houses, are made by women. Coconut-palm leaves are used for the more rough-and-ready woven work, while pandanus leaves or thin strips of bamboo are used for finer hats, bags and mats, which are often decorated with flowers or shells. Some of the finest work comes from the Australs.

Flowers & Shells

Flowers are omnipresent in French Polynesia. When you arrive at the airport, you'll be presented with a *tiare* (Tahiti's national flower) to sniff as you brave the customs queues. Both men and women tuck a *tiare* or other flower behind their ear in the world's most simple yet graceful gesture of physical adornment. Traditionally, a flower behind the left ear meant you were taken or married, while a blossom tucked behind your right ear meant you were available; while Tahitians love to tell tourists about this practice, in reality no one will try and deduce your relationship status in this way.

Flower crowns or necklaces are given as gifts on arrival while shell necklaces are given on departure.

Tattoos

Since the early 1980s, tattooing has enjoyed a strong revival, becoming one of the most expressive and vibrant vehicles of Polynesian culture.

Modern tattooing is completely for the sake of style or beautification; in ancient times it was a highly socially significant and sophisticated art. It was a symbol of community or clan membership and geographic origin; it was also an initiation rite, a symbol of social status and an aesthetic adornment that played a part in the seduction process. Finally, tattooing served to intimidate: in the Marquesas, warriors tattooed their faces to make themselves look terrifying.

Today, you'll find talented tattoo artists throughout the islands who will be happy to create an unforgettable souvenir on your skin.

French Polynesia in Popular Culture

For over 300 years French Polynesia has been painted as paradise via art and media. Throughout this time the clichés haven't changed much, but new Polynesia-based artists are starting to unearth the subtleties of their stereotype-ridden home.

Literature

Polynesia has been getting the Western pen flowing since the first European explorers returned with accounts of paradise. Early writers also offered valuable historical and ethnological details. Most modern fiction by non-Polynesians veers more towards fantasy, based only slightly on reality.

English-Language Writers

Pre-WWI Works

Through the 1800s and early 1900s several great authors travelled to French Polynesia looking for adventure. Herman Melville was the first, giving a fascinating account of his experiences living with an isolated cannibalistic tribe on Nuku Hiva in his book *Typee* (1846). He followed this with *Omoo* (1847), about his time on Tahiti. Robert Louis Stevenson came through the islands in the late 1880s before continuing through the Pacific. His book *In the South Seas* (1908) chronicles his voyage and his many encounters with local peoples. Jack London followed the footsteps of his idols Melville and Stevenson in 1906, visiting many of the places his heroes had written about. His travels inspired much of his writing, including *South Sea Tales* (1911). In 1917 Somerset Maugham visited Tahiti to research *The Moon and Sixpence* (1919), loosely based on Paul Gauguin's life.

Author Zane Grey spent many months in French Polynesia in the 1920s and 1930s. While there, he caught the first game fish (a marlin) to exceed 1000lb (over 450kg); he tells this story and more in his book *Tales of Tahitian Waters* (1931).

Mutiny on the Bounty & Beyond

The most famous books with a French Polynesian backdrop remain the *Mutiny on the Bounty* (1932) trilogy, written by James Norman Hall and Charles Nordhoff. Both authors lived on Tahiti for a good portion of their lives (you can visit Hall's house – see p54), and the books evoke all of the colours of the landscape and culture while telling one of the world's greatest adventure tales – it's based on a true story (see p223).

James Michener's *Tales of the South Pacific* (1947) and *Return to Paradise* (1951) contain a few stories based in French Polynesia, particularly during WWII. From the 1960s literature became dominated by French authors, but from the 2000s Polynesia began to appear more in romance and adventure genres, including books by Clare Coleman, Ferenc Máté and Suzanne Enoch.

MUTINY IN THE CINEMA

The story of the famous uprising aboard the *Bounty* has been embellished by big-budget film-makers three times in 50 years. If another version is ever made, audiences could be forgiven for having a mutiny of their own.

Mutiny on the Bounty (1935) Starred Charles Laughton as Captain Bligh and Clark Gable as Fletcher Christian. Very little was actually shot on Tahiti.

Mutiny on the Bounty (1962) Trevor Howard played Bligh and Marlon Brando was Christian. Filmed on Tahiti and Bora Bora.

Bounty (1984) Filmed mostly on Mo'orea, Anthony Hopkins plays Bligh and Mel Gibson is the more-handsome-than-ever Christian.

Polynesian & French Writers

Oral recitation was the fountain pen of the Pacific, and the written word only came into being after missionaries began producing texts in Tahitian in the 19th century. This dependence on the spoken word means that literature by Polynesians has only recently begun to grace bookshelves.

A number of Polynesian writers are slowly changing the literary landscape; few have been translated into English, but you can find them. Search for books by Henri Hiro, Turo Raapoto, Hubert Bremond, Charles Manutahi, Michou Chaze, Chantal Spitz and Louise Peltzer.

The *Materena* (2006) series, by Celestine Hitiura Vaite, a Tahitian living in Australia, is a trilogy of novels available in English about a headstrong but poor woman in contemporary Tahiti. Meanwhile, Franco American writer Alex du Prel (editor of Tahiti's French news monthly, *Tahiti Pacifique*) has been in French Polynesia so long he's an honorary local. His *Tahiti Blues* (2011) series recounts fascinating modern tales of the islands.

In the footsteps of Somerset Maugham, Peruvian author Mario Vargas Llosa wrote *The Way to Paradise* (2003), a story that mirrors the life of Gauguin with his feminist-socialist grandmother Flora Trist.

Painting

Even today, painting in the South Pacific is synonymous with Paul Gauguin, the French post-Impressionist painter. Gauguin spent much of his later life in Polynesia, and presented Europe with images of the islands that moulded the way Europeans viewed Polynesia. In his wake a number of predominantly European artists have sought inspiration in the region.

Matisse made a short visit to Tahiti, but his work on Polynesia is eclipsed by Jacques Boullaire, a French artist who first travelled to Tahiti in the 1930s. He produced magnificent watercolours, and reproductions of his work are readily available.

Other artists of French and Polynesian descent who have influenced the art scene locally and internationally include Christian Deloffre, François Ravello, Michèle Dallet, Bobby (also a singer and musician; he died in 1991), André Marere, Jean Masson, Garrick Yrondi, Maryse Noguier and Erhard Lux.

Cinema

Until the recent comedy *Couples Retreat* (2009), mostly filmed at the St Régis Resort on Bora Bora, French Polynesia's role as a movie backdrop is almost exclusively tied up with *Mutiny on the Bounty*. James Michener's *South Pacific* may have been about Polynesia, but it was filmed in Malaysia.

Tabu, released in 1931, was filmed on Bora Bora. This work of fiction explores the notions of *tapu* (taboo), and although it remains an interesting slice of history, it was a flop in its era. The IMAX movie *The Ultimate Wave Tahiti* (2010) brought surfing Teahupoo to the really big screen. There's stunning footage but, perhaps in an attempt to adhere to stereotypes, the film has a Hawaiian-music soundtrack and even the dancing has non-Tahitian choreography. As a result, the cultural parts feel canned.

Survival Guide

Directory A–Z

Accommodation

See the Which Island? chapter (p26) for details on accommodation options in French Polynesia.

Activities

French Polynesia's exceptional natural heritage lends itself to a range of activities. For scuba diving and snorkelling see the Diving chapter, p31).

Golf

There are two golf courses in French Polynesia – one on Tahiti and the other on Mo'orea.

Hiking

The high islands offer superb walks but the tracks are sometimes unmarked and are hard to follow: it's often a good idea to hire a guide. Tahiti and Mo'orea are the main islands for walking, but there are also good walks on Ra'iatea, Bora Bora Maupiti, Huahine, Rurutu, Raivavae and all around the Marquesas.

Horse Riding

There are equestrian centres in the Society Islands on Tahiti, Mo'orea and Huahine. Most places offer short jaunts and longer excursions that explore the island interiors. Horses are an important part of life in the Marquesas, and there are various places to rent them, with or without a guide; you can also horse ride on Rurutu in the Australs.

Surfing

Polynesia was the birthplace of *horue* (surfing) and Tahiti in particular has a thriving local surfing scene. The island is home to Teahupoo, one of the most powerful waves in the world and the site of the Tahiti Billabong Pro competition each year. Tahiti, Mo'orea, Ra'iatea and Huahine are the main islands for surfing, but many of the Tuamotu atolls have good breaks including Tikehau, Rangiroa and Fakarava. The best place for beginners is Papenoo on Tahiti.

Like surfers anywhere in the world, French Polynesians can be possessive of *their* waves. If you want to enjoy the surf, observe all the usual rules of surfing etiquette, give way to local surfers and smile and say hello. On Huahine and Ra'iatea in particular don't even think of taking surf pictures or of arriving at the wave in a big group.

There are several surf shops in Pape'ete – look out for the excellent, locally shaped Teva Tahiti boards. Elsewhere, the local surf shops all have boogie-board equipment as well as short boards and traditional surfboards. You won't need a wetsuit in the warm waters, but a lycra vest will protect you from the sun.

Windsurfing & Kitesurfing

French Polynesia's sheltered lagoons with their consistent trade winds are perfect for wind sports. The best time of year is May to October when the southeast winds blow strong.

The best spots on Tahiti are off Hiti Mahan Beach at PK45 on the east coast and Baie Phaeton in Taravao. Other popular islands include Mo'orea, Ra'iatea, Huahine, Bora Bora and Tikehau.

Yachting

Renting a yacht can be a fine way to explore French Polynesia, and you can choose from a bare-boat charter (which you sail yourself) or a cabin on a fully crewed luxury boat. Ra'iatea is the

BOOK YOUR STAY ONLINE

For more accommodation reviews by Lonely Planet authors, check out http://hotels.lonelyplanet.com. You'll find independent reviews, as well as recommendations on the best places to stay. Best of all, you can book online.

main yachting base in French Polynesia, although there are a number of yacht-charter operations around the islands with a flotilla of modern monohulls and catamarans. Cruises on a crewed yacht will usually include tour programs at the stops en route, and dive cruises are also possible.

The following are some of the companies offering cruises and charter boats.

Aqua Polynésie (☎73 47 31; www.aquapolynesie.com) Luxurious 14m catamarans with crews cruise around the Leeward Islands and the Tuamotus, plus there's a boat specially equipped for dive cruises. Departures are from Bora Bora, Nuku Hiva (Marquesas) or Fakarava (Tuamotus).

Archipels Croisières (☎56 36 39; www.archipels.com) Reasonably priced crewed cruises to the Leeward Islands and the Tuamotus on deluxe 18m catamarans. Departures are from Rangiroa (Tuamotus), Mo'orea or Pape'ete.

Atara Royal (☎79 22 40; www.motoryachtchartertahiti.com) Luxury, dive-equipped motor cruiser based in Ra'iatea. Visits the Leeward, Tuamotu and Marquesas archipelagos.

L'Escapade (☎72 85 31; www.escapade-voile.pf) Sail on a 14m monohull to Tetiaroa and the other Society Islands and to the Tuamotu Islands from Tahiti.

Moorings (☎66 35 93; www.moorings.com) Twenty different options, including bare-boat charters, hire with skipper and host, or cabin charters. It's based at Apooiti Marina at Ra'iatea and offers cruises to the Society and Tuamotu Islands.

Polynésie Croisière (☎28 60 06; www.polynesie-croisiere.com) Scuba-specialist catamarans based on Ra'iatea offering a host of cruises to the Leeward Islands.

Sailing Huahine Voile (☎68 72 49; www.sailing-huahine.com) This operation, based on Huahine, has monohulls and offers cruises in the Leeward Islands and the Tuamotus.

Sun Sail (☎60 04 85; www.sunsail.com) Based at the Apooiti Marina on Ra'iatea, this operation offers bare-boat charters, hire with skipper and/or host, and cabin charter. About 20 boats of a variety of types are available for hire. Cruises are in the Leeward Islands and the Tuamotus.

Tahiti Yacht Charter (☎45 04 00; www.tahitiyachtcharter.com) Catamarans and monohulls; bare-boat charter or hire with skipper and host. Cruises are possible in all the archipelagos. Vessels depart to the Society, Tuamotu and Marquesas Islands from Ra'iatea and Tahiti.

It's often possible to pick up crewing positions on yachts, particularly if you have had some relevant sailing experience. Check notice boards in popular restaurants and at the yacht clubs on Tahiti, Ra'iatea, Bora Bora and other popular yachting stops. Yacht owners have to complete complex paperwork when making crew changes, so make sure your own papers are in order.

Business Hours

The opening hours for banks vary from branch to branch but are typically from 8am to noon and 1.30pm to 5pm Monday to Thursday, and 8am to noon and 1pm to 3pm on Friday. Shops and offices normally open around 7.30am, close for lunch from 11.30am to 1.30pm and shut around 5pm, Monday to Friday. On Saturday, shops are typically open between 7.30am and 11.30am; almost everything (except a few grocery stores and boutiques on the more touristy islands) is closed on Sunday. Restaurant hours vary according to the type of food served and the clientele; most places open around 10.30am and stay open until about 10pm.

Climate

Atuona

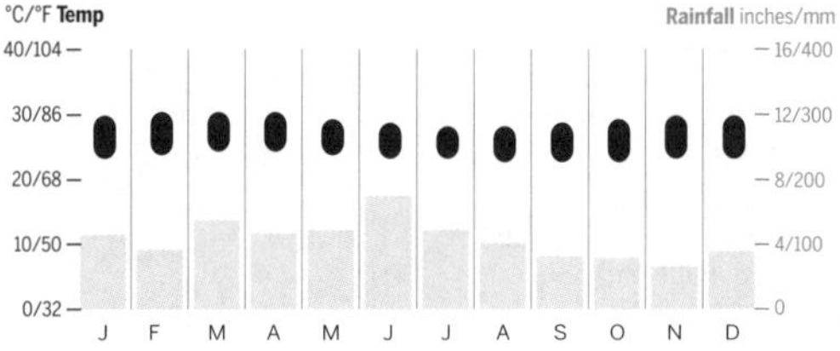

Pape'ete

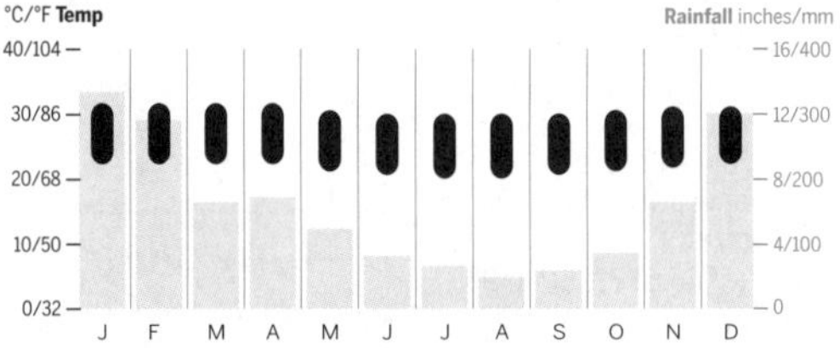

Customs Regulations

The duty-free allowance for visitors entering French Polynesia includes 200 cigarettes or 50 cigars, 2L of wine and 2L of spirits, two cameras, one video camera and 50mL of perfume. No live animals can be imported (if they're on a yacht they must stay on board) and certification is required for plants. For information on customs regulations for yachts, see p244.

On the way out of the country you're allowed to bring up to 10 undrilled pearls plus as much mounted jewellery as you like, tax-free.

Embassies & Consulates

Consulates in French Polynesia

Given that French Polynesia is not an independent country, there are no foreign embassies, only consulates, and many countries are represented in Pape'ete by honorary consuls.

The following consulates and diplomatic representatives are all located on Tahiti. Many are just single representatives and they do not have official offices, so you'll have to call them. BP here refers to '*boite postal*' (post office box).

Australia & Canada (☎46 88 53; service@mobil.pf; BP 9068, Pape'ete)

Austria, Switzerland & Leichtenstein (Map p56; ☎43 91 14; paulmaetztahiti@mail.pf; Rue Cannonière Zélée, BP 4560, Pape'ete)

Chile, Brazil, Paraguay, Argentina & Bolivia (Map p56; ☎43 89 19; c.chilepapeete@mail.pf; BP 952, Pape'ete)

China (☎45 61 79; BP 4495, Pape'ete)

Denmark (☎54 04 54; c.girard@groupavocats.pf; BP 548, Pape'ete)

Germany (☎42 99 94; BP 452, Pira'e)

Italy (☎43 45 01; consolato_polinesia@yahoo.fr; BP 380 412, Tamanu)

Israel (☎42 41 00; consulisrael@mail.pf; BP 37, Pape'ete)

Japan (☎45 45 45; nippon@mail.pf; BP 342, Pape'ete)

Korea (☎43 64 75; bbaudry@mail.pf; BP 2061, Pape'ete)

Netherlands (☎42 49 37; htt@mail.pf; Mobil Bldg, Fare Ute, BP 2804, Pape'ete)

New Zealand (☎54 07 40; nzcgnou@offratel.nc; c/- Air New Zealand, Vaima Centre, BP 73, Pape'ete)

Norway (☎42 89 72; amitahiti@mail.pf; BP 274, Pape'ete)

Spain (☎77 85 40; mlpromotion@mail.pf; BP 186, Pape'ete)

Sweden (☎47 54 75; jacques.solari@sopadep.pf; BP 1617, Pape'ete)

UK (☎70 63 82; BP 50009, Pira'e)

US (Map p52; ☎42 65 35; usconsul@mail.pf; US Info, Centre Tamanu, Puna'auia BP 10765, 98711 Pa'ea)

Electricity

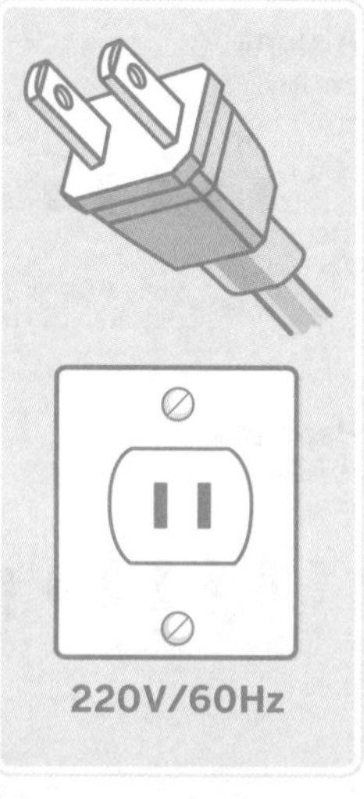

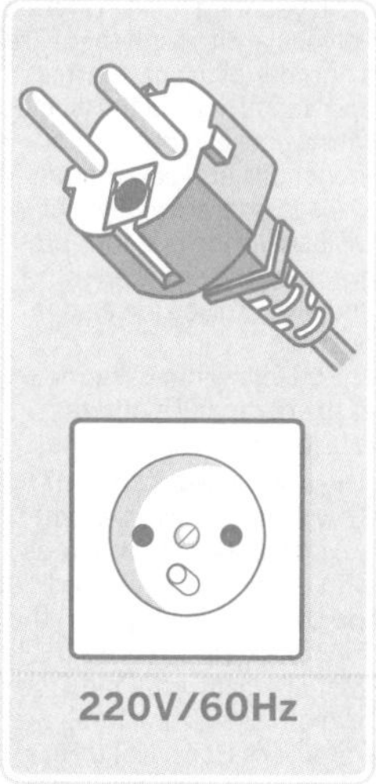

Food

Modern Tahitian food is a fairly balanced melange of French, Chinese and Polynesian influence; béchamel, soy sauce or coconut milk all have an equal chance of topping your meal.

Staples & Specialities

Ma'a Tahiti, traditional Tahitian food, is a heavy mix of starchy taro and *uru* (breadfruit), raw or cooked fish, fatty pork, coconut milk and a few scattered vegetables. On special occasions, the whole lot is neatly prepared and placed in a *hima'a* (cooking pit) where a layer of stones and banana leaves separate the food from the hot coals beneath. The food is covered with more banana leaves then buried so all the flavours and juices can cook and mingle for several hours. The result is a steamy, tender ambrosia of a meal.

Main Dishes

Open-sea fish (tuna, bonito, wahoo, swordfish and *mahi mahi* – dorado) and lagoon fish (parrotfish, jackfish and squirrelfish) feature

MEAL PRICE RANGES

The following price ranges are used in this guide and refer to a standard main course. Unless otherwise stated tax is included.

» $ less than 1200 CFP

» $$ 1200 CFP to 2400 CFP

» $$$ more than 2400 CFP

prominently in traditional cuisine. *Poisson cru* (raw fish in coconut milk) is the most popular local dish, though fish is also served grilled, fried or poached. Lobster is not plentiful but is available at finer restaurants; *chevrettes* (freshwater shrimps) however, often served in curry, are farmed locally and can sometimes be found even at budget restaurants. Salmon and trout generally come from Australia or New Zealand, and prawns may be imported or farmed locally.

Pua (pork) is the preferred meat for the traditional underground oven. Although chickens run wild everywhere, most of what is consumed is imported frozen from the US and is of low quality. Lamb and beef, from New Zealand, make regular appearances on menus and are as good as you'll find anywhere in the world. In the Marquesas, goat meat takes pride of place, and dog is still eaten on the remote atolls of the Tuamotus.

Among Chinese specialities, chow mein is the most popular. This fried noodle dish usually has pork and/or chicken in it, but vegetarians can always order a meat-free version. Pizza and pasta are also easy to find on the touristy islands.

Fruit & Vegetables

French Polynesia is dripping with tropical fruit, including mango, grapefruit, lime, watermelon, pineapple and banana. *Pamplemousse* (grapefruit) is the large, sweet, Southeast Asian variety. The rambutan, another Southeast Asian introduction, is a red spiny-skinned cousin of the lychee. Fruits on the high islands are seasonal; different ones will be available depending on when you're visiting. In the Tuamotus fresh produce is always scarce.

Vegetables are not a major component of Polynesian cuisine. *Uru* is a staple, and is eaten roasted or fried as chips. *Fei,* a plantain banana, is only eaten cooked and is much less sweet than a common banana. Taro root is usually boiled, as are sweet potato and manioc (cassava), but can also be fried as delicious chips. *Fafa* (taro leaves) are used to make *poulet fafa,* a stew with chicken and coconut milk. Carrots, Chinese cabbage, cabbage, tomatoes and bell peppers all make regular appearances in dishes like chow mein and *poisson cru*.

Drinks

Several delicious fruit juices are made locally, notably the Rotui brand. *Pape haari* (coconut water) is the healthiest, cheapest, most natural and thirst-quenching drink around. If you want a real coffee, order a *café expresso* (espresso coffee), otherwise you'll probably be served instant Nescafé. The further you get from the tourist hubs the further you get from espresso machines.

The local brand of *pia* (beer), Hinano, is sold everywhere, and foreign beers, notably Heineken, are also available. Allow at least 350 CFP for a beer in a bar or restaurant.

Most supermarkets stock red and white wines (from around 1000 CFP), imported from France. It can be excellent, but the tropical heat is a good wine's worst enemy, and you sometimes happen upon a crate of bottles that has spent time sitting in the sun at the port. The cheapest (and nastiest) is boxed (cask) wine for around 450 CFP for 1L. Restaurants enjoy a tax reduction on alcohol, which makes it affordable (allow 1500 to 3000 CFP for a bottle).

The classic Tahitian holiday drink is the *maitai,* a yummy cocktail made with rum, fruit juices, coconut liqueur and, in some cases, Grand Marnier or Cointreau. This concoction is also available readymade as Tahiti Drink in 1L cartons found at grocery stores.

Where To Eat & Drink

There is a wondrous array of restaurants on the island of Tahiti, where you can find

MENU DECODER

» **brochette** shish kebab of beef heart, beef or fish

» **carpacio du thon** thinly sliced sashimi: quality raw tuna with a sprinkling of olive oil, salt and pepper, and capers

» **casse-croûte** sandwich on a French-style baguette

» **chevrettes/crevettes** freshwater shrimp/saltwater prawns

» **chow mein** Chinese wheat noodles with carrot, cabbage, Chinese greens and chicken

» **poisson cru** raw fish marinated in lemon then doused in coconut milk and mixed with tomato and cucumber

» **sashimi** thinly sliced raw tuna served with a sauce

» **steak frites** steak and chips (French fries)

'SNACK' & ROULOTTE FOR GOOD, CHEAP MEALS

A *'snack'* in French Polynesia is actually a little snack bar–cum-cafe and sometimes may even be more like a small restaurant. These places are simple, cheap, and serve everything from sandwiches (made from French-style baguettes) and salads to *poisson cru* (raw fish in coconut milk) and meat or fish burgers. Even cheaper are *roulottes*, mobile vans with a kitchen inside and a fold-down counter along each side. The nightly gathering of *roulottes* near the tourist office in Pape'ete is a real institution and you'll find others dotted around all the bigger islands.

everything from French cuisine to sushi, but the rest of French Polynesia has more limited options. The prices are fairly intimidating – expect to pay 1200 to 2000 CFP for a main in a midrange restaurant – but the food is very good. Most resort restaurants host buffet and dance performances a few times a week, which usually cost around 8000 CFP.

Supermarkets of varying sizes can be found around the islands. Some have dusty little collections of tins and packaged goods, while others, particularly those on Tahiti, Mo'orea and Ra'iatea, are very well equipped. The biggest supermarkets on Tahiti are the Carrefour chains (in Arue and Puna'auia).

There are no vegetarian restaurants in French Polynesia, but you can usually ask the chef to tweak a dish for you.

Gay & Lesbian Travellers

French laws concerning homosexuality prevail in French Polynesia, which means there is no legal discrimination against homosexual activity. Homophobia in French Polynesia is uncommon, although open displays of affection in public should be avoided. French Polynesia does feel remarkably heterosexual, given the preponderance of honeymooning couples, but you will meet lots of *mahu* (men living as women) working in restaurants and hotels (see the boxed text, p229).

Health

You probably have less chance of getting sick in French Polynesia than in any major international city. There's no malaria, land snakes, poisonous spiders or crocodiles, and cold and flu bugs are brought in from elsewhere. Mosquitoes do exist in quantity, however, and dengue fever will be a concern when there is an outbreak. Your biggest worry will be sunburn and avoiding infection in minor cuts and scrapes. Health facilities in the country are generally of a good standard but some less-populated islands will have little to no medical services.

French Polynesia has doctors and dentists in private practice, and standard hospital and laboratory facilities with consultants in the major specialities. The outer islands, of course, have more basic services. Private consultation costs from 3500 CFP to see a GP; specialists are more expensive and anywhere you go, the waiting times can be very long. Direct payment is required everywhere except where a specific arrangement is made, eg in the case of evacuation or where prolonged hospital stay is necessary; your insurer will need to be contacted by you. Although most of the larger hospitals are coming into line in accepting credit cards, there will be difficulty with the more remote, small medical facilities.

Most commonly used medications are available. Private pharmacies are not allowed by law to dispense listed drugs without a prescription from a locally registered practitioner, but many will do so for travellers if shown the container. While the container should preferably specify the generic name of the drug, this has become much less of a problem with the use of internet search engines.

It's best to have a sufficient supply of a regularly taken medication as a particular brand may not be available and sometimes quantities can be limited. This applies particularly to psychotropic drugs like antidepressants, antipsychotics, anti-epileptics or mood elevators. Insulin is available even in smaller centres, but you cannot guarantee getting a particular brand, combination or preferred administration method. If you have been prescribed 'the very latest'

WATER

The municipal water supply in Pape'ete and other large towns can be trusted, but elsewhere avoid untreated tap water. In some areas the only fresh water available may be rainwater collected in tanks, and this should be boiled or otherwise treated. Water at restaurants, particularly resort restaurants, is safe.

oral antidiabetic or antihypertensive, make sure you have enough for the duration of your travel.

Infectious Diseases

The overall risk of illness for a normally healthy person is low. The most common problems are diarrhoeal upsets, viral sore throats, and ear and skin infections. The two following ailments are the only relatively common things you should know about, although the chances of contracting them are unlikely.

DENGUE FEVER

Dengue fever is a viral disease spread by the bite of a daytime-biting mosquito. It causes a feverish illness with headache and severe muscle pains similar to those experienced with a bad, prolonged attack of influenza. Danger signs include any sort of bruising or bleeding, vomiting or a blotchy rash – if you experience any of these alongside the fever get medical attention quickly. There is no preventive vaccine. Self-treatment involves paracetamol, fluids and rest. Do not use aspirin.

LEPTOSPIROSIS

Also known as Weil's disease, leptospirosis produces fever, headache, jaundice and, later, kidney failure. It is caused by a spirochaete organism found in water contaminated by rat and pig urine. The organism penetrates skin, so swimming in flooded areas or in rivers near pig farms is a risky practice. If diagnosed early it is cured with penicillin. This disease is often confused with dengue fever; if you have blood in your urine consider leptospirosis, which is considerably more serious.

PRACTICALITIES

» The weekly English-language tourist paper *Tahiti Beach Press* includes some local news coverage. If you read French, there are two Tahitian dailies, *Les Nouvelles de Tahiti* and *La Dépêche de Tahiti*.

» There are about 10 independent radio stations that broadcast music programs with news flashes in French and Tahitian along with the occasional interview. Among the best-known stations are Tiare FM (the pioneer nongovernmental radio station; 104.2FM), NRJ (103 FM) and RFO-Radio Polynésie (95.2FM).

» Radio France Outre-Mer (RFO) has two TV channels: Télé Polynésie and Tempo. TNTV is the satellite carrier and has its own channel as well.

» French Polynesia follows the international metric system.

Environmental Hazards

Threats to health from animals and insects are rare, but you need to be aware of them.

BITES & STINGS

Poisonous jellyfish and sea snakes are virtually unheard of in French Polynesia, but in the unlikely event you see these in the water or stranded on the beach, step or swim away. Tiny cubo-medusae jellyfish are abundant but produce only uncomfortably irritating stings; rarely they can cause generalised symptoms, especially in someone with poorly controlled heart disease.

More of a worry are extremely well-camouflaged stone fish, prolific on coral reefs and rocky areas – they are nearly impossible to see and have poison-injecting spines along their backs. If you do get stung apply heat immediately and head for the hospital. Wearing plastic, waterproof sandals provides the best protection.

Poisonous cone shells abound along shallow coral reefs. Stings can be avoided by handling the shell at its blunt end only and preferably using gloves. Stings mainly cause local reactions; nausea, faintness, palpitations or difficulty in breathing flag the need for medical attention.

On land, mosquitoes and noseums will be your biggest concern. Although there is no malaria in French Polynesia, there are occasional dengue-fever outbreaks spread by mosquitoes. Noseums aren't disease carriers but be careful not to over-scratch the bites or you'll risk infection.

SKIN & EARS

Coral ear is a fungal infection caused by water entering the canal. Apparently trivial, it can be very, very painful and can spoil a holiday. Apart from diarrhoea it is the most common reason for tourists to consult a doctor. Self-treatment with an antibiotic-plus-steroid eardrop preparation (eg Sofradex, Kenacort Otic) is very effective. Stay out of the water until the pain and itch have gone.

Staph infection of cuts and scrapes is very common and cuts from live coral are particularly prone to infection. As soon as you can, cleanse the wound thoroughly (getting out all the little bits of coral or dirt if needed), apply an antiseptic and cover with a dressing. You can get back in the water but healing time will be prolonged if you do. Change the dressing regularly, never let it sit wet and check often for signs of infection.

DIVING HAZARDS

There is one recompression chamber on Tahiti, at the Centre Hospitalier du Taaone.

GETTING MARRIED IN FRENCH POLYNESIA

Recent changes in local law mean that international visitors can now legally get married in French Polynesia. You'll need to plan in advance, fill out forms and make reservations for a civil service at a city hall (for information see www.tahiti-tourisme.com/weddings/tahitidestinationweddings.asp). Following this you can indulge in a traditional Polynesian wedding ceremony that is now offered through most big resorts and at Tiki Village on Mo'orea – a list of places is on the Tahiti Tourism website.

Even experienced divers should check in with organisations like **DAN** (Divers' Alert Network; www.diversalertnetwork.org) and check that their insurance covers costs both for local treatment and evacuation. Novice divers must be especially careful. If you have not taken out insurance before leaving home you may be able to do so online with DAN.

FISH POISONING

Ciguatera has been reported in many carnivorous reef fish, especially barracuda and very large jack, but also red snapper and napoleon fish; in French Polynesia it sometimes occurs in the smaller reef fish as well and this will vary from island to island. There is no safe test to determine whether a fish is poisonous or not. Although local knowledge is not entirely reliable, it is reasonable to eat what the locals are eating. Treatment consists of rehydration and, if the pulse is very slow, medication may be needed. Healthy adults will make a complete recovery, although disturbed sensation may persist for some weeks.

HEAT

Sunburn is an obvious issue so use sunscreen liberally. It's also important to stay hydrated; heat exhaustion is a state of dehydration associated to a greater or lesser extent with salt loss. Heat stroke is more dangerous and happens when the cooling effect of sweating fails. This condition is characterised by muscle weakness and mental confusion. Skin will be hot and dry. If this occurs, 'put the fire out' by cooling the body with water on the outside and cold drinks for the inside. Seek medical help.

Insurance

A travel-insurance policy to cover theft, loss and medical problems is vital. There is a wide variety of policies available and your travel agent will have recommendations.

Some policies specifically exclude 'dangerous activities', which can include scuba diving, motorcycling and even trekking. If such activities are on your agenda, you obviously don't want that sort of policy.

You may prefer a policy that pays doctors or hospitals directly rather than requiring you to pay on the spot and claim later. If you have to claim later, make sure you keep all documentation. Some policies ask you to call (reverse charges) a centre in your home country where an immediate assessment of your problem is made.

Check the small print: for example, whether the policy covers ambulances and an emergency flight home.

Internet Access

Internet cafes can be found on all the major islands – although the ones on the smaller islands often have only ancient computers and slow connections. Most post offices also have internet posts. Many top-end hotels offer internet access to their guests (sometimes at ridiculously high prices), and access elsewhere is fairly straightforward. You'll generally pay around 900 CFP per hour.

If you're toting your own computer through the Society, Marquesas or Austral Islands, consider buying online or from the local post office a prepaid **Mana Pass** (www.manaspot.pf; per hr 500 CFP) that allows you to access the internet at 'Mana Spots' (wi-fi zones) located in post offices and at some hotels, restaurants and public areas. Check the website for current locations.

Legal Matters

French Polynesia is a part of France, and is thus subject to that country's penal system. The police rarely hassle foreigners, especially tourists. Drunk driving is a real problem on the larger islands, and police sometimes set up checkpoints on Tahiti, Ra'iatea and Mo'orea.

Maps

The map *Tahiti Archipel de la Société* (IGN No 3615), at a scale of 1:100,000, is readily available in Pape'ete and from map specialists abroad. It covers the Society Archipelago and is the one really useful map for travellers. IGN also publishes maps at 1:50,000 for each island in the archipelago, although these are harder to track down. The SHOM navy maps of the Tuamotus are the best available; for the Marquesas there are SHOM maps and

IGN maps at 1:50,000 for Hiva Oa, Nuku Hiva and 'Ua Pou.

Money

The unit of currency in French Polynesia is the *cours de franc Pacifique* (CFP; Pacific franc), referred to simply as 'the franc', and it's pegged to the euro. Aside from the following options, there's also a money-exchange machine for US dollars in the domestic terminal of Faa'a International Airport.

ATMs

Known as *distributeurs automatiques de billets* or DABs in French, ATMs will give you cash via Visa, MasterCard, Cirrus or Maestro networks. International cards generally work only at Banque Socredo ATMs; luckily most islands have at least one of these. You'll need a four-digit pin number.

The exchange rate on these transactions is usually better than what you get with travellers cheques, and the charge your own bank makes on these withdrawals (typically about US$9) is far less than you'll be charged by banks in French Polynesia for changing money or travellers cheques.

See individual chapters for the availability of ATMs in the islands. There's a Socredo ATM at Faa'a International Airport.

WITHDRAWAL LIMITS

Check with your bank before you leave home to ensure that the card you plan to use to withdraw cash doesn't have a low daily or weekly limit. Some travellers (particularly those with European-based cards) find that they are only able to take out 35,000 CFP per week in French Polynesia – not nearly enough if you plan on going to smaller guesthouses or restaurants that don't take credit cards.

Banks

There are three major banks operating in French Polynesia: Banque de Tahiti, Banque de Polynésie and Banque Socredo.

All the main islands in the Society group, apart from Maupiti, have at least one banking agency. In the Tuamotus, only Rangiroa has a permanent banking service. In the Marquesas there are Socredo agencies on 'Ua Pou, Nuku Hiva and Hiva Oa. In the Australs group, Rurutu, Raivavae and Tubuai have some banking services.

Banking hours vary from branch to branch but are typically from 8am to noon and 1.30pm to 5pm Monday to Thursday, and 8am to noon and 1pm to 3pm on Friday. Some branches in Pape'ete do not close for the traditional French Polynesian lunch break, and a handful of Tahitian branches open on Saturday morning. The Banque de Polynésie and Banque Socredo has banking facilities at Faa'a airport for flight arrivals.

Credit Cards

All top-end and midrange hotels, restaurants, jewellery shops, dive centres and the bigger supermarkets accept credit cards, sometimes exclusively Visa or MasterCard (although American Express is gaining ground), but they usually require a 2000 CFP minimum purchase. You can also pay for Air Tahiti flights with a card. Most budget guesthouses and many tour operators don't accept credit cards.

Tipping

Tipping is not a part of life in French Polynesia. The price quoted is the price you are expected to pay, which certainly simplifies things. In special circumstances, such as an excellent tour or great service by the hotel cleaning crew, a tip is appreciated.

Post

The postal system in French Polynesia is generally quite efficient, and there are modern post offices on all the main islands. Mail to Europe, the USA and Australia takes about a week. Postcards or letters weighing up to 20g cost 100 CFP to France, 140 CFP to anywhere else.

Post offices are generally open from around 7.30am to 4pm Monday to Friday, although the main post office in Pape'ete has longer opening hours and the post office at Faa'a International Airport is also open from 6.30am to 10am Saturday and Sunday.

Fed-Ex (☎45 36 45; PK2.5 Faa'a) and **DHL Express** (☎83 73 73; across from Faa'a International Airport) have offices in Pape'ete. If you need to send something fast from the outer islands they can usually help out – although it will probably involve sending the item by freight on Air Tahiti.

Public Holidays

Public holidays, when all businesses and government offices close, include the following.

New Year's Day 1 January

Arrival of the First Missionaries 5 March

Easter March/April

Labour Day 1 May

VE Day (Victory in Europe Day) 8 May

Ascension Late May

Pentecost & Pentecost Monday Early June

Internal Autonomy Day 29 June

Bastille Day 14 July

Assumption 15 August

All Saints' Day 1 November

Armistice Day 11 November
Christmas Day 25 December

Telephone

Public phone boxes requiring a prepaid phonecard are becoming harder to find; buy phonecards from post offices, newsagencies, shops and some supermarkets in 1000 CFP, 2000 CFP and 5000 CFP denominations.

There are no area codes in French Polynesia. From a landline, local phone calls cost 17 CFP per minute or 22 CFP per minute to a mobile phone. To call overseas, dial ☎00 plus the country code followed by the phone number. French Polynesia's country code is ☎689.

Mobile Phones

Mobile phone services operate on 900 GSM and 98% of the inhabited islands have cellular coverage. SIM cards are available for 5900 CFP at most post offices on main islands bearing a 'Vini' sign and this price includes one hour of local minutes.

If you're from North America and your phone is locked by your phone company, there are often good deals at Champion and Carrefour supermarkets on phones – at the time of writing you could get a basic phone plus SIM card and one-hour of credit for 5900 CFP, the price of just the SIM card at the post office! Additional minutes can be purchased from 1000 CFP, also at the post office. Talk isn't cheap however: calls from a mobile cost 30 CFP to 50 CFP per minute.

Many foreign mobile services have coverage in Tahiti but roaming fees are usually quite high.

Time

French Polynesia is 10 hours behind London, two to three hours behind Los Angeles and three hours ahead of Sydney; the region is just two hours east of the International Date Line. The Marquesas are a half-hour ahead of the rest of French Polynesia (noon on Tahiti is 12.30pm in the Marquesas).

Tourist Information

The main and only real tourist office is the **Office du Tourisme de Tahiti et ses Îles** (☎50 57 00; www.tahiti-tourisme.com; Fare Manihini, Blvd Pomare; ⏰7.30am-5pm Mon-Fri, 8am-noon Sat & public holidays) in the centre of Pape'ete.

For information before you leave home, go to the **Tahiti Tourisme website** (www.tahiti-tourisme.com), which has several international tourism office links.

Travellers with Disabilities

With narrow flights of steps on boats, high steps on *le trucks* (public buses) and difficult boarding facilities on Air Tahiti aircraft, French Polynesia resembles a tropical obstacle course for those with restricted mobility. What's more, hotels and guesthouses are not used to receiving guests with disabilities. However, all new hotels and public buildings must conform to certain standards, so change is happening.

Visas

Everyone needs a passport to visit French Polynesia. The regulations are much the same as for France: if you need a visa to visit France then you'll need one to visit French Polynesia. Anyone from an EU country can stay for up to three months without a visa, as can Australians and citizens of a number of other European countries, including Switzerland.

Citizens of Argentina, Canada, Chile, Japan, Mexico, New Zealand, the USA and some other European countries are able to stay for up to one month without a visa. Other nationalities need a visa, which can be applied for at French embassies.

Apart from permanent residents and French citizens, all visitors to French Polynesia need to have an onward or return ticket.

Visa Extensions

It's possible to extend a month-long visa exemption for two more months but it can be tricky. Tahiti's Immigration Department states it's best to get an extended visa at a French embassy before arrival but we've found that this requires heaps of time and paperwork, and requests are often refused. Try at the **Police aux Frontières** (Frontier Police; ☎42 40 74; pafport@mail.pf; Blvd Pomare; ⏰airport office 8am-noon & 2-5pm Mon-Fri, Pape'ete office 7.30am-noon & 2-5pm Mon-Fri), at Faa'a International Airport and next at the tourist office in Pape'ete, at least one week before the visa or exemption expires. Dress nice and smile big.

Stays by foreign visitors may not exceed three months. For longer periods, you must apply to the French consular authorities in your own country for a residence permit; you cannot lodge your application from French Polynesia unless you have a sponsor or get married to a permanent resident.

Formalities for Yachts

In addition to presenting the certificate of ownership of the vessel, sailors are subject to the same passport and visa requirements as travellers arriving by air or by cruise ship. Unless you have a return air ticket, you are required to provide a banking guarantee of repatriation equivalent to the price of an airline ticket to your country of origin.

Yachties must advise the **Police aux Frontières** (Frontier Police; ☎42 40 74; ⏲7.30am-noon & 2-5pm Mon-Fri), next to the tourist office in Pape'ete, of their final departure. If your first port of call is not Pape'ete, it must be a port with a *gendarmerie* (police station): Afareaitu (Mo'orea), Uturoa (Ra'iatea), Fare (Huahine), Vaitape (Bora Bora), Taiohae (Nuku Hiva, Marquesas), Hakahau ('Ua Pou, Marquesas), Atuona (Hiva Oa, Marquesas), Mataura (Tubuai, Australs), Moerai (Rurutu, Australs), Rairua (Raivavae, Australs), Avatoru (Rangiroa, Tuamotus) or Rikitea (Mangareva, Gambiers). The *gendarmerie* must be advised of each arrival and departure, and of any change of crew.

Before arriving at the port of Pape'ete, announce your arrival on channel 12. You can anchor at the quay or the beach, but there are no reserved places. Next, you'll need to report to the **capitainerie** (harbour master's office; ⏲7-11.30am & 1-4pm Mon-Thu, 7-11.30am & 1-3pm Fri), in the same building as the Police aux Frontières, and complete an arrival declaration.

Women Travellers

French Polynesia is a great place for solo women. Local women are very much a part of public life in the region, and it's not unusual to see Polynesian women out drinking beer together or walking alone, so you will probably feel pretty comfortable following suit.

It is a sad reality that women are still required to exercise care, particularly at night, but this is the case worldwide. As with anywhere in the world, give drunks and their beer breath a wide berth.

Perhaps it's the locals getting their own back after centuries of European men ogling Polynesian women, but there is reportedly a 'tradition' of Peeping Toms in French Polynesia, mainly in the outer islands. Take special care in places that seem to offer opportunities for spying on guests, particularly in the showers, and make sure your room is secure.

Work

French citizens aren't required to comply with any formalities but for everyone else, even other EU citizens (with the exception of those with very specialised skills), it's difficult to work in French Polynesia. Unless you're a pearl grafter, a Chinese chef or a banking executive, you stand little chance. Authorisation to take up paid employment is subject to the granting of a temporary-residence permit, issued by the French state, and a work permit, issued by the territory.

Transport

GETTING THERE & AWAY

Entering the Country

» Entry procedures for French Polynesia are straightforward. You'll have to show your passport, with any visa you may have obtained beforehand (see p244). You'll also need to present completed arrival and departure cards, usually distributed on the incoming flight. You may also be asked to show proof of a return airline ticket – Polynesians don't want to share their paradise with you forever.

» You do not have to fill in a customs declaration on arrival unless you have imported goods to declare, in which case you can get the proper form from customs officials at the point of entry.

Air

Most visitors arrive by air. Faa'a International Airport, on Tahiti, is the only international airport in French Polynesia. There is no departure tax within French Polynesia.

Airports & Airlines

» **Faa'a International Airport** (PPT; ☎86 60 61; www.tahiti-aeroport.pf) is on Pape'ete's outskirts, 5km west of the capital. International check-in desks are at the terminal's eastern end.

» A number of international airlines serve French Polynesia from different parts of the world. The following airlines have offices in Pape'ete:

Aircalin (Air Caledonie International; airline code SB; ☎85 09 04; www.aircalin.nc)

Air France (airline code AF; ☎47 47 47; www.airfrance.com)

Air New Zealand (airline code NZ; ☎54 07 47; www.airnz.com) Code share with Air Tahiti Nui.

Air Tahiti Nui (airline code TN; ☎45 55 55; www.airtahiti.com)

Hawaiian Airlines (airline code HA; ☎42 15 00; www.hawaiianair.com)

Japan Airlines (airline code JL; ☎50 70 65; www.jal.com, jal@southpacificrepresentation.pf) Code share with Air Tahiti Nui.

LAN Airlines (airline code LA; ☎42 64 55; www.lan.com)

Qantas Airways (airline code QF; ☎43 06 65; www.qantas.com) Code share with Air Tahiti Nui.

Tickets

Many people choose to buy tickets with a package tour (see p30). Flights can be booked online at lonelyplanet.com/bookings.

INTERCONTINENTAL (RTW) TICKETS

If you're travelling to multiple countries, a round-the-world (RTW) ticket – where you pay a discounted price for several connections – may be the most economical choice.

A Circle Pacific ticket is similar to a RTW ticket but is cheaper and covers a more limited region. This ticket uses a combination of airlines to connect Australia, New Zealand, North America and Asia, with a variety of stopover options in the Pacific islands. Generally, Circle Pacific fares are a better deal from the USA and Asia than from Australia.

Online companies that can arrange RTW and Circle Pacific tickets that include French Polynesia:

» www.airbrokers.com

» www.airstop.be

» www.airtreks.com

» www.aroundtheworlds.com

» www.oneworld.com

Asia

Air Tahiti Nui operates flights between Japan (Narita/Tokyo) and Pape'ete. Return flights from Tokyo start at US$1400. This is often the cheapest connection to other parts of Asia, although it can be quicker to go via Australia or New Zealand.

Australia & New Zealand

All flights from Australia to Pape'ete are via Auckland. In Auckland, Qantas Airways flights connect with Air Tahiti Nui. Fares increase considerably in the high season (June to September and over Christmas). From

Sydney expect to pay about A$1050/1500 for a return trip in the low/high season with either Qantas or Air New Zealand.

As in Australia, fares from New Zealand increase during high season. From Auckland return fares start at NZ$850/1250 in low/high season. Both Air New Zealand and Qantas/Air Tahiti Nui offer connecting flights from Pape'ete to Los Angeles.

Other Pacific Islands

For Pacific islands other than those listed below, you'll have to connect with flights from Hawaii, Raratonga, Noumea or Auckland.

Pape'ete–Noumea – Aircalin (Air Calédonie International) has one weekly flight.

Pape'ete–Easter Island – One flight per week with LAN which continues on to Santiago, Chili.

Pape'ete–Honolulu (Hawaii) – Hawaiian Airlines once per week; has many connections to the US mainland, other Pacific islands and Asia.

Pape'ete–Rarotonga (îles Cook; Cook Islands) – Once per week plus one supplementary flight every two weeks with Air Tahiti.

South America

LAN Airlines operates flights between Santiago and Pape'ete; one flight a week has a stopover on Easter Island. Return fares to Easter Island cost around US$805 and round trip onward to Chile is around US$3300.

UK & Continental Europe

Air France and Air Tahiti Nui have flights to Pape'ete via Los Angeles; Air New Zealand also runs some of these flights with a code share with Air Tahiti Nui. Return fares from Paris and Frankfurt start at around €1650. From other destinations in Europe the easiest option is to travel to one of these cities and connect with flights to Pape'ete.

USA & Canada

Coming from the USA you can either fly direct from Los Angeles to Pape'ete or go via Honolulu (fare differences vary greatly depending on the season). Air New Zealand and Qantas do a code share with Air Tahiti Nui on this route, and Air France and Air Tahiti Nui flights from Paris to Pape'ete go via Los Angeles. Return fares from Los Angeles to Pape'ete range from around US$1485 to US$2000. If you are starting your trip in Honolulu, return fares from Honolulu to Pape'ete start from US$1140 in the low season (January to May) and US$1700 in the high season (November to December).

There are no direct flights from Canada, so you will need to go via Honolulu or the US West Coast.

Sea

Cruise Ships

Getting to French Polynesia by cruise ship can be a real challenge, although cruise ships from the USA and Australia occasionally pass through for a day or so.

Yacht

Travelling to French Polynesia by yacht is eminently feasible. Yachts heading across the Pacific from North America, Australia or New Zealand are often looking for crew and, if you're in the right place at the right time, it's often possible to pick up a ride. It's also possible to pick up crewing positions once in French Polynesia. Sailing experience will definitely score extra points, but so will the ability to cook soup when the boat's keeled over and waves are crashing through the hatch.

» On the eastern side of the Pacific, try the yacht clubs in San Diego, Los Angeles, San Francisco or Honolulu. On the western side, Auckland, Sydney and Cairns are good places to try. Look for notices pinned to bulletin boards in yacht clubs and yachting-equipment shops, and post your own notice offering to crew. Another great resource is the **Latitude 38** (www.latitude38.com) crew list where you can post yourself as a potential crew member and peruse ships that are looking for crew.

» Ideally you should do some sailing with the boat before you actually set off. A month from the next landfall is not the time to discover that you can't bear the crew or that the ogre of seasickness is always by your side.

CLIMATE CHANGE & TRAVEL

Every form of transport that relies on carbon-based fuel generates CO_2, the main cause of human-induced climate change. Modern travel is dependent on aeroplanes, which might use less fuel per kilometre per person than most cars but travel much greater distances. The altitude at which aircraft emit gases (including CO_2) and particles also contributes to their climate change impact. Many websites offer 'carbon calculators' that allow people to estimate the carbon emissions generated by their journey and, for those who wish to do so, to offset the impact of the greenhouse gases emitted with contributions to portfolios of climate-friendly initiatives throughout the world. Lonely Planet offsets the carbon footprint of all staff and author travel.

» It takes about a month to sail from the US West Coast to Hawaii and another month south from there to the Marquesas; with stops, another month takes you west to Tahiti and the Society Islands. Then it's another long leg southwest to Australia or New Zealand.

» There are distinct seasons for sailing across the Pacific in order to avoid cyclones. Late September to October and January to March are the usual departure times from the USA. Yachts tend to set off from Australia and New Zealand after the cyclone season, around March and April.

GETTING AROUND

Getting around French Polynesia is half the fun. There are regular and affordable (and dramatic and scenic) connections between the larger islands by boat and aeroplane. Getting to the remote islands can be time-consuming and difficult, but never boring.

On some islands there are paved roads, *le truck* (bus) services and myriad car-hire companies; on others there are rough dirt or coral tracks and public transport is unheard of. Generally, your best bet is to hire a car or a bicycle and be controller of your own destiny.

Air

There are some (expensive) charter operators with small aircraft and helicopters, but essentially flying within French Polynesia means **Air Tahiti** (☎86 42 42; www.airtahiti.aero). Air Tahiti flies to 47 islands in all five of the major island groups. Window seats on its modern fleet of high-wing turboprop aircraft offer great views, but for the nervous flyer these flights can be rather hair-raising.

» Note that Pape'ete is very much the hub for flights within French Polynesia and, with only a few exceptions, you'll generally have to pass through Pape'ete between island groups.

» Flight frequencies ebb and flow with the seasons, and extra flights are scheduled in the July–August peak season. Air Tahiti publishes a useful flight-schedule booklet, which is essential reading for anyone planning a complex trip around the islands. If you are making reservations from afar, you can reserve online and pay by credit card.

» Note that Air Tahiti and Air Tahiti Nui are different airlines: Air Tahiti Nui is the international carrier, while Air Tahiti operates domestic flights only.

Air Routes in French Polynesia

See the specific chapters for information on fares between the various islands of French Polynesia – we've listed only general routes in this section. Because distances to the remote islands are so great, some of the full fares are quite high and the cheapest way to visit a number of islands by air is to buy one of Air Tahiti's air passes.

THE SOCIETY ISLANDS

From Pape'ete there are frequent direct flights to Mo'orea and several times a day to other major islands in the group, except for Maupiti, where connections are less frequent (about five a week). There are daily connections on most routes between Mo'orea, Huahine, Ra'iatea and Bora Bora. On some routes, such as the busy Pape'ete–Bora Bora connection, there are up to 10 flights a day in the high season. The Society Islands are quite close together and the longest nonstop flight (between Pape'ete and Bora Bora) takes only 45 minutes. Other flights, such as the speedy trip between Pape'ete and Mo'orea, may be as short as seven minutes.

THE TUAMOTUS

Air Tahiti divides the Tuamotus into the busier, touristy northern Tuamotus (Ahe, Apataki, Arutua, Faaite, Fakarava, Kauehi, Manihi, Mataiva, Napuka, Rangiroa, Tikehau, Takapoto, Takaroa) and the much less frequented eastern Tuamotus (Anaa, Fakahina, Fangataufa, Hao, Makemo, Nukutavake, Puka Puka, Pukarua, Reao, Takume, Tatakoto, Tureia, Vahitahi).

Rangiroa is the main flight centre in the Tuamotus, with between two and three flights to/from Pape'ete daily (one hour). Three days a week one flight continues on to Manihi. Other flights from Pape'ete, either direct or via Rangiroa, include Fakarava, Ahe, Makemo, Mataiva and Tikehau.

Apart from Tahiti, the only Society Island with a direct connection to the Tuamotus is Bora Bora – but only in the direction of Bora Bora going to the Tuamotus. There's one daily Bora Bora–Rangiroa flight (from which you can easily connect to Manihi or Fakarava).

THE MARQUESAS

Flights to the Marquesas are direct from Pape'ete (about three hours) to Nuku Hiva or Hiva Oa. From Nuku Hiva there are flights to 'Ua Pou and 'Ua Huka, although at the time of writing Air Tahiti was threatening to halt these services.

THE AUSTRALS

Air Tahiti has four to five flights weekly from Pape'ete to Rurutu (1½ hours) and Tubuai with more flights in high season. There are also flights three days a week to Raivavae and Rimatara that stop in Tubuai and Rurutu before continuing back to Pape'ete.

BAGGAGE ALLOWANCE

Bring a copy of your international ticket when checking in to domestic Air Tahiti flights. The normal baggage weight allowance is 10kg per passenger but those with international tickets get 20kg. If you don't need the extra weight, consider offering it to an overburdened local. This will make their day.

GAMBIER ARCHIPELAGO

There is one flight every Tuesday to Mangareva from Pape'ete (about 3½ hours) and one flight every other Saturday.

CHARTER FLIGHTS

Based at Faa'a airport, **Pol'air** (www.compagniepolair.com) can arrange charter flights with small aircraft to any destination in French Polynesia.

Air Passes

There are six island-hopping air passes offering inclusive fares to a number of islands.

» Travel must commence in Pape'ete and you cannot connect back to Pape'ete until the end of the pass. You are only allowed one stopover on each island, but you can transit an island if the flight number does not change. If you stop at an island to change flights, it counts as a stopover.

» Passes are valid for a maximum of 28 days and all flights must be booked when you buy your pass. Once you have taken the first flight on the pass the routing cannot be changed and the fare is nonrefundable. The children's fares are for kids aged 12 and under.

» You can extend the Society Islands and Tuamotu Islands passes to include the Marquesas (Nuku Hiva and Hiva Oa) for an extra 65,000/41,000 CFP per adult/child fare. An extension to the passes to the Australs (Rurutu, Raivavae and Tubuai) costs 6,000/22,000 CFP.

DISCOVERY PASS

The Discovery Pass (Passe Decouverte; adult/child 32,000/20,000 CFP) is the most basic pass and allows visits to Mo'orea, Ra'iatea and Huahine from Pape'ete.

BORA BORA PASS

The Bora Bora Pass (Passe Bora Bora; adult/child 37,000/24,000 CFP) allows you to visit the six main islands in the Society group: Tahiti, Mo'orea, Huahine, Ra'iatea, Bora Bora and Maupiti.

LAGOONS PASS

The Lagoons Pass (Passe Lagons; adult/child 44,000/25,000 CFP) allows you to frolic in the vast lagoons of Mo'orea, Rangiroa, Tikehau, Manihi, Ahe and Fakarava.

BORA-TUAMOTU PASS

This pass (adult/child 59,000/35,000 CFP) allows you to enjoy the high islands of Mo'orea, Huahine, Ra'iatea, Bora Bora and Maupiti before heading to the atolls of Rangiroa, Tikehau, Manihi, Ahe and Fakarava.

MARQUESAS PASS

Visit wild and ancient Nuku Hiva, Hiva Oa, 'Ua Pou and 'Ua Huka for 74,000/42,000 CFP per adult/child. Of course, if Air Tahiti stops serving 'Ua Pou and 'Ua Huka, this pass will change or no longer exist.

AUSTRALS PASS

The Australs Pass includes Rurutu, Tubuai, Raivavae and Rimatara and costs around 62,000/49,500 CFP per adult/child.

Discount Cards

You can get these discount cards at the Air Tahiti office in downtown Papeete. You'll need to show a passport, pay the fee and give them an ID photo. Reductions are based on whether a flight is 'blue,' 'white' or 'red' and these flights are marked as such on the Air Tahiti schedule. In general the 'red' flights are the most popular and hence the most expensive.

Carte Jeunes (1500 CFP) 50% off 'blue' flights and 10% off 'white' ones for those aged 12 to 25 years.

Cartes Marama (1500 CFP) For those over 50 years old – you get the same price reductions given to Carte Jeune holders.

Carte Familles (2500 CFP) 50% off 'blue' flights for both parents and 75% off for children under 12. On 'white' and 'red' flights kids get 50% off. Parents get 30% off on the 'white' flights and 10% off the 'red'.

Bicycle

Cycling around the smaller islands of French Polynesia is a sheer pleasure, particularly if it's not too hot. The distances are rarely great, the traffic is rarely heavy (except in Tahiti) and the roads are rarely hilly. Bikes can be hired on many of the islands for about 1500 CFP a day, but you may find yourself riding an antique. Consider bringing your own bike if you are a really keen cyclist. Bicycles are accepted on all the inter-island boats.

Boat

Boat travel within the Society group isn't as easy as you'd hope unless you're only going to Mo'orea or taking a cruise or sailboat. A number of companies shuttle back and forth between Tahiti and Mo'orea each day; other routes between the islands are less frequent but served at least twice a week by cargo vessels.

In the other archipelagos travel by boat is more difficult. If you are short on time and keen to travel beyond the Society Islands you may need to consider flying at least some of the way.

Cargo ships, also known as *goélettes*, are principally involved in freight transport. Some take passengers, however, and for those who want to get off the beaten trail such a voyage can, depending on the circumstances, be anything from a memorable experience to an outright nightmare. The level of comfort is rudimentary: some ships don't have passenger cabins and you have to travel 'deck class', providing your own bedding to unroll on the deck and all your own meals. You may get wet and cold. And then there's seasickness... At the same time, the connection with the locals and the sheer street cred of travelling this way can make it worth it for a select few.

Cruise Ship

At the other end of the spectrum from rudimentary cargo ships are the luxury cruise ships that operate in the Society Islands. These ships are incredibly stylish and comfortable, and offer shore excursions at each stop – this is a long way from the leaky copra boats of traditional interisland travel.

You may see the enormous *Paul Gauguin* (seven-day voyages) and Princess Cruises' *Tahitian Princess* (10-day cruises) anchored in Pape'ete. They depart Pape'ete to visit the Society Islands and sometimes an atoll or two in the Tuamotus.

For a more intimate cruising experience **Archipels Croisières** (☎55 36 39; www.archipels.com) has five eight-person catamarans that cruise the Society Islands and Tuamotus. It's a full-service experience with all meals and activities.

See **Tahiti Tourisme** (www.tahiti-tourisme.com) for more information about cruising.

Ferry & Cargo Ship

THE SOCIETY ISLANDS

It takes between half an hour and an hour to travel between Tahiti and Mo'orea, depending on which company you go with. The car ferries, such as those run by Aremiti Ferry, are slower than the high-speed ferries, which take only passengers, motorcycles and bicycles.

Aremiti V & Aremiti Ferry (☎Pape'ete 42 88 88, Mo'orea 56 31 10; www.aremiti.net; per person/car one way 1450/4030 CFP) The Aremiti Ferry is a car ferry while the Aremiti V is a high-speed catamaran. The two boats jet between Tahiti and Mo'orea six or more times daily between 6am and 4.30pm. The trip takes about 30 minutes on the Aremiti V or 45 minutes on the Aremiti Ferry. You can buy tickets at the ticket counter on the quay just a few minutes before departure.

Aremiti IV (☎41 25 35; www.aremiti.net; one-way fare from Pape'ete to Huahine/Raiatea/Bora Bora 7350/8400/9450 CFP) This on-and-off service relaunched at the end of 2011 and hopefully it will stay in business. The Pape'ete–Huahine–Ra'iatea–Taha'a–Bora Bora round trip leaves Pape'ete once a week (Friday).

Hawaiki Nui (☎54 99 54; deck/cabin per person 2000/5600 CFP) Travels the Society Islands circuit on a twice-weekly schedule (Tuesday and Thursday at 4pm). Reserve well in advance.

Maupiti Express (www.maupitiexpress.com) Makes regular trips between Bora Bora and Maupiti (one way 4000 CFP) and between Bora Bora and Taha'a and Ra'iatea (one way 3000 CFP). Check the website for the schedule. Tickets can be purchased at the quay.

Raiatea–Tahaa Navette Taxi boats run between Ra'iatea and Taha'a every day except Sunday. See the Ra'iatea & Taha'a chapter for details.

Taporo VI & VII (☎41 25 35, 42 63 93) This boat runs cargo to Huahine, Ra'iatea, Bora Bora and Taha'a twice per week. They rarely take tourists but if you can talk your way on, the fare between two islands is 970 CFP.

THE TUAMOTUS

The cargo vessels that serve the Tuamotus Islands are true lifelines. Only the following take passengers (others take freight only) but their main purpose is to transport goods and petrol, and the standard of comfort is generally basic. Because of insurance changes in recent years there are limited places available. Still, this is the way to go if you're looking for adventure and have plenty of time on your hands.

The routes and fares mentioned here are just an indication and are subject to change. The offices are all in the Motu Uta port area in Pape'ete (take *le truck* 3 from the *mairie* – the town hall).

Cobia III (☎43 36 43; cobia@mail.pf; ⊙office 7.30am-3.30pm Mon-Fri, 8-11am Sat) A small boat (think lots more wave movement) that travels Pape'ete–Kaukura–Arutua–Apataki–Fakarava–Pape'ete once a week; there are no cabins and no meals are served. The fare is about 6300 CFP.

Kura Ora II & Kura Ora IV (☎45 55 45; ⊙office 7.30am-3pm Mon-Thu) These boats make a trip every 15 days to the remote atolls of the central and eastern Tuamotus, including Anaa, Hao and Makemo. Deck-class prices cost from around 7000 CFP, depending on the distance travelled, plus around 2500 CFP per person per day for meals. The complete trip takes two to three weeks.

Mareva Nui (☎42 25 53; ⊙office 7.30-11.30am & 1.30-5pm Mon-Thu) Runs a circuit from Pape'ete taking in Makatea, Mataiva, Tikehau, Rangiroa, Ahe, Manihi, Takaroa, Takapoto, Raraka, Kauehi, Aratika, Fakarava, Arutua, Apataki, Niau and Kaukura. Fares vary from 3900 to 23,200 CFP (including meals) for a bunk; the complete trip takes 10 days.

Saint-Xavier Maris-Stella (☎42 23 58; maris-stella@mail.pf; ⊙office 7.30-11am & 1.30-4pm Mon-Fri) Travels a circuit from Pape'ete every 15 days, taking in Mataiva, Tikehau, Rangiroa, Ahe, Manihi, Takaroa, Takapoto, Arutua, Apataki, Aratika, Kaukura, Toau, Fakarava, Kauehi, Raraka and Niau over two weeks. Departing from Pape'ete, allow 7100/10,000 CFP for deck-class/air-conditioned cabin to Rangiroa, 8500/15,000 CFP to Manihi and 10,000/17,000 CFP to Fakarava. Meals are included. This is the most comfortable option for the Tuamotus but it's still pretty grubby.

THE MARQUESAS

The **Aranui** (☎42 62 40; www.aranui.com) is a veritable institution, taking freight and passengers on 17 trips a year from Pape'ete to the Marquesas (see the boxed text, p176). The only other cargo ship, the *Taporo IX*, won't take passengers.

THE AUSTRALS

Services between the Society Islands and the Australs are limited, so make sure you plan ahead. While you'll need plenty of time to travel this way, it will save you lots of money.

The new boat **Tuhaa Pae IV** (☎50 96 05, 41 36 06; snathp@mail.pf) started chugging to the Australs in early 2012; it leaves Pape'ete three times a month. It stops at Rurutu, Tubuai, Rimatara and Raivavae on every trip, and Rapa once every two months. You can choose between berths and air-con cabins. From Pape'ete to Rurutu, Rimatara or Tubuai a berth/air-con cabin costs 6000/8500 CFP; to Raivavae it costs 8500/12,000 CFP. Three meals add another 3500 CFP per day. The office is in Pape'ete's Motu Uta, between the *Kura Ora* and *Mareva Nui* offices.

THE GAMBIER

This archipelago is the farthest away from Tahiti. Once a month the **Nuku Hau** (☎54 99 54; contact@stim.pf) takes a 15-day circuit from Pape'ete to Rikitea in the Gambier Archipelago via a few eastern Tuamotu atolls. Deck passage to Rikitea is 8400 CFP plus 2500 CFP per day for meals. The boat shares an office with the Hawaiki Nui.

Local Transport

Most islands in the Society group have one road that hugs the coast all the way around. Tahiti (where there is even a stretch of freeway), Mo'orea, Bora Bora, Ra'iatea, Taha'a and Huahine have paved and reasonably well-maintained roads. On all of these islands, tracks leading inland are often rough and ready and almost always require a 4WD.

There are far more boats than land vehicles in the Tuamotus, although there is a sealed road running the length of Rangiroa's major island – all 10km of it!

Outside the towns there are hardly any sealed roads in the Marquesas. Tracks, suitable for 4WDs only, connect the villages although slowly bits and pieces are being paved.

Sealed roads encircle both Tubuai and Raivavae in the Australs, and there are reasonable stretches of sealed road on Rurutu. Otherwise, roads in the Australs are fairly limited and little transport is available.

Bus

French Polynesia doesn't have much of a public transportation system; Tahiti is the only island where public transport is even an option.

The colourful, old *le trucks* (trucks with bench seats in the back for passengers) have now been almost entirely replaced by a more modern fleet of air-con buses, though some still run in and around Pape'ete. Buses (often still called *le trucks*) stop at designated spots (which are marked with a blue sign) and supposedly run on a schedule – although times are hardly regular.

Although there are official *le truck* stops, complete with blue signs, they are rather difficult to spot, and *le trucks* will generally stop anywhere sensible for anybody who hails them. Note that you pay at the end of your trip and that for many routes there is a set fare, irrespective of distance.

Car & Scooter

If you want to explore the larger islands of the Society group at your own pace, it may be worth hiring a car or scooter, particularly given the price of taxis and the dismal state of public transport outside Pape'ete.

DRIVING LICENCE

» Car-hire agencies in French Polynesia only ask to see your national driving licence, so an international driving licence is unnecessary.

HIRE

» There are many different car-hire agencies on the more touristy islands, but the prices really don't vary much: compared with rental costs in the rest of the world, prices are high. For a small car expect to pay from 10,000 CFP a day including unlimited kilometres and basic insurance – and that's not even including petrol. On some islands (Taha'a comes to mind) rentals start at 12,000 CFP. Rates drop slightly from the third day onwards. Fortunately, the cars available are pretty economical and you won't cover too many kilometres, no matter how hard you try. Off-road excursions into the interior are usually off limits to anything other than a 4WD.

» Most places offer four-, eight- and 24-hour rates, as well as two- and three-day rentals. At certain times of the year (July, August and New Year's Eve) it's wise to book vehicles a few days in advance, although at any time of year reserving in advance helps ensure that you get one in the price bracket you are hoping for.

» You'll need a credit card, of course.

» On Tahiti you will find the major international car-hire agencies such as Avis, Budget, Europcar and Hertz. On other islands such as Mo'orea, Huahine, Ra'iatea and Bora Bora, as well as on Rangiroa in the Tuamotus, the market is divided up between Avis and Europcar. Smaller local agencies exist on some islands, but the rates are almost as high.

» You can hire a car on Rurutu in the Australs, but in the Marquesas rental vehicles are mainly 4WDs with a driver (15,000 to 20,000 CFP per day). Rental without a driver is possible only on Atuona (Hiva Oa) and Taiohae (Nuku Hiva).

» Avis and Europcar rent scooters on a number of islands. It's a good way of getting around the small islands, but bear in mind you won't be wearing protective gear, so this is probably not the place to learn to ride a scooter. You'll pay around 6000 CFP a day. After numerous accidents, there are no rental scooters on Tahiti.

ROAD RULES

» Driving is on the right-hand side in French Polynesia. Although the accident statistics are pretty grim, driving here is not difficult, and the traffic is light almost everywhere apart from the busy coastal strip around Pape'ete on Tahiti. However, the overtaking habits of locals can sometimes get the heart rate up. Beware of drunk drivers at night, and of pedestrians and children who may not be used to traffic, particularly in more remote locations. Sometimes dodging sauntering dogs and chickens makes driving in Tahiti feel like a video game – take it slow.

Hitching

Hitching (*auto-stop* in French) is a widely accepted – and generally safe – way of getting around the islands in French Polynesia, and you'll see locals and travellers alike standing with their thumbs out on the roadside. Of course, hitching is never entirely safe, but if you're going to hitch, French Polynesia is an easy place to start – usually you'll never have to wait more than 15 or 20 minutes for a ride, plus you'll meet some interesting folks. Always take the necessary precautions and use your judgement before jumping into a car; drunk drivers are probably your biggest problem. It's not recommended for women to hitch alone.

Language

WANT MORE?

For in-depth language information and handy phrases, check out Lonely Planet's *South Pacific Phrasebook* and *French Phrasebook*. You'll find them at **shop.lonelyplanet.com**, or you can buy Lonely Planet's iPhone phrasebooks at the Apple App Store.

Tahitian and French are the official languages of French Polynesia, with Tahitian spoken more than it is written. Although French dominates, many of those working in the tourist industry can speak some English. If you venture to the more remote and less touristy islands, it's definitely useful to know some French, and even more so, a few Tahitian words which will be greatly appreciated. Other Polynesian languages on the islands include Austral, Marquesan and Tuamotuan.

TAHITIAN

Tahitian (also known as Reo Maohi) belongs to the group of Polynesian languages that includes Samoan, Maori, Hawaiian, Rarotongan and Tongan. There are several dialects of Tahitian, but the spread of Christianity through French Polynesia helped make the variety spoken on Tahiti the most widespread.

Most Tahitian sounds are also found in English. The vowels are pronounced as follows: a as in 'father', e between the 'e' in 'bet' and in 'they', i as in 'marine', o as in 'more' and u as the 'oo' in 'zoo'. All vowels have a longer version too, indicated in this language guide by a line over the vowel (ā, ē, ī, ō and ū). Note also that *r* is often rolled, and *h* is pronounced as in 'house' (but as the 'sh' in 'shoe' when preceded by i and followed by o). The apostrophe (') in this language guide indicates a glottal stop – the sound you hear in the middle of 'uh-oh'.

Basics

Hello./Good morning.	*Ia ora na, nana.*
Goodbye.	*Pārahi, nana.*
Welcome.	*Maeva, mānava.*
Thank you.	*Māuruuru.*
Excuse me./Sorry.	*E'e, aue ho'i e.*
No problem./Don't worry.	*Aita pe'ape'a.*
Yes.	*E, 'oia.*
No.	*Aita.*
Pardon?	*E aha?*
How are you?	*E aha te huru?*
My name is ...	*To'u i'oa 'o ...*
country	*fenua*
I don't understand.	*Aita i ta'a ia'u.*
Good luck!	*Fa'aitoito!*
I'm ill.	*E ma'i to'u.*

Accommodation & Food

bathroom	*piha pape*
bed	*ro'i*
breakfast	*tafe poipoi*
room	*piha*
Cheers!	*Manuia!*
beer	*pia*
coffee	*taofe*
food	*ma'a*
menu	*tāpura mā'a*
restaurant	*fare tāmā'ara'a*
water	*pape*

Shopping & Services

How much?	*E hia moni?*
bank	*fare moni*
chemist/pharmacy	*fare ra'au*
embassy	*fare tonitera rahi*
film (camera)	*firimu*
money	*moni*
police station	*fare mūto'i*
shop	*fare toa*
telephone	*niuniu paraparau*

Time & Numbers

When?	*Afea?*
What time is it?	*E aha te hora i teie nei?*
day	*ao*
now	*i teie nei*
today	*j teie nei mahana*
tonight	*i teie pō*
tomorrow	*ānānahi*

1	*hō'ē*
2	*piti*
3	*toru*
4	*māha*
5	*pae*
6	*ono*
7	*hitu*
8	*va'u*
9	*iva*
10	*'ahuru*
20	*piti 'ahuru*
100	*hō'ē hānere*
1000	*hō'ē tauatini*

Transport & Directions

bicycle	*pereo'o tāta'ahi*
boat	*poti*
bus	*pereo'o mata'eina'a*
car	*pereo'o uira*

Where is ...?	*Tei hea ...?*
address	*vahi nohoraa*
beach	*tahatai*
map	*hoho'a fenua*
plantation	*fa'a'apu*

TAHITIAN LEXICON

Although Tahitian borrowed a number of terms from English, it was not simply a case of adopting terms for items new to Tahitian culture. Tahitians use their own rich language to derive terms for words generated by modern technology. Some of the new terms are very colourful and expressive.

accelerator	*ha'a pūai ra'a pereo'o* (make-power-vehicle)
aeroplane	*manu reva* (bird-space)
airport	*tahua manu reva* (field-bird-space)
ambulance	*pereo'o ma'i* (vehicle-sick)
bank	*fare moni* (house-money)
bar	*fare inu ra'a* (house-drink)
battery	*'ōfa'i mōrī pata* (stone-light-switch on)
bedroom	*piha ta'oto* (room-sleep)
bicycle	*pereo'o tāta'ahi* (vehicle-pedal)
bra	*tāpe'a tītī* (hold-breast)
camera	*pata hoho'a* (click-image)
can opener	*pātia punu* (stab-container)
car	*pereo'o uira* (vehicle-lightning)
cathedral	*fare pure ra'a rahi* (house-pray-big)
cheese	pata-pa'ari (butter-hard)
dentist	*taote niho* (doctor-tooth)
drawer	*'āfata 'ume* (box-pull)
fork	*pātia mā'a* (spear-food)
glasses	*titi'a mata* (filter-eye)
goat	*pua'a niho* (pig-tooth)
horse	*pua'a horo fenua* (pig-run-ground)
hose	*uaua pipi tiare* (rubber-water-flower)
hospital	*fare ma'i* (house-sick)
motorcycle	*pereo'o tāta'ahi uira* (vehicle-pedal-lightning)
office	*piha pāpa'i ra'a parau* (room-write-word)
post office	*fare rata* (house-letter)
refrigerator	*'āfata fa'a to'eto'e ra'a* (box-make-cold)
submarine	*pahī hopu moana* (ship-dive-ocean)
telephone	*niuniu paraparau* (wire-speak)
television	*'āfata teata na'ina'i* (box-cinema-small)
toilet	*fate iti* (house-small)

FRENCH

The sounds used in spoken French can almost all be found in English. There are a couple of exceptions: nasal vowels (represented in our pronunciation guides by o or u followed by an almost inaudible nasal consonant sound m, n or ng), the 'funny' *u* (ew in our guides) and the deep-in-the-throat *r*. Bearing these few points in mind and reading our pronunciation guides below as if they were English, you'll be understood just fine.

Basics

Hello.	*Bonjour.*	bon·zhoor
Goodbye.	*Au revoir.*	o·rer·vwa
Excuse me.	*Excusez-moi.*	ek·skew·zay·mwa
Sorry.	*Pardon.*	par·don
Yes./No.	*Oui./Non.*	wee/non
Please.	*S'il vous plaît.*	seel voo play
Thank you.	*Merci.*	mair·see

How are you?
Comment allez-vous? ko·mon ta·lay·voo

Fine, and you?
Bien, merci. Et vous? byun mair·see ay voo

You're welcome.
De rien. der ree·en

My name is ...
Je m'appelle ... zher ma·pel ...

Do you speak English?
Parlez-vous anglais? par·lay·voo ong·glay

I don't understand.
Je ne comprends pas. zher ner kom·pron pa

I'm ill.
Je suis malade. zher swee ma·lad

Accommodation & Food

campsite	*camping*	kom·peeng
guesthouse	*pension*	pon·syon
hotel	*hôtel*	o·tel
room	*chambre*	shom·brer
youth hostel	*auberge de jeunesse*	o·berzh der zher·nes

Cheers!	*Santé!*	son·tay
beer	*bière*	bee·yair
breakfast	*petit déjeuner*	per·tee day·zher·nay
coffee	*café*	ka·fay
grocery store	*épicerie*	ay·pees·ree
market	*marché*	mar·shay
menu	*carte*	kart
water	*eau*	o

Shopping & Services

How much is it?
C'est combien? say kom·byun

I'd like to buy ...
Je voudrais acheter ... zher voo·dray ash·tay ...

credit card	*carte de crédit*	kart der kray·dee
internet cafe	*cybercafé*	see·bair·ka·fay
post office	*bureau de poste*	bew·ro der post
tourist office	*office de tourisme*	o·fees der too·rees·mer

Time & Numbers

What time is it?
Quelle heure est-il? kel er ay til

When?	*Quand?*	kon
yesterday	*hier*	yair
today	*aujourd'hui*	o·zhoor·dwee
tomorrow	*demain*	der·mun

1	*un*	un
2	*deux*	der
3	*trois*	trwa
4	*quatre*	ka·trer
5	*cinq*	sungk
6	*six*	sees
7	*sept*	set
8	*huit*	weet
9	*neuf*	nerf
10	*dix*	dees
20	*vingt*	vung
100	*cent*	son
1000	*mille*	meel

Transport & Directions

boat	*bateau*	ba·to
bus	*bus*	bews
plane	*avion*	a·vyon
train	*train*	trun

Where's ...?
Où est ...? oo ay ...

I want to go to ...
Je voudrais aller à ... zher voo·dray a·lay a ...

At what time does it leave/arrive?
À quelle heure est-ce qu'il part/arrive? a kel er es kil par/a·reev

GLOSSARY

See also the Menu Decoder boxed text, p239.

ahu – altar in a *marae;* in the *marae* of French Polynesia the *ahu* was generally a pyramid shape

aparima – dance with hand gestures

ari'i – high chief of the ancient Polynesian aristocracy; literally, 'king'

atoll – type of low island created by *coral* rising above sea level as an island gradually sinks; postcard atolls consist of a chain of small islands and reef enclosing a *lagoon;* see also *low island*

atua – god or gods

barrier reef – *coral* reef forming a barrier between the shoreline and the open sea but separated from the land by a *lagoon*

belvédère – lookout

bonitier – whaleboat or skipjack boat; used for fishing and for transferring passengers and cargo from ship to shore on islands that have no wharf or quay

boules – see *pétanque*

BP – *boîte postale;* post-office box

breadfruit – see *uru*

caldera – volcano crater

capitainerie – harbourmaster's office

CEP – Centre d'Expérimentation du Pacifique; the French nuclear-testing program

CFP – Cour de Franc Pacifique, usually known as *franc cour pacifique;* currency of French Polynesia

ciguatera – malady caused by eating infected reef fish

CMAS – Confédération Mondiale des Activités Subaquatiques; scuba-diving qualification; the Francophile equivalent of *PADI*

copra – dried coconut meat, used to make an oil

coral – animal of the coelenterate group which, given the right conditions of water clarity, depth and temperature, grows to form a reef

cyclone – tropical storm rotating around a low-pressure 'eye'; 'typhoon' in the Pacific, 'hurricane' in the Caribbean

demi-pension – see *half board*

fare – traditional Polynesian house; hotel bungalow

fare atua – house for the gods on *marae;* actually a small chest in the form of a statue

fare potee – chief's house or community meeting place; open dining room of a restaurant or hotel

fenua – country or region of origin

feo – coral outcrop

fringing reef – *coral* reef immediately alongside the shoreline, not separated from the shore by a lagoon as with a *barrier reef*

full board – bed and all meals (French: *pension complète*); see also *half board*

gendarmerie – police station

ha'e – traditional Marquesan house

half board – bed, breakfast and lunch or dinner (French: *demi-pension);* see also *full board*

hei – garland of flowers

heiva – celebration or festival; the Heiva is a huge festival of Polynesian culture (mainly dance) that takes place on Tahiti in July

high island – island created by volcanic action or geological upheaval; see also *low island*

hima'a – underground oven used for cooking traditional Polynesian food

himene – Tahitian-language hymn

Hiro – god of thieves who features in many Polynesian legends

hoa – shallow channel across the outer reef of an atoll, normally carrying water into or out of the central lagoon only at unusually high tides or when large swells are running; see also *pass*

kaveka – sooty tern

kaveu – coconut crab

lagoon – calm waters enclosed by a reef; may be an enclosed area encircled by a *barrier reef* (eg Rangiroa and Tetiaroa) with or without *motu,* or may surround a *high island* (eg Bora Bora and Tahiti)

lagoonside – on the lagoon side of the coast road (not necessarily right by the lagoon); see also *mountainside*

le truck – public 'bus'; a truck with bench seats that operates a buslike service

leeward – downwind; sheltered from the prevailing winds; see also *windward*

LMS – London Missionary Society; pioneering Protestant missionary organisation in Polynesia

low island – island created by the growth and erosion of *coral* or by the complete erosion of a *high island;* see also *atoll*

ma'a – food

ma'a Tahiti – Tahitian or Polynesian food; Tahitian buffet

mahi mahi – dorado; one of the most popular eating fish in French Polynesia

mahu – males who are raised as girls and continue

to live their lives as women; see also *raerae*

mairie – town hall

maitai – local cocktail made with rum, pineapple, grenadine and lime juices, coconut liqueur and, sometimes, Grand Marnier or Cointreau

makatea – *coral* island that has been thrust above sea level by a geological disturbance (eg Rurutu, and Makatea in the Tuamotus)

mana – spiritual or supernatural power

manahune – peasant class or common people of pre-European Polynesia

manu – bird

Maohi – Polynesian

mape – Polynesian 'chestnut' tree

maraamu – southeast trade wind that blows from June to August

marae – traditional Polynesian sacred site generally constructed with an *ahu* at one end; see also *me'ae*

me'ae – Marquesan word for *marae*

Melanesia – islands of the western Pacific; Papua New Guinea, the Solomons, Vanuatu, New Caledonia and Fiji

Micronesia – islands of the northwest Pacific including the Mariana, Caroline and Marshall groups, Kiribati and Nauru

monoi – coconut oil perfumed with the *tiare* flower and/or other substances

motu – small islet in a lagoon, either along the outer reef of an *atoll* or on a reef around a *high island*

mountainside – on the mountain side of the coast road (not necessarily up in the mountains); see also *lagoonside*

nacre – mother-of-pearl; iridescent substance secreted by pearl oysters to form the inner layer of the shell; shell of a pearl oyster

navette – shuttle boat

niau – sheets of plaited coconut-palm leaves, used for roof thatching

noni – yellowish fruit with therapeutic properties, grown in the Marquesas and popular in the USA; also known as nono

nono – very annoying biting gnat found on some beaches and particularly prevalent in the Marquesas

nucleus – small sphere, made from shells found in the Mississippi River in the USA, which is introduced into the gonads of the pearl oyster to produce a cultured pearl

'Oro – god of war; the cult that was superseding the *Ta'aroa* cult when the first Europeans arrived

pa – hilltop fortress

PADI – Professional Association of Dive Instructors; the most popular international scuba-diving qualification

pae pae – paved floor of a pre-European house; traditional meeting platform

pahu – drum

pahua – giant clam

pamplemousse – grapefruit

pandanus – palm tree with aerial roots; the leaves are used for weaving hats, mats and bags

pareu – traditional sarong-like garment

pass – channel allowing passage into the *lagoon* through the outer reef of an *atoll* or the *barrier reef* around a *high island*; see also *hoa*

pension – guesthouse

pension complète – see *full board*

pétanque – French game in which metal balls are thrown to land as near as possible to a target ball; also known as *boules*

petroglyph – carving on a stone or rock

pirogue – outrigger canoe (Tahitian: *va'a*)

PK – *point kilométrique;* distance markers found along the roads of some French Polynesian islands

Polynesia – islands of the central and southeastern Pacific, including French Polynesia, Samoa, Tonga, New Zealand and the Cook Islands

popaa – European or Westerner

pu – conch shell

purau – hibiscus

raerae – sometimes applied to *mahu* who are transsexual or homosexual

requin – shark

roulotte – mobile diner; a food van operating as a snack bar

seaward – side of an *atoll,* island or *motu* that faces the sea rather than the *lagoon*

snack – snack bar

Ta'aroa – supreme Polynesian god whose cult was being superseded by worship of *'Oro*, god of war, at the time of the European arrival

tabu – alternative spelling of *tapu*

tahua – faith healer; priest of the ancient Polynesian religion

tamure – hip-jiggling version of traditional Polynesian dance

tapa – cloth made from beaten bark and decorated with traditional designs; worn by the people of pre-European Polynesia

tapu – sacred or forbidden; the English word 'taboo' comes from *tapu* or *tabu*

taro – root vegetable; a Polynesian staple food

taxe de séjour – daily accommodation tax

tiare – fragrant white gardenia endemic to the Pacific; the flower has become symbolic of Tahiti

tifaifai – colourful appliquéd or patchwork material used as blankets, bedspreads or cushion covers

tiki – humanlike sacred sculpture usually made of wood or stone and sometimes standing more than 2m high; once found on many *marae*

tohua – meeting place or a place for festival gathering in pre-European Polynesia but especially in the Marquesas

tou – *Cordia subcordata;* tree, common in the Marquesas, that produces a dark, hard, grained wood popular with carvers

tupapau – irritating spirit ghosts of the ancient Polynesian religion, still much feared

tuu – ceremonial activities centre in the Marquesas

TVA – *taxe sur la valeur ajoutée;* a tax added to accommodation rates

ua ma – Marquesan food pit

umete – traditional Tahitian wooden dish or bowl

uru – breadfruit; starchy staple food of Polynesia that grows on a tree as a football-sized fruit (French: *arbre à pain*)

va'a – outrigger canoe (French: *pirogue*)

vahine – woman

vanira – vanilla

windward – facing prevailing winds; see also *leeward*

behind the scenes

SEND US YOUR FEEDBACK

We love to hear from travellers – your comments keep us on our toes and help make our books better. Our well-travelled team reads every word on what you loved or loathed about this book. Although we cannot reply individually to postal submissions, we always guarantee that your feedback goes straight to the appropriate authors, in time for the next edition. Each person who sends us information is thanked in the next edition – the most useful submissions are rewarded with a selection of digital PDF chapters.

Visit **lonelyplanet.com/contact** to submit your updates and suggestions or to ask for help. Our award-winning website also features inspirational travel stories, news and discussions.

Note: We may edit, reproduce and incorporate your comments in Lonely Planet products such as guidebooks, websites and digital products, so let us know if you don't want your comments reproduced or your name acknowledged. For a copy of our privacy policy visit lonelyplanet.com/privacy.

OUR READERS

Many thanks to the travellers who used the last edition and wrote to us with helpful hints, useful advice and interesting anecdotes:
Jose Branco, Kate Hammond, Erik Helmstetter, Martin Heng, Thum Herbert, Markus Kuhn, Denny Nolan, Dina Priess Dos Santos, Ian Schuyt, Ronald Wolff, Steve Wood

AUTHOR THANKS

Celeste Brash

Most thanks to Diana Hammer and Patrick Humbert for starting this adventure, and to my kids Jasmine and Tevai and my husband Josh for continuing it. This book wouldn't be what it is without the excellent input, collaboration and first edition written by author/superhero Jean-Bernard Carillet. Maryanne Netto has done a fine job putting this guide together in a calm, Polynesian way. All of my work on this book is in loving memory of my son's beautiful godfather, Ralph Ioane.

Jean-Bernard Carillet

Heaps of thanks to the South Pacific team at Lonely Planet, especially Maryanne and Errol, for their trust and support, and to the editorial and cartography teams. A heartfelt *māuruuru roa* to coordinating author Celeste, with whom I share the same passion for that trippy *fenua;* she was utterly helpful and patient throughout the process. In French Polynesia, a special mention goes to my second family, the Peirsegaeles in Mahina – thanks Yan, Vai, Sean, Majo and Hubert for having opened all doors, and the infectious *aroha* (despite a broken car). A big thanks also to all people who helped out and made this trip so enlightening, including Alain Buzenet (next time we'll be off to the *motu*!), Katou, Verly, Heikura, Moearii, Pam, Reata, Tepupu, Lucile, Céline, Lionel and Pascale, among others. And how could I forget Christine and my daughter Eva, who shared some of my Polynesian adventures and give direction to my otherwise roving life?

ACKNOWLEDGMENTS

Climate map data adapted from Peel MC, Finlayson BL & McMahon TA (2007) 'Updated World Map of the Köppen-Geiger Climate Classification', *Hydrology and Earth System Sciences*, 11, 163344.

Cover photograph: Green sea turtle, Marine Turtle Protection Centre, Bora Bora, Danita Delimont Stock/AWL. Many of the images in this guide are available for licensing from Lonely Planet Images: www.lonelyplanetimages.com.

This Book

This 9th edition of Lonely Planet's *Tahiti & French Polynesia* guidebook was researched and written by Celeste Brash and Jean-Bernard Carillet. The previous edition was also written by Celeste and Jean-Bernard. Celeste and Becca Blond wrote the 7th edition, with Jean-Bernard contributing the Diving chapter. This guidebook was commissioned in Lonely Planet's Melbourne office, and produced by the following:

Commissioning Editor Maryanne Netto

Coordinating Editors Carolyn Boicos, Victoria Harrison, Fionnuala Twomey

Coordinating Cartographer Julie Dodkins

Coordinating Layout Designer Clara Monitto

Managing Editor Barbara Delissen

Senior Editors Andi Jones, Susan Paterson

Managing Cartographer Shahara Ahmed

Managing Layout Designer Jane Hart

Assisting Editors Janice Bird, Helen Koehne, Saralinda Turner

Assisting Cartographer Mick Garrett

Cover Research Naomi Parker

Internal Image Research Aude Vauconsant

Illustrator Mick Weldon

Language Content Samantha Forge, Branislava Vladisavljevic

Thanks to Yvonne Bischofberger, Ryan Evans, Larissa Frost, William Gourlay, Trent Paton, Gerard Walker

NOTES

index

H

I

J

K

L

M

N

O

P

000 Map pages
000 Photo pages

U

V

W

Y

000 Map pages
000 Photo pages

how to use this book

These symbols will help you find the listings you want:

- Sights
- Beaches
- Activities
- Courses
- Tours
- Festivals & Events
- Sleeping
- Eating
- Drinking
- Entertainment
- Shopping
- Information/ Transport

These symbols give you the vital information for each listing:

- Telephone Numbers
- Opening Hours
- Parking
- Nonsmoking
- Air-Conditioning
- Internet Access
- Wi-Fi Access
- Swimming Pool
- Vegetarian Selection
- English-Language Menu
- Family-Friendly
- Pet-Friendly
- Bus
- Ferry
- Metro
- Subway
- Tram
- Train

Reviews are organised by author preference.

Look out for these icons:

- TOP CHOICE — Our author's recommendation
- FREE — No payment required
- A green or sustainable option

Our authors have nominated these places as demonstrating a strong commitment to sustainability – for example by supporting local communities and producers, operating in an environmentally friendly way, or supporting conservation projects.

Map Legend

Sights
Beach
Buddhist
Castle
Christian
Hindu
Islamic
Jewish
Monument
Museum/Gallery
Ruin
Winery/Vineyard
Zoo
Other Sight

Activities, Courses & Tours
Diving/Snorkelling
Canoeing/Kayaking
Skiing
Surfing
Swimming/Pool
Walking
Windsurfing
Other Activity/ Course/Tour

Sleeping
Sleeping
Camping

Eating
Eating

Drinking
Drinking
Cafe

Entertainment
Entertainment

Shopping
Shopping

Information
Bank
Embassy/ Consulate
Hospital/Medical
Internet
Police
Post Office
Telephone
Toilet
Tourist Information
Other Information

Transport
Airport
Border Crossing
Bus
Cable Car/ Funicular
Cycling
Ferry
Metro
Monorail
Parking
Petrol Station
Taxi
Train/Railway
Tram
Other Transport

Routes
Tollway
Freeway
Primary
Secondary
Tertiary
Lane
Unsealed Road
Plaza/Mall
Steps
Tunnel
Pedestrian Overpass
Walking Tour
Walking Tour Detour
Path

Geographic
Hut/Shelter
Lighthouse
Lookout
Mountain/Volcano
Oasis
Park
Pass
Picnic Area
Waterfall

Population
Capital (National)
Capital (State/Province)
City/Large Town
Town/Village

Boundaries
International
State/Province
Disputed
Regional/Suburb
Marine Park
Cliff
Wall

Hydrography
River, Creek
Intermittent River
Swamp/Mangrove
Reef
Canal
Water
Dry/Salt/ Intermittent Lake
Glacier

Areas
Beach/Desert
Cemetery (Christian)
Cemetery (Other)
Park/Forest
Sportsground
Sight (Building)
Top Sight (Building)

OUR STORY

A beat-up old car, a few dollars in the pocket and a sense of adventure. In 1972 that's all Tony and Maureen Wheeler needed for the trip of a lifetime – across Europe and Asia overland to Australia. It took several months, and at the end – broke but inspired – they sat at their kitchen table writing and stapling together their first travel guide, *Across Asia on the Cheap*. Within a week they'd sold 1500 copies. Lonely Planet was born.

Today, Lonely Planet has offices in Melbourne, London and Oakland, with more than 600 staff and writers. We share Tony's belief that 'a great guidebook should do three things: inform, educate and amuse'.

OUR WRITERS

Celeste Brash

Coordinating Author; Plan Your Trip, Understand and Survival Guide Celeste first visited French Polynesia in 1991, fell in love with her now husband as well as Polynesian culture, and moved to the country in 1995. Her first five years were spent living off fish and coconuts on a pearl farm on an atoll sans plumbing, telephone and airstrip, and the next 10 years were spent on Tahiti. Now in Portland, Oregon, she often complains of the cold. Her award-winning travel stories have appeared in *Travelers' Tales* books, and her travel articles have appeared in publications such as the *Los Angeles Times* and *Islands* magazine. She's written over 30 Lonely Planet guides, but she considers the *Tahiti & French Polynesia* guide to be her pièce de résistance.

Read more about Celeste at:
lonelyplanet.com/members/CelesteBrash

Jean-Bernard Carillet

Diving, On the Road Paris-based journalist and photographer Jean-Bernard is a diehard Polynesia lover and diving instructor. So far, he has explored 28 islands in the five archipelagos. On this research gig he searched for the most idyllic *motu* (small islet), the best manta-ray encounters, the most thrilling lagoon tours, the tastiest *poisson cru* (raw fish in coconut milk) dish, the most romantic spots, the most enjoyable hikes and the best-value accommodation. His favourite experiences included following the Hawaiki Nui canoe race by boat and attending the Marquesas Arts Festival on Nuku Hiva.

Jean-Bernard has contributed to many Lonely Planet titles and he writes for travel and dive magazines.

Published by Lonely Planet Publications Pty Ltd
ABN 36 005 607 983
9th edition – Sep 2012
ISBN 978 1 74179 692 6

10 9 8 7 6 5 4 3 2 1
Printed in China